Quest for
Decisive Victory

Quest for
Decisive Victory

• • • • • • • • • • • • •

FROM STALEMATE TO

BLITZKRIEG IN EUROPE,

1899–1940

ROBERT M. CITINO

University Press of Kansas

Published by the University Press of
Kansas (Lawrence, Kansas 66045), which
was organized by the Kansas Board of
Regents and is operated and funded by
Emporia State University, Fort Hays State
University, Kansas State University,
Pittsburg State University, the University
of Kansas, and Wichita State University

British Library Cataloguing in Publication
Data is available.

The paper used in this publication meets the
minimum requirements of the American
National Standard for Permanence of Paper
for Printed Library Materials Z39.48-1984.

Library of Congress Cataloging-in-
Publication Data
Citino, Robert Michael, 1958–
Quest for decisive victory : from stalemate to
Blitzkrieg in Europe,
1899–1940 / Robert M. Citino
p. cm.—(Modern war studies)
Includes bibliographical references and index.
ISBN 978-0-7006-1655-8 (pbk. : alk. paper)
1. Military history, Modern—19th century.
2. Military history, Modern—20th century.
3. Military art and science—History—19th
century.
4. Military art and science—History—20th
century.
5. Tactics—History—19th century.
6. Tactics—History—20th century.
7. Lightning war.
I. Title. II. Series.
U41 .C52 2002
355'.009'04—dc21
2001007627

Printed in the United States of America
10 9 8 7 6 5 4 3 2

For my daughter Allison

CONTENTS

• • • • • • • • • • • • • •

ILLUSTRATIONS

• • • • • • • • • • • • • •

Photos

Maps

PREFACE

• • • • • • • • • • • • • • •

THE PROBLEM

Judas Maccabaeus had just received a piece of bad news. The leader of the Jewish revolt against Antiochus Epiphanes in the second century B.C. had been commanding his ragged force of rebels for some time against the regular troops of the royal army under Appolonius. The struggle had been difficult enough, but now he heard that a second enemy army was coming up out of Syria, under the command of Seron, to link up with Appolonius and crush the rebellion once and for all. This new force had entered Judea by the coastal plain and was just now beginning to make the ascent to the Judean hills through Beth-horon, the pass that has played such an important role in the military history of Israel. Judas knew that he had to prevent the two armies from uniting against him. After speaking a few words to quiet his edgy troops and to instill confidence in them, he marched out to battle against Seron.

His men had reason to be afraid. Either enemy army alone had them greatly outnumbered. "How can we, few as we are, fight such a mighty host as this?" they asked. But Judas was equal to the situation. Marching with lightning speed over ground that he knew far better than his adversary, he reached the head of the pass well before Seron. Deployed in an advantageous position, he launched a surprise attack on Seron's columns as they were strung out and isolated in Beth-horon. The story is told in 1 Maccabees:

When he finished speaking, he rushed suddenly against Seron and his army, and they were crushed before him. They pursued them down the descent of Beth-horon to the plain; eight hundred of them fell, and the rest fled into the land of the Philistines. Then Judas and his brothers began to be feared, and terror fell on the Gentiles all around them. His fame reached the king, and the Gentiles talked of the battles of Judas. When Antiochus heard these reports, he was greatly angered.[1]

And well he might be. Despite all its seeming advantages, Seron's over-confident host had been destroyed. Compared with Judas's force of irregulars, it was better armed, better trained, and certainly better organized for war. Motivation was probably stronger among the Maccabeans, fighting as they were for their homes, wives, and children—"our lives and our laws," as Judas exhorted them in a prebattle address. Seron's men, however, especially his officers, had their own lives and careers to think about, and that is powerful motivation in any event.

The single advantage enjoyed by the Jews in this encounter was their superior mobility. They knew the land: every fold, ridge, and mountain pass. They had no real supply train or heavy equipment to drag around, and their lack of these "impedimenta" meant that they could get around much faster than their adversaries. Judas exploited this advantage to get his army into a position from which he could offset Seron's numerical superiority, trapping him in a narrow pass where the Syrian could not deploy his main strength.

The battle itself, although not described in detail by the ancient author, is still a perfectly valid working model for a decisive military encounter. The more mobile opponent deploys in a position of strength, then launches a rapid assault. The enemy, surprised or discomfited or both, eventually reaches the point when the survival instinct overcomes the will to victory. He turns and runs, a moment called by the ancient Greeks the *trope,* or "turning," of the battle (and giving its name to the memorial that the victorious side would erect on the spot, the "trophy"). Now, with the enemy throwing off discipline and fleeing the battlefield, comes the time for the pursuit.

It is this last phase that is the most important. The enemy is beaten, but that is really only a momentary thing, a loss of nerve that could last a day or even a week but might last only a few minutes. The victor, therefore, must pursue, not allowing the enemy to reform, reorganize, or regain his confidence. The pursuer does not have to kill every last soldier in the enemy army in order to destroy it as an effective fighting force. He only needs to scatter it and destroy its organization.

It is the pursuit that turns a victorious battle into a victorious campaign. In modern terms, the pursuit is the link between warfare at the level of *tactics* (the technique of winning a battle) and the level of *operations* (the art of winning a military campaign). The "assault-turning-pursuit" model is flexible enough to serve as a guide to many centuries, even millennia, of military history. When one reads accounts of a decisive victory, one is usually reading about a successful pursuit.

Over 2,000 years later, in the course of the nineteenth century, this model began to break down. It seemed to be a paradox. Armies had never been larger. The troops had never been better trained or equipped, and there had never been more gifted and intelligent minds contemplating and designing military doctrine. But something was happening that even a mildly intelligent observer could see. Battles were still being fought—vast, bloody, horrible battles—but they were not being fought to any good purpose. Throughout most nineteenth-century wars (the Crimean War of 1854–55, the Italian War of 1859 between the Austrian and French armies, the American Civil War), the great battles were curiously indecisive. One side, usually the more aggressive, attacking side, won; the other fled. And then . . . nothing. There was rarely a pursuit. The unharassed enemy had a breathing space in which to re-form, forcing another battle somewhere up the road, in which the entire process would repeat itself.

It was not difficult to see the reasons for the lack of pursuit, and the resulting sterility of great battles. Fire weapons were undergoing a transformation unparalleled since their introduction into European warfare in the fifteenth century. Smoothbore weapons—both musket and artillery pieces— were giving way to rifled ones; spiraled grooves inside the barrel imparted spin to the projectiles that these weapons fired, greatly increasing their range and accuracy. Where a smoothbore musket might have an effective range (defined as a 50 percent chance of hitting the target) of much less than one hundred yards, and probably less than fifty, a rifled musket (or simply "rifle") had a range of five hundred to eight hundred yards, terrain and line of sight permitting. It was no longer necessary for defenders to wait until they could "see the whites of their eyes" before opening fire. Attacking troops became targets at greater distances and for longer periods, and their casualties grew. Of course, they had their own weapons, but the stationary defender squeezing off carefully aimed rounds had an advantage over an attacking infantryman rushing to get forward as quickly as possible.

This is not to say that there were no successful assaults at all during the nineteenth century. The attacker might even the odds, or even tip them in his favor, with superior artillery, forcing the defenders to keep their heads down and suppressing their fire. He might enjoy a moral superiority, or have used his mobility to seize advantageous terrain, like Judas Maccabaeus at Beth-horon. Even a successful attack, however, often found the attacker so mauled by defensive fire that asking the troops to re-form for a vigorous pursuit was simply impossible. Not only were casualties much higher than in previous eras, but the loss of cohesion and organization, the intermingling of men from different units, the chaos of the high-firepower battlefield all conspired to eliminate the pursuit as an integral component of battle.

A second, related problem was the decline of cavalry, the arm traditionally entrusted with carrying out the pursuit. As the century wore on, fire weapons continued to increase in power. Breech-loading firearms, in which the operator loads the weapon through an opening in the rear of the barrel, replaced the old muzzle-loaders. Far easier, faster, and more convenient to reload than the muzzle-loader, the breechloader allowed a man to use the weapon while lying on the ground and thus presenting almost no target to enemy fire. Now, compare his target profile with the man on horseback, who became a nearly impossible-to-miss target on the nineteenth-century battlefield. Cavalry found it increasingly difficult even to get near its own front line, let alone play a role in the assault on an enemy position. And since the horsemen were not there in the assault, it was not easy to suddenly bring them forward for a pursuit. Even small bands of the enemy, a rear guard for example, could keep them at a distance. Finally, there was the impact of a modern firefight on the terrain to consider. Repeated explosions of modern artillery shells churned up the ground severely, and the infantry on both sides often dug entrenchments and put up obstacles to protect themselves from enemy fire. On ground such as this, it was difficult for cavalry to operate in any aggressive sense, or even to move. During most nineteenth-century battles, armies triumphed, opponents fled, and friendly cavalry looked on.

A third cause of this lack of pursuit was the increasing size of nineteenth-century armies and the difficulty in commanding, controlling, and communicating with them. Armies of 200,000 men were now common, operating over hundreds of miles of open country. No longer was it possible for a commander to stand on a hill and direct his battalions to trouble spots on the battlefield—the "Napoleonic mode," we might call it. As a result, even where opponents were fleeing the battlefield and fresh forces were in place to pursue them, there was no guarantee that commanders would recognize the opportunity that beckoned or that they would be able to exploit it in time if they did recognize it. The technology was improving in this area, the introduction of the radio telegraph (or simply telegraph) being the best example, but it was too slow and inflexible to offer a commander any real control over a battle or pursuit. Usually chalked up to bad commanders, the problems in this area were much too systemic and complex to be attributed to individual failings.

And yet the dream of the defeat, pursuit, and annihilation of the enemy lived on in the minds of European military professionals. One German officer wrote on the eve of World War II:

Without a tireless pursuit, no tactical gains—however great they may appear or however large the booty may be—have any lasting effect. Once an attack has been successful and there are indications that the opponent is retreating or has intentions to do so, all arms must immediately take up the pursuit, if the complete annihilation of the hostile forces, which is the object of any pursuit, is to be accomplished.[2]

The inability to achieve this vision had become the single greatest military problem facing armies as the twentieth century dawned. How they met it, analyzed it, and eventually overcame it—once more restoring the pursuit to its rightful place and resurrecting the possibility of decisive warfare on the operational level—is the theme of this work.

THE WORK

Quest for Decisive Victory is intended to be a broad synthesis of European warfare during the first half of the twentieth century, centered around the loss and recovery of operational decisiveness. Mobility will be one key theme. While war is usually said to consist of "fire and movement," the former came to dominate the battlefield in this period, and the latter seemed in danger of disappearing altogether. In this era, victorious armies were the ones that managed to keep moving; that maintained the momentum of their advance even in the face of the withering firepower generated on the modern battlefield; and that somehow succeeded in limiting the mobility of their enemies. The problem of mobility, however, deals with more than the relative speed of the hostile armies. Mobility was, and is, a function of a number of factors: the length and quality of one's supply lines; command and control; leadership; the relative morale of the adversaries; prewar campaign planning; and many more. This book will take a detailed, operational-level look at military conflicts from 1899 to 1940 and will also discuss the vigorous debates over military doctrine during that period in order to see how European armies managed the difficult task of coordinating these elements in the quest for decisive operational victory.

The analysis will not limit itself to the two world wars. The first conflict to be discussed will be the South African, or "Boer," War (1899–1902), in which the British army was taught a hard lesson in modern tactics by a nation of farmers. Although there has been a tendency to focus on the British disasters in the first few weeks of the war (the battles of the Modder River, Magersfontein, Stormberg, and Colenso), this was a long and immense struggle, as the two adversaries maneuvered around a theater of war as large as France and Spain combined. The latter phase of the war, the "guerrilla," or more accurately the "commando," phase, is highly instructive in the problems of modern military operations, as a much larger British force gradually managed to fix the Boers in place and finally force their surrender.

The Russo-Japanese War (1904–5), with its machine guns, barbed wire, heavy artillery, and extremely long casualty list, will be discussed next. In two diverging drives, one southward to Port Arthur, the other northward into Manchuria, the Japanese army pushed the Russians back again and again but never managed to destroy them. In three great battles (at the Yalu, Liaoyang, and Mukden), the Japanese attempted to encircle and destroy their foe. They failed each time, due to a recurring combination of factors—the inadequate mobility of the traditional arms; the increasing unwieldiness of the mass armies attempting the maneuvers; and the difficulty the Japanese had in commanding and controlling them.

The Balkan Wars of 1912–13 form an important part of the book. The small powers of the Balkan Peninsula put aside their historic differences and united for a war against Ottoman Turkey. While the outside world expecting an easy Turkish victory, the Balkan States in fact inflicted a devastating defeat on the Turks that essentially cost the latter their centuries-old position in Europe, and along the way showed that even small and relatively impoverished states could master the increasingly complex art of modern military operations. The armies of Serbia and Bulgaria, in particular, demonstrated to the world that highly motivated infantry could overcome even the heaviest concentrations of defensive firepower.

World War I (1914–18) was the most vivid illustration of the problems to be examined in this study. This first "total war" destroyed Europe's dominant position in world affairs and still stands as the nadir of the military art. It was a static "positional war" *(Stellungskrieg)* of trenches, barbed wire, machine guns, and artillery, a brutal contest of firepower that was almost completely devoid of maneuver, a war in which the Allies finally triumphed "through attrition and not through any far-ranging operation,"[3] in the words of a German officer in the 1930s. It was out of this grisly stalemate that the two solutions to the problem of operational and tactical mobility arose. One was the German development of *Stosstrupp* (often mistakenly called "infiltration") tactics; the other was a British invention given the code name of "tank."

The interwar period (1918–39) was the era of the "great debate" over the future of warfare. While everyone could agree that the war just ended had been a disaster and that trench warfare on such a scale should never be repeated, no one could agree on what steps to take to avoid it. Two schools of futurist thought came forward, each one championing a piece of new technology that it claimed had changed the face of warfare forever. A British officer writing in 1935 described these groups, with some exaggeration, as "those whose gospel may be epitomized as 'The air and nothing but the air,' for whom the only weapon is the gun and the bomb of the aeroplane, and for whom ground troops are simply aerodrome guards. After these we have the tank enthusiasts in whose minds the air arm and even the artillery are mere accessories."[4] The futurists argued that the traditional arms had outlived their usefulness and needed to disappear. They were speaking not just of cavalry but of infantry and artillery as well. All of them were too slow for the pace of machine warfare, not to mention too vulnerable to the ghastly effects of modern firepower.

While this lively debate proceeded, complete with exaggerated claims for various new weapons, ad hominem remarks, and sometimes vicious name-calling, the badly named "interwar" era saw its share of wars: the Russo-Polish War (1920–21), for example, was a highly mobile conflict of cavalry charges and armored trains advancing and retreating rapidly across an immense theater of operations. The great counteroffensive led by Marshal Josef Pilsudski in front of Warsaw was one of the highest achievements of the operational art. Likewise, the Paraguayan-Bolivian conflict known as the Chaco War (1932–35) offered a number of examples of decisive operational maneuver, allowing the outnumbered Paraguayans to surround and destroy much larger Bolivian forces and eventually to triumph in the conflict. This discussion will focus on the two greatest wars of the period. The Italo-Ethiopian War of 1935–36 was of intense interest to contemporary observers. It saw the Italian army—motorized, equipped with modern weapons, and enjoying absolute superiority in the air—come within a hair of being driven out of Ethiopia altogether by an army consisting of irregular infantry. Even more closely studied was the Spanish civil war of 1936–39. Its gritty trench warfare seemed to some to be reminiscent of 1916; its use of tanks, aircraft, and bombardment of defenseless cities like Guernica pointed forward to 1939.

During World War II, the German army (Wehrmacht) solved the problem that had bedeviled military planners since 1914: highly mobile, massed formations of tanks (panzers) working in close cooperation with the air force (Luftwaffe) proved capable not only of blasting through static enemy positions on the tactical level but also of sustaining their operational advance into open country, moving forward 150 miles per day, linking up far behind the enemy lines, trapping and destroying hostile formations in great battles of encirclement. The world would call it "blitzkrieg" (lightning war), although the Germans themselves did not use the term. It was the basis for the dramatic German victories in Poland, France, and the first year of the invasion of the Soviet Union—victories that still stand at the pinnacle of the modern military art.

Quest for Decisive Victory will concentrate on that level of war between tactics (the movement of battalions, companies, and squads on the battle-field) and strategy (the realm of the politico-military leadership of the respective warring nations). It was the Germans who first coined the term *operations* to describe this intermediate level. Involving the movement of corps and divisions, it might be described as the analysis of the campaign (rather than the battle or the war). Nowhere else is the creativity (or lack thereof) of the higher commander so important to the outcome. Both tactics and strategy are essentially sciences; warfare on the operational level is an art. A commander may feint in the center with one corps while massing over-whelming forces on one or both flanks; he might employ surprise or take advantage of the terrain to march a force into position in the enemy's rear. Operational possibilities are limited only by the commander's creativity. The tradition in the German army was for the commander to "shape" the campaign so that it resulted in a great battle of annihilation. His primary task was to concentrate overwhelming strength at the decisive point of the battle, the "point of main effort," or *Schwerpunkt*, rather than frittering away his forces on diversionary thrusts or nondecisive sectors of the theater. Each well-conducted campaign and battle would have a *Schwerpunkt* that would, in a sense, define it, give it shape and meaning. In the words of the great German field marshal Paul von Hindenburg, "A battle without a *Schwerpunkt* is like a man without character, who leaves everything to chance."[5]

It is a fundamental assumption of this book that while the machines may have changed, certain fundamental principles of the military art (including, for example, concentration of force, unity of command, Clausewitz's definition of war as "an act of force to compel our enemy to do our will," or Moltke's warning that "no plan long survives contact with the enemy's main body") have remained more or less constant. The interplay and tension between technology and doctrine, what we might call a "hardware-software dichotomy," is another important theme of this study.

Attempting to acknowledge all those who helped me to write this book is difficult. It is a long list and risks two equally bad outcomes: trying the reader's patience and leaving someone out. My students at Eastern Michigan University have stimulated me with good questions for ten years now, and many of the issues under discussion in my classes have found their way into the book. Randy Talbot, formerly my graduate student and now a Staff Historian at the U.S. Army Tank-automotive and Armaments Command (TACOM) in Warren, Michigan, has been an excellent resource: patient, thorough, and unfailingly helpful. A recent graduate of Eastern Michigan's program in geography, Kristine Inman, drew the maps. A public thank-you is also in order to Louise Arnold-Friend, Librarian in the Historical Services Division of the U.S. Army Military History Institute at Carlisle Barracks, Pennsylvania. She is a dedicated and extremely helpful professional who guided me through the incredible collection of materials there. Both Janice Mullin and Emma Cummings of the Imperial War Museum offered valuable assistance and expertise in helping me find suitable photographs for the book. Dennis Showalter and James Corum read the manuscript and offered help, encouragement, and advice well beyond the call of duty. The demand for excellence that is so much a part of their own scholarship has, I hope, found its way into the present work. As always, I would like to thank Barbara and Charles Jelavich; every book I publish is a tribute to the intellectual formation I received under them while a graduate student at Indiana University. Finally, to my wife, Roberta, and my daughters, Allison, Laura, and Emily: thanks for your help, understanding, and love. Of course, any failings in the work are mine alone.

Chapter 1

• • • • • • • • • • • • • • •

Nineteenth-Century Warfare:
The Breakdown of the Napoleonic Doctrine

INTRODUCTION: THE RISE OF FIREPOWER

The popular view of nineteenth-century warfare holds just enough truth to be useful. Briefly, it runs something like this: during the century, the introduction of new technologies, especially in the field of weaponry, made war an ever more terrible undertaking. The introduction of rifled muskets, the development of rapid-fire artillery, and the transition from muzzle-loading to breech-loading weapons greatly increased the firepower of the nineteenth-century army. The increased firepower rendered impossible the old-style assault by bayonet-wielding infantry formations. Unfortunately, a generation of generals schooled in the example of the great Napoleon kept trying. A typical history will usually bring forth one or more failed assaults during the American Civil War (Burnside at Fredericksburg, Pickett's Charge at Gettysburg, Grant at Cold Harbor) as proof of the impossibility of getting through the fire zone of the defending force.[1]

The analysis then usually fast-forwards to the fateful year 1914, when the Great Powers launched themselves into the horrendous bloodletting that was known, for a time at least, as the Great War.[2] Here, the firepower of the defender took a quantum leap forward. New and ever heavier artillery was capable of chewing up enemy concentrations even before they reached the battlefield. Artillery forced the infantry on both sides to dig trenches in order to survive. The war also saw the integration of the machine gun, the "concentrated essence of infantry," into the European battlefield. A machine gun could literally sweep the area before it clean of attackers, turning the assault zone into a "no-man's-land" that no one could cross. While the weapons were new and powerful, however, the generals were old and mentally flabby—still pursuing the ghost of Bonaparte. They either could not believe or simply refused to believe that the bayonet charge was as dead as the spoke-wheeled chariot or the Macedonian phalanx. An entire generation of European manhood would be sacrificed in four years of futile assaults on impregnable defenses that no contemporary army was capable of penetrating. The examples usually entered in evidence include a number of images that have burned their way into our historical consciousness: the first day of the battle of the Somme, when German machine guns annihilated the hapless infantry formations of the British army as they tried to "assault" across no-man's-land; the battle of Verdun, with the infantry on both sides sitting helplessly under an unceasing rain of high-explosive shells; and the horrible struggle in the mud of Passchendaele, as the British and Canadian attackers struggled forward in a morass of waist-deep mud while German machine gun fire flickered around them, doing its deadly business.[3]

This view of nineteenth-century warfare, still prevalent today, is true in many particulars. First of all, the new weapons did greatly increase firepower. The rifled musket ("rifle") easily outranged the old smoothbore. Artillery dramatically increased its range, accuracy, and power. Breech-loading increased the rate of fire of both small arms and artillery, abolishing the complex series of motions involved in loading and firing muzzle-loading weapons.

Second, the new firepower was more effective in the defense than in the offense. The attacker, after all, was still trying to get forward to use his bayonet on the defender, a form of killing unchanged since the dawn of recorded history—and probably well before that. An assaulting infantry formation had to move out into the open and charge across an area well beaten by enemy fire. The defenders, particularly if they were hunkered down in entrenchments or fortifications, were, by contrast, hidden and protected from enemy fire. The destruction of Pickett's division at Gettysburg is not the invention of some journalist or historian with an ax to grind; neither was the Somme or Verdun. No historian will ever be able to rehabilitate the generals of the Great War who ordered these assaults, men caricatured in Great Britain as know-nothings with enormous mustaches, "Colonel Blimps." No one will ever find much good to say about the horrors of trench warfare, nor should anyone wish to.

And yet, when viewed over the course of the entire century, the case for the "impossibility of infantry assault" is hardly ironclad. The truth is much more complex. The history of warfare from 1815 to 1914 included an impressive series of well-planned and executed assaults, spearheaded by infantry, that resulted in the penetration and destruction of rifle-armed defenders who were well supplied with artillery. The supposed "lessons of the nineteenth century" (or "the lessons of Pickett's Charge," for that matter) are not so clear-cut when one takes into account the military history of all the century's wars, and not just a small number of carefully selected battlefield disasters.[4] The fact that the legion of generals who tried to emulate Napoleon failed was, in the final analysis, simply a reflection of the greatness of Napoleon. It was not due to their ignorance of the new technology of warfare.

THE PARADIGM: NAPOLEON

Any analysis of modern warfare must start with this greatest of commanders. During his career—first as a young general in the revolutionary armies, then as "first consul" of the Republic, and finally as "emperor of the French"—Napoleon led his Grande Armée to a series of astonishing victories. His list of battle honors is incomparable: he crushed the Austrians and Russians at Austerlitz in 1805; the Prussians at Jena and Auerstädt in 1806, the Russians again at Friedland in 1807; and the Austrians one more time at Wagram in 1809. In the process, he overran most of Europe, transforming its laws, government, and social structure.[5]

Napoleon's "art of war" became the paradigm for succeeding generations of field commanders.[6] Its essential component was mobility, marching harder and faster than his enemies. "Marches," he once said, "are war." Speed was everything—whether manifested in rapid movement, in surprise maneuvers, or in hard-hitting, bold attacks. The aim was to discomfit, even bewilder, his opponent. His men, fired by revolutionary zeal and fanatical loyalty to their leader, and led by a group of talented young commanders (the "marshals"), consistently outmarched every other army of the day. Napoleon himself once said that his entire art of war consisted of marching twenty-five miles per day and fighting in the afternoon.

There is a limit to how far and fast men can march, but Napoleon was able to increase the mobility of his forces in several ways. First, in a throwback to the seventeenth century, he dispensed with supply lines and had his men live off the land, "foraging" or "requisitioning" their supplies.[7] While these are fancy terms for stealing and looting from the civilians among whom they campaigned, Napoleon also made use of purchasing officers. Sent out in front of the army, their mission was to arrange for food and fodder. His enemies, tied to bulky supply convoys, might as well have been moving in slow motion.

Second, he used a system of organization based on the "army corps" *(corps d'armée)*. His forces marched dispersed into corps, separate formations of all arms (infantry, cavalry, and artillery), perhaps 20,000 men apiece. The corps were typically arranged in a "battle square" *(bataillon carré)*, with each corps one day's march from its neighbors. Theoretically, each corps was able to engage and fight even a much larger foe on its own for one day, by which time it would be reinforced by the others.

The system offered many advantages. It allowed for the most rapid possible movement by breaking up a huge force into smaller chunks. It was capable of sudden changes of direction while on the march (as in the lightning campaign against the Prussians that ended in the twin victories of Jena and Auerstädt in 1806). Finally, it disguised Napoleon's true objective, giving the appearance of an ill-coordinated scatter while allowing very rapid concentration and bringing the largest possible number of men to the battlefield in the shortest possible time. When later generations paid testament to Napoleon's genius, they were usually praising his skillful use of the *corps d'armée.*

Of special importance was the fact that Napoleon enjoyed unprecedented command and control over his forces. The Grande Armée possessed an expert General Staff, led by Marshal Alexandre Berthier, whose task it was to execute Napoleon's commands. Each corps had its own staff, as did each division. The archaic armies of France's foes had nothing to parallel this command system. The dramatic victories from 1805 to 1807 are attributable not just to Napoleon's own genius but also to French superiority in this crucial area.[8]

The purpose of his maneuvering rarely varied: Napoleon sought to bring the enemy's main force to battle and to crush it, a great change from the limited wars of the eighteenth century. To do this, he used three basic operational maneuvers, alone or in combination. First, where space and numbers allowed, he sought a maneuver onto the rear *(manoeuvre sur les derrières)*, engaging the enemy main body with one corps, while his main body sought, via a flanking maneuver, to drive into the enemy's rear and get astride his line of communication. Screening and protecting this flank march might be a river, a forest, or, more likely, an aggressive screen of French cavalry. Second, in a move that was most effective against coalition armies, he might employ the "strategy of the central position." Preventing the junction of enemy forces with his cavalry, he would typically detach a strong "observation corps" *(corps d'observation)* to keep an eye on the weaker of the two forces. Concentrating rapidly against the stronger, he would crush it. Then, detaching a corps to pursue the beaten foe, he would march back to the support of the observation corps. Finally, Napoleon was as capable as anyone of conducting a frontal attack in order to bludgeon an enemy into submission. In all three cases, prebattle maneuver usually ended two days' march from the enemy. At this point, Napoleon would usually order a forced march, a last-minute pounce on the foe under cover of darkness, which would bring about battle against a surprised and rattled enemy who was a full day away from being prepared. This was the key to victory over the Austrians at Lodi in 1796 and, once again, the Prussians at Jena.[9]

The classic example of Napoleonic maneuver was the opening of the 1805 campaign. Breaking camp along the Channel, where he had been contemplating an invasion of England, Napoleon took his entire Grande Armée across northern France with lightning speed. Covering his forces with an active screen of cavalry, he crossed the Rhine into Germany. Unable to discern his true line of march, the allied armies facing him were paralyzed. Freed from supply lines, he was a simultaneous threat to Vienna, Berlin, and northern Italy. An Austrian army under General Mack sat at its forward base in a fortified camp at Ulm. Suddenly wheeling his force to the south, Napoleon swooped down on Mack with five corps, using forced march. Mack, quite literally, went to bed one night with reports that Napoleon was several days' march away, then awoke the next morning to find himself cut off from home. Fifty thousand Austrian troops surrendered with hardly a shot fired. "I am the unfortunate General Mack," the defeated commander said by way of introducing himself to Napoleon. He could not have been more correct. Mack was a perfectly competent general, trained in the warfare of his era, forced into a one-on-one encounter with the greatest field commander of the modern era, and catching him in his prime.

Once battle had been joined, Napoleon's tactics featured an intricate system of formations and combined arms. He added nothing particularly new here; he just handled his forces more effectively, more often, than any of his enemies. His infantry fought in line *(ordre mince)* to maximize firepower, three ranks deep (although British troops fought in what would become known as the "thin red line," just two ranks deep, which maximized its fire). It could also adopt column formation *(ordre profond)* for rapid forward movement and shock action (i.e., assault with the bayonet). A battalion in such a formation might form a column of divisions (eighty men wide by twelve men deep) or a column of companies (forty men by twenty-four). Finally, there was the so-called open order, with the infantry fighting as small, irregular groups of skirmishers *(tirailleurs)* to harass the enemy and screen friendly formations. In fact, it is today clear that French infantry often deployed in a combination of all three *(ordre mixte)* for maximum flexibility. Infantry in line provided the firepower, infantry in column provided the threat of assault, and skirmishers screened the formed units from enemy fire and assault.[10]

Battle usually opened with Napoleon concentrating his artillery into one large formation, a "grand battery" that he used to soften up enemy formations. The guns could fire ball ammunition, effective at long range against anything unlucky enough to be struck by it. For shorter-range work, they could fire canister. The canister disintegrated when fired, and the small lead shot inside it dispersed into a cone of fire capable of shattering even the most resolute attacking formations and inflicting horrible injuries. With the enemy formations disrupted, infantry columns would launch the assault, charging with bayonets leveled, often supported by a charge of the heavy cavalry *(cuirassiers,* so-called from the armored breastplate, or cuirass, that they wore) or a flank attack by a newly arriving corps. Once the enemy line was shredded, light cavalry (known variously as *lanceurs, chasseurs,* and *hussars)* would begin the pursuit—harrying the retreating foe, butchering his stragglers, and finishing his destruction. The cavalry was the glamour arm of Napoleonic armies. It attracted some of the most fascinating personalities of the period and generated some of the most absurd uniforms in the entire history of war.

Two observations should be made regarding this tactical system. First, it was finely tuned, with each arm having its strengths and weaknesses. Infantry in line or column, for example, was highly vulnerable to cavalry charges, and when threatened had to defend itself by forming an immobile square *(carré)* bristling with bayonets. Squares, in turn, were extremely vulnerable to enemy artillery, which could be wheeled up to hammer such a dense, stationary target. Gun crews, however, were highly vulnerable to skirmishers and cavalry and had to be supported closely by infantry or cavalry formations. There has been no end to commentators who have likened Napoleonic tactics to the children's game of rock, scissors, paper, and it is an apt description. As it had been since the days of Philip of Macedon, combined arms warfare was still the key to success on the Napoleonic battlefield.

Second, given the weapons in use in the era, a well-executed assault stood a very good chance of succeeding. As the infantry columns charged forward in the assault, they had to brave the fire of an opposing line armed with smooth-bore muskets, for France the Model 1777, for Great Britain the so-called brown Bess. Well-trained infantry might get off three shots per minute. The effective range of these muskets was well under one hundred yards, yielding perhaps one or two volleys at the attackers as they came forward.[11] An assault column therefore had a solid chance of getting at the foe with the bayonet—although most sensible defenders would flee long before it came to that.

Napoleon's tactical masterpiece was Austerlitz. The occasion was hardly auspicious. He was deep inside enemy territory; he was outnumbered 68,000 to 85,000; his army was exhausted and running low on supplies. Desperately needing a decisive victory, Napoleon coolly took the measure of the enemy commanders, the Habsburg emperor Francis I and the Russian tsar Alexander I. Well aware that these men, born to the purple, despised him as an upstart and a social inferior, he laid a very clever and, as it proved, irresistible trap for them. He deliberately left both of his wings weak, in order to invite attack. As he knew they would, the allies split their forces, launching simultaneous thrusts on both his left wing, anchored on Santon Hill, and his right, along the Goldbach stream. The attack across the Goldbach, opening at 7:00 A.M., turned into the principal allied thrust. A handful of French regiments holding the villages of Telnitz and Sokolnitz here bore the brunt of the assault for two hours. They had to hold, and although it was a desperate fight, hold they did. More and more allied troops were fed into the fighting here, eventually some 50,000. This was just what Napoleon wanted. Unknown to the allies, he had deployed the main weight of his force in the center behind a low ridge, further hidden that morning by a thick fog. At 9:00 A.M. the sun suddenly broke through, revealing to Napoleon that the allies had taken his bait. He now ordered IV Corps under Marshal Soult to storm the weakened center of the enemy line along the Pratzen Heights, supported by the Cavalry Reserve under Marshal Joachim Murat. Although there was some tough fighting here, the French soon secured the Pratzen. With the allied center broken, Napoleon wheeled his forces to the right, onto the rear of the attacking allied columns crowded along the Goldbach. Taken suddenly in their rear, the allies panicked and tried to flee. French cavalry pursued them—and butchered them in great numbers. Thousands more drowned when the ice on Lake Satschen gave way as they were trying desperately to retreat over it. At a cost of just 1,300 killed in action, Napoleon had inflicted 30,000 casualties on the allied armies and taken 12,000 prisoners of war. The two defeated emperors fled from the wrath of this self-made man, this walking testimony to the "career open to talent." It was one of history's most decisive battles.[12]

Napoleon was no god. He made his share of blunders, and given the sheer number of campaigns that he fought, it would be foolish to expect otherwise. On numerous occasions, only the talents of a subordinate, the bravery of his soldiers, or some unspeakable blunder on the part of his foes saved him from the consequences. At Jena, for example, he believed that he was facing the main body of the Prussian army, when it was actually concentrating against a single French corps at Auerstädt, commanded by Marshal Louis Davout (who, by the way, beat it single-handedly). The same thing happened before the battle of Eckmühl. This time it was against the Austrians, and once again Davout had to take on the enemy's main body single-handedly (and once again he gave it pretty rough treatment; perhaps we should speak of "Davout's art of war").[13] But even after taking into account the catastrophe in Russia and the final defeat at Waterloo, the emperor's moral ascendancy over every other general of the day is indisputable. Wellington once stated that Napoleon's mere presence on the battlefield was worth 50,000 men. We should take the duke at his word.

One final point about Napoleon is in order. Historians still debate how much he owed to the military reforms of the French monarchy in the years before 1789. The *corps d'armée,* for example, was not Napoleon's idea. Nor was the *ordre mixte* that he used so successfully in battle.[14] There was no real advance in weaponry during the Napoleonic period. French infantry continued to use the same firearm it had used in prerevolutionary times. Other historians downplay his achievements by arguing that he was merely the creation of the French Revolution. The *levée en masse* of the French Revolution, the total mobilization of the nation for war against the European monarchs, gave France the benefit of much larger armies than its neighbors. The popular enthusiasm unleashed by the Revolution, which made ordinary French men and women feel that they had some stake in defending the country, gave the French a willingness to persevere that was lacking in the hostile powers that Napoleon fought, with the exception of Great Britain.

All of these arguments are worthy of consideration. Still, while granting that we are all products of a specific time and place, none of them detract from the genius of Napoleon. He took the men, the weapons, and the systems of organization available to him, put them together in new and unique ways, and used them to build an unrivaled reputation of success that even his ultimate defeat has not tarnished. For the rest of the century, every battlefield commander either consciously or unconsciously wanted to emulate him. Nearly 200 years later, Napoleon still dominates any discussion of "the great captains."

THE PROPHETS

No human activity, with the possible exception of love, has proved so immune to rational analysis as war. That fact has not stopped some very gifted individuals from trying. So immense had been Napoleon's achievement that the aftermath of Waterloo saw numerous attempts to analyze and codify the reasons for his success. One of the most enduring was that of Baron

Antoine Henri de Jomini, a Swiss officer who had served with both the French and allied armies during the long years of war.[15] A son of the eighteenth-century Enlightenment, Jomini tried to distill Napoleon's art of war into a small number of universal, easily teachable principles, or maxims. In his magnum opus, the two-volume *Précis de l'art de la guerre*, published in 1838, he went so far as to identify "the one great principle underlying all operations of war," expressing it in four maxims:

1. To throw by strategic movements the mass of an army, successively, upon the decisive points of a theater of war, and also upon the communications of the enemy as much as possible without compromising one's own.
2. To maneuver to engage fractions of the hostile army with the bulk of one's own forces.
3. On the battlefield, to throw the mass of the forces upon the decisive point, or upon that portion of the hostile line which it is of the first importance to overthrow.
4. To so arrange that these masses shall not only be thrown upon the decisive point, but that they shall engage at the proper times and with energy.[16]

These maxims give a good idea of the flavor of Jomini's analysis. Although there is much sound advice scattered throughout his volumes, the view of war that they describe is tidy, geometric, full of precise angles and mathematical relationships. It is filled with detailed, often hairsplitting, definitions of terms that cascade one upon the other: strategic lines, strategic points, objective points, strategic positions, strategic fronts, operational fronts, pivots of operations, and pivots of maneuver. He manages to define each, in the words of one modern scholar, "with the precision of a medieval schoolman." The result is "a general synthesis in a manner calculated to baffle the simple and fascinate the worst sort of intellectual soldier."[17] Jomini describes the zone of operations, for example, as a rectangle, with two sides defined by the opposing armies, a third often consisting of impassable terrain. Victory, then, was a simple matter of seizing control of the fourth, a theorem that he attempts to establish with the aid of geometric diagrams replete with line segments standing in various relation to one another.

In discussing actual operations, he stressed the advantages that Napoleon was able to derive from his use of "interior lines." A centrally placed army can use its position, he argued, to deal successively with external threats in turn. The enemies are operating on the edge of a circle, widely separated from one another, and are therefore unable to coordinate their activities in any effective way. Here is Jomini at his best: coldly analytical, using numerous historical examples in a simple, effective way, and drawing them together into a new and convincing synthesis.[18]

Jomini's theories, based on the Enlightenment belief that war is a teachable science, as subject to natural law as any other natural phenomenon, were widely popular in the nineteenth and early twentieth centuries. They still affect the way we view war—and the way soldiers are trained. They have proved to be irresistible to the modern military professional, in that they claim to offer secret knowledge that can tame the unruly beast of war.

The Prussian writer Carl Maria von Clausewitz disagreed in every possible way with Jomini. Where Jomini's work offered prescriptions, Clausewitz offered analysis. Seeking to formulate a "metaphysic of war," he argued that war could never be distilled into a few short formulas. It was not a science to be taught, not a measured, structured object, but an organism, operating under an internal logic that we can only dimly penetrate. In *Vom Kriege (On War)*, published in 1832,[19] he describes war as the domain of violence, of danger, of physical exertion and suffering, of uncertainty, where "everything is very simple, but the simplest thing is difficult," where both sides develop plans, then have to watch helplessly as they are ground down in an inexorable process of "friction." War is not a question of technique and form and rules but "an act of force to compel our enemy to do our will." War is never a mathematical certainty but a matter of assessing probabilities, a gamble: "No other human activity is so continuously or universally bound up with chance."

Clausewitz did have definite ideas on war, to be sure, but little of what he had to say could offer comfort to a military professional. War was not an end to itself but "merely the continuation of policy by other means." It could never be considered apart from its political objective. While in operational terms he held that an aggressive defense ("a shield of blows") was by far the stronger form of war, with the defender falling back until his opponent had outrun himself, then launching the decisive counterattack, he still ended up by rejecting all systems of war, Jomini's included: "In the rules and regulations they offer, they are absolutely useless," he wrote. They ignored moral factors, such as the experience of the troops or their patriotic spirit. Worse, they ignored the role of the great commander, his boldness, audacity, and will. Genius, he wrote, "rises above all rules"; it can "ignore or laugh at them." In fact, Clausewitz wrote that "what genius does is the best rule."[20] This phrase is the Napoleonic legacy in its purest form.

THE CRIMEAN WAR

The first general conflict in post-Napoleonic Europe was the Crimean War.[21] It confirmed the truth of Clausewitz's view of war as the province of uncertainty and friction, and on every level it was a muddled affair. While the long-term cause of the war, the decline of the Ottoman Empire and the resulting instability in the Near East, is clear enough, the outbreak of the conflict stemmed from an incredible collection of miscalculations and blunders that would be humorous if so many men had not died as a result.[22] In December 1852 a dispute arose between Russia and the Ottoman Empire over the status of certain shrines in the Holy Land. Negotiations broke down, and in July 1853, Russian forces occupied the principalities of Moldavia and Wallachia, then under nominal Turkish control. The empire declared war on Russia in October. British and French naval units entered the Black Sea to support the Turks. On November 30 a naval squadron of Russian steamships operating from Sevastopol destroyed a Turkish fleet of thirteen sailing vessels off of Sinope, with great loss of life, some 4,000 in all. Under heavy pressure from public opinion, inflamed by the barbarity of this "massacre," Great Britain and France declared war on Russia in March 1854.

Did the Turks need help? After declaring war, Ottoman forces had carried the fight over the Danube, seizing and fortifying a number of positions on the northern bank. The Russians were unable to break through the Turkish defenses here and in April 1854 began a siege of the fortress of Silistria. Thus, by the time allied forces arrived in the theater in May, the justification for their presence had vanished. Unfortunately, returning home without a victory—or even a defeat, for that matter—was politically impossible. The Crimean War proved beyond dispute the validity of Clausewitz's idea on the relationship of war and politics. The allies now landed at the Turkish port of Varna on the Black Sea, making it their base of operations against Russia. Poor sanitation almost immediately brought on a cholera epidemic, killing thousands. There they sat, while the Russians, unable to take Silistria, decided to abandon the siege in June; that same month, after an ultimatum from neutral Austria, the Russians evacuated the Principalities altogether.

With the French and British public still demanding action, the allies decided on a campaign to seize the Russian naval base of Sevastopol, a place they might take but certainly could not hold for long. Five British and four French divisions sailed from Varna for the Crimea, landing at the small port of Eupatoria on September 14. They came ashore without transport and with little equipment beyond rifles. The British did not even bring any tents.

Operations were just as haphazard, simple to the point of dullness. Making no attempt to maneuver, the allies organized themselves and drove straight down the main road from Eupatoria toward Sevastopol. The Russians came up to block them. There was no surprise, hardly any reconnaissance, no attempt at all on the part of either side to find the foe's flank or rear. The two sides met on the Alma River on September 20. It was the greatest battle Europe had seen since Waterloo: 62,000 French, British, and Turkish forces versus some 35,000 Russians.[23]

In command terms, the Alma was hardly a clash of titans. The British commander was Lord Raglan. Sixty-six years old, he had lost an arm at Waterloo, and, if the reports can be believed, he had a tendency to refer to his French allies as "the enemy." An unimaginative officer, he gave orders that rarely went beyond "halt" or "march." His plan for the battle on the Alma was simple: a simultaneous crossing of the river by all the forces at his command, followed by a frontal assault. The French were not much better off. Marshal Antoine de Saint-Arnaud not only was dying of cancer but also had caught a severe case of cholera in Varna. His conception of the upcoming battle was just as simple as Raglan's. Reviewing his troops on the eve of the battle, he cried out, "With men such as you I have no orders to give, I have but to point at the enemy!" And that is essentially what he did.

The Russian commander, General Menshikov, matched them in imagination. He held a position of great natural strength: a height, the Kourganie Hill, looming up behind a winding river covered by vineyards and farmhouses, but he did little to augment it. He had his men dig one fortification on his right (the "Great Redoubt"), a breastwork with twelve guns and rifle pits for the infantry, but that was it. On his left, facing the French, he relied on the steep cliffs on the southern bank of the river to impede attack. He failed to destroy several trails in the area, however, and the French would use them during the battle to muscle their guns up to the heights. The rest of his position was open ground.

Menshikov's troop dispositions were also less than inspired. While he concentrated his forces on his right, against the English, his left was completely open, dangling in the air, due mainly to allied warships stationed at the mouth of the Alma. He seems not to have considered the sensible proposition that the presence of the allied flotilla, in fact, rendered his entire position along the Alma untenable. Finally, he wasted his one real advantage: a great superiority in cavalry (3,500 horse against just 500 for the allies). He arrayed it in a thin screen protecting his right flank—although it is hard to see just what threat he had in mind from that quarter—rather than concentrating it for a blow at the allies when they would be most vulnerable, at the moment they were crossing the river.

The battle opened at noon, with the allied fleet opening fire on the Russian left. Three British divisions (the Light, the 2nd, and the 1st) now advanced to the south, and as soon as they came within range of the Russian guns, they deployed from column into line and halted. It was 1:30. Raglan decided to wait until the French had crossed on his right and then make a combined charge with both armies. That plan soon went awry. Although the French were facing no real opposition, they were having a tough time negotiating the steep cliffs in their sector and eventually had to abandon their packs in order to proceed. The British lines north of the Alma began to suffer grievously from Russian artillery in the Great Redoubt and received orders to lie down. Here they lay for ninety minutes, fully exposed on ground that actually sloped down toward the river. At 3:00, Raglan could wait no more: "The troops will advance!" he commanded, his one order of the battle, and then rode off. He would be incommunicado for much of the rest of the day, and a controversy has arisen about his whereabouts during the fighting. Two full divisions, some 10,000 men in all, now rose to their feet, dressed ranks, and advanced shoulder to shoulder into the Alma—a magnificent, Napoleonic moment. Just at this moment, the lead French division under General Bosquet finally appeared on the plateau after crossing the Alma at its mouth. Menshikov responded by ordering his reserve (eight battalions of the Minsk and Moscow regiments) on a forced march to the west. When he arrived at the village of Ulokol Touiets, however, allied naval fire immediately killed four of his staff. Deciding that the area was too dangerous, he evacuated the village and ordered his regiments back whence they had come.

His indecision gave the British enough breathing space to cross the Alma. The 2nd Division was slowed by flames from the village of Bourliuk, set on fire by Russian skirmishers. The Light Division made better progress. As it crossed the Alma, the vineyards and bends in the river robbed its formations of all order. Once over the river, however, the division stormed the Great Redoubt, driving out the Russian defenders.

How had the Light Division managed this triumph? It is tempting to speak of bravery, determination, and even British "pluck," but technology also had something to do with it. The British troops on the Alma were equipped with a new firearm that would revolutionize nineteenth-century battle tactics. This was the minié rifle, firing a conical bullet of soft lead that expanded to fit the rifled grooves. Its effective range was over 300 yards. Although the British fought in a fragile-looking line only two ranks deep, they were able to generate enormous amounts of firepower. The Russians, by contrast, were not only still using smoothbore muskets but also fought in dense columns, battalions of four companies apiece, some fifty men wide by sixteen deep. In their long gray coats, they were a closely packed, hard-to-miss target.

Nevertheless, if those Russian columns could close to hand-to-hand fighting, they were a formidable foe. Immediately after the fall of the Great Redoubt, four battalions of the Vladimir Regiment launched an impetuous counterattack. In the confusion of battle, a British officer apparently mistook their identity, crying "Don't fire! The column's French!" The pause enabled the Russians to retake the Redoubt, driving the Light Division back down toward the river. But now the Russians in turn were repulsed by a spirited assault of the 1st Division, consisting of the Highland and Guards Brigades, the cream of the British army. Their assault not only outflanked and overran the Great Redoubt but also drove the Russians off Kourganie Hill altogether. Facing two advancing and converging armies, the Russians began streaming away to the south, abandoning their equipment and throwing off all discipline. The time had come for Raglan to unleash his cavalry (the ill-fated Light Brigade) in a pursuit to destroy the fleeing enemy, à la Napoleon. With characteristic caution, however, he refused. The British troopers, trained for this moment and eager for action, sat by cursing, watching their opportunity for glory slip away. The French also hesitated to launch a pursuit, with St. Arnaud giving the lame excuse that his men could not follow the beaten enemy until they had retrieved the packs that had been left back across the Alma.

The casualties in the battle of the Alma tell the tale: the Russians had lost over 5,000 men in being evicted from their strong defensive position. The British had suffered 362 killed and 1,640 wounded in taking it. The French had done much marching and climbing but little fighting and had suffered just 60 killed and 500 wounded.[24]

The Russian rout did not stop until it reached Sevastopol. The force that reached the fortress was a beaten rabble, however, not an army. The allies could almost certainly have taken the city by assault but, showing an exaggerated concern for their supply line back to Eupatoria, decided to cut themselves loose from the port, executing a long flank march around Sevastopol to attack it from the south. While this allowed them to switch their bases of supply to the more conveniently located ports of Kamietch (for the French) and Balaklava (British), it also took a great deal of time. The allies did not bombard Sevastopol until October 17, by which date any hope for a speedy victory was gone. Instead, there would be that most sterile, costly, and difficult military operation: a siege of an enemy fortress.

The rest of the year saw two vain attempts by the Russians to break the siege. On October 25, they launched a great cavalry attack against Balaclava but were thrown back by a single regiment of infantry, the 93rd Highland, the "thin red line tipped with steel." The battle is best known for the senseless cavalry charge by the British Light Brigade, which arose from imprecise orders and resulted in the brigade's total destruction. On November 5, the Russians launched a second attempt to relieve Sevastopol, launching some 20,000 men against the British position at Inkerman. In a thick early morning fog, the ponderous Russian columns were unable even to penetrate the British outpost line, held by perhaps 1,000 men in all, let alone get at the main British position. Once again, British minié rifles took a heavy toll on the attacking Russians. Inkerman was an action totally without higher direction on either side, a classic example of a "soldier's battle."

There is no reason to describe the siege. After a terrible winter, in which the allies suffered horribly in their trenches, spring brought them huge reinforcements, and the issue was not in doubt.[25] The British built a five-mile railway from Balaklava to their battery positions (another first in warfare), which could bring up 700 tons of ammunition per day to their siege guns.[26] Over the next few months, the city was pulverized. In September 1855, an allied assault—spearheaded by French troops—broke through the main Russian defense line, and the Russians evacuated Sevastopol. Both sides were ready for a negotiated peace, leading to the Treaty of Paris in April 1856. The Crimean War was over. Both sides combined had taken some 500,000 casualties—the vast majority from disease. Despite the modern touches (rifles and telegrams and daily media coverage), the Crimean War will stand forever as the classic example of a senseless war. Fought for no good reason, under terrible leadership, it killed vast numbers of men and in the end settled nothing.

TECHNOLOGY: RIFLES AND RAILROADS

The nineteenth century was an era of dramatic change in warfare. Just as industrial technology revolutionized society, economy, and culture, it also transformed war. Historians typically speak of the age of "railroads and rifles." The railroad, and the industrial revolution that had spawned it, offered mechanized transport to armies. They could now "maneuver" twenty-four hours per day, and the problem of the slow-moving supply column that had bedeviled military operations from time out of mind seemed to have been solved. The kingdom of Prussia led the way, adding a Railway Section to its General Staff in 1860 to study the application of the railroad to warfare, and the entire European military establishment studied carefully the use of railroads by both sides in the American Civil War. In battle the introduction of the rifle dramatically improved the range and firepower of infantry. The 1860s saw another breakthrough with the introduction of the breech-loading rifle, greatly increasing the individual soldier's rate of fire. Again Prussia led the way, with the Dreyse needle gun, named for the narrow firing pin that struck the back of the cartridge and ignited the charge.[27] Industry and railroads also made possible a great increase in the size of armies, with industry churning out the necessary mountains of supplies and ammunition and the railroads to haul them. Finally, to railroads and rifles must be added an even more important invention, the telegraph, "the first real technological advance in the field of communications to take place in millennia."[28]

The new technology, as it always does, imposed its own peculiar, even contradictory requirements on nineteenth-century war. The railroad not only made possible the transport of mass armies and their supplies but also chained them to the existing rail net. The larger an army, the more rapidly it would wither and die should it be cut off from rail supply. The telegraph might have offered the nineteenth-century commander the comforting vision of tight control of an army in the field. He could now send orders to far-flung units, receive acknowledgment of their receipt, and coordinate his forces with a much greater degree of precision than Napoleon had enjoyed. Tied to a static system of poles and wires, however, it was much more useful to the defender than to the attacker.

The dream of centralized control remained just that. The huge size of the armies made it necessary to disperse them widely while they were on campaign. Concentrating them in one place for long was impossible; how could they be fed? In the words of the chief of the Prussian General Staff, General Helmuth von Moltke, these hosts were too large "either to live or advance," their one option being to fight a decisive battle as soon as they could.[29] Dispersal of such huge forces was bound to have negative consequences on the ability of a supreme commander—even a gifted one equipped with the telegraph—to control it. In combat, the increased range of rifles meant that the contending armies had to spread themselves out much more than in any earlier age, deploying farther away from the enemy, not to mention from their own commanders. Technology, therefore, was pulling the conduct of war in two contradictory directions, toward greater centralized control, on the one hand, and the need for decentralization and flexibility, on the other.

The most obvious impact of the new technology, and the one felt most immediately by the soldier at the front, was the increased firepower of the rifle. Military historians today generally make the argument that rifles made the Napoleonic assault obsolete. The argument is compelling: with long-range rifles now in the hands of the defenders, assault columns could be shot to pieces long before they struck home. In place of the old-style assault, there now arose the firefight, with extended skirmish lines on both sides replacing the formations of line and column. An "open order revolution" took place, with the soldiers physically dispersed on the battlefield, much farther away from their commanders, and thus far more difficult to control.[30] While there were some clearheaded progressives among the European officer corps who recognized these obvious facts, so runs the argument, there were too many still wedded to the Napoleonic tactics of yore. These conservatives felt that the bayonet was still the supreme arbiter of battle, and that to de-emphasize its use in training would mean the end of any chance for successful attacks and decisive victories.

Although this argument is generally true, the picture at the time was not so clear-cut. A good example is the War of Italian Unification (1859) between Austria and an alliance of France and the kingdom of Piedmont.[31] Analyzing its operations, we see, first of all, that railroads played a very small role. Austrian troops, already in the theater, invaded Piedmont on April 26, crossing the Ticino River from the Austrian province of Lombardy. The Austrian commander, Count Ferenc Gyulai, had 107,000 men versus 60,000 Piedmontese under King Victor Emmanuel II. But Gyulai moved quite slowly, taking four full days to get his five corps over the river, with some units barely moving three miles a day. For the next month he sat, complaining about lack of gun carriages, wagons, and supplies. The French, however, failed to take advantage of his hesitation. They, too, were having problems getting into gear. Their railroad net, consisting exclusively of single-track lines, was choked with bottlenecks. Mountains of supplies came by sea to Genoa, then sat there. It was all a colossal improvisation. As one French staff officer remarked, "On s'organisera en route" (We'll get organized along the way).[32]

Still, by the end of May, the French had assembled five army corps in northern Italy. After early encounters at Montebello and Palestro, Gyulai ordered a retreat back over the Ticino into Lombardy. As always seems to be the case with such generals, he managed to leave much more quickly than he had arrived. The French pursued, and on June 4 the armies met at Magenta. After a tough daylong battle, the French triumphed due to a combination of aggressive infantry and superior guns. Gyulai now evacuated Lombardy altogether, retreating to the heavily fortified "Quadrilateral" of Verona, Legnago, Mantua, and Peschiera.

While Napoleon III entered Milan on June 8, Emperor Franz Josef arrived to take command of the Habsburg forces. It would have made sense for him to stay in the Quadrilateral and let the French get mired in the Austrian fortified zone. There were no alternate routes forward. With the Alps and a series of lakes to the north and the mighty Po River to the south, northern Italy has all the operational subtlety of a bowling alley, with the Quadrilateral at the end; that is why the Austrians had spent so much money on the fortresses in the first place. But the presence of the emperor, eager to make his name on the battlefield, made it impossible to simply sit there and wait. Too much prestige—his and that of his dynasty—was on the line. After intense debate among his staff, Franz Josef brought the army out of the Quadrilateral to attack the advancing allies. The armies met at Solferino on June 24, with some 150,000 Austrians facing a Franco-Piedmontese force of 120,000. In a bloody day of seesaw fighting, the Austrians were again forced back. They had suffered much higher losses than the allies, 22,000 against 11,000 French and 5,000 Piedmontese. The fighting was over, as the demoralized Austrian army stumbled back to Verona.

Tactically, the battles had been confused meeting engagements. In both, bold attacks by small, fast-moving French columns, screened by aggressive waves of skirmishers, managed to break the Austrians again and again. The Austrians had a rifle, the Lorenz muzzle-loader, but it hardly seemed to matter. Most of the troops hardly knew how to fire it, and their columns often did little more than stand and get hit by aggressive French charges. Both problems were due to a lack of trained noncommissioned officers, who, in the highly bureaucratized Habsburg state, tended to get assigned to desk jobs. The army in the field consisted of a great mass of untrained conscripts, few of whom understood the official language of command, German, including even such basic commands as "halt" and "fire."[33] Like all minié rifles, the Lorenz also had a curved trajectory, and the untrained troops made the problem worse by tending to aim high. Finally, the French had much more effective artillery, rifled guns made of bronze called "Napoleons," that far outranged the Austrian smoothbore pieces and inflicted heavy casualties on nearly immobile Austrian columns.

Contemporary observers were shocked by the bloodiness of both battles, especially Solferino, from which Napoleon III had to be escorted after becoming physically ill. A Swiss businessman who was present, Henri Dunant, was so appalled by the plight of the wounded lying untended in the hot summer sun that he formed an organization for the impartial relief of wartime suffering, the Red Cross.[34] Still, despite the horrors, the lesson of Solferino seemed to be that well-led and highly motivated infantry was still capable of storming a rifle-armed position.

Soon after, of course, the American Civil War seemed to teach the opposite lesson. Again and again, infantry charges were shot to pieces by the defenders' rifle fire—the Union charge against the Sunken Road at Fredericksburg (1862), Pickett's Charge at Gettysburg, the sickening carnage suffered by Grant's assault force at Cold Harbor (1864). To many Europeans, however, these were battles fought by amateurs, both men and leaders, and its battlefield lessons—quite apart from its innovative use of railroads—were therefore without a great deal of significance for the professional soldier.

THE NEW NAPOLEON? THE CAREER AND INFLUENCE OF MOLTKE

The military history of the late nineteenth century is dominated by General Helmuth von Moltke, chief of the Prussian General Staff.[35] More than any other figure, he seemed to be able to square the circle, reconciling the new technology with the unchanging nature of war. As the American Civil War had shown, war had become a complex affair of mass armies, railroads, and telegraphs. It could no longer be improvised as in Napoleon's day. More than anyone who had gone before, Moltke put war on a scientific basis. He expanded the Prussian General Staff and extended its influence, using it for systematic, peacetime war planning. The Mobilization Section, for example, drew up detailed plans for the initial moves of a future war, compiling railroad schedules in huge volumes. The Geographical-Statistical Section was responsible for estimates of foreign armies, cartography, even weather charts of potential theaters of war. The Military History Section wrote histories of past campaigns, distilling the key lessons for modern officers. Moltke also drew up a series of standardized regulations. His *Instructions for Large Unit Commanders* (1869) is a groundbreaking work, the first handbook for warfare on the operational level and still worthy of study.

To teach both tactics and operations, the General Staff ran a busy schedule of maneuvers and war games *(Kriegsspielen)*, played on large sand tables and umpired by senior officers. There was also an annual staff ride *(Führerreise)*, in which staff officers played a simulated war while touring the actual terrain over which they were fighting. Each game featured an initial scenario *(Lage)*, the issuing of realistic orders, situation reports from the umpires, and, by far the most important component, a final discussion *(Schlussbesprechung)* analyzing each side's performance.[36] These may have been games, but they were *very* serious business. A slipup in a war game, or a shoddily prepared analysis in a final discussion, could mean the end of a career. The perhaps unreachable goal was to mold officers into one mind, guided by one overall operational doctrine.

Moltke demanded almost monastic devotion from General Staff officers, and in fact many were bachelors. Recruited by a highly competitive process, just twelve officers per year, and amounting to just one hundred men in all, the General Staff was the army's brain, a collective genius in the place of a once-in-a-millennium figure like Napoleon. In wartime, each army, corps, and divisional commander had a chief of staff at his right hand, an officer from the General Staff, to guide his thinking and actions onto the right path.

Beyond administrative and staff reforms, however, Moltke was also one of history's great field generals, commanding the Prussian army in the three wars of German unification: the Danish War of 1864, the Seven Weeks' War against Austria in 1866, and the Franco-Prussian War of 1870–71. As one analyzes his campaigns, it is possible to detect three constants in his art of war. The first was the importance he attached to the initial deployment *(Aufmarsch)* of the army. Due to the fixed nature of the railroad, a mistake made here could be a disaster. As he wrote, "A mistake in the initial concentration of the army can hardly be made good in the entire course of the campaign." Advantages could also be decisive. The classic example of a war won by the initial mobilization was the Franco-Prussian conflict. It began on July 15, and by the end of the month, a combination of careful planning by Moltke's staff and the highly developed Prussian rail net had resulted in the smooth mobilization of over 400,000 men. Deployed along the border of the French province of Lorraine, this great mass was organized into three armies, based respectively on Trier (1st Army), Homburg (2nd), and Landau (3rd). By the time the Prussians were fully mobilized and ready to march on July 31, the French had mobilized only individual corps, which were still being formed into armies as the fighting began. In Lorraine itself, French forces consisted of just two corps. In the opening battles, therefore, three coordinated Prussian armies faced individual French corps and beat them one by one, a classic example of a "defeat in detail" and a demonstration of the key place that advanced planning holds in the operational art.[37]

Second, Moltke had a distinct preference for the battle of envelopment, that is, pinning the foe in the front with one army, then hitting him simultaneously in the flank and rear with another. The result was a *Kesselschlacht* (cauldron battle), or more simply a battle of encirclement.[38] Achieving this goal required widely separated armies that had to "march separately but fight jointly,"[39] linking up only on the battlefield. It was a risky scheme, since armies that were dispersed during their initial deployment invited an enemy concentration and attack against one of them, but it also offered the possibility of decisive victory.

Finally, Moltke saw no certainty in war. "Strategy," he once wrote, "is a system of expedients," and on another occasion, "No plan survives contact with the enemy's main body." While it was on the march, an army had to be ready for anything, not hamstrung by rigid orders. "Only the layman perceives the campaign in terms of a fixed original conception, carried out in all details and rigidly followed until the end," he wrote.[40] His solution was something called *Auftragstaktik* (mission tactics). The commander devised a mission *(Auftrag)*, explained it in a short, clear order, then left the methods and means of achieving it to the officer on the spot.[41] In the wars of German unification, Moltke's touch was light indeed. Often, his army commanders did what they thought was correct and reported it to him afterward. On several occasions in the 1866 campaign, for example, armies of over 100,000 men went a day or two without any orders at all—an incredible notion by our modern standards.

The flexibility implicit in *Auftragstaktik* was a trademark of Moltke's entire art of war. By 1866, for example, the Austrians' infantry tactics had become much more aggressive, as a reaction to their experience against the

French in 1859. They now emphasized aggressive shock tactics, the assault with the bayonet, and the use of "storm columns."[42] Against Austria, Moltke tended to keep his troops on the defensive, trusting in the superior firepower of the needle gun. In 1870, however, the French had a fine breech-loading rifle of their own (the chassepot), even a primitive machine gun (the mitrailleuse). Relying on firepower, they fought much more defensively. Against France, Moltke risked a much bolder series of infantry attacks, supported by the fire of his modern artillery, new breech-loading guns made of steel, manufactured by the firm of Krupp.[43] The result was a pair of close-fought, very bloody victories at Spicheren and Wörth that shattered the nerve of the French army, driving it back onto its fortresses of Metz and Sedan, where it was eventually encircled.

The 1866 campaign is illustrative of Moltke's operational art.[44] Mobilizing more rapidly than their foe, the Prussians invaded Habsburg territory with three widely separated armies dispersed in an arc stretching over 200 miles of terrain. In a sense, it was an inversion of Napoleonic warfare: Moltke was using his rail net to operate on "exterior lines." There was no shortage of dissenting voices in the Prussian army warning of the dangers of Moltke's heresy. Why, he was ordering three unsupported and isolated armies into enemy territory! Betraying their lack of understanding of the age's military problems, many advised a simple concentration of the whole Prussian army at some selected point on the border for an irresistible advance into the enemy heartland, though the problems of feeding and supplying such a massive phalanx would have been insurmountable.

Moltke had his way in the end. As operations commenced, 1st Army under Prince Friedrich Karl, the "Red Prince," drove southward with his three corps into Bohemia. The 2nd Army, four corps under the command of Friedrich Wilhelm, the crown prince, invaded Moravia to the east. A third force, the "Elbe Army," was much smaller, a little over 40,000 men; its mission was to march through the territory of Austria's ally Saxony, sweep up the small Saxon army, and join 1st Army in Bohemia. Moltke's plan could not have been more flexible: advance in a concentric fashion, find the Austrian main body, fix it in place, then effect a junction of all three Prussian armies to destroy it. It was a simple but effective concept that would not require much in the way of fine-tuning or close control from the center, two things that Moltke felt were impossible in any event.

The war opened with a series of sharp engagements along the mountain passes into Bohemia. In these battles, the Austrians employed their newly designed shock tactics—charging forward in deep battalion columns with fifty-man frontages—and were torn apart by Prussian riflery. Austrian losses in these encounters were five times those of the Prussians. The steep price

The adversaries at Königgrätz. For most of the day, the battle was a contest between entrenched Austrian forces under Marshal Ludwig Benedek (above) and the Prussian 1st Army, led by Friedrich Karl, the "Red Prince" (opposite). Author's collection.

resulted from the combination of two factors: the Austrian turn toward shock since 1859 and the deadliness of the Prussian needle gun. The entire Austrian position in Bohemia was in shreds after two weeks of fighting.

The Austrian commander, General Ludwig Benedek, now decided to retreat, concentrating his army at Sadowa, west of the Elbe. Here his engineers fortified a position on the Chlum Heights behind the Bistritz (Bystrice) River.[45] As in all campaigns, intelligence was highly imperfect. Moltke believed that Benedek's main body actually lay to the east of the Elbe, until July 2, when 1st Army literally bumped into the Sadowa position. The Red Prince now decided, on his own initiative, to attack the Austrians at 10:00 A.M.

the next day. He sent a dispatch to the crown prince, instructing him to send a corps to support the attack, and only at that point did he inform Moltke. A rider brought Moltke the message in the night. Moltke immediately realized the significance of the news—and the opportunity that beckoned. He drafted two short orders: one to the crown prince, telling him to send not just a corps but his whole army to support 1st Army's attack; and one to the Red Prince, ordering him to attack earlier in the morning, to pin Benedek in place until 2nd Army could arrive to destroy him.

Military historians have a way of making every victory sound inevitable. That would be a mistake for Königgrätz. The Red Prince's attack went in at 8:00 A.M. in a heavy rain and was quickly pinned by Austrian fire. Rifled artillery on the Chlum Heights silenced the Prussian batteries, then began grinding up the infantry. For seven hours, the Red Prince was trapped in a killing ground between the Bistritz and Chlum, his men lying in the mud and rain, unable to advance, equally unable to retreat. It looked bleak, so much so that Wilhelm I, present with 1st Army, began muttering about retreat. "Moltke, Moltke, we are losing the battle," the king told his chief of staff. There are witnesses who heard Moltke calmly disagree with his sovereign. "Your majesty will today win not only the battle but the campaign," he is supposed to have said.[46] Still, it must have been a long morning for Moltke.

Benedek felt that he had won the battle. He even began preparing a counterattack with his I and VI Corps, as well as his large and excellent force of cavalry. He knew that 2nd Army was nearby, but he had deployed IV and II Corps on his right wing in entrenchments to keep watch. Unfortunately, IV Corps commander, Count Festetics, itching to get into battle, had made an unauthorized advance from his position into a patch of woods known as the Swiepwald. Count Thun, commander of II Corps, had orders to stay aligned with Festetics, and he did so. Soon both corps were engaged in a confused fight in the forest with the Prussian infantry and, incidentally, suffering horrible casualties from the fire of the needle gun.[47]

At noon, Benedek discovered what had happened and ordered his two corps back to the start line. He was ready to begin his counterattack when word came that Prussian 2nd Army was arriving on the field. Believing his line to be intact, he met the news with calm, a calm that was shattered the next moment when Festetics's chief of staff arrived to argue *against* pulling out of the Swiepwald. The attack by Prussian 2nd Army, spearheaded by the elite Guard Corps, was thus virtually unopposed, driving into Maslowed village at 1:00 P.M., then charging up the Chlum Heights by 2:00, overrunning the guns there, and scattering the Austrian reserves. The Austrian army, which just two hours previously had stood on the brink of a historic victory, now came apart, fleeing in confusion. One counterattack, by Austrian VI and I Corps, broke on the rocks of Prussian rifle fire at 3:30 P.M. By 5:00, it was over. The last Austrian formations were streaming away to the south, across the Elbe River into Königgrätz fortress, their flight skillfully and bravely covered by their cavalry and artillery. Austrian losses were 20,000, plus another 20,000 prisoners of war. Prussia's were just 10,000, a small price to pay for the mastery of central Europe.

It is not necessary to romanticize any of this or to make claims for Moltke's infallibility. It is clear that luck played a role in the Prussian victory. If the crown prince had arrived even an hour later, the battle could easily have gone the other way. The Prussian army was not the well-oiled machine of the history books. Moltke's army commanders seemed, at times, to have no understanding of his strategy. The Red Prince seemed particularly at sea for much of the campaign, forming his huge army into as compact a mass as possible with cavalry deployed in the rear, ready to deliver the final charge in battle.[48] As a result, he marched much more slowly than he might, and with no reconnaissance arm out in front of his main body, he often had no idea what he was facing. Moltke himself, as the years went by, made it seem as if every last move of the campaign had been his personal inspiration and intention. Given the praise heaped on his head by Germans and non-Germans alike, it is understandable if he began to believe in his own legend.

Still, he deserves most of the accolades. He had devised a simple, sound operational plan, based on his clear insight into the difficulties of commanding mass armies in the field. As the campaign unfolded, he had altered that plan as circumstance and opportunity dictated. He had given his subordinate army commanders a great deal of leeway, and although he and they made a number of miscalculations and mistakes, when the time came, he still managed to direct the crucial maneuvers of the campaign, bending it to his own will. In battle, he had persevered through the difficult morning in front of the Chlum Heights, coolly watching what looked like a disaster in the making, no doubt glancing occasionally to the north to look for signs of the arrival of the crown prince's army, yet still displaying admirable calmness under fire. If any nineteenth-century general deserves to be described as Napoleonic, it is Moltke.

CONCLUSIONS: THE NINETEENTH-CENTURY MILITARY REVOLUTION

What lessons does the military history of the nineteenth century offer us? First of all, it is clear that war had become a much more complicated undertaking than in any previous era. New technologies had radically transformed the way wars were fought. The successful general had to be more than the charismatic warrior of days past. He had to be a thoroughly trained professional grounded in the technical aspects of war-making, equally at home in the study, the foundry, the railway depot, or the battlefield.

Adding to the complexity was the dramatic growth in the size of armies. The contending forces at Königgrätz, for example, raised within mere weeks of mobilization, numbered around 450,000 men. Where nations had formerly raised a wartime army of, perhaps, 250,000 men, they could now raise several armies of that size. There was no textbook that explained how to handle armies this large; how to transport them by rail; how to feed, clothe, and supply them; and especially how to command them on campaign or in combat. While the railroad allowed massive conscript armies to mobilize rapidly and to advance into enemy territory within days of mobilization, what they did after that point was another story.

Two systems of handling these hosts immediately suggest themselves. In the first, the army, after crossing the hostile frontier, would pause in its advance until new orders, possibly the result of laborious argument among the commander, his staff officers, and the politicians, arrived. The advantage of this system was close direction of the war effort by those with sufficient political power, and enough facts at their disposal, to make the correct decision. The disadvantage, greatly outweighing the former, was the danger that while waiting for orders to arrive, the invading force would lose momentum and likely miss opportunities for favorable action against the enemy. In a sense, this was what had happened to British forces in the Crimea. Strategic indecision at home meant hesitancy and vacillation in the field. Nor was this "centralized strategy" to be salvaged by the simple expedient of having the political leadership present in the field. The example of Napoleon III and Franz Josef in the Italian War of 1859 proved that combining the operational command and political leadership into one man's hands was an obsolete and dangerous concept under modern conditions.

The second solution to the problem was the one adopted by Prussia. Command of immense, far-flung armies was a difficult undertaking, certainly beyond the ability of a single commander who was tucked away safely in the capital city hundreds of miles away. Army commanders in the field had to be able to react immediately to favorable opportunities as they presented themselves, without asking for permission. The supreme commander's job was to shape the campaign with a series of short, crisp orders, then let the army commander choose the means and methods of carrying them out.

There was an obvious danger to this scheme, of course. The army commander might, through foolhardy or mistaken decisions, torpedo the entire operational plan of the supreme command. This is what nearly happened in the Königgrätz campaign. In the Prussian system, the presence of a trained staff officer at the right hand of every army commander at least reduced the possibility of such a disaster. While there could never be certainty on this point, the identical education and training of the staff officers would tend to give them the same view of various military problems and their solutions. One thing was certain: the nineteenth century produced no better solution to the problem of command.

What, then, of the standard view of the century as an age in which the technology of war outstripped the ability of the generals to assimilate it? At issue here is the alleged supremacy of the defense created by the introduction of breech-loading rifles, and the refusal of the generals to recognize it.

This is a blatant example of anachronism. Historians have simply read the horrible experience of World War I back into the nineteenth century.

By and large, the armies of the age adopted the new technology about as smoothly as one could expect. Breech-loading rifles, railroads, telegraphs, and steamships—all entered the military establishment as fast as the constantly expanding military budgets would permit. The period from 1815 to 1914 was a testing ground for new weapons and new tactics to employ them most effectively, as was evidenced by the nonstop series of revised tactical manuals generated by virtually all European armies. Certainly, the rifle-armed defender could get off more shots at a greater distance than in Napoleon's time. What was not so clear was that the defense had thereby become supreme. The wars of the century saw the attacking side triumph again and again. The French in Italy, the Prussians against Austria and the French, and the Russians in their war with Turkey (1879) all have two things in common. All were forces on the strategic (and often the tactical) offensive, and all three were victorious.

Historians often criticize a so-called cult of the offensive, a wrong turn that European officers took in the late nineteenth century. Such an accusation stands on questionable evidence, at best. Given the historical record, why would the offensive not be the favored method of warfare?[49] The lesson of the century, in fact, might be stated thusly: the side that waits to be attacked, and then defends passively in place, loses every time. At Königgrätz, the Austrians occupied a solid defensive position, on a dominating height, fortified by the best efforts of skilled military engineers, with wide fields of fire for both artillery and infantry. At the end of the day they were streaming back to Königgrätz fortress a defeated mob. Not a typical nineteenth-century battle? It was more typical than Fredericksburg.

No one can deny the impact of the rifle on modern tactics. Its increased range, accuracy, and rate of fire made obsolete the old-style column assault. Cavalry, in particular, found itself unable even to approach the battlefield, let alone charge forward in the old style to deliver the decisive blow. In addition, the rifle changed modern battle by spreading it out across ever larger stretches of terrain. Napoleon could stand on an elevated piece of ground and survey the entire battle raging around him. That was no longer possible. With enemy fire—both rifles and long-range artillery—able to poke ever more deeply into any friendly position, the armies had to deploy farther away from one another. What had formerly been tightly packed formations of infantry and cavalry closely supported by artillery were now much thinner lines deployed across tens, sometimes hundreds, of miles of terrain. A kind of chaos—a command and control nightmare—had descended onto the battlefield.[50]

The combination of heavier firepower and the dispersed battlefield was the inspiration for the last of the great nineteenth-century "prophets" of modern warfare. Charles-Ardent du Picq was a French colonel who served in the Crimea, Syria, Algeria, and finally the Franco-Prussian War, in which he was killed at the age of thirty-nine. Although his *Études sur le Combat* was not printed in its entirety until 1902, it became a sensation and was one of the most widely read books in the French trenches during World War I.[51] Writing in the midst of the technological revolution, he claimed that technology hardly mattered at all. Basing his research on a questionnaire that he had circulated among his fellow officers, he concluded that "success in battle is a matter of morale." Moral forces, not material ones, came into conflict on the battlefield. "The stronger conquers."

But what makes a soldier "stronger"? Since the days of the Roman legion, he argued, a man took strength from the formation of which he was a part. Whether in line or column, a soldier could look up and see his fellows, reach out and touch them, and gain a sense of strength from the mass. The new battlefield, with the units spread far and wide by necessity, was a very different environment. "The soldier is unknown often to his closest companions," he wrote. "He loses them in the disorienting smoke and confusion of a battle which he is fighting, so to speak, on his own." It was a lonely place, an empty battlefield, where "cohesion is no longer ensured by mutual observation."

Du Picq argued that the best way to enforce cohesion in an army was to order it to attack, since the boldness of coming to close quarters with an enemy imbues the attacker with a moral advantage over an adversary who is conducting a passive defense. The bayonet charge, he wrote, "in other words the forward march under fire, will every day have a correspondingly greater effect." Du Picq is perhaps at his best in destroying the myth of hand-to-hand combat. A charge succeeded or failed based on moral factors. If the enemy yields and runs, the charge succeeds—and the slaughter begins; if the enemy stands firm, the charge fails and is repulsed. It is decided, in other words, before the two parties make contact. "Shock," he wrote, "is a word." The notion of huge masses of cavalry colliding with one another, an idea featured in so many nineteenth-century military histories, was "poetry, never reality."

Despite the terrors of du Picq's empty battlefield, it was almost always possible in the nineteenth century to attack an enemy position, to reach it, and even to drive through it, given sufficient will, sufficient manpower, and enough preparatory fire on the part of friendly artillery. Then the troubles began. How could the commander, by necessity deployed far behind the lines and "armed" only with an immobile telegraph network, get his orders

forward to the unit that had just assaulted successfully? How far would reserve forces, deployed well in the rear to avoid presenting attractive targets
to enemy artillery, have to march in order to reinforce the success? How many
casualties had the assault force taken, even from a weak defending screen, if
the defenders were armed with rifles? This was the great military problem
of the day: in the German parlance, how might the attacker transform his
"break-in" *(Einbruch)* into a "breakthrough" *(Durchbruch)*?[52]

Solving this problem was not so much a firepower issue as an issue of
command, or, in the words of twentieth-century analysts, "command, control, and communications" ("C³"). The command problem foiled most of
the nineteenth-century generals, even quite gifted ones. In the American Civil
War, the commonly discussed examples given in support of the "supremacy
of the defensive" are hardly typical of the century, or even of the war itself.
At Fredericksburg, Gettysburg, and Cold Harbor, assault forces met their
doom by charging into the teeth of solid defenses that were almost completely untouched by preparatory fire. Of course all three suffered horrendous casualties and failed dismally. The same tactics had failed at Agincourt
in 1415, where the French knights went to their doom in a hail of English
longbow fire. In fact, the American Civil War could hardly be called a show-
case of long range rifle fire, the allegedly supreme arbiter of the nineteenth-
century battlefield. The vast majority of skirmishes and firefights took place
well under maximum rifle range.

A more instructive Civil War battle was Chancellorsville.[53] Here General
Robert E. Lee launched a bold flank march under his most talented subordinate, General Thomas "Stonewall" Jackson. Marching clear around the
dangling flank of General Robert Hooker's Union army south of the Rapidan
River, Jackson achieved almost complete surprise. He crashed into the flank
of the utterly unprepared XI Corps as it was lining up for supper and simply rolled it up. The XI Corps had neither time nor room to deploy, and in
any case its command structure had collapsed, its commanders being swept
up in the rout alongside the men. With his flanks caved in and facing the
always dangerous Lee to his front, Hooker beat a hasty retreat back over
the river.

While Chancellorsville was a Confederate victory, it was no Austerlitz.
The Union army had been thoroughly mauled, but it had not been destroyed.
After launching Jackson on his way, Lee had no way of coordinating the
activities of the flanking force with his own; Jackson himself had precious
little control over his own assault once it got under way. Almost immediately after making contact, the charge began to lose momentum. The assaulting units became intermingled with one another and disoriented, as dusk
settled on the Virginia wilderness. Scattered Federal units came up into the

line, delaying, disrupting, and harassing the Confederate advance. Jackson's attempt at personal reconnaissance, riding on ahead to see the situation at the front for himself, ended in disaster when his own soldiers mistook him for a Union officer and shot him dead. This most "Napoleonic" of Civil War battles, featuring Lee's elegant version of a *manoeuvre sur les derrières,* illustrated how dramatically war had changed since Napoleon's day.

As the nineteenth century gave way to the twentieth, a war was raging in faraway South Africa. The course of the war, and the seemingly insurmountable tactical and operational problems that it posed, shocked the general staffs of all the great powers. Had the traditional infantry army, even one equipped with rifles and backed with its own powerful artillery, lost its ability to maneuver, and thus to triumph? Had the defense finally triumphed over the attack? Had the age of decisive victory ended?

Chapter 2

●　●　●　●　●　●　●　●　●　●　●　●　●　●

Firepower Triumphant:
The South African War

In most military histories, the year 1914 is the great divide. So dominant is the Great War in our historical consciousness that it is sometimes hard to remember that the fifteen years before it saw no fewer than three "great wars." While each of them was unique in many respects, they all faced their participants with a similar set of problems: how to command and control the mass army spread out over vast stretches of terrain; how to maintain the momentum of the advance in the face of the heavy casualties inflicted by modern firepower; how to achieve decisive, "Napoleonic" victory under modern conditions; and, finally, how to develop any firm principles of war at all, when the technology was in such a constant state of flux. As we shall see, no one had a very good solution to any of these problems.

THE BOER WAR: FIRST PHASE

The shock of Great Britain's war with the "Boers" (more accurately, with the Orange Free State and the South African Republic, or Transvaal) still reverberates around the world.[1] Looking simultaneously backward to the American Revolution and forward to the national liberation struggles of the

An unusual opponent for a European army. Three generations of Boers prepare to face the British in 1900. From left, P. J. Lemmer (age 65), J. D. L. Botha (age 15), and G. J. Pretorius (age 43). Courtesy of the Imperial War Museum, London (Q 101767).

mid–twentieth century, it has lost none of its ability to fascinate in the century since it ended. What scholars now call the "South African War" was really two distinct conflicts. The first was a conventional struggle between two very different armies that featured some of the most shockingly lopsided outcomes in all of military history. The second is often described as one of the greatest guerrilla struggles ever waged. In every way, the conflict was a fitting curtain-raiser on the warfare of the twentieth century.

When war broke out in October 1899, British officers viewed their Boer adversary as a half-educated simpleton, a drastic underestimation for which they would pay dearly. The Boers (Dutch for "farmers") of South Africa were a hardy folk, independent-minded and deeply religious, of the same Calvinist stamp as the Puritans who had settled America. In war they proved to be a tough lot. Entirely at home in their rugged environment, the Boers fought as mounted infantry, riding to battle, then dismounting to fight on foot. They had no need of supply lines. By law, each man had to carry his own ammunition and eight days' worth of rations (dried beef and biscuits), and the endless grasslands (the "veld") on which they lived fed their ponies.

They knew each fold of the terrain intimately, every donga, spruit, drift, and kloof, and each man among them was a crack shot, armed with his modern Mauser rifle with five-shot magazine and smokeless powder. In battle, the Boer was a formidable mix of fire and movement. He would entrench on a commanding height, or kopje, a terrain feature he had inevitably reached before his slower-moving enemy, lay down withering fire against the advancing foe, then mount up and gallop back to the next one.

The Boers' one real weakness, in the end a fatal one, was a lack of central command. They fought in irregular, independent units, or commandos, who elected their leaders and tended to go on leave whenever they felt like it. They had no real order of ranks, since each man was a citizen, or burgher, as good as any other. He had to be persuaded, not ordered. The great guerrilla leader Christiaan De Wet, who ought to know, wrote after the war that "real discipline did not exist among the burghers," not even in combat.[2] Describing one early action, he noted that many of his men "remained in the first safe position they reached—a frequent occurrence at that period."[3] By contrast, British forces in South Africa consisted of a regular army corps of three divisions, under General Sir Redvers Buller. Discipline under fire, a regular structure of command, the presence of a reliable supply train—all these would stand the British army in good stead over the next two years.

The British had other disadvantages, however. Buller and his staff were working from poorly drawn maps. His command was almost completely infantry, no match in the veld for Boer mobility. His entire force was tied to three single-track railroads for a theater of war bigger than France and Spain combined. The main line northward from Cape Town to De Aar Junction was 400 miles of single-track line. The town of Mafeking, soon to figure prominently in British strategy, was 850 miles from Cape Town; the capital of Transvaal, Pretoria, was over 900 miles.[4] Finally, even though it had provoked the war, Great Britain began the conflict outnumbered, with only 20,000 men against some 30,000 Boers, although Boer strength at any given time in the war can be extremely difficult to pin down. Summing up the problem, British general Ian Hamilton likened the war to a struggle between "city-bred dollar hunters" and "Deer-slayer and his clan," and those are apt metaphors.[5]

The war began in a conventional manner with Boer forces invading the British territories of Cape Colony to the west and Natal to the south and east. The outnumbered British forces ran to the nearest towns, and soon the Boers were besieging British garrisons at Kimberley and Mafeking, on the western frontier of the republics, as well as Ladysmith in Natal. None was ever in real danger of being taken, as siege was not the Boers' game.

Apart from a few modern guns purchased abroad from the firms of Krupp and Schneider-Creusot, they had no real siege train. Still, the surrounded garrisons were important in the war's early months by dictating British strategy. With the London dailies screaming for action, and an avid reading public seconding them, Buller had to take action before he was fully prepared.

In the western theater, his main thrust was by 1st Division, 10,000 men under Lord Methuen, moving up the railroad line to relieve Kimberley, a march of some seventy-five miles to the north. Methuen made use of the standard British tactic against native forces, which was, after all, what the Boers were in British eyes: a night march followed by a dawn assault. Skirmishes took place at Belmont (November 23) and Graspaan (November 25). In both, the Boers inflicted heavy casualties, then retreated.

Believing that he had the foe on the run, Methuen kept on to the north and on November 28 met the main Boer force at the Modder River.[6] These were Free Staters under the command of Jacobus Prinsloo and Transvaalers under Piet Cronje and Koos De la Rey. In the prebattle council, standard practice for the democratically minded Boers, De la Rey argued for digging in not on a kopje, as the Boers had traditionally done, but on the plain in front of the river itself. This would better exploit the flat trajectory of the Mauser, which had a range out to 2,200 meters. In the early encounters, the kopje had also proved vulnerable to the one arm in which the British were clearly superior: artillery. Entrenched on the flat and covered with brush, the Boers would be nearly invisible, the best protection, De la Rey argued, from British shellfire.

Methuen arrived at the Modder after a night march. Reconnaissance was poor, as it would often be in this war. His scouts, a few weak cavalry units, reported a light screen of just 400 Boers in front of him. There were in fact 3,500. Methuen was not even sure of the river's exact course. Nevertheless, at 5:30 A.M., he ordered the advance. His men were less then 1,000 yards from the river, all was quiet, and Methuen had just turned to an aide to say, "They're not here," when a hail of bullets ripped out of the unseen Boer trenches, hitting the Guards Brigade moving up on the right and sending them to the ground.[7] All day long, the Guards lay pinned to the veld, unable to move, slowly being ground up by an enemy they could not even see, on an "empty battlefield." This battle has as much claim as any to being that elusive moment: the birth of modern war. British losses topped 500 men, against just 50 Boers, and it could have been worse. The Boers, having concentrated against the Guards, had no real strength on their own right flank. During the day, small groups of British infantry, units of the 9th Brigade under General R. Pole-Carew, managed to find a dry riverbed through which they could advance relatively immune from Boer fire. They managed to evict

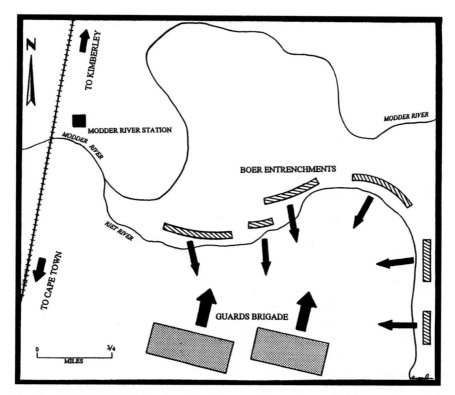

The "empty battlefield": Battle of the Modder River, November 28, 1899.

a group of Boers from a small farmhouse south of the Modder and then used it as a strongpoint to protect their advance over the river. With a British force, albeit a small one, over the river, and with his reinforcements coming up by late afternoon, Methuen could have taken up the attack the next day. The Boers, apparently satisfied with their day's work, retreated from the Modder that night. Methuen called it "one of the hardest and most trying fights in the annals of the British Army."[8] While casualties had not been exceptionally heavy, most of the British soldiers had spent the whole day lying out in the open, unable to reply to Boer fire or even see a single Boer. The fight on the Modder was a completely new experience.

Methuen was now just twenty-nine miles from Kimberley, but blocking his way was a prominent hill, the Magersfontein kopje.[9] It seems incredible after his experience at the Modder, but Methuen's plan called for a night march up to the foot of Magersfontein, followed by a frontal assault at dawn on the southern ridge of the hill. His assault force was the newly arrived

General Andrew Wauchope led the Highland Brigade, arrayed in a thick mass of "quarter columns," to its destruction at Magersfontein. Wauchope was killed in the initial Boer volley. Author's collection.

Highland Brigade, under the command of General Andrew Wauchope. This time, however, a huge artillery bombardment would precede the assault, destroying the Boer entrenchments and demoralizing the defending burghers. The Boers were not where he thought they were, however. Now some 8,000 strong, they had dug their trenches not on the hill, nor even at the foot of the hill, but well in front of it. They had also dug another trench at a right angle, to the east of the British line of advance. Finally, they had placed whitewashed stones at intervals in front of their position, giving an easy range reference, as well as trip wires tied to tin cans to announce the arrival of the enemy.

Not that they really needed such quaint devices. The bombardment opened on the afternoon of December 10 but did hardly any damage to the deeply entrenched Boers. A little after midnight on December 11, the Highland Brigade began its march to the north. It had been drizzling since the previous afternoon, and now suddenly the skies opened in a downpour. There was not a long distance to go, just two and a half miles, but in the darkness of night on the veld, any march might go astray. To keep the column on its heading, the Highlanders came up to the hill in close formation of quarter columns, a great mass of men forty men wide by ninety-six deep. The Black Watch was in the van, followed by the Seaforth Highlanders and the Argyll and Sutherland Highlanders in succession. The Highland Light Infantry brought up the rear. Methuen, like all European commanders of the age, knew that once his troops were deployed into line and began to exchange fire with the enemy, command and control would become impossible. Hence, he delayed the deployment until the last possible moment. Now, just minutes away from the base of Magersfontein, that moment had come. His plans called for deployment into line a few hundred yards from the Boer trenches. The Black Watch would hold the center, the Seaforths would extend to the left, and the Argyll and Sutherland Highlanders would do the same on the right, with the Highlanders in reserve.[10] The men would then fix bayonets and charge.

Methuen would bear the brunt of the blame for this unimaginative plan of battle. However, the same scheme could have resulted from the mind of nearly every officer in the British army. The night march, as risky and as disruptive as it appears to us, was the prudent way for the Highland Brigade to get across two miles of open ground in front of the Boers. The quarter columns were necessary to keep the force concentrated for the assault. Likewise, while many readers are shocked to find that the leftmost files of the column were knotted together with rope, they had to be, to keep the column in order until the time came to deploy. For many years, published accounts on the battle have claimed that Wauchope objected strenuously to Methuen's orders. "I do not like the idea of this night march," he is supposed to have said to Methuen's chief of staff.[11] Although the charge even made the official history, more recent research has labeled it a myth. It appears that the plan made sense to Wauchope, as indeed it would to most professional officers of the day.

After repeated halts on the march, the Highland Brigade had reached its objective by 3:30 A.M. Daylight was just moments away, and because it would take the brigade a full fifteen minutes to change formation, it was imperative to get started. Wauchope hesitated, however. He peered at the kopje, but in the semidarkness it was impossible to gauge its exact distance. He thought the brigade was still too far away from the Boer trenches, which he expected to find at the foot of the hill. It was crucial that the break of dawn not find the brigade too far out in the open. That would be a disaster. The advance continued for several hundred more yards. The men of the Black Watch got tangled in a patch of prickly mimosa, and Wauchope let more minutes pass so they could negotiate it. By now, he and the brigade were 700 yards from the hill, and perhaps 400 from the hidden Boer trenches.

Finally, all was in readiness. Wauchope had just given the order to deploy into line when the air literally exploded with rifle fire. The Highlanders could not have been in a worse situation, bunched up, dazed, and soaked through. Even worse, they were in the midst of the always disruptive and confusing process of changing formations. According to one officer,

> Had the Highlanders been deployed when the Boers opened fire the pipers would have sounded the charge and the impetus of the first rush would have carried the brigade into the Boer trenches before the enemy could stop it. [However, as Wauchope] gave the order to deploy, the Boer fire commenced at that instant. It caught the brigade at its greatest disadvantage—halted and partly deployed.[12]

The fire was point-blank, well under 500 yards, a range at which a single bullet could pass through more than one man. In ten minutes, Wauchope was killed, and hundreds of his men were dead or dying.

This was far worse than the Modder. For nine hours, the Highland Brigade lay pinned to the veld. The slightest movement of a hand, a sneeze, the glint of a belt buckle, or the raising of a head brought down a hail of lead. It was December, high summer on the veld, and the men lay tortured by heat and thirst and ravenous ants, the backs of their bare legs (these were Scotsmen) burned raw by the sun. Methuen, in classic understatement, wrote, "The Highland Brigade was of little use to me, during the remainder of the day, greatly owing to the paucity of officers."[13] The British official history matched him, stating only, "The unfortunate incidents of the early morning had gravely compromised Lord Methuen's battle array."[14] No doubt the men being chewed up on the veld would have chosen different words.

By 2:00 P.M., the cream of the British army had had enough. A trickle of men began to work their way back. The trickle grew, and then what was left of the Brigade began to withdraw en masse. The Boer defenders stood up in their trenches to empty their magazines into the retreating force, and the retreat became a rout. The Highland Brigade was essentially destroyed, with losses topping 1,000, and many of the men had died with their backs to the enemy. "Then I saw a sight that I hope I may never see again," wrote one observer, "men of the Highland Brigade running for all they were worth, others cowering under bushes, behind the guns, some lying under their blankets, officers running about with revolvers in their hands threatening to shoot them, urging on some, kicking on others."[15] This time the Boers stayed put in their trenches, as a dazed Methuen retreated back to the Modder.

Magersfontein was just one of three disasters during what the British press dubbed "Black Week." On December 10, one day before the battle, a force under General Gatacre had tried to surprise the Boers at Stormberg in the Cape Colony, after a long night march. The Boers were not surprised. They not only inflicted 135 casualties on Gatacre's force but also took 696 prisoners. Then, on December 15, Buller had his own personal introduction to the Mauser rifle. Marching to the relief of Ladysmith through some of the most difficult terrain in South Africa, described by one correspondent as mountain "disarranges," Buller tried to force a crossing over the winding Tugela River at a place called Colenso.[16] Here the British met a force under thirty-seven-year old Boer general Louis Botha, entrenched behind the river.

In the aftermath, observers and participants in the battle of Colenso would describe it as "one of the most unfortunate battles in which a British army has ever been engaged," a "deplorable tactical display," and "a devil of a mess."[17] None of those phrases really does justice to what happened. Buller approached the river, whose winding course and variable depth he only dimly understood, with a massive force and all its impedimenta: four infantry brigades under Generals Barton, Hildyard, Lyttelton, and Hart (the last named commanding the Irish Brigade); five field batteries; fourteen naval guns, including two 4.7-cm pieces; and a huge contingent of cavalry and mounted infantry, including the 1st Royal Dragoons, the 13th Hussars, and large contingents of the South African and Imperial Light Horse, all under the command of Lord Dundonald.

Although Buller had given consideration to turning Botha's position by crossing the river at Potgieter's Drift, some twenty-five miles to the west, in the end the horrible news from Stormberg and Magersfontein impelled him to force a decisive action as soon as possible. He now launched this huge force, which outnumbered the Boer defenders by perhaps eight to one, on a frontal assault against Colenso: Hart's Irishmen on the left to cross the river at a drift imprecisely marked on Buller's map; General Hildyard in the center, to "cross the iron bridge" over the river, even though there were two iron bridges over the river, one road and one railroad;[18] and Dundonald's cavalry on the right, to seize Hlanghwane Hill; Barton and Lyttelson's brigades were in reserve.

They approached the Tugela on a front two miles wide and about a mile deep, throwing up a thick pall of dust that announced their arrival to the Boers. The battle opened with Hart's brigade heading for its assigned crossing. Just west of Colenso, the Tugela bends sharply around and then back, describing a neat loop toward the Boer side of the river. Into that loop, apparently to the amazement of his native guide, Hart now ordered his brigade. The leading regiment, the Dublin Fusiliers, was deployed into line; the rest of the Brigade was in the same formation of quarter columns as the Highlanders had been when the shooting started at Magersfontein. The sudden appearance of one of the most amazing target profiles in all of military history was too much for the Boers to resist. Although Botha had impressed on his men the necessity for holding fire until he ordered it, a heavy fire, "the most terrific I have ever heard or thought of in my life,"[19] according to one British participant, now erupted from the unseen Boer trenches. Even though the first volleys went high, apparently out of excitement, the Irish Brigade was finished. For the rest of the day, its men lay as flat as they could under whatever cover they could find, watching bullets strike all around them, being hit, wounded, or killed one by one. By the end of the day, the brigade had suffered 532 casualties. For the record, some brave men managed to crawl forward to the river, to the point at which the drift had been marked on their maps. They found the river in that place to be deep and swift, completely unfordable.

While Buller's left was being ground up, another disaster occurred in the center. Here were Buller's field guns, under the command of Colonel C. J. Long, twelve 15-pounders and six naval 12-pounders. Although Buller had ordered Long to deploy them well to the rear, Long saw a chance for glory. Galloping his gun teams to within 1,000 yards of the river, he unlimbered them in what might be called Napoleonic fashion, if he had not far outraced the supporting infantry of Hildyard's brigade. From his perch on the opposite side, Botha was amazed. Once again, his men anticipated his order to open fire— it was impossible to resist the opportunity. The magazines of 1,000 Mauser rifles now emptied into the hapless British gun crews, a true hail of bullets. This was a situation that most of the contemporary manuals did not yet discuss: total helplessness. Those who could flee—the trailing gun crews, for

The Colenso battlefield, seen from the heights on the northern bank of the Tugela. The loop in the river in the upper right of the photo is the site where the Irish Brigade blundered into the Boer ambush. Courtesy of the Imperial War Museum, London (Q 68469).

example—fled. Those who could not tried to get their guns into action, failed, and eventually were shot. By the end of the day, after Buller had ordered a general retirement, ten British guns stood, uncrewed. Small parties of Boers crossed to the south of the river and made off with them.

Compared with these two unmitigated disasters, the rest of the battle was simply a failure. Dundonald's cavalry and mounted infantry fought their way to the foot of Hlanghwane and worked their way around its eastern flank but could not seize it, due partially to the refusal of General Barton to support him. Hildyard's attempt to cross the bridge, by now reduced to a simplistic frontal assault without any support on either flank, did manage to get to the bridge, then was called off by Buller's order to retire.

Colenso was a catastrophe, but, again, it could have been much worse. Botha had been shooting for the big prize, apparently intending to let the British cross the river, then blow the road bridge in their rear and bag the entire force. He went so far as to credit Colonel Long and General Hart with upsetting his plans, although it is difficult to credit them with anything other than having their units act as target practice for the Boers entrenched along the riverbank. Whatever Botha's intentions had been, Colenso was bad enough. When finally added up, British losses had amounted to 1,138: 143 killed, 755 wounded, and 240 prisoners, not to mention ten field guns. The Boers, incredibly, lost 6 men killed and 21 wounded. Colenso requires a new definition for the word *battle,* which has traditionally meant a test of arms in which both sides give and take punishment. The Dublin Fusilier who stated after Colenso that "it was no fight, no fight at all" was absolutely correct.[20] Botha was better able to make sense of it, in the way that any Boer could understand: "The God of our fathers has today granted us a brilliant victory," he cabled President Kruger.[21]

In these three battles—Magersfontein, Stormberg, and Colenso—Buller's army was essentially destroyed. More slaughter was to come, such as the battle of Spion Kop in January 1900, where the Boers managed to work around the flank of a British force entrenched on a hill and subject it to a devastating enfilade fire. Each disaster had its excuses and rationalizations. Buller's defenders, for example, argued that he was operating in country that was designed for the defense and very unsuited to the attack. But all were essentially reruns of the same story: simplistic frontal attacks, laid out along the rail line; lack of reconnaissance; maps that were often incorrect on basic information like the course or depth of a river. And yet all these pale in comparison with the shock of Boer rifle fire. Mauser magazine rifles, firing smokeless powder, seemed to be a new kind of infernal machine, an awesome wonder weapon loosed upon the world that would carry all before it. Past meetings with the Boers had testified to their ability with the rifle. When Winston Churchill was in South Africa as a correspondent in the war's early days, Boers ambushed the armored train in which he was riding. As he tried to flee on foot, he saw two armed Boers raising their rifles at him and later recalled that the only two words that passed through his mind at that moment of destiny were "Boer marksmanship."[22] This was two months before Black Week.

But now, a new age in warfare had apparently begun, one in which the rifle had made all other weapons obsolete. Artillery, as presently built and used, was useless, since it could no longer get close enough to the front to support the infantry in the old manner. And when the defender was in his entrenchments, it really did not matter where the artillery was. One observer wrote that "a fortified position may be shelled for half a day without the enemy being driven so far from it that he cannot return in time to meet a charge of infantry."[23] As for cavalry, it was increasingly clear that the man on horseback represented nothing on the modern battlefield so much as a huge, hard-to-miss target for the rifle-armed defender. It seemed that the magazine rifle had upset the delicate combined arms balance that had obtained in battle since Napoleon's day.

There is danger in overstating what had happened, however. The Boers were not invulnerable. At Elandslaagte on October 21, the British had launched a well-coordinated assault that destroyed the Johannesburg commando. Infantry under the command of soft-spoken Colonel Ian Hamilton, later of Gallipoli fame, worked their way toward a Boer position on a kopje in short rushes, utilizing extremely open order to reduce casualties. The Devonshire Regiment attacked frontally, to pin Boer attention; the Manchesters and Gordon Highlanders worked their way carefully along the flank. Once the flanking forces were in place, a bayonet charge sealed the victory. At this point, with some Boers waving white flags and others simply trying to get away, the commander of the British cavalry, Major General John French, ordered a charge by his 5th Lancers and 5th Dragoon Guards. With sabers drawn and lances at the ready, the troopers rode down a group of retreating Boers. Their retreat turned into a rout, then into a massacre as the lancers began stabbing and hacking at men who clearly had no more fight left. One lancer wrote, "We charged them and they went on their knees, begging us to shoot them rather than stab them with our lances, but in vain. The time had come for us to do our work and we did it."[24] But one hears hardly anything these days about Elandslaagte. Moreover, despite their tactical skill, the Boers had all the strategic acumen of a group of farmers. Defending the land was the sum total of their vision. Pursuing and destroying defeated forces, linking victorious defensive battles together into some kind of successful campaign, carrying the fight to the British rather than waiting to be attacked—these were entirely beyond them.

Second, the hysteria about Boer firepower tended to ignore the skill with which the Boers handled their small amount of artillery. Both republics together probably owned 100 field guns at the outset of the fighting. But they used them cleverly, manhandling them into positions that a more modern army would never have considered. They also made good use of a piece that the British army had rejected, the 37-mm Vickers-Maxim automatic gun. Known as the "pompom" for the sound it made, it could unlimber quickly, lay down a lightning barrage against its target, then disappear. At Colenso, the pompoms played a key role in the destruction of the unfortunate British gun crews.

Black Week had the paradoxical result of generating a tremendous outpouring of popular enthusiasm for the war in Britain. Men volunteered by the thousands, and soon huge reinforcements had arrived in South Africa, eventually reaching 450,000 men. In February a great British force under Lord Roberts set out from the Modder. It consisted of 60,000 infantry, a full cavalry division under General French (assisted by an able young staff officer, Major Douglas Haig), contingents of mounted infantry, and recently raised units of colonial guides like Rimington's Tigers. British newspapers spoke of "Bobs's steamroller," but in fact Roberts handled his force with a great deal of skill and finesse. Keeping two brigades in front of Magersfontein to screen the Boers, he launched his main body on a flank march to the east, invading the Orange Free State and forcing the Boers to slide along with him.

An important part of this great flank march was the relief of Kimberley. On February 15, French assembled a "flying column" of regular cavalry, mounted infantry, and irregular horse formations like the New South Wales Lancers and the New Zealand Light Horse. They took off around the Boer left flank, while a feint by the Highland Brigade distracted the Boer right. Almost immediately they had broken through into the clear, as the dust raised by almost 5,000 horsemen temporarily blinded the weak screen of Boer riflemen in the area. By afternoon he was within sight of Kimberley, and he entered the town that evening. Significantly, the great pace of the ride killed off the vast majority of the regular cavalry's mounts, due to the heavy equipment they carried. This was still a force accoutred for shock combat. The irregulars, lighter and leaner in every way, made it in much better shape.[25]

Cronje, now leading the main Boer force, began to retreat eastward along the Modder, then made a fatal error of drawing up his ox wagons into laager, the traditional Boer all-around defensive stance. By February 17, Roberts had him surrounded near Paardeberg. The British launched an assault that day, nearly 20,000 infantry against fewer than 5,000 defenders. The Boers repulsed it bloodily, inflicting some 1,200 British casualties, before Roberts did the sensible thing: bringing up his artillery and pounding Cronje into submission. For eleven days the Boers in the Paardeberg laager endured bombardment by new high-explosive lyddite shells. Men and horses suffered terribly, not to mention the women and children who were present in the camp. Largely based on his fears for their safety, Cronje surrendered on February 27 with 4,000 men. Continuing east along the Modder, "Bobs" took Bloomfontein on April 4. From here the steamroller moved north against increasingly scattered opposition, taking the surrender of demoralized Boers as it went. Roberts entered Pretoria on June 5. Great Britain annexed both republics, and it appeared that the war was over.

DE WET'S WAR

Despite the annihilation of their field army and the occupation of their republics, many Boers refused to give up the struggle. Young commanders like Louis Botha, Jan Christiaan Smuts, and De Wet met at a war council (*Krijgsraad*) in March 1900 and swore to fight on. Calling themselves "bitter-

Christiaan De Wet was one of the most successful Boer leaders during the irregular phase of the war. Author's collection.

enders," they took to the veld in small bands, launching a furious guerrilla war against the British and sometimes against fellow Boers who had surrendered ("hands-uppers," they were called). They destroyed railroad lines, shot up isolated outposts, ambushed supply columns, inflicted heavy casualties, then faded into the vastness of the veld. They would lie low as British patrols passed, then reemerge with redoubled fury.

De Wet's adventures form one of the most exciting chapters in the military history of the twentieth century, a story he tells exceedingly well in his memoirs, *Three Years' War*. He was a master of terrain, of the coup d'oeil that allows a commander to take in the possibilities of the ground with a single glance of the eye. Living in the Heilbron district in the northern reaches of the Orange Free State, he was elected vice commandant of the district commando at the outset of the fighting. On November 30, 1899, he played a leading role in the battle of Nicholson's Nek in Natal, battling a British force established on Swartbooiskop, a kopje about six miles from the Nek.[26] The British occupied the southern end of this flat-topped, irregularly shaped hill. As so often proved to be the case in this war, they had not even reconnoitered the higher, more rugged northern side, since it seemed unlikely that any force could get up there. De Wet led a party of 300 men up the northern slopes, and by 5:00 A.M. they began to pour a heavy fire into the British positions. The Boers, operating in small groups, moved constantly forward, ducking and darting and generally trying to avoid British fire as much as possible. The British, trained in volley fire, never found a lucrative enough target. By noon the Boers had crept closer and closer, and the British began to fall back to the extreme southern end of the mountain. Here they were crowded together under intense Boer fire, suffering heavy casualties. By afternoon the entire force had surrendered. De Wet counted 203 British casualties and 817 prisoners. The Boer force engaged was never larger than 200 men; their losses were 4 dead and 5 wounded.

At Paardeberg, De Wet led 500 men and two guns in a daring stroke against the British position near Stinkfontein. They seized a series of ridges to the south of the encircling forces, about two and a half miles southeast of the laager. For nearly three days, they beat off all British attempts to storm the ridges, holding open a small corridor through which Cronje's encircled force could have made its escape.[27] Unwilling to abandon the women and children in the laager, Cronje instead chose to surrender.

The period between Paardeberg and the fall of the capitals marked a transition between the two phases of the war. The British had no time to celebrate their victory. De Wet, by now the commandant of all Free State forces, ambushed an English supply column, 128 wagons and their entire escort, at Sanna's Post on March 31. Keeping his men concealed in a shallow depression along the riverbanks of Koorn Spruit, he allowed each wagon to enter the ravine, disarmed the crew and escort, warned them they would be shot if they made any sound, then let the next wagon come in.[28] This amazing occurrence took place within twenty miles of Lord Roberts's headquarters at Bloemfontein. Among other things, the victory left the pumping station of the British-held capital city in the hands of the Boers. By the time

Roberts had dispatched a typically ponderous column to punish De Wet, the raider was long gone, launching an attack on an isolated column of the Royal Irish Rifles at Reddersburg and taking 470 prisoners.[29]

Within weeks of the fall of the capitals, Lord Roberts had come to recognize these raids as a serious threat to his rear. On July 7, De Wet led a tiny force of eighty burghers and one Krupp gun in an attack on Roodewal Station, one of the largest supply depots on the Central Railway. It netted him a number of prisoners and an incredible amount of booty, 600 cases of Lee-Metford ammunition, blankets, boots, cigars, and over 1,500 bags of British mail. This last he and his men scattered over the veld. "Undoubtedly, Lord Roberts would be very angry with me," De Wet wrote, "but I consoled myself with the thought that his anger would soon blow over."[30] As a result of simultaneous attacks against British garrisons on the Rhenoster River and at Vredefort, De Wet now controlled large stretches of the rail line upon which the British host was absolutely dependent for supplies.

Lord Roberts now dispatched a number of mobile columns, under the overall command of Lord Kitchener, to run down De Wet. By July 1900, the British seemed to have snared their quarry. Relentless pressure by columns under Generals Clements and Paget had compressed him and the remnants of the Free State army into the mountains along the border with Basutoland. A large British force had entered Bethlehem. De Wet occupied good defensive terrain in some hills a half dozen miles to the south. But with British forces moving up and closing the passes out of the mountain refuge one by one, he had managed to slip through Slabbert's Nek in the dead of night—threading his way through British lines with 2,600 men, five guns, and 400 wagons—to make his getaway.

Roberts was in something of a quandary. He knew he had to catch De Wet in order to stabilize his own rear. At the same time, he could not shake the traditional conviction that all he had to do was continue his advance along the railroad to the east. Once he had reached Komatipoort on the border of Portuguese East Africa, he would sever the last Boer link to the outside world. The war would be over. Torn between the two options, he decided to do both. His main body duly undertook the march to Komatipoort and reached it after some sharp fighting on September 24, 1900. One modern writer put it nicely: "The British could now look about them and see no more armies to fight, no other cities to conquer, no more railways or other installations to capture. The soldiers began to think of returning home."[31]

But such thoughts were highly premature. First they had to finish the "hunt for de Wet." It began in August 1900. Correspondent Frederick Hoppin Howland was with the pursuing British, and his account makes plain the difficulties, the long stretches of boredom, and the occasional moments of drama that followed. The British force consisted of a complex array of columns and generals, including a mounted infantry brigade under General Ridley, the Household Cavalry under General Broadwood, the columns of Generals Clements and Paget, and columns under Colonels Little and Ewart moving down toward Bethlehem with a large convoy from Lindley. The plan was simple in concept but difficult in execution: "to keep as close behind the enemy as possible and harass his rear until another force could be stationed across his path."[32] Getting "across his path" proved to be the hard part.

The chase began badly. Little and Ewart received orders to cooperate too late, and De Wet managed to slip between them, giving himself a good eighteen-mile head start. Moving to and fro, doubling back repeatedly, De Wet, "with consummate cunning," kept the British in doubt as to his true line of march. The British columns had to stop often to get their bearings and to interrogate the local residents. Howland's account is filled with the language of doubt. While the columns seemed to be going "in a generally correct direction," there was no indication that "we were closing the gap," and at times, "the scent failed us altogether."

Nevertheless, on the fourth day of the chase, while making a figure S near Lindley (passing southward of the town in an easterly direction, then northward of the city heading west), Broadwood's column caught sight of some Boer wagons in the far distance. Because the wagons always moved first in a Boer column, it was evident that the rear guard was somewhere close. An hour later, Howland saw a familiar sight to the British in this war: "figures standing out clearly on the skyline some four miles ahead." They had caught De Wet.

As Generals Broadwood and Ridley moved forward to reconnoiter some fifty yards ahead, they came under Boer fire. "The wily Boer commander had purposely placed his men in plain view on the skyline, in order to draw our attention away from a ridge below, and within fourteen hundred yards of us." Trouble was apparent from the spurts of dust on the ground all around the British party. One man was hit as the rest took cover deliberately and calmly. "It's the only way to do when you have men with you," Ridley told him. "If I had been alone, though, I'd have run like hell." Broadwood now brought up some guns, and the Boers promptly withdrew from their advanced positions.

With his quarry near, Broadwood decided to gather his light wagons and carts and cut loose from the rest of the baggage train. Re-forming the column took some time, and it was five days until contact had been reestablished with the enemy. De Wet took advantage of the pause to cut the rail and telegraph lines for several miles south of the Rhenoster River and to capture another train laden with supplies. He then began to move north toward Vredefort and, finally, the Vaal, where he began to entrench. It was clear that he intended to make a stand on the river. After taking Vredefort hard on the heels of the Boers, Broadwood entrenched along a ridge a few miles to the south. There the adversaries faced one another for nearly two weeks, De Wet facing generally southward, his naturally strong position like a fortified bridgehead over the Vaal. Broadwood, holding what had now become the front line, immediately requested reinforcements. His cordon around the southern face of De Wet's position was fourteen miles long, and De Wet could have chosen a spot almost anywhere and concentrated superior strength against it. There was a mood of growing anxiety in the British camp that he would do just that, but it was clear that nothing could be done until reinforcements had arrived. Broadwood was not about to storm the Boer camp with insufficient force. That would be a recipe for another Magersfontein.

For two weeks, Broadwood's men sat, watched for movement out of De Wet's camp, and waited for reinforcements. The days of waiting featured desultory artillery duels that did little damage, the occasional skirmish by outlying pickets, and an exciting incident when General Ridley, riding out to Broadwood's camp, was fired on by a party of his own men. Lord Kitchener, who was coordinating the forces involved, did not want to send Broadwood more troops, wasting them on "a stern chase." What would they be able to achieve? De Wet was not about to sit and wait to be attacked by superior forces; he would simply slip away north over the Vaal. The British would have to start all over again. Instead, what was needed was a strong British force marching down from Pretoria to close the trap and turn De Wet's encampment along the Vaal into another Paardeberg.

De Wet himself had been unusually quiet since reaching the river. His horses were tired; his burghers, Free Staters, had little desire to cross the river and leave their country. Strong reinforcements to Broadwood might have allowed him to bring on a general engagement under favorable circumstances, but this is second-guessing. While Broadwood had to worry about Boer firepower, higher command had to worry about Boer mobility. Trapping De Wet was the key, not smashing into his position.

The column chosen to close the trap was under the command of the unfortunate General Methuen, marching down toward Potchefstroom, on the northern bank of the Vaal. His approach brought matters to a head. By August 5, Kitchener had six columns marching on De Wet and felt that the time had come to settle the issue. De Wet, constitutionally incapable of inaction for long, recognized that it was time to move on. He had made good use of the previous two weeks, replacing his worn-out mounts and reprovisioning his force. The men were refreshed and steeled to the concept of abandoning their homeland. Still, De Wet was in trouble. His enemy had apparently closed the ring. British forces now stood to his south and west (Vredefort), northeast (Wildehonde Kop and Groot Eiland Kop), and north (Methuen, across the Vaal at Potchefstroom). Moreover, Paget and Clements were moving up from Kroonstad, due at Vredefort on August 11.

This moment of high drama ended in what Howland called "a fizzle." Methuen failed to move his force up close enough to the Vaal. He apparently wanted to avoid a general engagement as much as his colleagues did; no one had greater reason to avoid another Magersfontein than he did. De Wet found two fordable drifts, the appropriately named De Wet's and Schueman's. Sending a diversion across the first, he and his entire force crossed the Vaal at the second. Soon he was trekking at top speed to the east along the northern bank of the Vaal. Methuen engaged his rear guard but to little effect. There was no clue as to De Wet's future intentions. Perhaps he would recross the Vaal at Lindeque's or Viljoen's Drift, reentering the Free State; perhaps he would strike north for Pretoria and Johannesburg. What little intelligence British patrols could gather favored the former. They moved to block him, rushing a force to Lindeque's Drift to block any attempt to recross the river. Kitchener vowed to catch De Wet this time if he had to kill every mule in the British army, and for a time, things looked bad for the mules. But, of course, De Wet moved to the north, slipping the trap again. Howland describes the last moment of the hunt: "That afternoon, I climbed to the top of a high kop with General Ridley and his staff and signalers, and thence for over three hours we watched the whole Boer force trekking off to the northward, safely out of range, while Lord Methuen dropped ineffectual shells into his rear guard."[33]

The failure to bring down De Wet is a good example of the dynamics of this phase of the war. Throughout this campaign, the Boers moved faster, had better knowledge of the land, and had no supply lines to defend. They could attack anywhere they wished, while the British had to defend everywhere, all at once. They could concentrate; the British had to disperse. Howland is in the company of scores of writers and eyewitnesses who argued that the failure was due to incompetent officers, that it was "a reflection upon the incapacity of a few of the British generals still in the field," by whom he meant primarily Methuen. "Every commander had to trust a part of his effective force to some incompetent subordinate. Hunter had his Hart and his Barton and his Paget; Buller, and after him Kitchener, had his Methuen."[34] This is simplistic analysis. Superior Boer mobility was far more important.

As 1901 opened, the war in South Africa showed no signs of ending. The British had annexed the republics and had heavy forces in place in the major towns along the railroad. Between those towns, however, lay immense stretches of territory held by small British garrisons that proved, again and again, to be incapable of defending themselves. The garrisons usually had to be supplied by wagon, and wagons, both escorted and unescorted, were falling into De Wet's hands at an alarming rate. In addition, in June 1901, leaders from both the Transvaal and the Free State, meeting at Standerton, decided to launch an invasion of the Cape Colony.[35] Led by a young lawyer, Jan Christiaan Smuts, the commandos broke into the colony and led British forces on a merry chase. It is one of those military campaigns that one must follow on a map in order to appreciate fully. Setting out from Vereeniging in June, Smuts and his handpicked force of 362 men, with Jacobus van Deventer and Ben Bouwer as his lieutenants, trekked across the Orange Free State, eluding no fewer than seventeen British columns sweeping between the blockhouses. On September 5, they crossed the Orange River into the Cape. Past Jamestown and Dordrecht and then due south toward Adelaide the little band rode on, through British patrols and a storm so bad the Boers called it "the big rain." With his men looking like scarecrows, food hard to come by, and the horses dropping by the dozen, Smuts caught a British force encamped near the Klaas Smits River, launched a surprise assault, destroyed it, and replenished his column from the supplies. Reaching the town of Adelaide, he could stand on a hill and see the lights of Port Elizabeth to the south, the Indian Ocean to the East. From here, he trekked clear across the Cape Colony, from the eastern to the western cape. He was still in the field, unsuppressed, having ridden 2,000 miles, when the war ended.

What followed is usually described as a guerrilla struggle, but it was more than that. De Wet's memoirs make it plain that he saw no real distinction between the two phases of the war. At the start of the war, he led an irregular commando of several hundred men, with a gun or two; its aim was to discomfit the English flanks, to destroy isolated garrisons, and to seize rich stores from poorly guarded supply convoys. This was exactly what he was doing at the end of the war. In fact, such a large percentage of the republics was still in Boer hands in mid-1901 that De Wet could deny the applicability of the term *guerrilla* to the Boer war effort: "The only case in which one can use this word, is when one civilized national has so completely vanquished another, that not only is the capital taken, but also the country from border to border is so completely conquered that any resistance is out of the question."[36] That, he argued, was clearly not the case in 1901.

It was not a classic "insurgent" struggle so much as a conventional war being waged by irregulars. The battles from this phase of the war were hardly distinguishable from the Modder River or Magersfontein. In November 1900, for example, a force of 500 burghers under Ben Viljoen was active along the Rhenoster River, launching punitive raids on the farms of pro-British Boers. Patrols brought in reports of a large British column, perhaps 5,000 in all, marching from the direction of Pretoria and along Zustershoek. It was the 20th Infantry Brigade and a large force of mounted infantry, under the command of General A. H. Paget. Choosing his position carefully, Viljoen entrenched his force on a hill called Rhenosterkop, his Johannesburgers on the right, a unit of Johannesburg police in the center, and a commando from Boksburg on his left. After careful reconnaissance, Paget opened his assault on November 28. Viljoen described the scene: "It gave me a turn when I suddenly saw the gigantic army of 'Khakis' right in front of us, slowly approaching, in grand formation, regiment upon regiment, deploying systematically, in proper fighting order, and my anxiety was mingled with admiration at the splendid discipline of the adversary."[37] All day and deep into the night, the British came on in skirmish order. They began with an assault on the Boer right, then switched to the center, and finally the left—all equally fruitless and decimated by accurate Boer rifle fire and Viljoen's tiny complement of artillery: several pom-poms and one Krupp gun. During the entire battle, Viljoen knew that he had a secure line of retreat to the north, so he could hang on as long as possible to the kopje and inflict the greatest possible damage. Paget made no attempt to maneuver or to take the Boers in the flank, something to which they were extremely sensitive, as the British well knew, or at least should have known by now. By the end of the day, he had suffered several hundred casualties, in an action that hardly rates mention in many general histories of the war. Viljoen had suffered two killed and twenty-two wounded. That night, he and his men, short of ammunition, retired from Rhenosterkop. Paget's battered force occupied it the next morning.

Another example of the fierce nature of these "guerrilla" battles was the action at Tweefontein, on Christmas Day, 1901. Here De Wet launched a successful ambush on a British brigade encamped and entrenched on a hill called Groenkop. Traveling light, his men approached the British force undetected. After several days of personal reconnaissance, De Wet noted that the western, steeper side of the hill was lightly defended. His commandos began their ascent in the dead of night on Christmas Eve. At 2:00 A.M. they were in position, within sight of the white tents of the sleeping British camp. At De Wet's call of "Burghers, storm!" they launched a brisk attack that virtually wiped out the British force inside. British losses included 116 casualties and 240 prisoners, twenty wagons, a great deal of ammunition, 500 horses and mules, and one wagon full of rum, "so that the burghers,"

De Wet wrote, "who were not averse to this, could now satisfy their thirst."[38] Tweefontein was an instant replay of the Boer triumph at Nicholson's Nek, in the early months of the war's "conventional" phase.

Whatever one calls this phase of the fighting, whether "guerrilla" or "irregular," it became increasingly tiresome to the British commanders and their men in the field. A restless population and Parliament at home were also clamoring for an end to the war. The British commander in South Africa by this time was Lord Kitchener, an officer who had a firm understanding of the unique problems that he faced in this war. His first task was to find a way to limit the guerrillas' mobility. Too many ponderous columns of several thousand men had tried and failed to run down De Wet and his 300. The solution was a network of concrete blockhouses, built at one-mile intervals across the veld, garrisoned and connected by barbed wire barricades. Mobile British columns composed of irregular horse, mounted infantry, and cavalry, often using hands-uppers as their guides, carried out regular sweeps between them. The lines grew in density until whole sections of veld were literally walled off. Guerrilla activity was thus slowly compressed into a smaller and smaller area. Second, Kitchener launched a war against what we today would call the infrastructure that was supporting the guerrilla movement, the Boer civilian population and their farms. It was a brutal, repressive policy. His men burned the Boers' farms, killed their livestock, and, worst of all, rounded up their women and children, incarcerating them in concentration camps. These were crowded and filthy, with inadequate water and sanitation. Of 125,000 prisoners, some 25,000 died, ravaged by epidemics of measles, pneumonia, and dysentery. There was a loud outcry back home in Great Britain when news of the camps leaked out, with Liberal MP David Lloyd George accusing Kitchener of pursuing "a policy of extermination against children" in South Africa and likening him to Herod. Although no one could see it at the time, it was the beginning of the end of the British Empire. But with their once lovely veld a fenced-off, blackened ruin, and with their families dying in camps, the bitter-enders had no real choice but to lay down their arms. Kitchener had triumphed.

CONCLUSION: THE "LESSONS" OF THE SOUTH AFRICAN WAR

The Boer War was a subject of intense interest to contemporary military men and civilians alike. The international situation was increasingly tense, and the outbreak of a general war seemed possible at any time. Perhaps, many reasoned, the events of this war held the key to the future of military conflict. Unfortunately, attempting to distill the "lessons" of any war is a tricky business.[39] So much depends on the point of view of the observer, whether he is a soldier or a civilian, the place he occupies in the military hierarchy, whether or not he was an eyewitness to the events he is discussing (which has its pluses and its minuses), not to mention the number and type of axes he feels like grinding. In addition, the things that appear to later generations as clear lessons of a given conflict are much less obvious to contemporary observers. There were many things about the nature of war that seemed "obvious" to all the world in 1915 that no one had thought about just a few short years before.

That being said, what were the military lessons of the Boer War? Examining the first phase, it struck many observers that modern battlefield conditions had rendered the infantry assault difficult, or perhaps even impossible. In battle after battle in the war's early months, the role played by some of the finest units in the British army—regiments with long histories and gallant traditions—was to lie down and get shot at by the Boers, an entrenched enemy they could not even see. Military planners pondered the question of how to get the assault moving forward again. Within virtually all European armies, "Boer tactics," essentially replacing lines and columns with extended fronts of skirmishers, became the dominant order of attack prescribed by the tactical manuals.[40] The first of the great civilian analysts, Ivan S. Bloch, calculated that a superiority of eight to one in favor of the attackers was the minimum necessary for a successful assault, and that 100 men in a trench would be able to put out of action 336 of the 400 men attacking them.[41]

As always, there were contrary voices among Europe's military professionals. Many argued, quite rightly, that extended and dispersed groups of skirmishers would be uncontrollable in combat and could never gather the force necessary for a successful assault. France was the center of the reaction against "Boer tactics." General Hippolyte Langlois, for example, mocked what he saw as the new regulations' preoccupation with casualties. It was a new disease, he said, "acute Transvaalitis."[42] He even started a new journal, the *Revue Militaire Générale,* to preach the virtues of bold attack and shock combat. In his lectures at the École Supérieure de Guerre, General Ferdinand Foch stressed the importance of "preparation, mass, and impulsion," argued that "action is the governing rule of war," and told his students that "the laurels of victory are at the point of enemy bayonets. They must be plucked there. They must be carried by a fight hand to hand." With the rewriting of the French tactical manuals in 1913 and 1914, these ideas became official French army doctrine.

One of the world's most respected military analysts, American admiral Alfred Thayer Mahan, felt that all the hand-wringing about Boer firepower was much ado about nothing:

The battle of the Modder showed that, with the modern improvements in rapid-firing arms, it is possible for troops well-entrenched over an extended front to sweep a plain field of approach with such a volume of fire as is impossible to cross. This it shows, but otherwise the lessons to be derived have been greatly exaggerated. Witnesses exhaust their descriptive powers to portray the evidences of the innumerable falls of bullets, shown by the kicking up of the dust. "A fire so thick and fearful that no man can imagine how any one passed under or through it. . . ." Yet, as far as the result was concerned, it was an immense expenditure of ammunition and little loss of life. The frontal attack was so clearly impossible that it was at once abandoned and the men lay down.[43]

His tactical analysis of the Modder was curiously bloodless but contained a germ of truth: "The battle may be summarized by saying that the British line held the enemy in front until a couple of detachments, by daring rushes, had established themselves in positions of command on the western flank, whence they worked themselves round, crossed the river, and fairly turned the hostile flank. And that, so stated, is a very old story."

One might add that, with its fixation on what had happened to the British, much of this debate ignored the plight of the defender in a modern firefight. Even many of the most dramatic Boer victories did not appear so lopsided and easy to the Boers themselves. Their accounts of Modder River, Magersfontein, and especially Spion Kop often emphasize their own casualties, not the ease with which they destroyed the British forces opposite them. Deneys Reitz was at Spion Kop, fighting with a group of volunteers from Pretoria under "Red Daniel" Opperman, and it is clear from his account that this was a hard-fought and discouraging battle for both sides, not another pushover of a poorly handled British force:

> We were sustaining heavy casualties from the English *schans* immediately in front of us, and the men grew restive under the galling point-blank fire, a thing not to be wondered at, for the moral effect of Lee-Metford volleys at twenty yards must be experienced to be appreciated. . . . We were hungry, thirsty, and tired; around us were the dead men covered with swarms of flies attracted by the smell of blood. We did not know the cruel losses the English were suffering, and we believed that they were easily holding their own, so discouragement spread as the shadows lengthened. Batches of men left the line, openly defying Red Daniel who was impotent in the face of this wholesale defection, and when at last the sun set I do not think there were sixty men left on the ledge.[44]

Reitz's description reminds us that the "empty battlefield" cuts both ways. The defenders are often just as much in the dark about the true nature of the battle as are the attackers.

In addition, in concentrating on the issues of fire and protection, the debate missed an even more important point: the pressing problem of command. It is clear today, as it was clear at the time, that many British commanders had proved themselves totally unsuited to the modern battlefield, and they had kept on proving it up until the last days of the war. The battle of Rhenosterkop, for example, fought a year after the Modder, called into question the entire concept of a British "learning curve" in this war. Even the Boer commandant, Viljoen, was aghast, writing of his British opponent's "incompetence" and "stupidity."[45]

And yet the problem of command went deeper than the commanders themselves. Even when British forces managed to break into the Boer position, as for instance the 9th Brigade's success during the Modder referred to by Mahan, they were unable to sustain momentum, to break into open country, to turn a tactical success into operational victory. As bad as Colenso had been, by the end of the day it appeared that Hildyard's brigade might yet salvage the battle by forcing a passage across the rail bridge. He had just reached the objective when he received the order for a general retirement. Eyewitnesses always treated these events—assaults mysteriously called off on the verge of success, the lack of pursuit—as an anomaly, but in explaining them they always turned to a suspiciously similar set of reasons: intense fatigue, heavy losses on the part of the attackers, intermingling of units. No field commander was yet capable of solving that knotty complex of problems, not with the primitive means of communication at his disposal. At Colenso, for example, Buller's link to his units consisted of "heliograph and ragged bits of bunting."[46] Likewise, the sum total of communications into besieged Ladysmith from the outside world was a mirror used by an enterprising young British officer, Captain Cayser.[47]

Related to the command problem was the problem of reconnaissance. Contemporary accounts from both the British and the Boer side refer repeatedly to British shortcomings in this area. Partly it was due to a certain British arrogance about their "primitive" and "uncivilized" enemy, partly to the increasing problems that cavalry was experiencing getting close enough to a position occupied by rifle-armed infantry. But above all, it was due to the immense size of the theater of war. The British could have doubled, or even tripled, the size of their force in South Africa and still have had trouble locating the Boers or finding out exact information about their deployments. As a result, they had to operate in an information-poor environment, often with devastating consequences.

The Boers did not suffer the same difficulties. Reconnaissance was a simple matter for these tough frontiersman. As for command, accounts of the war often focus on the difficulties that Boer leaders had in keeping a force in being, since the burghers might depart for home any time they felt like it. But the much smaller size of their force and the fact that, for the most part, they were engaged in a war of positional defense often allowed Boer commanders to get by on argumentation and personal charisma. Returning once again to Spion Kop, Reitz describes the Boers awakening the morning after the battle thinking that they had been beaten. They were in the midst of preparing their own retreat when the commandant-general, Louis Botha, arrived on the scene, and it was only his personal charisma that kept them in the trenches:

> Fortunately, just as the foremost wagons moved away and the horsemen were getting ready to follow, there came the sound of galloping hoofs, and a man rode into our midst who shouted to them to halt. I could not see his face in the dark, but word went round that it was Louis Botha, the new Commandant-General. . . . He addressed the men from the saddle, telling them of the shame that would be theirs if they deserted their posts in this hour of danger; and so eloquent was his appeal that in a few minutes the men were filing off into the dark to reoccupy their positions on either aside of the Spion Kop gap.[48]

The second phase of the war received much less attention at the time, although the British victory seems today to be a much more impressive achievement than Lord Roberts's triumph over the tiny Boer field army. It was an entirely new kind of war for the British, and in fact one would have to go back to the Spanish struggle against French occupation in the Napoleonic period to see its like. Individual terrain formations practically ceased to matter. The British had the strength to march an army wherever they wished, but it was often to no good purpose. What counted was being swift enough to find and fix in place a major force of Boers so that they could be destroyed. This imposed a certain logic on the struggle: with the target no longer being capital cities or population centers, but small groups of Boers fighting in dispersed groups, the British had no choice but to disperse in search of them. In scattering across the countryside, however, they were vulnerable to Boer "surge capacity," helpless before an enemy who knew the land intimately, who could concentrate for battle far more rapidly, and who had a simplified command structure of independent units linked only by ties of language, culture, and a determination to fight to the bitter end. British columns were still marching off to their doom mere months before the Boer surrender.

The British certainly did come to understand the importance of mobility in the course of the war. The British force in South Africa changed dramatically during the war, from a predominantly infantry force, to a mix of infan-

The Boer War posed almost insurmountable problems for modern military operations. The country was huge and rugged and the communications inadequate. Here is a primitive British communications outpost (above), as well as a typically unwieldy supply column (opposite). Courtesy of the Imperial War Museum, London (top, MH 29376; bottom, Q72044).

try and cavalry units, to an army of mounted infantry. Mobility increased accordingly. In the summer of 1900, General Barton's brigade marched from Christiana to Vryburg, a distance of 120 miles, in just seven days.[49] It was an impressive achievement for light infantry over some tough country but, of course, nowhere near fast enough to chase down a Boer force on horseback. "De Wet seldom failed to cover twenty-five miles a day to his pursuers' twenty," was Howland's melancholy characterization.[50] Although the British were far more mobile at the end of the war than they had been at the beginning, they were never quite fast enough to catch the Boers.[51]

Commentators often remark on the immense size of the British host in South Africa by the end of the war, but given the even more immense size of the country, the British force was barely adequate to its task. As a twenty-three-year-old subaltern, J. F. C. Fuller commanded a force of seventy African scouts. He recounted a conversation with his captain:

> I asked him about my duties. "Well," he replied, "find the enemy, report his whereabouts and keep him under observation." "And what is my area to be?" I then asked. To which he answered: "Rather indefinite. Roughly, shall we say between the railway and the Vaal, the Rhenoster River, and the Vet River?" Looking at the map I hazarded: "Rather a large area to watch? (about 4,000 square miles). "Well," he replied, "make it what you like."[52]

It was, Fuller remarked, "not a bad mouthful for a youngster of twenty-three."[53]

Major F. M. Crum was with the mounted infantry when the war broke out, a detachment of the 1st Battalion, King's Royal Rifles. With a training emphasizing "shooting and stalking," his unit started the war by operating regular mounted patrols along the border with the republics, and by mounting flank and rear guards for larger forces on the march. He describes the problems of going on patrol in late 1900: "The line was continually threatened. Small patrols were frequently in difficulties. Raids on the cattle or horses grazing beyond the camp were of daily occurrence. We lived in momentary expectation of the order, 'Saddle-up!' Many a time we did saddle-up, but however quick we might be we were never quick enough." At daybreak, he wrote, individual Boers were to be seen on every height around the column, watching it. When the patrol was over, the column would return to the line. Then "each Boer, as seemed to him best, was galloping, stalking, shooting, or working round our rear guard." Nearly every patrol ended with men hit by rifle fire. "Thus it was no wonder that we failed to agree with the home papers when they insisted that the war was over."

Crum's account makes for depressing reading. At the Olifants River in October 1900, he and 60 troopers had to guard twelve miles of railroad. On November 19, seven of his men came under attack by thirty Boers. In January 1901, a Boer ambush hit his company near Uitkyk and nearly had a bigger prize: a train carrying Lord Kitchener. In April 1901, he was part of a column consisting of about 3,000 men patrolling between Piet Retief and Middelburg. This relatively huge force caught nothing and did no fighting. He was with a force almost as large in October 1901 near Bakenlaagte that was hit hard by a particularly skillful Boer ambush. Over 300 Boer horsemen allowed the column to pass by a farmhouse, then charged the rear guard, being suddenly joined by 700 more who had been hidden by the buildings and terrain. By the end of the day, Crum's company had suffered badly, suffering 10 killed and 14 wounded. In previous colonial wars, Crum mused, Bakenlaagte would have "been looked upon as a national calamity." In this one, "it was merely an incident."[54] In the course of the war, Crum's single company would suffer 25 killed and 29 wounded, an expensive bill indeed. Crum's memoirs show the conundrum well. Tiny patrols were vulnerable to Boer raids; larger columns were too ponderous to catch anything worthwhile.

A word about Kitchener's war on civilians is in order. It hit the Boers in their vulnerable spot. While they were on commando picking off isolated British outposts and columns, they could not be at home protecting their families. Kitchener's decision to turn both conquered republics into prison camps, with large sections walled off by wire and concrete, and with an increasing portion of the civilian population treated as inmates, both figuratively and literally, was a solution of sorts to the military problem. It only worked, however, because there were so few Boers that the huge British Empire could have arrested the entire civilian population of the two republics had it been necessary. Such a strategy certainly would not have worked in guerrilla campaigns later in the century, such as the conflict in Vietnam. Although the British had "solved" the Boer problem, the situation was unique, and it offered very few hints for future wars elsewhere.

The most interesting example of the "lessons learned" literature on the South African War came from the pen of Ernest Swinton. Having served during the war as a captain in the British army, he wrote a pamphlet in 1905 entitled "The Defence of Duffer's Drift."[55] Framed in the style of a dream sequence, it is the story of Lieutenant "Backside Forethought," whose platoon has the mission of defending "Duffer's Drift," the only ford for miles around on the "Siliaasvogel River" suitable for wagons. He prepares his defenses, is ambushed and overrun, and is led off into captivity. During the long trek under guard, he muses over the lessons he has learned. These lessons are then carried over into the second dream, and the lessons of the second into a third, and so on for six dreams.

The first dream is worth a detailed look, since it describes Swinton's view of British tactics at the start of the war. The lieutenant's training and military education left him completely baffled by his assignment. "Now, if they had given me a job like fighting the battle of Waterloo, or Sedan, or Bull Run, I knew all about that, as I had crammed it up and been examined in it too. I also knew how to take up a position for a division, or even an army corps, but the stupid little subaltern's game of the defense of a drift with a small detachment was, curiously enough, most perplexing. I had never really considered such a thing."

As a result, he makes every error imaginable. He decides to pitch the camp on a spot just south of the drift, on slightly rising ground, "which I knew should be chosen for a camp whenever possible." The proximity to the drift was also in the site's favor, "for, as every one knows, if you are told off to guard anything, you mount a guard quite close to it, and place a sentry, if possible, standing on top of it." Since the men are tired after their long march and "as the enemy were not within a hundred miles," he postpones defensive preparations until the following day. He starts by a personal reconnaissance to the north, since that is where the Boers were reported to be. "I knew naturally that there must be a front, because in all the schemes I had had to prepare, or the exams I had undergone, there was always a front, or—'the place where the enemies come from.'" Since the south was his rear, he sees no need to scout in that direction.

During his tour, he finds no Boers but does come across a kindly "surrendered" farmer, Mr. Andreas Brink, who invites him into his farmhouse, introduces him to his sons (who take a great interest in his gear, especially his new, latest pattern field glasses), and declares his opposition to the war and his loyalty to the crown (a fact confirmed for the young lieutenant by the portrait of the queen hanging on the living room wall). Since his men need victuals, he agrees to let the Brinks visit the camp to sell milk, eggs, and butter to the men. He returns to his camp, which he can clearly spot by the blue threads of smoke rising in the air from the cooking fires, and which he can hear by the "indistinct and cheerful camp noises, which gradually grew louder as I approached." The Brinks arrive and begin to sell their wares: "The three of them stroll about the camp, showing great interest in everything, asking most intelligent questions about the British forces and the general position of affairs and seemed really relieved to have a strong British post near."

After drawing up orders for the digging of trenches in the morning, the lieutenant falls asleep, dreaming of promotion, VCs, and DSOs, the call of the sentries ringing in his ears as security: "Number one—all is well!" At some point in the night, the sentry's call of "Halt! Who goes . . ." and the recognizable "plip-plop" of Mauser fire jerk him out of his sleep.

> There was some wild shooting in return from my men, but it was all over in a moment, and as I managed to wriggle out of my tent the whole place was swarming with bearded men, shooting into the heaving canvas. At that moment I must have been clubbed on the head for I knew no more until I found myself seated on an empty case having my head, which was dripping with blood, tied up by one of my men.

His losses were ten killed, including both sentries, and twenty-one wounded. The Boers had one man killed and two wounded. As he strips off his waistcoat and pants at the orders of the "very frowzy" Boer commander, our lieutenant notices the Brinks in animated conversation with the Boer commando that had just overrun them. Mr. Brink was "curiously enough, carrying a rifle and bandolier and my new field glasses. He was laughing."

In the course of his dreams, the lieutenant begins to get the hang of things. He learns not to let the Boers into his camp, then to take them into custody as soon as he arrives, then to take their women and children and threaten to burn their farm if they do not cooperate. He digs a trench behind the drift, then farther up on the high ground, then on Waschout Hill to the southeast of the camp. None of these things works: his positions are still far too visible ("In the end the trench looked quite neat—'almost as nice as mother makes it'—with the fresh red earth contrasting with the yellow of the veld"); perched on the high ground behind a horseshoe bend in the river, the camp is still too vulnerable; the Boers employ artillery to great effect. Finally, he makes a radical decision: entrench not on the high ground, nor on the hill behind, but dispersed inside the riverbed itself. This stratagem defeats an attack and drives the Boers back in confusion from the drift. Interestingly enough, it is not primarily a matter of firepower to Swinton. In the most revealing passage in the book, he discusses the real problem of dispersing the men along the steep riverbank: "At dusk, when we had nearly all the pits finished and some of the clearance done, tents and gear were hidden, ammunition and rations distributed to all, and orders in case of an attack given out. As I could not be everywhere, I had to rely on the outlying groups of men fully understanding my aims beforehand, and acting on their 'own.'" When military experts of the day discussed firepower, what they often meant, even if they did not know it, was the problem of command under fire.

Chapter 3

· · · · · · · · · · · · ·

The Russo-Japanese War

The Russo-Japanese War clearly demonstrated the interrelated problems of fire, maneuver, and command under modern conditions.[1] Sandwiched between two celebrated events at sea (the surprise naval attack on the Russian fleet in Port Arthur and the annihilation of the Russian Far Eastern Squadron at Tsushima) came a land campaign that dwarfed anything the world had seen up until that point. Two mass armies, equipped with the latest in modern firepower (machine guns and so-called rapid-fire artillery, equipped with recoil piston), crashed into one another in battle after battle, and the slaughter was immense. Both sides found their operations severely limited by supply, and both had to rely on a very tenuous supply line: for Japan the sea, for Russia the 5,000-mile, single-track Trans-Siberian railroad. While many observers saw the Boer War as an atypical conflict, and thus tended to discount the lessons it taught, this was a conflict between an established European power and a rising, fast-modernizing nation that relied on a German-trained officer corps. Although the Japanese drove the Russians back in every battle, they failed to achieve the decisive victory that so often appeared to be within their grasp.

In the supercharged international climate of the early twentieth century, this was a very carefully watched war. Despite the great distance from Euope of these events, a virtual horde of journalists, military attachés, and military experts of every description were in the theater observing the fighting, sending back a flurry of articles, dispatches, and eyewitness accounts. All were looking desperately for some sort of clue as to how the next great European war would be fought.

OPENING ACT: FROM THE YALU TO TELISSU

On February 8, 1904, Japan opened hostilities by launching a surprise attack on the Russian 1st Pacific Squadron in Port Arthur. Ten Japanese destroyers approached the roadstead undetected, loosed their torpedoes at the anchored Russian vessels, and sped off. Two of Russia's seven modern battleships *(Retvizan* and *Tsarevich)* and the cruiser *Pallada* were seriously damaged. The next morning the Japanese battle fleet attacked Port Arthur. Led by Admiral Heihachiro Togo, six modern battleships and nine cruisers steamed past in line-ahead formation, opening fire at 10,000 yards, some six miles. Stark refused to come out, sheltering under the protective fire of his shore batteries, and after an hour in which four more Russian cruisers were damaged, Togo sailed off. It was an inconclusive, disappointing affair. Togo now settled in for a blockade of the port, with operations limited to patrolling and minelaying.

Despite their frustration, the Japanese had bottled up the Russian battle fleet in Port Arthur and could now begin the land war. On February 16, the Japanese 1st Army began landing in Korea, at Chemulpo (modern Inchon). Led by Baron Takemoti Kuroki, it consisted of the 2nd, 12th, and Guard Divisions, some 42,000 men, supported by the fire of twenty heavy howitzers at army level, as well as each division's own artillery. From Chemulpo it entered Seoul, then began its march to the north. On May 1, it reached the Yalu River and encountered a much smaller Russian force dug in along the northern bank. The Russian force here included the III Siberian Corps under General Zasulitch, about 16,000 men, plus a brigade of 5,000 cossack cavalry and sixty-two guns. Contemporary observers, especially British military attaché Ian Hamilton, criticized the composition of the force. The Yalu formed the extreme left flank of the Russian strategic position, a 400-mile arc across southern Manchuria, virtually all of which was exposed to Japanese attack from the sea. It was, therefore, impossible to concentrate along the river. A smaller force of cossack cavalry, mounted infantry, and horse artillery would have been useful in delaying the Japanese approach to the Yalu through northern Korea, as well as in blocking any attempt to cross the river. Not only was Zasulitch's corps too small to

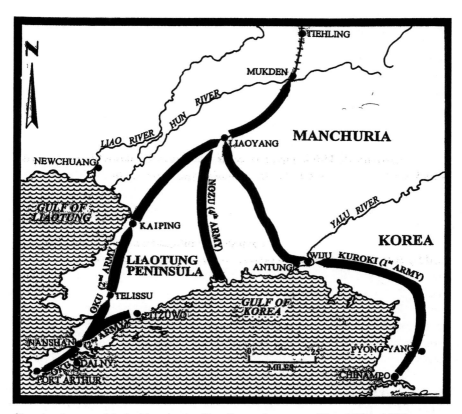

The great campaign in Manchuria: The Russo-Japanese War, 1904–1905.

defend against an entire Japanese army, it might also be too large and immobile to get away if it were beaten.[2]

Kuroki handled the approach to the Yalu skillfully and boldly. On April 8, the army's advance guard, under Lieutenant General Asada (hence, the "Asada Detachment") entered the town of Wiju on the south bank of the river. Asada's force was originally a brigade, but lack of supply and transport had whittled it down to a mere regiment of infantry and one of cavalry, with two artillery batteries in support. Kuroki was running a risk, deploying a force of less than 2,000 infantry and 500 cavalry well within cannon shot of the Russian force over the Yalu, but he had no real choice. His orders were to cover the port of Chulsan, immediately to the southwest, intended as the main supply port for the heavy guns, munitions, and supplies for 1st Army. Kuroki also seemed to have taken the measure of his adversary on the march from Chemulpo. The Russians had hardly contested the march at all, even though the terrain was ideal for flanking attacks on the long, strung-out Japanese columns. As the Asada Detachment staggered into Wiju, over 6,000 men, 1,000 cavalry, and sixteen guns sat just across the river—the forward elements of Zasulitch's main body. This greatly superior Russian force missed its chance to do serious damage to the Japanese. By April 20, 1st Army was concentrated at Wiju.

Now began the game that every good attacking commander plays before a river-crossing operation, as Kuroki tried to deceive Zasulitch as to the intended crossing point. A detachment under General Sasaki marched to Changsong, some thirty miles upriver (i.e., on the Russian left). Japanese naval units demonstrated near Antung, at the mouth of the Yalu (the Russian right). Zasulitch was forced to keep his corps dispersed along some twenty-five miles of front, while Kuroki had his units concentrated and well in hand at Wiju.

The terrain opposite Wiju should have favored the defenders. It is here that the much smaller tributary river Ai (or Aiho) flows into the Yalu, forming a right angle at the confluence. There are beaches of smooth, yellow sand, very little foliage or cover, and excellent fields of fire. Entrenched infantry on the northern bank would have been nearly invisible, much as Botha's burghers at Colenso, and in fact Hamilton remarked more than once on the similarities between the topography of this battle and that slaughter along the Tugela. Yet the Russians did very little to strengthen the position. There were no trenches of any note, just extremely simple breastworks thrown together from boughs and branches, which would offer Japanese artillery a conspicuous target during the battle. Similarly, the gun emplacements looked like they were designed, in Hamilton's words, like something out of "grandfather's text-book." There was, he said, "a flimsy parapet, just enough to attract attention, not enough to give cover, and there was no trench for the personnel."[3] Tactically, the Russians seemed interested in nothing but defending their line in a passive fashion. Two obstacles in the Yalu might have been serious blocks to any Japanese attempt to cross. These were Chukodai village and Tiger Hill, a promontory at the exact confluence of the rivers. Unfortunately, the Russians left the village untouched and the hill unfortified.

On the southern side of the river, there was careful, methodical preparation. On the night of April 25–26, Japanese units landed on the islands of Kyurito, Osekito, and Kinteito, quickly securing them, although the Russians did open fire on one of the boats carrying elements of the Guards Division and killed or wounded thirty men. The next day, Japanese infantry began work on the first of ten bridges they would build, linking the southern bank with Kinteito; some were made of their own pontoons, others of Chinese junks anchored with Korean plows, found to work just as well.

The original Japanese plans for attacking the Yalu position called for a flanking march upriver by the 12th Division, while 2nd and Guards Divisions pinned Russian attention in front.[4] The main question was, how wide should 12th Division's swing be? A wide flanking march could bring the division down the Kuantienchen road, practically in the rear of the Russian position; the danger was that the division would be out of contact with the rest of the army for three or four days. A shorter swing to Suikaochin offered less chance of a decisive surprise but would allow the division to make contact with the neighboring Guards Division on the day of the battle. Kuroki chose the latter course. At 3:00 A.M. on April 30, the division began to cross the Yalu at Suikaochin.

This was not at all a surprise to the Russian commander, and in fact he had already prepared his defensive positions along the Aiho. His line from the battle's outset, then, resembles a backward L, the base of the letter being his line in the heights overlooking the northern bank of the Yalu, and the stem being the Aiho. Most histories describe a great flanking maneuver that levered the Russians off the Yalu. In fact, Zasulitch was not defending on the river itself but in the heights north of it, and he concentrated his strongest forces against the flanking maneuver that he knew was coming, along the Aiho.

That same morning, the Japanese finished massing their artillery, thirty-six field guns and twenty howitzers, on Kinteito island—this represented 2nd Division's artillery plus army assets. The guns had orders to fire at any lucrative target of opportunity. By contrast to the Russians, the Japanese had taken great care in the placement of their batteries, even to the point of transplanting trees to hide the flash of the discharge from Russian eyes, and they had also built covered shelters, roofed over with timber and earth, proof against even a direct hit from Russian guns.

Most important, the Japanese had made careful provisions for fire control, and their preparations give a good idea of how fundamentally artillery had modernized since the Boer War. The Japanese established two observation stations some 3,000 to 4,000 yards to the rear of the batteries, on high ground that commanded the Russian position. Connected to the howitzer batteries by field telephone, the observer could call down fire on any point on the map grid, the birth of "indirect fire," or firing at a target that the gunner himself cannot see.

At 10:00 A.M., the guns on both sides opened up. Within thirty minutes, the Japanese batteries had silenced their Russian counterparts. It was not much of a fight, occurring as it did between a smaller number of guns in obvious positions and a much larger number that were well concealed and protected. With the Russian guns out of action, Kuroki could be bolder. Japanese infantry built more bridges over the Yalu, especially in front of the 2nd and Guards Divisions, the left flank and center of the Japanese line. By the morning of May 1, most of the divisional artillery had been ferried across the main stream of the Yalu, along with supporting battalions of infantry.

Their preparations completed, and the 12th Division having reached the line of the Aiho, the Japanese launched their attack at 7:00 A.M. on May 1, with the infantry of all three divisions moving forward into the assault. A Russian battery that attempted to intervene drew a deadly response from the Japanese batteries of the Guards Division. The Japanese artillery had fire superiority from the outset and in fact completely destroyed the Russian battery as it attempted to withdraw from the field. As the Japanese center and right crossed the Aiho, however, the rifle fire of Russian infantry came into play. It was volley fire, not at all the well-aimed fire of individual marksmen, and the Japanese casualties were lighter than they might have been if there had been Boers in the breastworks (as Hamilton was quick to point out). Still, they were a sharp target, with their blue uniforms against the white sand, and there were losses. Some Japanese units hesitated; others even fell back. Hamilton also saw clear evidence of that tendency to "flee to the front" that military analysts since du Picq had been writing about: "It was quickly realized by regimental officers and men that the fire was too hot to admit of a prolonged duel between troops in the open and troops under cover, and that the only alternative to going back was to go forward. Instinctively, the whole line endeavoured to press on."[5]

Although strong Russian resistance had balked the Japanese right and center, the Japanese 2nd Division was facing much lighter fire. It easily overran the village in front of it, Chiuliencheng, as well as Suribachiyama, the bowl-shaped hill directly behind the village. With his right wing driven in, Zasulitch gave the order for a general retreat. By 9:00 A.M., the Japanese had evicted the Russians from the Yalu position, at a cost of some 1,100 casualties (318 killed, 783 wounded). They had inflicted 3,000 casualties on the Russians, including 600 prisoners. Contrary to the vast majority of published accounts of the battle, it was not the Japanese flanking maneuver against the Russian left but the collapse of the Russian right that was the decisive factor in the battle's outcome.

Up to now, the actions of the Japanese command at the Yalu had been beyond reproach. Kuroki and his staff had assembled an overwhelming force, kept it concentrated, forced the enemy to stay dispersed, then picked the time and place of its choosing for the assault. Well supported by heavy artillery fire, 1st Army had stormed into the Russian positions with only moderate losses and after some delays was triumphant all along the line. So much for the impossibility of assaulting a line of rifles. Now it was time for the pursuit.

But the pursuit never came. With the Russians evicted from their position and streaming back to the rear, the command problems that tormented every nineteenth-century commander arose to plague the Japanese. Their units were in contact with the enemy and out of contact with their own army command. They had suffered losses, to be sure, but more important, they had lost the cohesion and close contact with their command structure that had characterized the concentration at Wiju. Field telephones were fine for static positions and defense but were worthless for a mobile assault. Rather than re-form and reorganize their units for a pursuit into the unknown, lower unit commanders did what seemed the sensible thing. They went for the first target of opportunity, allowing themselves to be sucked into a prolonged rearguard action at Hamatong. This heroic Russian stand managed to delay the Japanese advance long enough for the rest of the Russian force to escape into Manchuria proper.[6] This pattern of skillful assault, Japanese victory, and lack of pursuit would characterize virtually every battle of the war.

The official explanation for the lack of pursuit, that 2nd and Guards Divisions were tired and hungry, hardly seems sufficient, given the fact that the battle had lasted only several hours. Hamilton himself was able to identify command as the heart of the problem but was not aware of the true nature of that problem. The reason for this "strangely inconclusive ending," he thought, was psychological. Here is a passage from his memoirs that gives us as much insight into the mind of this sensitive man, the future British commander at Gallipoli, as it does the problems of command:

> It is perhaps necessary to have been a responsible commander during an attack to realize the immense reaction of relief when success is attained, a reaction coincident with an intense longing to tempt fate no further. "You have won your battle," a voice seems to whisper in your ear; "the enemy are going; for God's sake let them go; what right have you to order still more men to lose their lives this day."[7]

One last factor deserves mention. Pursuit was the mission of the cavalry. Traditionally armed and equipped cavalry had taken its lumps in South Africa, as we have seen, and would continue to do so in this war. It was not so much that it suffered heavy losses but that it did nothing at all, being completely out of place in the new firepower-rich battlefield environment. Mounted infantry might have played a role at the Yalu, especially for the flanking maneuver of the 12th Division, but neither side had mounted infantry.

Still, the Yalu had been a Russian defeat, and the rest of the Japanese operational plan could now unfold. On May 5, the 2nd Army under General Yasukata Oku landed at Pitzuwo, about halfway up the southern shore of the Liaotung Peninsula. Consisting of three divisions, the 1st, 3rd, and 4th, it had an interesting pair of missions: first, advance to the south and seize the port of Dalny as a base for later operations by other forces against Port Arthur, then completely reverse its direction of march and begin an advance to the *north* up the railroad toward the major fortified cities of Liaoyang and Mukden. Once again, clever and methodical planning was the Japanese hallmark. Easing the landing immeasurably was a series of Japanese naval feints on the northern shore of the peninsula, between Kaiping and Newchwang, which deceived Russian forces, mainly cavalry under General Mishchenko, as to the actual site of the disembarkation. In fact, Pitzuwo lay very near the site of the Japanese landing in the 1894 war against China.

Brushing aside the small Russian forces he encountered, Oku had by May 25 reached one of the most incredible military bottlenecks anywhere in the world, the Nanshan position.[8] As it extends to the south, the Liaotung Peninsula narrows into an isthmus linking it to the Kwantung promontory. At its narrowest point, the isthmus is just 3,500 yards wide, although low tides on either side can add a considerable amount of breadth. Looming up over it is Nanshan, a ring of hills about one mile in diameter. To the east lies Talien (Hand) Bay, to the west Chinchou Bay, so any attack on Nanshan would by necessity be frontal, although the sudden broadening of the terrain to the north of Nanshan did give the Japanese some room for maneuver. The slopes of Nanshan are bare and open, giving the defenders an even better field of fire than they had enjoyed on the Yalu, and the Russians had fortified the position with trenches, barbed wire, and machine gun nests. The artillery positions were much better, with the guns dug in deeply and connected by telephone. Russian engineers had brought up a generator, which powered searchlights in the front lines. Fronting the eastern side of the position were thick minefields and a double fence of barbed wire. The western side was weaker, relying mainly on barbed wire, since the smaller room for maneuver made the Russians doubt that an attack on this side had much chance of success.

With the port of Dalny lying about fifteen miles to the south, and with the great prize, Port Arthur, just twenty miles beyond that, the Russians had to defend Nanshan. And as even this cursory description indicates, if ever a position could be held, this was it. The military observer for the *Times* of London wrote that "the Russian position had everything in its favor. It was short and strongly fortified; its flanks were apparently secure, and it was held by a garrison more than ample for its defense." If the Russian army could not hold Nanshan, he continued, "it is hard to say what position it can expect to defend with success."[9]

Defending Nanshan was the 4th East Siberian Rifle Division under General Fock. While his four full regiments gave him sufficient force, Fock would start the battle with his command well dispersed. He is often criticized for his failure to concentrate, but he had a legitimate worry about enemy landings on the coast to his south, further proof of the importance of command of the sea. In addition, his supreme commander, General A. N. Kuropatkin, advised him from the start not to delay too long in withdrawing from Nanshan, intending the division to be part of the defenses of Port Arthur. Thus, when the battle opened, three of Fock's regiments were well to the rear. That left a single regiment, the 5th East Siberian under Colonel Tretyakov, defending the Nanshan position itself. The fate of the battle would hinge on two factors: the ability of Oku's men to brave heavy fire from the Russian trenches, and Fock's ability to handle the significant force he held in reserve.

Oku launched his assault on Nanshan on May 26. It will not go down in history as an example of finesse, nor, given the topography, could it be. Thick waves of Japanese infantry, three divisions deployed abreast (from right to left, 4th, 1st, and 3rd), tried to storm Nanshan and were mowed down by machine gun fire, as well as by artillery deployed far to the rear, using indirect fire called in by Russian forward observers. Heavy rains the day before the battle washed away enough of the topsoil to expose Russian mines and wires, but the Japanese infantry still had to be careful to avoid them. Over the course of the day, there were nine separate charges against Nanshan, all repulsed with heavy losses, and by 6:00 P.M., the situation was a stalemate. Only 4th Division, on the right, or northwestern, flank, had managed any progress, although that was due mainly to fire support from a nimble flotilla of Japanese gunboats in Chinchou Bay, including the *Tsukushi*, *Saiyen*, *Akagi*, and *Chiokai*, mounting fifteen guns in all.[10]

The advance of the 4th Division was an epic, with the men advancing in deep water and thick mud as they outflanked Nanshan along the coast. Spotting this threat to his left, Tretyakov wired Fock a request for reinforcements from the three reserve regiments. Fock did send reinforcements, but they amounted to just two companies. While his dispersed deployments can be justified, Fock had failed to recognize what the Germans call the *Schwerpunkt* of the battle (the decision point, or point of main effort) and to reinforce it accordingly.

The two Russian companies now marched into 4th Division's path. Desperate hand-to-hand fighting took place along the beach and even into the bay itself, which according to the Reuter's dispatch, left the water crimson with blood. Despite their bravery, the outnumbered Russians were overwhelmed. The Japanese fought their way back inland, overrunning a pair of redoubts in the area. Fock had moved closer to observe what was happen-

The Russian commander in Manchuria, General A. N. Kuropatkin, failed to make use of his numerical superiority, either to concentrate for the attack or to defend in place. Author's collection.

ing here, and he did not like what he was seeing. With 4th Division driving in his left and threatening his path of retreat, he decided that the time had come to withdraw.

He began by ordering the companies in his immediate vicinity to withdraw, then gave orders for the destruction of his reserve ammunition dumps to the rear, at Tafangshen. The shells and cartridges went up with a great roar, and in fact one major and twenty Russian enlisted men were killed in the explosion, due to faulty communications.[11] The first news that poor Colonel Tretyakov had of the retreat was the sound of this tremendous explosion. He was still holding firm in the center at the time: he had Japanese 1st Division pinned 300 yards in front of his trenches, and Japanese 3rd Division was suffering heavily from enfilade fire by Russian forces deployed to the south of Talien Bay. Still, he had no choice but to retreat. It began as an orderly withdrawal, but poor Russian command and control allowed it to degenerate into a rout. Oku had taken Nanshan, at a cost of 739 killed and 5,459 wounded. Russian losses amounted to a little over 1,000 killed and wounded.

The situation facing Oku on the evening of May 26 was not a happy one. His artillery was nearly out of ammunition; his three divisions were fought out, and, once again, as his exhausted men bivouacked on the hills they had stormed with such heavy loss, there was no possibility of pursuing and destroying the beaten Russians. The extremely heavy losses suffered by the Japanese (some 6,000 out of a total attacking force of perhaps 40,000, with losses concentrated among the assault units) had weakened them so thoroughly that they were, for the time, incapable of further offensive action. Units were so intermingled and their command structures so thoroughly disrupted that merely mustering them into some semblance of organization was a daunting task. Finally, how could the Japanese cavalry, waiting impatiently behind the lines, possibly negotiate the broken ground of the Nanshan position, further torn up by a day of shelling and foot-slogging infantry? It was four full days before the Japanese could re-form and reorganize themselves enough to resume their advance, entering Dalny on May 30.

With Port Arthur now sealed off from the rest of the Russian forces, Kuropatkin ordered his first offensive action of the war in order to relieve it. It was a curiously halfhearted effort, involving troops of the I Siberian Corps under General Stakelberg, a force of 30,000 men. In the first week of June, Stakelberg began to move south from his concentration area at Liaoyang, bearing confused, even contradictory, orders that told him, at one and the same time: (1) to move rapidly and energetically against any covering detachments he met; (2) to avoid decisive action against superior forces; and (3) to remember that the ultimate objective aim of his southerly movement was Nanshan and the relief of Port Arthur! On June 15, Stakelberg's force made contact with the Japanese 2nd Army, just starting its move up the rail line to the north, at the village of Telissu.[12] Stakelberg immediately went into a defensive posture, which seems to be a logical decision, based on the dissonance of his orders. Oku handled his force with skill, hitting the Russians frontally at Telissu with his 5th and 3rd Divisions, while working 4th Division around their right, or western, flank along the Fuchou River. Soon the Russians were in full retreat through the narrow mountain defile north of Telissu, under heavy fire from several batteries of captured Russian guns, the shrapnel cutting great gaps in the ranks of the retreating columns. It was one of the grisliest moments of the war. Only the sudden onset of a thunderstorm ended it, allowing Stakelberg to get the rest of his force back to where it had started, Liaoyang.

PORT ARTHUR

While the two armies were joined in battle at Telissu, Japanese 3rd Army (the 1st Division, detached from Oku's 2nd Army, plus the 9th and 11th) was landing at Dalny. It was under the command of Baron Maresuki Nogi, the old warrior who had conquered Port Arthur in the Sino-Japanese War of 1894. He marched on the fortress with his three divisions and on August 19 launched his first assault. The "siege of Port Arthur" may be the glamour event of the Russo-Japanese War, but it was not really a siege at all. Instead, it was a series of three assaults, and it offers greater insight into the nature of early twentieth-century field battle than it does into the classic art of siege.[13]

Since the nineteenth century, it had been clear that a field army could use a great city as a strong unflankable point upon which to base its defenses. The American Civil War consisted of three years of open-field maneuver and a fourth year of trench fighting in front of Petersburg; the Franco-Prussian War consisted of six weeks of campaigning in the open and five months in front of Paris. In the end, the Russo-Turkish War of 1877–78 came down to a struggle for the fortified city of Plevna.[14] None of these were sieges in the ordinary sense, in that the fall of the city was not the only issue involved. Besides being an important strategic position in its own right, each of the cities involved was also a fortified, all-around defensive position, a "hedgehog" in the parlance of World War II. The purpose of besieging such a position went beyond merely seizing it; it included destroying the enemy force that was using the city as a strongpoint. Thus, siege warfare and battle in the open field had become increasingly difficult to tell apart. The operation in front of Port Arthur fits the bill of the "new siege" perfectly, with the city being at one and the same time a Russian strongpoint in the rear of any Japanese drive into Manchuria and an important naval base in its own right.

Baron Maresuki Nogi, the commander of the Japanese 3rd Army and the conqueror of Port Arthur. Equal parts modern operational commander and traditional Japanese warrior, he would commit ritual suicide in 1912 upon the death of Emperor Mutsuhito. Author's collection.

Assaults on walled fortresses have always been bloody affairs. Given Nogi's determination to carry out a quick seizure of the Russian fortress, the size of the forces he commanded, and the firepower in use by 1904, losses were bound to be high. But even an assault on a fortress can have more subtlety than Nogi showed. When he sailed from Tokyo in May, the Japanese General Staff was still debating the posture to be adopted in front of Port Arthur: a long, gradual siege or a rapid assault. Apparently, the success at Nanshan, in which Japanese infantry had shown that it was capable of chewing its way through any sort of defense, no matter how intricate, threw the scales in favor of a quick assault. Rather than long weeks of preliminary bombardment, typical of siege operations, Nogi decided on three days of heavy fire followed by a direct assault on the Russian fortifications, which he was sure would succeed at a cost of one of his three infantry divisions. The *Daily Telegraph*'s war correspondent David H. James was with Japanese forces at Port Arthur, and he described Nogi's strategy as "three day's hammering with artillery" and a "heavy butcher's bill."[15] Nogi was so sure of success that on August 19 he had the correspondents brought to the front to see the fall of the city, which he assured them would be in Japanese hands in three days. He stuck to this plan even after disaster struck. On June 16, vessels of the Russian Vladivostok squadron sank the Japanese freighter *Hitachi Maru* in the Straits of Tsushima. It was carrying eighteen of Nogi's 280-mm siege howitzers, a major part of the Japanese siege train.

A great deal had changed since that day back in 1894 when he had taken the city at the head of a regiment and suffered minimal casualties. In fact, a great deal had changed since the start of the war. It is generally accepted that Port Arthur had not been ready to defend itself in February 1904.[16] In the ensuing six months, however, the garrison had been quite active, filling in gaps in the fortified positions, throwing up earthworks, mounting naval guns of large caliber, building redoubts and small advance works ("lunettes") in positions where they could be supported by fire from the permanent forts, laying out miles of barbed wire, digging trenches all around the perimeter, even sinking painted range stones into the path of the Japanese advance for instant fire registration, à la the Boers. Even more important, the troops had recovered their morale since the dark days after Nanshan. Nevertheless, Nogi believed that the indomitable will to conquer of his troops would be sufficient, and he also knew how badly his 3rd Army would be needed for the showdown to the north.

Even if it had been completely unfortified, Port Arthur would still have been a tough nut to crack. Lying on the southern coast and near the tip of the Liaotung Peninsula, it is surrounded by an arc of rugged hills and broken gullies that opens out into a broad valley to the east. Any approach to the town from that direction, the most direct and efficient route, would have to run a gauntlet of Russian fire from both the permanent and the newly constructed forts on the Ehrlung hills in that sector, which essentially followed—and in some places made use of—the old Chinese wall around the fortification. The tactical positions here included the Ehrlung Lunette, Sungshu Fort, Ehrlung Fort, West Panlung, East Panlung, "P" Fortification, North Keekwan Fort, "Q" Fortification, and South Keekwan Fort, moving from north to south. Backing up this sector, and dominating all the positions in front of it, was the fortified village of Wantai. An approach from the north would be even worse, coming up against the permanent forts in the center of the Russian line on the hills of Itzushan, Antzushan, and Taiyangkou, plus Sueishi village and the lunettes directly in front of it. These were tough concrete fortifications of the most modern type. A detailed description is in order, so that the term *heavily fortified* does not become mere military history boilerplate:

> The glacis, or long outer slope, of the hill selected was carefully cleared of dead ground and leveled for purposes of a clear field of fire. . . . After the hill had been leveled, a moat, some thirty to forty feet wide and deep, was hewn out of the country rock around the position selected for the construction of the fort. Then, ten feet or more under the glacis, a subterranean gallery was excavated in the central front and flanks of the counterscarp wall of the moat. This gallery was then reconstructed with concrete walls and roof of a uniform thickness of three feet. This, known as the caponiere gallery, was designed for the defense of the moat, and its casemated interior was fitted with loop-holes in the concrete wall facing the moat, which enabled the entire space in the moat to be swept with rifle, machine gun, and light artillery fire. Against these caponieres the shells of the heaviest known artillery are ineffective.
>
> The opposite wall of the moat—the escarpment—was leveled off and then glazed over with cement until it presented a smooth, perpendicular face. At the top of this wall there are the parapet defenses in the form of bomb-proof shelters. Then come the first of the interior defenses, a series of earth and timbered traverses, behind which lay the light guns of the first line of defense. More traverses follow, and shelter the line of heavy fortress cannon. Behind these concrete platforms are underground magazines and concrete shelters for the gunners, while passages lead to the underground concrete barracks of the garrison, with kitchens, sleeping quarters, etc., etc. In these barracks the infantry are as safe from shell fire as in the caponiere galleries.[17]

An approach from the northwest would be marginally easier, but a large force concentrated here would be vulnerable to a sally from the city itself against its left flank and rearward communication. And even here an assault would have to overcome a clump of individual hills containing a number of impressive fortifications. Two of the hills, known as 174 Meter Hill and 203 Meter Hill for their height, boasted an impressive array of works:

> The trenches circling the summit of 174 Meter were roofed over with wooden beams and railway sleepers, which were further topped with earthwork. The breastwork of these trenches was stiffened with rows of sandbags, and inlaid with steel ace-of-club shaped loopholes. Just off the sky-line were emplaced two 4-inch cannon and five fieldpieces, while machine guns were hidden in the trenches. 203 Meter Hill had all this and more, for here the sleepers were overlaid with a double layer of ¼ inch steel plates, and the trench ends braced across with railway iron and rails.[18]

Protecting the lower slopes of all these hills were barbed wire entanglements, fastened around stout piles of wood every three feet.

This was the position against which Nogi now hurled 3rd Army. His plan was the direct approach, following the railroad to drive toward Wantai in the northeast sector of the Russian line. Once they had penetrated the Russian position, his assault columns would take Ehrlung and Sunshu Forts from behind. They would use the captured ground as a base for an advance into the town. There would be little use for finesse. Bold and aggressive attacks would maintain the momentum through the secondary Russian defenses, take the city by storm, and mop up its garrison. He had his three divisions arrayed abreast, 1st on his right, occupying a line from the coast of Louisa Bay to Sueishi village; 9th in the center, from Sueishi to a point half a mile due east of the Panlung forts; and 11th on his left, from the east coast along the Russian parallels to the foothills of the Takushan hills. His artillery included some 300 cannon in all, including ten batteries of 150-mm and 120-mm howitzers, all emplaced on reverse slopes, masked, and hidden by both terrain and man-made artifice.

Nogi's communications with his army were state-of-the-art for the era, that is to say, totally inadequate. He was in touch by telephone with each of his divisions, ammunition columns, depots, pioneers, and auxiliary arms. He was also in wireless communication with the Japanese fleet blockading the port. His artillery commander, General Teshima, controlled the bombardment from a point on "Observation Hill" (part of the Feng-hwang-shan chain in the center of the Japanese position). He, too, relied on telephone to reach his batteries, observation posts, and even the balloon section operating in the rear.[19] In both cases, the smoke and chaos of the shellfire soon rendered any sort of tight control impossible.

The assault opened at 9:00 A.M. on August 19 with a feint by 1st Division, launching its right wing against 174 Meter Hill. Rifle fire from the Russian trenches and well-placed shrapnel fire from the Russian guns soon drove it back. Essentially a canister of steel balls and a bursting charge triggered by a time fuse, shrapnel was then the standard round for the light field gun. Its detonation produced a shotgunlike effect, with a cone-shaped blast zone 25 meters wide and 150 meters long. Deadly against troops in the open, it was much less effective against entrenchments and fortifications. At 2:00 P.M., the 1st came back for another try and again had to fall back in the face of Russian fire.

The main Japanese thrust needed all the help it could get. The Russian positions on the eastern face of the Port Arthur perimeter faced a long, sloping valley. It was an ideal target for shrapnel fire, and the Japanese infantry would have to get through a lot of it before they were anywhere close enough to open fire on the Russian defenders. That night, howitzer fire rained down on the Russian positions all night long, and the Japanese used the cover of darkness to muscle a field battery to within a few hundred yards of the enemy line. It continued the next morning, while the 1st kept up its attack on 174 Meter Hill (taking far too many casualties for a feint). At noon, Japanese gunners, believing that they had destroyed the fortifications in front of them, switched to shrapnel to target the Russian infantry and gunners themselves. About 3:00 P.M., the 9th Division launched its assault on the eastern fortifications, going forward in small groups against the Ehrlung Lunette. The field battery that had been hauled into position during the night fired in direct support, and soon joining it was a tremendous barrage by all Japanese guns within range. At first, no reply came from the defenders of the lunette. As the assaulting infantry rushed against the moat of the work, however, a furious volley of rifle and machine gun fire erupted from within; then came the shrapnel, fired from guns on the neighboring positions of Ehrlung Fort and Itzushan. The assaulting infantry, those who survived at least, now came stumbling back to their start line, thankful for the tall stalks of kaoliang (a variety of millet that can grow ten to twelve feet tall), which partially hid their rout. As the second day of the fighting died down, the Japanese pounded the entire eastern sector with shrapnel, and flames were soon to be seen in the rear of East Panlung Fort, evidently the result of an ammunition explosion.

Night brought no rest. The Japanese continued their bombardment (although its effect was difficult to determine), Russian searchlights joined the action, seeking out the Japanese infantry, and at 3:00 A.M. a general assault began. There were three main axes of attack: against the hills in the west, against the Panlung forts, and against the Keekwan forts. None made any real headway, although a subsidiary thrust at 8:00 A.M. succeeded for a time

in occupying the Russian "P" Fortification. A Russian counterattack soon
took it back.

At midnight, the Japanese renewed the assault on their center and left. Again
and again they found it impossible to get through the Russian wire, which
was proving to be far more of an obstacle than the Japanese had imagined.
Even in areas supposedly cleared by their engineers, the gaps in the wire were
far too small for easy passage, and the injuries that came from trying to cut
fresh paths through it were gruesome. Russian electronic mines were used for
the first time, but their detonation was usually too late to hit the most lucrative massed targets—the Russian operators were too slow on the trigger finger. Russian searchlights once again did good duty, easily locating the masses
of assaulting Japanese infantry. This night attack made an unearthly scene.
Frederick de Villiers, an English correspondent with 3rd Army, described it:

> The deep purple of the mountain against the nocturnal blue, the pale
> lemon of the moon, the whitish rays of the searchlights, the warm incan-
> descent glow of the star bombs, the reddish spurt of the cannon's mouths,
> and the yellow flash from the exploding shell, all tempered to a mellow-
> ness by a thin haze of smoke, ever clinging to hilltop and valley, make the
> scene the most weird and unique I have ever looked on.[20]

Although morning found shattered Japanese columns limping back to their
start lines, they did succeed in getting a toehold in the Panlung forts, the
work of a single heroic regiment, the 7th (of the 9th Division).

The next day found the Japanese trying to continue their drive by assaulting Wantai. Here, however, they crashed head-on into a gigantic Russian
sortie from the neighboring fortifications ("Q," Ehrlung, and Wantai). Although it suffered heavily from Japanese fire, and was eventually repulsed,
it had succeeded in throwing off the timing of the Japanese assault, which
never developed any momentum. The Japanese had also encountered trouble
on their right flank, thanks to a clever Russian stratagem:

> In the west the first division commenced some pretty artillery practice
> on the western searchlights, and shells so frequently blanked the face of
> the lights that we were not surprised to see two lights die out. . . . A de-
> tachment of the left wing of the 1st Division, taking advantage of the ab-
> sence of the two powerful searchlights in that part of the field, were
> advancing in skirmishing order, and making their presence felt by the
> Russian outposts, when suddenly the extinguished searchlights reflashed,
> swung over the sky, and illuminated ranks of the Japanese infantry.[21]

A hail of shellfire from the neighboring hills of Itzushan, Antzushan, and
the nearby ridges now opened up on the unfortunate men, along with rifle

fire from a concealed line of infantry in front of them. The feint of 1st Division against 174 Meter Hill had come to a bad end.

The great assault was over. Nogi had gravely underestimated the strength of the Russian position he faced, and his men had paid the price. After six days of carnage, 3rd Army had suffered approximately 18,000 casualties. It had taken precisely two outlying Russian forts, the Panlungs. Both were of doubtful value, completely dominated by Wantai village, the objective of the last failed assault in the east. The Japanese had to garrison each fort with a company, and with Russian batteries a mere 500 yards away, each took a hundred casualties per day, although Japanese improvements to the position drove that figure down dramatically in the following weeks. Despite all the new technology evident in the assault, especially in the area of firepower, the casualties were in line with those of any great frontal assault—Napoleon at Borodino, for example.

THE BATTLE OF LIAOYANG

By now the thrust to the north had begun, with three armies—the 1st, 2nd, and 4th (under General Michitsura Nozu)—converging on the city of Liaoyang.[22] The chief of the Japanese General Staff, Marshal Iwao Oyama, was now in the theater and acting as supreme commander. Highly influenced, like so many of his contemporaries, by Moltke's operational ideas, he and his brilliant chief of staff, General Gentaro Kodama, refused to draw up detailed operational plans for each army. Instead, they merely constructed a framework: a concentric advance by all available Japanese armies would fix the Russian main body in place, then destroy it. The exact shape of the climactic battle could only be decided when the Russian deployment was clear. The logical candidate to play the role of the Prussian crown prince at Königgrätz was Kuroki's 1st Army. Coming up out of the southeast after its victory on the Yalu, it was ideally placed to hit the Russian left flank. Oyama ordered the two remaining Japanese armies, the 2nd and 4th, to launch a frontal assault along the railroad toward the heavily fortified city, while Kuroki made a wide turning movement round the Russian left across the Taitsu River, advancing toward the Yentai coal mines, cutting the railroad northeast of the city, and bagging the Russians in the greatest *Kesselschlacht* of all time.

Very little went right with his plan. The Russian commander Kuropatkin had dug three concentric rings of defensive works around Liaoyang, making the Japanese advance slow and costly. Opening on August 26, the battle raged for ten long days—an unprecedented thing in military history up to that point in time. The Russians were slowly driven back but not bagged. This fierce resistance slowed Kuroki's advance, which was crucial to the plan,

Marshal Iwao Oyama, the Japanese commander in Manchuria, displayed a thorough grounding in Moltke's art of war, seeking constantly to achieve a concentric attack by all his combined forces. Author's collection.

to a crawl. Kuropatkin spotted the flanking movement early—he was a perfectly competent general, if not a particularly inspired one—and kept shifting reserves to block it, eventually withdrawing his forces in the south to the inner line of defenses surrounding Liaoyang so that he could throw ever more men in front of 1st Army. By September 1, Kuroki had crossed the Taitsu with one of his three divisions, but he was clearly in trouble, trapped between the Russians to his front and the river to his rear. Making matters worse, the river was just entering its flood stage, isolating 12th Division altogether. Nevertheless, over the next three days, displaying will and determination if nothing else, Kuroki slowly ground his way up to the railroad and the Yentai coal mines. On September 4, with its railroad lifeline threatened but not yet choked off, the Russian army began a retreat to the north in fairly good order. Losses had been heavy on both sides: perhaps 17,000 for the Russians and 23,000 for the Japanese. For the latter, losses fell heaviest on the 2nd Army, which had done the hard slogging up the railroad into the teeth of Kuropatkin's trenches. The Japanese took no Russian guns. Unit cohesion was so thoroughly disrupted that the victors, once again, had to let their beaten adversary go without a pursuit.

The battle of Liaoyang was a huge, sprawling struggle—the Russian defensive front at the outset stretched over fifty miles—that in the end came to naught for both sides. The Russians had once again failed to carry out the simplest play in the book: defend themselves in a heavily fortified position. The Japanese had, on the surface, performed much more effectively, but a closer look reveals grave weaknesses in their conduct of the battle. Perceptive observers present at the battle compared it to Moltke's handling of the Königgrätz campaign, with three armies marching along different lines of communication in order to face the enemy with a concentric assault. In point of fact, however, the plan was a watered-down version of Moltke's great achievement. Two of the three Japanese armies were already in contact with one another as they approached Liaoyang, rather than widely dispersed and linking up only at the climactic moment. As a result, Kuroki's great flanking movement, intended by Marquis Oyama to be a swift coup de grâce, instead had to fight forward every inch of the way against a tenacious Russian defense. In fact, what 1st Army had done at the battle's outset was to hit the Russian army's left wing, not its left flank.

The ordeal of the 1st Army commander is an object lesson in the command problems of modern war, and in fact he fought them as much as he fought the Russians. On August 27, in preparation for the crossing of the Taitsu, Kuroki tried to concentrate his force, giving orders for all three divisions to close up to a line between Shuisenpu and Kotagai, a distance of just eight miles. Each of his divisions (the Guards, 2nd Division, and 12th

Division, reading left to right) was already heavily engaged with Russian forces to their front, however. Guards Division was trying to fight its way through the heaviest opposition of the entire battle, taking minor positions (usually hills and/or entrenchments) with great loss and then being thrown back out of them, in the pattern that would become distressingly familiar in World War I. The logic of engagement dictated where these divisions would go far more than did Kuroki's orders.

When the moment finally came to cross the Taitsu, Kuroki had precisely one division available, the 12th, less than that if we take into account how heavily it had been engaged in the previous five days of the battle. The weakness of the thrust against the Russian left ended Japan's chance for decisive victory at Liaoyang. One observer commented: "General Kuroki was forced to undertake this hazardous and decisive operation with first one and then two incomplete divisions, eventually strengthened by one mixed brigade—a force manifestly incapable of carrying through its task with the desirable vigor and completeness should the enemy display the slightest knowledge of war."[23]

In fact, with the crossing to be made at the Taitsu's bend, the 12th Division first had to disengage and march to the east, and was thus for a time actually moving away from the main battlefield. This was a faulty application of the *Schwerpunkt* concept, to say the least. As it attempted to fight its way around the Russian flank, the division (plus one brigade from the neighboring 2nd Division that had crossed the river and joined it on the following day) faced not only an unbroken Russian line but also an attempt by the Russians to extend and lap around its own flank. It was nearing harvest time in Manchuria, and the tall stalks of kaoliang made even elemental reconnaissance difficult, ruining both sides' field of fire and leading to the occasional lost unit.

Finally, to complete Kuroki's list of problems, telegraph communications between 1st Army and Oyama's headquarters went down for over twenty-four hours, from evening on September 1 to midnight on September 2, whether due to sabotage or equipment failure no one could say.[24] Under the impression that the neighboring armies (2nd and 4th) were making good progress, and realizing how important it was that he keep pace with them, he rode his men hard on September 1, ordering a series of attacks on the Russian positions in front of him: a turtle-backed little hill, about seventy-five feet tall, that the Japanese named Manjuyama (rice-bowl hill), as well as Mountain 131. Futile attacks on the latter position, in particular, led to heavy casualties, with one 600-man detachment from the 4th Regiment losing 270 killed and wounded. Those who were there testify to the almost unbearable atmosphere of tension in 1st Army headquarters. As September 2 wore on, Japanese artillery came near to running out of ammunition and began to hoard its barrages for last-ditch defenses of important positions.

The Russian guns, firing from positions hidden by the kaoliang, held the field, reaching a crescendo toward evening with over one hundred rapid-fire pieces pounding the Japanese infantry on Manjuyama, while the Japanese guns remained dead silent. Imagine Kuroki's chagrin when communications were restored and he found that the neighboring armies had not even fought their way up to the Taitsu River, let alone crossed it. He had needlessly set a "killing pace" for his men.

With the Russians in full retreat on September 4, Kuroki's order of the day began with the stirring words, "The 1st Army will now pursue."[25] Once again, however, there was no pursuit. How much could anyone reasonably expect from a flanking force of one and a half detached divisions that had been fighting continuously for ten days and nights, separated by a flooding river from the main body of its army? One Japanese staff officer gave a revealing explanation of what had happened. The divisions were unable to carry out their orders:

> Not at once, that is to say. Not as had been intended. The 2nd Division did not begin its march until almost dusk. Both brigades lost their way in the kaoliang, and, after struggling in vain for some time to make head against their difficulties, lay down where they were to await the morning light, having covered some two or three miles only instead of the six expected of them. The 12th Division did not commence its advance until after 10:00 P.M."[26]

This time, there is no mention at all of the cavalry, which, even if it could have been pushed up close enough to the front, would have found it impossible to negotiate a battlefield torn up by the fire of thousands of infantrymen and hundreds of heavy guns. Speaking of the action of September 3, the head of 1st Army's Operations Section, General Fukuda, said, "Even at a supreme moment such as this there was, however, one group of men who were idle. This was the cavalry. So they were employed to go back to the river and cook food for their companions of the infantry." While castigating that account as "unduly sarcastic," another officer from the 1st Army staff was not much more complimentary to the horse arm: "It was the same with the cavalry on the south side of the Taistsuho. Major-General Akiyama commanded the mixed brigade of cavalry, but although he was supported by field guns, machine guns, and infantry, he could accomplish nothing against the right of the Russian army. The Cavalry Brigade had two men wounded."[27] In the entire battle, the Cavalry Brigade suffered nineteen casualties. Nor did the Russians, with far more cavalry than the Japanese, manage to use it in any effective way. As 12th Division was crossing the Taitsu, small parties of Russian cavalry had looked on, then fell back without firing a shot.

Russian operations since Telissu had generally not gone beyond defending in place. In early October, Kuropatkin ordered the second offensive action of the war. He massed huge forces on both of his wings, a "Western" and an "Eastern Force," and launched them against the Japanese. The Western Force of two corps under the command of General A. A. Bilderling would attack down the railway, holding the Japanese in place for a flanking maneuver by the Eastern Force (General G. K. Stakelberg). This army, consisting of three corps, would swing down on the Japanese right, rolling past the Yentai coal mines and across the Taitsu River, and catch the Japanese forces in a battle of annihilation. The plan was a solid one that, properly handled, could have threatened the Japanese line of communications and perhaps even have taken back Liaoyang; it was, in a sense, a mirror image of Oyama's original plan for the battle of Liaoyang.

In the resulting battle of the Sha-Ho (October 9–17), little went right for Kuropatkin.[28] With the Russians attacking in ponderous, parade-ground columns, and a huge complement of artillery on both sides, the attack was more sanguinary than effective, but the operational conception fell apart early. For a time the Russian advance appeared to pose a threat to the extreme Japanese right at Pingtaitsu and Penchiho. Japanese 1st Army, on the right wing, once again saw heavy fighting. A cavalry division under General Rennenkampf actually slipped across the Taitsu River into the Japanese rear. But a Japanese cavalry brigade under Imperial Prince Kanin, well supported by machine guns, restored the situation. Driving off the Russian horse, Kanin seized a copse, quickly established his four machine guns on it, and enfiladed the left flank of the Russian position. His fire even hit the rear of a battalion of Russian infantry lining up for dinner.[29] It was the high point for Japanese cavalry in the war.

Much of the battle was a fight in the dark, fought over terrain that neither side knew well at all. Hamilton compared the situation to the Boer War:

> Evidently Kuroki is himself somewhat vague about the progress of events opposite his right wing. The Japanese have no maps, as the captured Russian maps upon which they have been mainly dependent until now do not show the Pingtaitsu or Penchiho country. As one of the staff ingenuously declared: "Our ideas of the theater of war to the north of Liaoyang were bounded on the east by the Yentai coal mines; now we begin too late to realize that on our right hand there extends a very continent of mountains!"
>
> Henceforth, the British War Office will be able perhaps to pluck up spirit to defend itself when attacked by absurd critics who, airily ignoring politics as well as finance, blame it for not having mapped out the whole South African subcontinent in anticipation of a possible war![30]

The fighting soon drifted into stalemate. Russian gains on the Japanese right were more than offset by losses on their own. The pinning attack of the Western Force failed totally. On this wing, Japanese 2nd and 4th Armies seized the initiative and once more began to grind their way up the axis of the railway. One British observer stated that "the Western Force cannot be said even to have attacked the Japanese 2nd and 4th Armies, much less engaged them closely while the Eastern Force turned their flank. All that the Western Force did was to make a slow forward movement, marked by the construction of defensive positions."[31] In a problem that had become typical for the Russians, they had plenty of troops in the reserve but failed to commit them to battle in a timely or effective manner. Kuropatkin had always made a fetish of security, but he went to extremes at the battle of the Sha-ho: of his eight corps, three and a half were in reserve. Besides his two maneuver forces, he had a general reserve, two "flank guards," two "extreme flank guards," and a "rearguard."[32] Finally, command and control were problem areas for the Russians, as they were in virtually every battle of the era: Kuropatkin had little real control over his large formations in this battle. The telegraph failed to function at key times and was used only rarely. As a result, his orders often took several hours to reach his subordinates.

This had been the bloodiest battle yet, with about 40,000 casualties on either side. It had exhausted both the men and the staff, and the amount of ammunition used was unprecedented. The Russians alone had fired 130,000 shells and 5 million rounds of small-arms ammunition at the Sha-ho. In fact, supply services on both sides had broken down during the fighting, silencing individual batteries from time to time and forcing the I Siberian Corps to go without rations for two days. Both sides now had to pause for breath. By the end of the battle, the opposing sides were in trench lines, often a mere 200 to 300 yards apart, and here they would sit in what the attachés euphemistically referred to as "winter quarters," if such a term can be used for camping outdoors in mountainous, snowy, wind-whipped Manchuria.

THE FALL OF PORT ARTHUR

The focus of the action now shifted to Port Arthur. On October 28, Nogi was ready for a second general assault on the outer works of the fortress. Again, the target was to be the toughest spot in the Russian line, the eastern fortifications. He began with three days of bombardment against the forts, from Sungshu to Keekwan, this time with newly arrived siege guns joining the smaller pieces. It was the greatest bombardment in military history up to that point. A Russian correspondent, E. K. Nojiine, described the shelling:

For forty-eight hours the works on the northeast front were incessantly pounded, the enemy deciding to break down and annihilate everything with their fire, and then to dash on the defenders with the bayonet. The night of the 30th was black, and the sky cloudy. Morning came, and the fire increased, and by 10:00 am the whole front was enveloped in dense smoke: the hills were literally reeking.[33]

The Japanese had fired 150,000 shells, but when their infantry came out to the assault, they found that the impact had been negligible. This time there was no feint, no diversion. Five columns of infantry stormed out of their trenches toward Ehrlung and Sungshu. "A bright sun, set high in a blue unflecked sky, painted the tips of the bayonets that glistened coldly in spite of the caressing light," wrote David James. "It was magnificent, and it was war." But now the Russian guns opened up, drenching the advancing Japanese columns with shrapnel. The rifles and machine guns joined in, reaping a deadly harvest of the advancing troops. Forts supposed to have been vaporized by the intense bombardment suddenly sprang into life; infantry supposed to have been suppressed suddenly appeared all too active. What had been a glorious sight, a dream vision of disciplined troops advancing to glory on a beautifully clear day, suddenly turned into a nightmare. Japanese troops who had appeared so invincible a few short moments before now turned tail and tried to run to safety. Others pushed on in a mad rush, their only hope to escape the deadly fire being a "flight to the front." One group of fortunate attackers managed to get to the moat of Ehrlung Fort. They laid down their ladders, specially designed for this mission, and found them to be thirty feet too short. A similar thing happened at Sungshu. What began as an assault had become a melee, without form or order or any direction at all from higher commanders. David James's comment on the assault is revealing: "The general attack, now in full swing, was out of control as far as immediate touch with the commander-in-chief or divisional commanders [was] concerned, and things were in a horrible mess."[34] A party of Japanese infantry did manage to get up under the parapet of South Keekwan Fort but then found themselves under a murderous, nearly uninterrupted fire from three sides, as enemy machine guns and field artillery on the neighboring works opened up on them. The Russians mowed down scores of them as they tried to run down the glacis of the fort back to safety. Another group, from the 35th Infantry Regiment, managed to seize the "P" Fortification, lose it to the Russians during the night, then recapture it before morning. It was the one Japanese gain of the entire assault, and it cost Nogi 4,500 men. Some of his regiments, like the 12th and 44th, lost hundreds of men in the first thirty minutes. As in the first assault, the lesson of the second one seemed to be the near invulnerability of concrete fortifications. Many Russian forts had withstood repeated direct hits by Japan's 280-mm siege guns.

By now the pressure on Nogi was almost unbearable, both from the Japanese High Command and from public opinion at home. Voices from all quarters were blaming him for the slow pace of the operations and the high casualties, and there were even rumors of his dismissal. He dutifully launched a third assault in November. It was a ghastly, inexcusable operation. Without any real preliminary bombardment, the Japanese infantry poured out of their trenches at 1:00 P.M. on November 26, advancing toward Ehrlung, Sungshu, and the North Fort. Once again, the target was the eastern face of the Russian perimeter, and once again, defensive firepower slaughtered the attacking infantry. The "lesson learned" was a pedestrian one: bombardment might not work against concrete fortifications, but neither did nonbombardment. The cost for such an important advance in military doctrine was 6,000 casualties.[35]

The third assault blended almost imperceptibly into another Japanese attempt against 203 Meter Hill.[36] Assaults on the eastern face had broken themselves on the network of interlocking fortification and firing positions in that sector. The Russian line to the northwest of the city, although heavily fortified, consisted more of independent, discrete positions. The loss of 203 Meter Hill, in particular, would fatally compromise the entire Russian defensive posture in this sector. That could not be said of any individual position in the east. Possession of the hill would also give the Japanese a direct line of sight down into the town and harbor, so that they could bring down direct artillery fire onto the Russian fleet and systematically destroy it. And as heavily fortified as 203 was, it really had the support of only one neighboring position, the lower hill (about 160 meters high) lying just to the southeast known as Akasakayama. Heavy Russian guns from the permanent forts in the center of their perimeter could also lend a hand to the defenders.

The attack on 203 began on November 27, after a week of artillery preparation finally succeeded in silencing the Russian guns on the hill. Spearheading the assault was the Japanese 1st Division, with its regiments deployed abreast at the foot of the hill: 15th Regiment on the Japanese right, 1st in the center, 38th on the left, this last regiment aimed more at Akasakayama than 203 itself.

The fighting for 203 Meter Hill was an incredible, back-and-forth struggle as the hill changed hands repeatedly. There has rarely been a better example in military history of bravery under fire, and that is referring to the conduct of both sides. Even a mere chronology tells the tale. The attack began at night, with a Japanese assault (1st Regiment) rather quickly gaining the crest of 203. A hastily assembled Russian counterattack threw the Japanese back down the hill, with explosive grenades playing a key role for the attacking infantry. At 8:30 the following morning, a coordinated assault by the 1st and 15th Regiments once again won them the crest of the hill, but intense Russian shelling from the heavy guns in the permanent forts succeeded in driving the Japanese from their new positions by noon. Ten minutes later, the Japanese again stormed up the crest of the hill. This time, enfilade fire from the infantry galleries on neighboring Akasakayama quickly drove them off again. At 3:00 P.M., there was another fresh Japanese assault. Rifle fire, shell, shrapnel, and grenade all working together tore great holes in the attacking formations, and once again, barbed wire proved to be the battlefield obstacle par excellence, the defender's best friend. By 7:00 P.M., the Japanese had failed to effect a lodging on the hill. The attempt by the 38th Regiment had likewise failed to take Akasakayama. By now, Nogi's trump card had arrived on the field. It was an entire fresh infantry division, the 7th, consisting of the 26th, 27th, and 28th Regiments. He hurled them at Akasakayama, which now more and more appeared to be the key to 203. The Russians threw them back; they tried again in the night, and again the Russians threw them back.

At dawn on November 30, the Russians were still holding firm to all their positions. Repeated frontal attacks had failed. That day featured a determined Japanese attempt against Akasakayama. Both the 1st and 7th Divisions attacked the hill and managed to seize a position in the center of the Russian trench, just below the crest. Here they managed to stave off repeated Russian counterattacks and then fell victim to a barrage of their own shrapnel, mistakenly delivered onto the hill after a report that the Russians were still in occupation. Caught out in the open, they sustained heavy casualties and had to retire.[37]

That night was the turning point. What infantry could not achieve, engineers could. Japanese pioneers began to sap their way at right angles to the parallel at the western foot on 203 Meter Hill, the 15th Regiment's position. By dawn, they had advanced about two-thirds of the way up the hill. The next morning, Japanese howitzers began to pound the top of the hill systematically. At 3:00 P.M., the infantry began to work its way up the sap and dig hasty entrenchments. From December 2 through 4, sappers continued to work their way up the hill, digging in the bitter cold and the hard, frozen ground. The Russian defenders had to sit and endure nearly uninterrupted fire from the Japanese 280-mm batteries, firing a 485-pound projectile. On the morning of December 5, every available Japanese artillery piece subjected 203 and Akasakayama to a hurricane of fire, which managed to keep the defenders' heads down and prevent them from interfering

· ·

with Japanese preparations. That afternoon, eight battalions of picked men under Major General Saito launched the long-awaited assault on the hill. A half hour later it was all over. The remnant of the Russian defense force was streaming back down the slope, and 203 Meter Hill was in Japanese hands.

The two armies lost over 12,500 men in the fight for this single hill. The worst-hit Japanese units lost more than 90 percent of their effectives.[38] David James wrote, "In no solitary instance in the history of the world was so much horror contracted into so small a space, for the revolting destruction wrought by dynamite bombs and high explosive shells was never more hideously exemplified than at the battle of 203 Meter Hill." It was not just the numbers, however, that shocked him:

> The corpses of the belligerents—and there were over 2,000 of these on the hillside the day I visited the hill—were mostly denuded of their clothing, scorched, deformed, and defaced beyond recognition, and in the trenches there was a pulp of mutilated humanity. The sight of those trenches heaped up with arms and legs and dismembered bodies all mixed together and then frozen into compact masses, the expressions on the faces of the scattered heads of decapitated bodies, the stupendous magnitude of the concentrated horror, impressed itself indelibly into the utmost recesses of my unaccustomed brain—there to remain and ever remirror itself in my eyes, and shame me for my very callousness that I did ever look on it.[39]

In fact, the fighting had killed the hill itself. The repeated detonations of high explosive had reshaped its distinctive twin crest perceptibly, and it was no longer 203 meters tall.

This was the decisive moment in the siege. In December, Japanese siege artillery rained down on the helpless Russian fleet in Port Arthur. Firing specially designed armor-piercing shells, the 280-mm guns made short work of the Russian ships. In January 1905, Port Arthur surrendered under controversial circumstances. There were stores and supplies of all sorts in the city to support a much longer struggle, not to mention approximately 20,000 able-bodied soldiers and sailors. In the course of the operations before Port Arthur, Nogi's army had suffered over 60,000 casualties, the result of marrying the ancient art of siege to modern firepower. The dead included two of his sons. He ended the siege, fittingly, with a traditional Shinto ceremony on January 14. Feeling a need to make amends for his own ineptitude, he gathered his entire army, all 120,000 men, before a shrine to the dead and personally read the invocation: "My heart is oppressed with sadness when I think of all you who have paid the price of victory, and whose spirits are in the great hereafter."[40]

THE BATTLE OF MUKDEN

With the fall of Port Arthur, all Japanese forces, five full armies since the arrival of 5th Army under General Kageaki Kawamura, could now be concentrated for what both sides hoped would be the decisive battle in Manchuria. With the war a year old, the Japanese were scraping the bottom of their manpower barrel. They had thus far made an epic march into Manchuria but were no closer to ultimate victory. In January 1905, the vulnerability of their supply line had been demonstrated by a large-scale Russian cavalry raid under Colonel P. I. Mishchenko.[41] With 6,000 horses and six batteries of light guns, he had slipped around the Japanese left flank, riding toward the crucial supply depot outside of Newchwang. Japanese infantry arrived just in time to stop him from reaching his goal. He did moderate damage to the rail line supplying the Japanese but caused maximum anxiety at Oyama's headquarters.

Up to this point, the Russians had been hammered in every engagement, whether they were attacking or defending, but they were still in the field, and their army was growing dramatically in size with the arrival of every troop train. But even Russia had its limits, as the revolutionary disturbances that were already beginning to convulse the empire proved. The Russians' own supply lines in vast Manchuria were none too safe, either, as a Japanese cavalry detachment proved in early February by slipping around the Russian flank and destroying a railway bridge some 160 miles *north* of Mukden.

In mid-February 1905, advancing up the by-now-familiar axis of the Southern Manchurian railroad, the Japanese met the Russians entrenched in front of the great city of Mukden.[42] It was the largest battle in military history up to that point: nearly 300,000 Russians (275,000 infantry, 16,000 cavalry, over 1,200 guns) faced 200,000 Japanese infantry, 7,300 cavalry, and 992 guns. The Russian line south of Mukden was ninety miles long, with three armies deployed abreast (moving west to east, they were 2nd Manchurian, 3rd Manchurian, and 1st Manchurian). It was a desperate fight between two desperate adversaries in appropriately godforsaken weather, featuring bitter cold and blinding snowstorms. With two more armies at his command, Oyama's plan could be much more complex than the one he had used at Liaoyang. On February 23, 5th Army, which had come up on the right of 1st Army and thus represented the extreme right of the Japanese line, led off the attack by making a thrust through the mountainous terrain to the southeast of Mukden. This was Oyama's attempt to resurrect a ghost in his opponent's mind. For Kuropatkin, the flank march against his left could mean only one thing: a replay of Liaoyang. Kawamura's army did not need to be especially powerful to achieve its mission, and it was not, con-

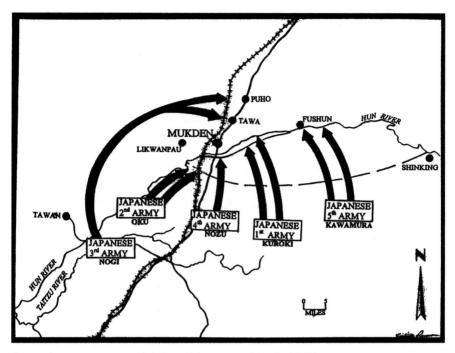

Oyama's maneuver on Mukden, February to March 1905.

sisting of one full division (the 11th, veterans of the Port Arthur fighting) and a smattering of reservists of indifferent quality. In fact, mounting losses were forcing all the Japanese armies to rely more and more on reserve *(kobi)* formations, with consequent loss of efficiency.

The ploy worked perfectly. Kuropatkin countered this thrust by shifting two-thirds of his reserve units to the east. Then, on February 25, a frontal assault began by the three armies in the center, advancing on the Russian trenches. They took terrible losses but, supported by the fire of the feared 11-inch howitzers, dealt out a great deal of punishment to the entrenched Russians, as well. One sympathizes with General Oku, whose 2nd Army had launched the assault on the Nanshan entrenchments, drove headfirst into the fortifications of Liaoyang, and was now playing the same role at Mukden.

With Kuropatkin now pinned in place, and most of his reserve committed against a secondary thrust far to the east, Oyama was ready for the main blow. The recently arrived 3rd Army under General Nogi now began a thrust from the west, aimed ultimately at the railroad, the lifeline of the Russian armies in Manchuria. Nogi began on February 27, moving up from his bivouac area north of Liaoyang and setting out on a northwesterly course to find and get around the Russian right flank. As he had demonstrated conclusively at Port Arthur, he had a tendency to move too slowly, a characteristic exacerbated by the tough Russian resistance and the truly horrible weather. His methodical pace allowed Kuropatkin to organize hasty counterattacks by small reserve detachments. At one point the Russians even had to throw their cooks and bakers into Nogi's path. Still, Nogi slowly ground his way forward, inexorably driving in the flank of the Russian line, which by now was a crescent 100 miles long in front of Mukden, drawing ever nearer to the railroad. As at Liaoyang, Kuropatkin first withdrew his armies in the center (3rd and 1st Manchurian) from their positions on the Sha River and re-formed behind the Hun, just south of Mukden. He apparently intended to use the troops saved by shortening the line for a counterstroke against the Japanese but lacked the time to carry out his plan. By March 9, his left flank had crumbled altogether. That night, with his reserves used up, Kuropatkin ordered a retreat to the north. With the withdrawal taking place through what was by now a very narrow corridor of Japanese fire, it soon became a rout, with many Russians throwing off their equipment and all discipline as they hurried to the north before the Japanese could slam the door.

And now the familiar denouement. In his new operational orders for March 7, drawn up after it was clear that the Russian armies of the center were withdrawing, Oyama wrote, "I intend to pursue in earnest."[43] It is doubtful, by this time in the war, that he believed his own words. The losses on both sides had been simply stupendous, some 75,000 Japanese to 99,000 Russians (the latter figure swelled by almost 20,000 Russian prisoners). There would be no pursuit of the defeated Russians.

It is difficult to evaluate Mukden in any final sense. On the one hand, it was an amazing achievement on the part of the Japanese army, and not for the usually specious reasons given about "Asians defeating Europeans." Instead, the Japanese had managed to concentrate a mighty army at the end of a very long supply line; they had hurled that army against a well-armed and even larger force entrenched in a position of tremendous strength and backed up with all that modern firepower that had supposedly made the defender invulnerable; their staff had devised an elegant double envelopment of the sort that was all the rage among European military men, a modern Cannae; and although it had not worked to perfection, it had worked well enough to lever the Russians out of their entrenchments and send them reeling back to the north in a full-fledged rout.

On the other hand, this was as good a chance as any army since Hannibal had had of actually achieving a Cannae. Although the Russian soldier fought tenaciously and bravely, his training was behind the times, field officers seemed to know little about the handling of their formations, and the higher staff was thoroughly unimaginative. Kuropatkin had defended in place at the Liaoyang, and he had defended in place at Mukden. The Japanese could do almost anything they wished, take as many risks as they desired, in the confidence that Kuropatkin probably would do nothing but continue to hold the positions he held. And still, the Japanese had failed.

Neither the commander, Oyama, nor the chief of staff, Kodama, had made any significant error at Mukden, with the possible exception of allowing Nogi to lead the flanking maneuver. This analysis rejects the tendentious journalistic reports that seem to reappear after every battle. "If only General X had done Y," or "If only he had not missed the opportunity that was staring him in the face," they say, breaking down the battle into a number of "magic moments" on which the fate of the armies supposedly hinged, and often falling into a loose psychoanalysis, discussing his "will" or "grit." Military professionals are often quite angered by this approach, and they, in turn, are free with comments about "armchair generals" who have a great deal of information at their fingertips that the commander did not. It is an understandable criticism, and one who has never commanded or fought in a war should consider it. Oyama's defeat (and his failure to destroy the Russian army was just that)—the failure of this gifted general in a situation that was absolutely suited to the plan he had devised—was due not to any particular failing on his part, nor to any allegedly mistaken decision in the heat of battle. Instead, it was the fault of systems of command that no longer sufficed for the immense armies they had to direct. The *Times* gave a good summary of the problem:

> Whatever the true reason of the stagnation on the Sha-ho, it will certainly afford no one any surprise if many mistakes are made in the command of great armies by generals on both sides who have no experience of the leading of such masses of men save what they are now in course of accumulating day by day. . . . Even Napoleon himself, like any common mortal, made mistakes, and allowed Mortier in 1805 and Vandamme in 1813 to be attacked and overwhelmed by the enemy's united columns. Can we expect a Kuropatkin or Oyama to fail to err where Napoleon sinned?
>
> Modern science, it is true, enables a directing staff to retain close touch with commanders, no matter how far away; but only experience can utilize these new powers to the utmost advantage, while the withdrawal of the personal influence of the commander from the critical points of contact makes it more and more indispensable that subordinate officers of all ranks should possess initiative and the resolution necessary to carry on the battle when unforeseen events occur.[44]

The problem with this analysis is that "initiative" is not enough. The double envelopment that Oyama envisioned requires control, direction, and split-second timing. The jaws must close together, or the quarry escapes. Perhaps he is mauled, even routed, but he escapes to fight another day. In this war, no one solved the problem of coordinating far-flung forces, literally hundreds of thousands of men, in any complicated operational maneuver. It would remain unsolved for several wars to come.

THE "LESSONS" OF THE RUSSO-JAPANESE WAR

Although the drama of Tsushima still remained to be played out, for all intents and purposes the great land war was over. What were its lessons? Poring over the reports of the observers, military attachés, and experts, we may distill three. First, artillery had become the dominant arm on the battlefield. It dictated where and when assaults could succeed and defenders could hold. Its ability to suppress enemy fire was just as important as the casualties it caused directly.[45] As one battle followed another, the amount of artillery in use had steadily increased. At the Yalu the Russians had 48 guns; at Mukden, 1,219; Japanese totals for those two battles were 132 and 992, respectively.[46] These guns had a voracious appetite for ammunition, with Russia's average monthly expenditure reaching 87,000 shells.[47]

The war had featured the first large-scale test of indirect fire, and most observers felt that it had passed with flying colors. Since the Franco-Prussian War, it had become plain that the increased range of both artillery and small arms meant that it was no longer possible, or even necessary, for guns to support the infantry in the traditional manner. Guns that unlimbered in small-arms range suffered tremendously. The Prussians were the first to advocate hidden positions for the guns, well out of the range of enemy rifle fire, even if it meant that the crew could not observe the target directly. Thus, field artillery was now doing what siege guns had done from time immemorial: fire at positions on a map rather than targets that it could see.[48] Indirect fire had been a matter of debate among artillerists before the war, with many traditionalists arguing that it was not "gentlemanly" to fire from protected positions, and that the task of the gunner was to go into harm's way and to do whatever was necessary to support friendly formations. The idea was not as reactionary or silly as it is usually portrayed: certainly there was nothing that improved the morale of friendly forces more than the sight of their own guns coming into the line and opening fire. But the events of this war made it hard to argue for the continuation of such methods. The battle of the Yalu River had been a contest between hidden Japanese guns and Russian guns out in the open, and the former had quite obviously been superior.

Second, cavalry had become increasingly worthless on the attack, was of little use even on the defense, and in fact was no longer even particularly effective as a flank guard or security force. Major J. M. Home, British army, was with the Russian cavalry at Telissu and described its attempt to defend the Russian right as "absolutely futile."[49] Any movement at all on its part brought down a hail of Japanese shrapnel fire. Likewise, the cavalry raids on both sides, although they formed an exciting chapter in the war, had hardly been worth the effort. Especially disappointing was cavalry's seeming inability even to carry out a decent reconnaissance. It could not get close enough to hostile infantry to say for certain whether it was facing a picket of 10 men, a skirmish line of 100, or a full division.

Third, despite all the prophecies of doom since the Boer War, infantry had proved itself capable of prosecuting a successful assault, provided that it had the support weapons it needed, especially artillery. Discussion of the machine gun, which plays such a major role in histories of the Russo-Japanese War, actually takes up a very tiny portion of reports by contemporary observers. Overall, the bloody nature of modern combat seemed to be a lesson of the war, along with this important corollary: the offensive was clearly the superior form of warfare. General Kuropatkin, of all people, identified this as one of the war's key lessons:

> The ability to assume the offensive bestows an immense superiority, for it gives the initiative to the side which undertakes it. The defender's leading troops are compelled to fall back, his less prepared troops are perhaps crushed, while his reinforcements are destroyed piecemeal. The result is that the *moral* of the attacker increases, while that of the enemy inevitably diminishes.[50]

Victory went to the side that attacked, that kept attacking, and that was sufficiently strong-willed to accept the inevitable losses caused by modern weaponry. Liaoyang and Mukden seemed to provide European armies with the cure to "acute Transvaalitis."

Chapter 4

• • • • • • • • • • • • • • •

The Balkan Wars, 1912–1913

As in the Great War that would break out just twenty months later, all the participants in the conflict that broke out in late 1912 between the Ottoman Empire and the small states of the Balkan Peninsula (Montenegro, Serbia, Greece, and Bulgaria, the so-called Balkan League) expected a short war.[1] "I would stake my head on it that we shall beat the Turkish Army in a few days," said the Bulgarian chief of staff and warlord, General Mikhail Savov.[2] Feti Pasha, the former Turkish ambassador to Serbia, countered with, "We shall soon invite our friends to dinner in Belgrade."[3] Unlike in 1914, predictions of a short war came true, although Feti Pasha never did get a chance to send out those invitations. How the allies of the Balkan League managed to inflict a decisive defeat on the immense Turkish force facing them is an instructive and worthwhile lesson in twentieth-century warfare. This largely ignored or forgotten war deserves greater study.

The First Balkan War was a highly mobile, swirling affair, in which the forces of the four small Balkan allies swept the Balkan Peninsula clean of Turkish forces that had been in occupation of the region for almost 400 years. It featured a Bulgarian siege of the immense fortress of Adrianople (Edirne), three great set-piece battles (the Serbs at Kumanovo, the Bulgarians at Kirk Kilisse and Lule Burgas), a pounding Serbian march down the valley of the Vardar River, and a well-conceived and almost perfectly executed *manoeuvre sur les derrières* against the Turkish forces in Thrace by the Bulgarians. It ended, fittingly, in a failed Bulgarian attempt to storm the Turkish trenches of the Chatalja position, the last defensive line before Constantinople. Within two years, the rest of Europe would have a good understanding of why Chatalja had stopped the Bulgarians.

Despite its short duration, it was a huge war. Estimates of manpower vary, but the Balkan allies mobilized well over 700,000 men, while Turkish forces numbered at least 500,000.[4] Bulgaria alone put over 490,000 men in the field, an amazing proportion out of a population of 4,430,000.[5] Both sides used a large number of second-line troops alongside their regular forces, as well. The Serbs differentiated their troops as belonging to the first or second "call-up" *(ban);* Turkish forces were *nizam* (active) or *redif* (territorial militia), not to mention a considerable number of irregulars in the mountains of Albania and Macedonia.

SERBIAN OPERATIONS IN MACEDONIA

It is difficult to summarize this war briefly, involving as it did the operations of four separate armies attacking Ottoman holdings in Europe from every direction. In the north, the Serbs mobilized three field armies, concentrated along the Turkish border at Vranje (the 1st, under Crown Prince Alexander); the Bulgarian town of Kustendil (the 2nd Army, under General Stepa Stepanovich, consisting of a mixed Serbian-Bulgarian force); and Kursumlie, southwest of Nis (the 3rd Army, under General Bozidar Jankovich). A small force, called the "Army of the Ibar" but really only a reinforced division, deployed at Kraljevo on the Ibar River, under General Mihailo Zivkovich.[6] The crown prince's 1st Army was the largest, with 131,000 men. It contained three of the Serbian army's six first-class infantry divisions, its only cavalry division, plus most of the guns—one battery of mountain artillery, three batteries of howitzers, and three batteries of siege guns, 154 guns in all. Both 2nd and 3rd Armies had roughly 75,000 men apiece; the Ibar Army, 37,000. Altogether, tiny Serbia managed to put over 300,000 men into the field.[7]

The Serbian operational plan, the work of chief of staff General Radomir Putnik, offers an interesting mix of the military and the political. Its heart was a Moltkean maneuver, a concentric advance by all three armies on Skoplje. The strong 1st Army would attack frontally in the center, while 2nd and 3rd Armies would encircle both enemy flanks. It was an elegant plan, drawn up by a gifted general and a very solid staff. In a liberation war of this sort, however, politics will always play a strong role in shaping operations. Thus, the

Army of the Ibar, along with the independent Javor Brigade, had orders to move into the Sanjak of Novi Pazar, the narrow forested strip that separated Serbia from Montenegro. Likewise, 3rd Army's mission was not only to function as the right wing of the Serbian field army but also to overrun the province of Kosovo, long claimed by Serbia for a host of historical and cultural reasons, even though most of the population were not ethnic Serbs.

The drives into the Sanjak and Kosovo, peripheral to the task of defeating the Turkish main force but central to the political character of the war, determined the course of the first encounters. Zivkovich's Army of the Ibar crossed into the Sanjak and, in cooperation with a Montenegrin force under General Janko Vukotich, secured it after minimal fighting, mostly with Turkish irregulars. Likewise, 3rd Army began the war with a drive into Kosovo. Jankovich had to move over some of Europe's most forbidding terrain, mountainous and poorly served by roads. He also had to throw out patrols to make sure that mountains on either side of the road were clear of Turks. As he crossed the border early in the morning of October 19, with thick fog hampering his reconnaissance, he crashed almost immediately into a Turkish force of six battalions of infantry, deployed well forward, practically on the border in fact, at Podujevo. Turkish rifle fire forced the 3rd Army's lead elements to deploy, and soon the Turkish guns joined in. It was ragged fire and did little damage to the Serbs. It did, however, betray the Turkish artillery positions. The ninety-six guns of the 3rd Army now joined the battle, and for the next several hours, the Serbian infantry sat and watched an artillery duel unfold. Turkish fire soon slackened, and the Serbian infantry prepared to launch its assault. As the assault columns moved forward, however, they found Podujevo deserted. Within hours, 3rd Army had regrouped and was back on the road. On October 21, 3rd Army entered Pristina, the district capital of Kosovo, similarly evacuated by the Turks.[8]

Podujevo was a small action and is hardly remembered today. However, it is the First Balkan War in microcosm. The Turkish forces were deployed well forward along the border rather than in the relative safety of the Macedonian interior. Since Turkey faced a large number of enemies, with a huge and convoluted border, prudence would have dictated a concentration of maximum possible force at some central point, perhaps Skoplje in Macedonia. There the Turks could have waited for the first enemy column to come within reach and hit it hard. Altogether, the Turks faced no less than *ten* separate advancing columns (one Montenegrin, four Serb forces, two Greek, and three Bulgarian), which, although posing a number of simultaneous threats to Turkish possessions, were also too numerous and widely separated to be coordinated to any significant extent.

There are two ways of looking at this situation, depending on which "military textbook" one uses. According to Jomini, who based his analysis on Napoleonic conditions, the Turks enjoyed the immense advantage of interior lines, sitting at the center of a circle while their opponents had the much more difficult task of coordinating their widely separated thrusts along the outside of the arc. Most observers took this analytical line and predicted disaster for the allies, who, after all,

> were advancing from five different points separated by hundreds of miles, against a formidable enemy possessing a large army organized by competent instructors along modern lines, fully equipped with modern armament, established in strongly fortified positions within easy supporting distances, and able, by moving along interior lines, to throw a preponderating force against an isolated detachment of any strength and in any direction.[9]

Adding to the Turks' advantage was the fact that the Balkan League was trying to coordinate the advance of four national armies using three different languages of command (both the Serbs and Montenegrins spoke Serbo-Croatian) over some of the worst terrain in Europe.

However, if the "textbook" is Moltke's, then the analysis is different. Now it is the Balkan League that is enjoying the advantages of "exterior lines," that is, launching converging thrusts by widely separated armies that will come together at a predetermined point for a climactic battle on advantageous terms.[10] After the fact, seeking to explain the rapid and totally unexpected victory by the forces of the Balkan League, many contemporary commentators, both military men and journalists, took this line and used exactly these terms. Such a description, however, is true only in a partial sense. The various national contingents of the Balkan League, taken as a whole, were not "converging" on anything. Each had its own territorial claims against the Turks, and each sought to march on those objectives as rapidly as possible. Of the four Serbian columns, one marched into the Sanjak and one into Kosovo. Likewise, the Montenegrin army marched directly on the fortress of Scutari and spent the rest of the war trying to reduce it. For the Greeks it was the fortress of Janina and the great port of Salonika. Only five of the invading columns (two Serbian and three Bulgarian) can be described as carrying out operations in the modern, Moltkean sense. That, however, proved to be more than enough.

The Turks chose an operational posture that appears in neither textbook, although it captures the spirit of the age in military affairs: attack everywhere. Disregarding their German advisers, who recommended a careful mobilization and then a strategic defensive, they threw individual units into the attack as they mobilized, marching them toward the border and ordering them to hit the first Balkan army they could find. From the start it was clear to Turkish field commanders that their mobilization was going very poorly. Supplies, ammunition, and even men failed to show up where they were assigned. Rather than wait to sort things out, the War Ministry in Constantinople gave orders to launch these incomplete forces toward the front. If the aim was political, that is, if it was intended to cow the Balkan allies into submission, then it failed. Even worse, it took an army that had still not digested the reforms begun by the Young Turk revolution in 1908 and shattered its morale in the first two days of the war. The Turkish forces that performed so poorly in these battles were badly trained and equipped, undersupplied (especially with artillery ammunition, as was clear at Podujevo), and lacking in cohesion. The decision by the Young Turks to end the draft exemption for Balkan Christians and to enroll them into the forces, while understandable from the standpoint of the empire's manpower requirements, was particularly disastrous, filling the ranks with malcontents even before a shot had been fired or a reverse suffered.[11]

With Turkish forces deployed so far forward, however, Putnik's plan for all three armies to unite was a dead letter almost as soon as the fighting began. We have already seen that the 3rd Army had to stop and fight at Podujevo. The same thing happened in the center. After a short, sharp fight in the Rujan Mountains with the Turkish covering force on the border, 1st Army marched on the small town of Kumanovo, about halfway to Skoplje.[12] It was the evening of October 22, and the neighboring armies were still quite a distance away: 2nd Army was coming up on its left but was only at Kratevo, forty-five kilometers from Kumanovo, that is, two days' march away; 3rd Army, on its right, was at Pristina, two or three days away by forced march. The Serbs believed that the Turks were still far off. Patrols had detected Turkish activity near Kumanovo, but no one could imagine that the Turks were there in enough strength to attack. Still, the Serbs were in the presence of the enemy, and they began building redoubts and digging entrenchments. It was not until 3:00 A.M. that the Serbian Danube Division of the first *ban*, or Danube (1), determined that there was a Turkish main force in front of it. In fact, the Serbs were facing a Turkish army of three corps under Zekki Pasha, carrying out an offensive of its own to the north.

Zekki Pasha's decision had been a bold one, a typical example of Turkish strategy in this war. Deciding not to wait until his mobilization was complete, he left behind a perfect defensive position right next to his concentration area in Skoplje, the plateau known as Ovce Polje, and brought his units fifty kilometers to the north by forced march. But as admirable as his fire for battle might have been, his decision was ill-advised. As one German observer argued, even if the Turks beat the 1st Army in front of them, they would subsequently have been hit by 2nd Army coming up on their right and 3rd Army from their left, and would probably have been destroyed. The following analysis from the same source illustrates the hold that Moltke and the campaign of 1866 still had on the European imagination:

> Zekki Pasha's operation is highly reminiscent of Benedek's war plan, which also aimed at the destruction of one of the Prussian armies invading Bohemia before they could unite. . . . The Serbian war plan, too, was reminiscent of Moltke strategy in 1866. Just as the armies of Crown Prince Friedrich Wilhelm and Prince Friedrich Karl, coming from the east and north, respectively, united during the battle of Königgrätz and inflicted a decisive defeat on the Austrians, so now the 2nd Serbian Army (from the northeast) and the 1st Army (from the north) were to unite and, with possible support from 3rd Army in the west, face the enemy with their combined strength.[13]

Despite that gloomy prospect, the Turks held some fairly good cards at Kumanovo. Zekki Pasha commanded 90,000 men and 200 cannon, he had his units concentrated for battle, and his force was ensconced in the mountainous terrain northeast of the town. Here they had erected field fortifications and entrenchments that commanded the roads into Kumanovo. All in all, it was a suitable spot for a tenacious, successful defense.

That is not why Zekki Pasha was at Kumanovo, however. He opened the action by launching an attack. At 9:30 A.M., his right ring (VII Corps, under Kara Said Pasha) began a vigorous and sustained attack on the left flank of the Serbian position, the Danube (1) Division, whose trenches lay forward of the rest of the Serbian line. The Turks attacked frontally, then began to work their way around the division's flank. The fight went on all morning. The Danube (1) Division held out and even managed to launch several local counterattacks in the course of the morning, foiling the Turkish attempt at envelopment. While this was taking place, Turkish VI Corps (under Feti Pasha) opened an attack of its own on the opposite wing, against the Serbian Morava (1) Division. This was a demonstration only, but it did have the effect of hindering the Serbs from sending help to the beleaguered Danube (1) Division. In the center, the Serbian Drina (1) Division had lagged a bit behind its fellows in the approach march. Due to the difficult terrain and barely passable roads, it was not able to send Danube (1) any help either, and in fact was barely in the fight all day. The roads also prevented Danube (1) from getting its artillery forward. Only through an immense amount of human and animal muscle power was it possible to bring several batteries into position by noon. Still, an entire artillery battalion did not see action at all.

The Danube (1) Division's situation became increasingly critical as the main Turkish body bore down on it through the course of the day. Several units of its 7th and 18th Regiments, exposed to Turkish artillery fire without any fire support of their own, were literally ground up, and survivors fled from the battlefield. Two factors worked to restore the situation. First, the Serbian Cavalry Division performed gallantly. Brought up alongside and to the left of the Danube (1) Division, it dismounted and fought on the extreme left wing of the Serbian line. With its machine guns and artillery established to the rear, on the Orlovatz hill, it helped repulse repeated Turkish flanking attempts and even hit several attacking enemy columns with flanking fire. Second, the Serb artillery, brought forward with such effort, finally began to tip the balance in the Serbs' favor. Its fire was very effective, and by 3:00 P.M. the Turkish attacks began to fade in intensity. Kara Said Pasha's men drew back to their entrenchments. The Serbs breathed a sigh of relief. The Turks had thus far fought well in the attack, with "great vigor and admirable bravery," and they had kept coming back, all day long, even after heavy losses.

Unfortunately for the Serbs, the Turks were simply regrouping. Taking a page from the Japanese army in Manchuria, Zekki Pasha renewed the assault on the Serbian left with a night attack at 7:00. The battle raged on a pitch-black battlefield until 11:30 P.M., with Turkish attacks on Danube (1) thrown back "by fire and cold steel."[14] Once again, Serbian artillery had played a crucial role in defeating this night attack. Even though darkness hindered target registration, the Serbian guns kept up an uninterrupted fire, which had a positive effect on Serbian morale and a correspondingly negative one on the Turks. The next day, Serbian infantry were to be seen hugging and kissing the barrels of their artillery pieces, calling them their saviors.

On the evening of October 23, with the Turkish attack finally contained, Crown Prince Alexander gave orders for a concerted attack by all his divisions for dawn the next day. In the early morning hours, the Drina (1) Division came up into the line after a short march in the darkness. The Timok (2) and Danube (2) Divisions, likewise, came up to lend support, with Timok (2) behind the center and Danube (2) behind the left, site of the day's crisis. Five Serbian divisions now faced the enemy, with the army's heavy artillery located behind the center.

October 24 dawned in a thick, nearly impenetrable fog. The crown prince opened the action by launching a heavy blow by his center and his right. The assault met stiff Turkish resistance and made only small gains. The fog meant that the Serbian guns, which had established their superiority during the previous day's action, could not really come into play. Around 11:00 A.M., however, the fog burned off, and the Serbs opened up a devastating fire on the Turkish guns in order to silence them. Several Turkish batteries had taken advantage of the fog and, in eagerness to get at the attacking Serbs, had established themselves well forward without any real cover. They were now caught out in the open and pulverized. With the enemy guns silenced, the Serbs switched their targets to the Turkish infantry, inflicting heavy losses. The Turks began to waver.

Now came the battle's decisive moment. The Morava (1) Division, the Serbian right wing, began to work its way around the Turkish left, moving up the railroad. It was a mirror image of the Turkish attempt the previous day. Three Turkish batteries were brought over to hinder the movement. Two were unlimbered to the east of the rail line out in the open. They attracted the fire of every available Serbian gun, and the crews of both were soon killed. A third battery, however, found shelter to the west of the rail line, where a copse of four trees hid its telltale muzzle flashes from Serbian observers. Its fire caused heavy losses to the Serbian attackers, until observers called in indirect fire by both field and heavy artillery to destroy it. Assault columns from the Morava (1) Division continued their advance, and by noon the Turkish left flank had crumbled.

That was the signal for the disintegration of the entire Turkish force at Kumanovo. First their fire began to slacken, and then small groups began to flee their trenches in haste and increasing disorder. Under constant Serbian shellfire, and without any fire support of their own, the disorder became outright panic, and the retreat turned into a rout. They fled in all directions, and only about 5,000 men made it to Skoplje under the command of Zekki Pasha. They did not pause there, however, boarding troops trains almost immediately for Koprulu to the south, where he hoped to re-form some semblance of a cohesive force.

The Serbs were too exhausted to pursue. They had made a hard approach march to get to Kumanovo in the first place, and the battle had gone on, nearly uninterrupted, for a day and a half. Turkish losses had been some 12,000 casualties and 327 prisoners, plus an enormous amount of equipment. The Serbs had suffered 1,126 killed and 3,468 wounded. It was two full days before the Serbs continued their march, entering Skoplje on October 26 and capturing another mountain of supplies, weapons, and ammunition.

Kumanovo had been a well-planned battle on both sides, and bravely fought, showing that the Great Powers did not have a monopoly on the military virtues or the ability to carry out maneuver under fire. Major Otto Gelinek, the Habsburg military attaché, described the Serbian infantry as "calm and cool-headed" in battle. Likewise, the British military attaché was filled with admiration as he watched the deployment of two Serbian battalions under heavy artillery fire: "They did the maneuver according to all the rules, as if it happened on a military exercise. Regiment and battalion commanders, young lieutenant colonels and majors between 32 and 40 years of age headed the assaults of their troops. Many higher ranking officers were killed or wounded. The lower ranking officers deserve the same praise."[15]

Despite the victory, Putnik's leadership has had its share of critics. He had expected to find the Turks at Ovce Polje, and the Turkish attack had clearly taken him by surprise. His two flanking armies were far too heavy for the rapid marches they needed to make on the primitive road network of the area, and that was one reason they were not able to be present on the field at Kumanovo. Some have criticized his decision to hand the Cavalry Division over to 1st Army rather than keeping it in his own hands for reconnaissance and pursuit duties. In fairness to him, however, the question arises: How could he have predicted the nearly suicidal Turkish decision to concentrate forward and then attack a numerically superior army? Since the neighboring 2nd and 3rd Armies did not arrive in the course of the battle, it is difficult to say whether General Putnik deserves to be ranked alongside Moltke. Nevertheless, the ability of the Serbs to scuttle their operational plan and to win with only one of their armies is impressive. So, frankly, was the Turkish attack, carried out by a force whose mobilization was incomplete and whose unit cohesion was tenuous at best.

As in all the battles of this era, there was no pursuit, nor could there be— Serbian disorganization and casualties prevented it. In addition, neither Putnik nor the men could believe that they had just encountered and thrashed the main Turkish force in Macedonia. Based on all prewar intelligence, Putnik still believed that the Turks would make a stand somewhere, most likely at Ovce Polje. This was another reason for the cautious nature of the Serbian follow-up to their victory. Looking back in 1928, Stanoje Stanojevic wrote: "The Serbian soldiers were relaxing in the calm and clear night. No one on the entire front thought that he had participated in an event of historical significance; no one was aware that on this day the centuries-old struggle of the Serbian people with the Turks came to an end, and that the Turkish Empire was defeated."[16] In this case, the lack of pursuit was a moot point. The Turkish army had disintegrated.

The campaign was not yet over. For the next three weeks, the Serbian army continued its drive to the south, down the Vardar valley. It was fighting the terrain and weather more than the Turks, but the achievement is no less impressive for that. By now, the crown prince's 1st Army included most of the main-force Serbian units. He split them up into two columns on the available roads to the south, his right through Tetovo and Kirtchevo, his left marching down the Vardar River and the railroad to Veles, and from there to Prilep. He met the Turks at Prilep, beat them there on November 3–5, then reunited his columns in front of Monastir. Worthy of mention is that fact that the Serbs also sent a column into Albania that reached the Adriatic Sea at Alessio, and two complete divisions to assist the Bulgarians at the siege of Adrianople. The scope of the Serbian war effort was impressive.

At Monastir, the Serbs met and, from November 14 to 19, destroyed a hastily reformed Turkish force in a six-day battle.[17] With much of the battlefield flooded by recent rains, and with large stretches of the front covered by an unfordable river (the Crna), much of the fighting took the form of an artillery duel. With the Serbs quickly establishing their superiority in guns, their infantry took position after position away from the demoralized Turks, an army fighting without supply, poorly commanded, and, above all, without hope of reinforcement. The fighting in Macedonia was over.

BULGARIAN OPERATIONS IN THRACE

While Kumanovo was a disaster, the Turks suffered an even more decisive defeat in Thrace, a debacle that brought the forces of tiny Bulgaria to the very gates of the Ottoman capital. The Bulgarians mobilized three armies under the overall direction of the military adviser to King Ferdinand, General Mikhail Savov. His plan was the most "Napoleonic" that European warfare had seen for some time. The problem facing him was that the direct route into Ottoman territory, and the road and rail network besides, passed through one of Europe's greatest fortresses, Adrianople. The Bulgarians might march on Adrianople, and with their complement of heavy artillery (eighteen batteries of field howitzers, pieces of 120-mm and 150-mm caliber) might even take it.[18] Unfortunately for Bulgaria, that would require a long campaign. With virtually every able-bodied Bulgarian male at the front (estimates run to 80 percent of the males of military age) and the budget strained to the utmost, a long war was not possible. A lengthy conflict would also allow the Ottomans to call up forces from the Asian heartland of the empire, and that would certainly spell defeat for Bulgaria.

Savov's solution was a *manoeuvre sur les derrières*. One army, the 2nd (under General Nikola Ivanov), would march from the west directly on Adrianople, via the important rail station of Mustapha Pasha. Two others—the 1st, under General Vassil Kutinchev, and the 3rd, under General Radko Dimitriev, considered by many to be the most gifted military mind in Bulgaria—would bypass the fortress to the east, crush the Turkish field army near the fortified town of Kirk Kilisse (Bulgarian Lozengrad), and from there drive deep into the Ottoman flank and rear, cutting off the retreat of the Turkish forces from Adrianople and perhaps even taking an undefended Constantinople. If successful in breaking through at Kirk Kilisse, the Bulgarian army could

General Mikhail Savov proved himself to be a master of the operational art during the campaign in Thrace versus the Turks, October to November 1912. Author's collection.

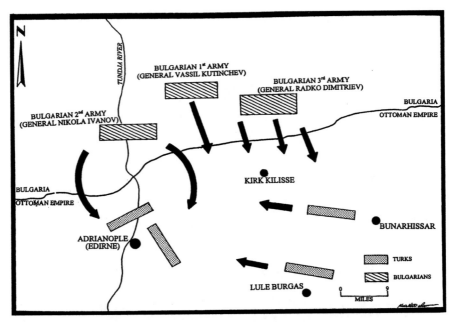

Savov's art of war: The Bulgarian maneuver in Thrace, October 1912.

present a simultaneous threat to two strategic targets at once and force the Turks into a no-win decision as to which one to defend: their fortress or their capital. The Bulgarian army was not capable of any long-distance advance, relying as it did on the bullock cart as its primary means of hauling supplies.[19] The beauty of Savov's plan was that it required a short, energetic advance—perfectly suited to the temperament of his soldiers, the limitations of his supply lines, and the geography of the relatively small Thracian theater. Adrianople and Kirk Kilisse alike were but two days' march from the Bulgarian border, and it was only eight to ten marches to the last defensible Turkish position before Constantinople, the Chatalja bottleneck.

It was an elegant plan, drawing deeply from the Napoleonic sources and yet as modern as anything the Great Powers would concoct in 1914. It calls into question the alleged "primitivism" of the Balkan nations and the condescending way that most Western observers tend to treat their conflicts. Consider the 1912 training program of the Bulgarian officer corps:

1. The solution of tactical problems on a map, done weekly in groups.
2. Map maneuvers and war games led by the division and brigade commanders and their staffs.
3. Weekly technical assignments for the specialized branches.

4. Practical field exercises without troops, carried out under the direction of the respective commanders from company to division in June and December.

5. Field exercises with officers of the general staff, carried out each summer.

6. Lectures. After 1905, about a third of the officers were working on topics in military history by critique and analysis of operations in a particular war.

7. Summer training in camp with the troops.

8. Grand royal maneuvers every September, involving several divisions supplemented by reserves. Such maneuvers took place in 1888, 1896, 1902, 1904, 1905, 1906, 1910, and 1912.[20]

The Bulgarian officer corps was as talented and as well trained as any in Europe in 1912 and was particularly well schooled in warfare on the operational level. If Mikhail Savov or Radko Dimitriev had been German, one suspects that today there would be a half dozen biographies of them in English.[21]

The Turks were defending Thrace with 1st Army, consisting of four army corps, the I (Constantinople), II (Rodosto), III (Kirk Kilisse), and IV

Mobile war in the Balkans. A Bulgarian supply column, consisting almost exclusively of ox-drawn wagons, prepares to advance through Thrace on the road to Chatalja. Author's collection.

General Radko Dimitriev, commander of the Bulgarian 3rd Army in 1912
and one of the most gifted operational commanders anywhere in the early
twentieth century. Author's collection.

(Adrianople), containing altogether twelve regular *(nizam)* and six reserve *(redif)* divisions. About 220,000 men in all, it was suffering from the same sort of mobilization, supply, and personnel problems already cited in Macedonia: general officers with little experience in the handling of large masses of men; a serious shortage of regimental officers; an untrained reserve; and the same problem of newly enlisted Christians in the ranks. Finally, much of the army had just returned from Tripoli, where it had been fighting the Italians in the war of 1911–12, a factor that played no small role in encouraging the Balkan States to launch their attack. Of equal importance, the fortifications of Adrianople had been neglected in recent years, as had the fieldworks around the Kirk Kilisse position, which was recognized by Bulgarian and Turk alike as the eastern key to Adrianople. Still, this was territory much closer to the Turkish heartland than was Macedonia, and 1st Army seemed, on paper, to be quite capable of defending it.

What it was not capable of doing, as events proved, was launching an early offensive of its own. When Bulgarian forces crossed the border on the night of October 17–18, they were as surprised as the Serbs had been. Far from digging into tough defensive positions, the Turks—three full corps, the I, III, and XVI—were advancing on a front of about twenty-five miles between Adrianople and Kirk Kilisse. They therefore ran head-on into the junction of two advancing Bulgarian armies, the 1st and the 3rd. After sharp scraps at Eski Polos, Erikler, and Petra, in which heavy Bulgarian artillery fire put the Turks to rout, the main bodies collided at Kirk Kilisse (October 23).[22] The Turkish III Corps under Mahmud Mukhtar fought the right and center of Bulgarian 3rd Army. In a day of tough fighting, vigorous frontal attacks by the Bulgarian infantry drove the Turks from their advanced positions back into the town. The Bulgarians kept up the pressure at night, working their way around the Turkish right flank and capturing the important heights of Demirkapu and Demirdza. As their guns came up, the Bulgarians emplaced them on this high ground. When morning came, they began systematically to bombard Kirk Kilisse, quickly setting it on fire. The Turks, who had outrun most of their artillery during their advance, now began to waver. The Bulgarian infantry, which by this time practically had the town surrounded, began a general assault with the bayonet at 10:00 A.M. Making a breach in the Turkish positions in the vineyards to the northwest of the town, it soon pushed into the streets of Kirk Kilisse itself. By this time, the same sort of panic that had gripped the Turkish force at Kumanovo had begun, and Mahmud Mukhtar's command was soon streaming away in a rout, southeast toward Bunarhissar. A Bulgarian column thrown out to the southeast rounded up some 1,500 prisoners, although a tough rearguard action by a small Turkish force kept the gate open for most of the Turkish force to escape. Once again, the booty taken by the Bulgarians was prodigious: seven batteries of modern artillery that had just arrived, a mountain of ammunition, stores, tents, even two airplanes, not to mention Mahmud Mukhtar's personal baggage.

The Turkish commander has left his memoirs, and they paint a highly unflattering portrait of Turkish war preparations. Although they are generally silent, as such memoirs are, on the author's own failings, it is possible that Napoleon himself could not have triumphed commanding the Turks at Kirk Kilisse. At the outbreak of the war, Mahmud Mukhtar's III Corps was concentrating at Kirk Kilisse. Its original mission, to serve as a covering force for the army's general mobilization to the rear near Lule Burgas and Viza, soon gave way to attack orders. The supreme army commander in Constantinople, Nazim Pasha, sent orders that as soon as 150,000 men had been gathered, the "Army of the East" in Thrace would launch a general offensive. Mahmud Mukhtar observed, rightly, that "it was not from the standpoint of a completed mobilization or whether the troops were capable of carrying out such orders, but in the end only the number of men." When the offensive movement began, III Corps had just 23,000 men with the colors, out of an authorized strength of over 30,000. A cavalry division that was crucial to flank security contained only 200 men. Here is Mahmud Mukhtar's description of his corps on the eve of action:

> The III Corps had still not completed its mobilization; several Nizam battalions had at most two hundred men. The process was slow. Equipment was lacking. Fitting out the personnel was very difficult. Many of the necessary supplies had to come from Constantinople. While the corps's head count grew, full magazines were lacking, and there were difficulties in procuring provisions. When I arrived the corps had one to two days of supplies of food and grain, and we had to requisition daily needs from the surrounding area. The situation in I Corps was no better. Instead of an interrupted stream of soldiers arriving by rail, it would have been better to receive the necessary provisions for the men. In fact I had to send the War Department an urgent request for provisions and biscuits, instead of men.[23]

By October 23, the 8th Division had mustered exactly four battalions (out of its authorized strength of nine) and two batteries. The munitions columns were only slowly approaching III Corps. The same could be said for the entire complex apparatus of the modern army corps: the field hospitals, sanitation troops, field bakeries. And Mahmud Mukhtar claimed, rightly from the evidence, that his corps mobilized faster than any other in Thrace. Intelligence also lagged far behind that of their Bulgarian adversary. "We knew nothing exact about the enemy," Mahmud Mukhtar wrote. "We were in complete ignorance about the concentration areas of the Bulgarians, as well as their army organization and unit strength." Although prewar staff studies had warned of the possibility of a Bulgarian thrust against Kirk Kilisse, the fortifications of the town had fallen into disrepair. Finally, in the opening actions at Erikler and Petra, lower unit commanders required detailed instructions in the most elementary evolutions of their troops, such as forming the men into a firing line. "The inability of the men, the officers, and the regimental and battalion commanders was obvious," he wrote, although the artillery performed well. The Turks were unprepared in every way.

And then there was the problem of morale. He had just, on the morning of October 22, ordered an attack for 6:00 A.M. At 6:15, he went out to the front to watch it unfold and found most of his left wing in a panicky flight out of its positions, apparently spooked by the approach of a small Bulgarian column. He managed to halt the flight by ordering his entire complement of artillery to open fire in the general direction of the Bulgarians. The effect on infantry morale of friendly guns opening up was "remarkable."

Mahmud Mukhtar's memories of Kirk Kilisse do give a vivid portrait of the problems of command in a disintegrating army. As he rode in the midst of the retreat from Petra on the night of October 22, his command consisted of a handful of troops in good order and a horde of refugees. His steadiest unit, 7th Division under Hilmi Bey, consisted of three or four *nizam* battalions in relatively good order, one or two machine gun companies, and a field artillery battalion already in Kirk Kilisse. Officers were desperately trying to round up as many of the stragglers as possible and sort them out into their units. After ordering these officers to perform their task to the rear, he came across a column of the Officers' Training Battalion, marching to Kirk Kilisse in good order. A wonderful sight it must have been, and he now ordered its commander to occupy and defend the trenches in Kirk Kilisse against an attack from the northwest. When the commander showed little enthusiasm for the task, Mahmud Mukhtar sent a staff officer along with him, "partly in order to show him the way, partly in order to make sure that my orders were followed."[24]

Ten minutes later, riding through the dark, he arrived at Kirk Kilisse, which had been abandoned by much of its civilian population. As he entered the town, he received an urgent message to report to the telegraph office and inform the war ministry of the day's events. In the midst of the report, the artillery commander of 7th Division burst in: the guns were poorly emplaced in swampy terrain, and he feared they might be lost; his ammunition was gone; the batteries lacked infantry support. Mahmud Mukhtar ordered ammunition brought up and, perhaps suspecting the artillery commander's intentions, ordered the guns to stay where they were. Then the staff of 7th Division arrived. Good men, even they were in a state of great agitation: many of the trenches in front of Kirk Kilisse were undefended; the local Greek and Bulgarian population was probably reporting every Turkish move to the enemy; the Bulgarians were nearby, and would surely be there shortly. At their urging, Mahmud Mukhtar, who had after all just arrived, moved his headquarters to a hospital outside of town. When orders arrived from army command that all corps should retreat to Lule Burgas and Bunarhissar, his corps now literally came apart. The 9th Division was already far gone in a process of disintegration since the retreat from Petra. By the time it arrived at the designated position, its commander, Hassan Izzet Pasha, was alone.

The experience of the 7th Division sheds a different light on the corps' performance. Its commander, Hilmi Bey, decided on his own to launch the division in a counterattack against the approaching Bulgarians, whose presence had been reported by cavalry. Unfortunately, the cavalry had been patrolling so short a distance before the infantry that the report and the Bulgarians showed up simultaneously. Still, 7th Division fought well in the defense, and for one of the few times so far was well supported by artillery. With field and howitzer batteries opening fire on the thick Bulgarian columns about five kilometers away, Hilmi Bey said that the effect was visible: "Columns fell into complete disorder and appeared much smaller when re-formed."[25] The fire of the howitzers was especially effective, he noted. He was just about to launch a flanking attempt against a Bulgarian force that was trying to get around his right when the order for retreat arrived. His right, well handled and with reserves in echelon, managed to get away in good order. His left, however, encountered much more difficulty. Troops were in closer contact with the enemy here, in the vineyards to the northwest of Kirk Kilisse. Their regimental commander, without orders, had brought companies given to him as a reserve into the firing line itself. There was, therefore, no reserve, and thus no force to act as a rear guard. He even had a reserve machine gun company in the line, a place it had no business being, according to Hilmi Bey. The commander of the machine gun company had argued with him about this, but to no avail. Finally, he had refused permission to open fire on a Bulgarian column coming up on his left, from the direction of Eski Polos, insisting that it was Turkish. As the Bulgarian column struck his left, the regiment was thrown into the greatest confusion, at which point the regimental commander ran to division headquarters for further orders.

The Bulgarian victory at Kirk Kilisse, over a single shaky division of a half-mobilized corps, had essentially decided the Thracian campaign. The Turks were now in deep trouble. Forces of the Bulgarian 2nd Army had surrounded Adrianople and its garrison of 60,000 men. It was a well-run operation, the fruit of a great deal of theoretical preparation in the prewar period by army commander Ivanov. In addition, two Bulgarian armies were pouring into the gap east of Adrianople, driving a demoralized army before them. The issue was no longer merely Thrace; it was Turkey's entire position, its very presence in Europe.

Following Kirk Kilisse, Bulgarian 3rd Army pursued its course to the southeast, with 1st Army to the right of and behind it, moving due south. It was not so much a pursuit as an uncontested advance: the Bulgarians were not in contact with the Turks, and in fact a panicked man will always move faster than one under orders. With the situation verging on disaster, the Turks remained true to the operational principles that had brought them to this pass: they attacked. As the Bulgarians continued their advance, they suddenly encountered large Turkish forces drawn up in a position from Lule Burgas in the southwest to Bunarhissar to the northeast, a line of approximately thirty-five miles. The ground here is extremely unusual, consisting of sharp, rolling undulations that reminded many observers of waves on the sea, as well as numerous water courses flowing north to south into the Ergene River.

Once again, Mahmud Mukhtar and Turkish III Corps stood at the center of attention. His command had essentially melted away twice, after Petra and after Kirk Kilisse. And both times he had managed to re-form it. Commanding a force of his III Corps reinforced by two reserve corps, XVII and XVIII, he now formed the right wing of the Turkish position, that is, behind Bunarhissar, with II, I, and IV corps laid out, in that order, to his left.[26] On October 29, on orders from the supreme commander Nazim Pasha, he launched an attack on the left wing of the Bulgarian 3rd Army. Although the 3rd had been the Bulgarian spearhead in the opening battles, its task here was to stay in place and act as the pivot so that 1st Army, currently behind and to the right, could come up alongside it. In the course of the maneuver, 1st Army would shift its own axis from south to southeast. The Bulgarian 5th Division was the first enemy unit to reach Bunarhissar, and it bore the brunt of Mahmud Mukhtar's attack for an entire day. Fighting alongside it was the Bulgarian Cavalry Division, whose mission was to make sure the Turks undertook no forward maneuver to the right of 3rd Army, preparing the position that 1st Army would assume upon its arrival. During the course of the day, the rest of 3rd Army arrived, with 4th and 6th Division entering the line, in that order, to the right of 3rd Division. Still, the Bulgarian left flank was essentially the 5th Division against Turkish III Corps for the better part of the day.

But what of that corps? On closer inspection, Mahmud Mukhtar's command appears to be less than meets the eye. Since the debacle at Kirk Kilisse,

Mukhtar Pasha was the most gifted Turkish commander in the First Balkan War. He managed to rebuild his corps on three separate occasions in the course of this rapid campaign, and he successfully defended the Chatalja bottleneck against the Bulgarians. Author's collection.

he had managed to scrape together three "combined divisions," hardly more than detachments, under commanders whose original commands had disappeared.[27] Two of them would spearhead the attack. His "1st Division," under Colonel Djemal Bey, consisted of the 20th, 21st, and 27th Regiments, two machine gun companies, and six field batteries. His "3rd Division," under Fuad Bey, was an incredible collection of units: the 8th Jäger Battalion, two battalions of the 23rd Regiment, one of the 25th, and three of the 26th, plus a motley collection of militia troops. These were units that did not know their officers, officers who did not know their units, batteries that had no idea of how to cooperate with the infantry, and infantry that had no liaison to its batteries. His total strength consisted of twenty-one *nizam* battalions, and most of his battalions were at less than half strength.[28]

But one factor compensated for Turkish organizational weakness: the rapidity of the Bulgarian advance meant that the infantry had temporarily outrun its artillery. As the action began, most of the Bulgarian guns were still strung out on the route of advance, making their way slowly on the muddy roads far behind the line of battle. For the first time in the war, then, the Turks managed to achieve local artillery superiority. For several hours in the morning, Turkish guns were able to concentrate on the enemy infantry formations without having to worry about counterbattery fire.

The attack on Bunarhissar opened early on the morning of October 29, and at first it went quite well. Mahmud Mukhtar watched as his "1st Division" debouched from the Sudjak Woods and struck the Bulgarians hard in the front and left flank, supported all the way by the fire of the Turkish guns. The enemy had to give way in some disorder, and the Turkish commander had no problem in calling it "our first victory in this unfortunate war."[29]

He did not have long to enjoy it. The next few hours saw the remainder of the Bulgarian 3rd Army arrive in the line, as well as the guns, and by midday it was the Turks who were on the defensive. The same combination that we have seen at Kirk Kilisse—dominant artillery and vigorous, even rash, infantry attacks—soon mastered the Turkish center and left. Both anchors of the front, Bunarhissar in the north and Lule Burgas in the south, were in Bulgarian hands by 5:00 P.M. The Bulgarian artillery ruled the entire battlefield. One eyewitness, who had been in Port Arthur during the siege, described the scene:

> The whole of the battle front for twenty miles was clearly shown by the masses of bursting shrapnel shells. Never before have I seen such an artillery fire. For every battery the Turks seemed to have in action, the Bulgarians were able to produce half a dozen, and, whereas the Turkish fire was desultory, and generally ill-directed, the Bulgarian shells burst in a never-ceasing storm on the Turkish positions with a maximum of effect. In fact,

the enemy seemed to have so little respect for the Turkish batteries that they seldom directed their fire against them, but concentrated it on the infantry, who suffered enormous losses, and became sadly demoralized.[30]

Although it had been a bloody, exhausting day, night did not bring the fighting to an end. Both Bulgarian armies were now in the front line, and it was evident from the massing of Bulgarian troops that they intended to make II Corps, in the center of Turkish line, the target for the next day's assault. That night, in fact, a bold attack by the Bulgarians seized the town of Turk Bey directly in the heart of the enemy position. The town, a bridgehead over the Karagach River, was the scene of hot fighting until dawn. The next morning, October 30, saw a coordinated assault by the two Bulgarian armies, supported by massed artillery fire. It simply cracked open the Turkish left and center. The Turks were fighting in unfamiliar units, under commanders they hardly knew, and, worst of all, their supply arrangements had broken down completely.[31] Not only were the guns silent due to lack of ammunition; the last meal brought forward for the troops had been on October 28.

The commander of the Army of the East, Abdullah Pasha, was present at the battle, but he spent much of the two days on a mound behind the lines, watching the fighting through field glasses, his sole companions his staff and personal escort. The British journalist Ellis Ashmead-Bartlett commented on the depressing scene, which fittingly enough took place in an old cemetery close to the front:

> Not a line of telegraph or telephone had been brought to the front, and not a single wireless installation, although the Turkish Army on paper possesses twelve complete outfits for its army corps; and not an effort had been made even to establish a line of messengers by relays to connect headquarters with the various army corps. I need hardly add that not a single aeroplane was anywhere within 100 miles of the front, and if any exist there was no one to fly them.
>
> Thus, throughout the entire day, Abdullah remained for hour after hour without any exact information, except that which he obtained hours too late by dispatching various staff officers to his corps commanders. . . .
>
> Thus the battle, instead of being directed by one master-mind, practically resolved itself into four isolated engagements with four separate commanders, each completely ignorant of his comrade's movements, and each having the same difficulty as his Commander-in-Chief in communicating with his divisional and brigade commanders.

Mahmud Mukhtar writes in his own memoirs that he had not heard from Abdullah since Kirk Kilisse. The Turks were, essentially, out of command. There was no one to stem the rout.

So ended the battle of Lule Burgas. It had featured continuous fighting for nearly forty-eight hours on a twenty-mile front, and the losses had been heavy on both sides. The Turks had suffered 25,000 casualties, lost 3,000 prisoners and 42 guns; Bulgarian losses were about 15,000. Some regiments of the Bulgarian 5th Division could muster only one-tenth of their strength on the morning of October 31. The Turkish army that fought there, hastily cobbled together and poorly supplied, disintegrated, fleeing en masse toward the east and the Chatalja line. There are any number of witnesses, Mahmud Mukhtar among them, who believed that had the Bulgarians mounted any sort of pursuit at all, they would have had a very good chance of marching into Constantinople. Ashmead-Bartlett corroborates that thought:

> Throughout the day we had all been wondering why the Bulgarians had not pursued the masses of fugitives streaming over the open plain without any semblance of order, who would have offered no resistance had they been attacked. . . . The thousands of fugitives crowded on to the banks of the river at Chorlu, who had only one bridge over which they could pass, would have been at the mercy of the cavalry, and, had the latter possessed a few batteries of horse artillery, it is awful to contemplate the disaster which would have ensued.

The Turks in hurried retreat after their defeat at Lule Burgas. Courtesy of the Imperial War Museum, London (Q 99884).

The extreme exhaustion of the Bulgarian troops, the high casualties and disorder caused by the fighting, the complete inability of the cavalry in the face of modern firepower, and above all, the impossibility of getting orders and commanders forward into the carnage of an early twentieth-century battlefield: all of these prevented any pursuit.

Still, the rout was total. Most observers—and there was literally a horde of correspondents covering this war—could think of only one thing as they saw the Turkish rout after Lule Burgas: the Grande Armée in Russia. The Turks had thrown off all military organization and become a starving, ravenous horde. Soon panic gave way to despondency, and there could hardly have been a more depressing sight in military history than the Turkish army stumbling home after defeat.

> The further we receded from the battlefield, the worse the scene became, because many of the wounded, having dragged themselves thus far, could go no further, and, crawling off the track, lay down to die by the roadside without a curse or reproach at the authors of all their miseries. Sometimes when a man had died his comrades would stop a moment and dig a shallow grave, but the majority of the corpses were left just where they fell.[32]

The number of corpses, problems with sanitation, and lack of a secure water supply had the predictable consequence: an outbreak of cholera.

Despite the horrors of this great Turkish retreat, Bulgarian problems with supply and organization meant that two weeks passed before the Turks again had to face the test of fire. And this time, at Chatalja, they were in an unflankable line of entrenchments with ideal fields of fire, and they were well supported by a full complement of field and heavy artillery. Both served to remedy the real Turkish deficiency in this war: troop morale. Facing the Turks was a Bulgarian army that was operating at the uttermost limit of its supply radius, short of artillery ammunition, exhausted from the fighting, and already forced to call the class of 1913 to the colors in order to make good its losses, not to mention suffering its own cholera outbreak.

The battles for the Chatalja line offer us no real lessons in higher operations, or even tactics. In fact, they would be of no interest whatsoever if all the Great Powers were not about to be plunged into nearly identical fighting that would stretch over the next four years. Located just twenty-two miles from Constantinople, the position was about twenty-five miles wide, although watercourses that intrude along both coasts reduce the frontage to just fifteen miles. Two streams, the Kartachi and Karasou, cross it in a generally north-south direction, adding further obstacles to the attack. With the Turkish navy still supreme in the Black Sea and Sea of Marmora, the flanks of the position were secure, while those of the Bulgarians were vulnerable to either naval bombardment or even an amphibious landing.

Although its Army of the East had been ruined, the empire was huge and could call upon the labor of thousands of men to fortify the line, digging entrenchments, preparing artillery emplacements, hauling the guns into place. A second line of entrenchments appeared behind the first, and eventually a third supported the second. Troops were pouring into the position from Asia. Finally, the thoroughly demoralized Abdullah Pasha was no longer the Turkish commander, whether voluntarily retired or dismissed it is difficult to say. With the battle raging at the gates of Constantinople itself, the more capable war minister, Nazim Pasha, was now in the field as commander in chief.

The Bulgarians arrived in front of the position on November 14, occupying the town of Chatalja itself (although the name is still used to refer to the entire Turkish position).[33] They occupied the high ground to the west, five to seven miles from the Turkish positions ensconced on the high ground to the east. Over the next three days, Bulgarian staff officers carried out a reconnaissance of the valley between the opposing lines, noting the most suitable approaches, choosing assault sectors, and determining the emplacement of the supporting guns. Much of this was reconnaissance by fire, both rifle and artillery, which searched out both the Turkish strongpoints and the weaker sectors where the assaulting infantry units might be able to force the line, since they obviously could not turn it.

By November 16, the preparations were finished. Two Bulgarian armies now faced the Chatalja lines: 3rd Army on the left and 1st Army on the right. The former had four divisions, two in the front line and two in reserve: on the right, 9th Division lay to the west of Kastania; on the left, 3rd Division, west of Lazarkoi. Its 5th and 4th Divisions were in support. First Army had three divisions, two in the front and one in support: 6th Division lay west of Ezetin, 1st Division in the center, in Chatalja itself; to the right and rear, 10th Division. Finally, the Cavalry Division occupied the extreme right of the Bulgarian line. It had dug a line of trenches in front of the village of Arnautkoi, where it guarded against any attempts by the Turks to land a force in the rear of 1st Army.

On the night of November 16–17, the frontline Bulgarian divisions began a general advance into the plain between the two armies, driving back the Turkish pickets and emplacing artillery for direct support of the infantry. There was heavy fighting in the south, as 1st Army tried unsuccessfully to force passage of the railway bridge over the Karasou, near the village of Bakceiskoi. At dawn on November 17, the Bulgarian infantry began moving up toward its assault positions, and at 9:00 A.M., a general Bulgarian bombardment

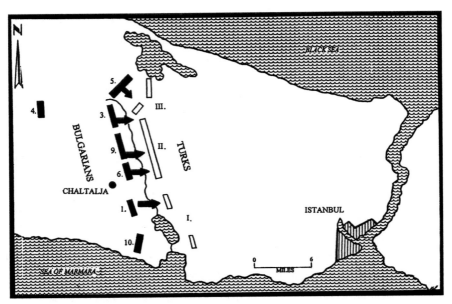

Opposing lines at Chatalja, November 1912.

opened up all along the line. In the south, 1st Army concentrated its effort on its left, against the Mahmudije Fort, in the center of the Turkish position, and also continued the thrust toward the rail bridge. In the latter struggle, the Turkish gunboats *Messoudieh* and *Barbarossa*, anchored in the Bay of Chekmedije, weighed in against the Bulgarians. The terrain was open and swampy, due to previous rains, and the naval shellfire drove the Bulgarians back in some confusion. The Turks then attempted a landing on that flank, with some 200 men coming across Lake Chekmedije on launches. They did not get far inland, being hit by Bulgarian rifle and artillery fire almost as soon as they landed. The entire force was killed or taken prisoner.

At Mahmudije, the Bulgarians managed some forward progress, but this time the artillery of the Turkish II Corps—well handled, well supplied, and hidden from Bulgarian sight in dugouts—inflicted horrible losses on the attacking infantry. Soon there was a Turkish counterattack that threw back the attackers, capturing two supporting batteries that had been emplaced virtually in the open. Three times they were captured and recaptured, since it was impossible to get horses forward in the heavy fire and drag them off. For the rest of the afternoon, those three batteries held the attention of Bulgarian 1st Army and Turkish II Corps. When night fell, the two forces held the same ground they had held in the morning.

In the northern sector of the battlefield, 3rd Army had launched a sustained assault of its own. Facing it was the redoubtable III Corps, under Mahmud Mukhtar, or perhaps one should call it "III Corps (mark III)," for once again it had been substantially reconstituted. This time, however, it had the successful assault at Bunarhissar to its credit. The assault of the Bulgarian 3rd Army was hit hard by rifle fire from the trenches opposite it, as well as hidden Turkish batteries. Aided by terrain that forced the Bulgarian guns to come out onto the plain, the Turkish artillery had clear fire superiority. The Bulgarian assault made some minor gains but as night fell was barely clinging to them.

Once again, night did not bring an end to the fighting. Just before midnight, units of the Bulgarian 9th Division, the right wing of 3rd Army, managed to break into the center of the Turkish line near Ordzunli. When the fog lifted the next morning, however, they suddenly came under heavy rifle fire from the Turkish trenches on their flanks, and then from Turkish artillery; this would become a familiar predicament to the regimental commander of World War I. Likewise, just after midnight, 3rd Division (the left of 3rd Army) had some success striking toward the town of Lazarkoi, seizing a small redoubt and penetrating about a kilometer past it to the southeast. However, with the arrival of morning, a counterattack led in person by Mahmud Mukhtar succeeded in retaking the lost position. He was seriously wounded in the encounter while riding out on reconnaissance with his staff. No news had come about the fall of the Turkish redoubt, and when he saw soldiers emerge from it, he thought that they were Turkish. As the situation sorted itself out, he and his entire staff suddenly found themselves between two firing lines. He took a bullet to the knee, had a horse killed under him, and broke both legs in the fall before dragging himself to safety.[34] He was the great Turkish hero of the war.

As morning dawned on November 18, both Bulgarian armies had suffered heavy losses, perhaps 10,000 men. Rather than push matters to a conclusion one way or the other, the Bulgarian command now decided to withdraw back across the valley, entrench, and wait for political developments. The Turks had already raised the possibility of an armistice. The Great Powers were watching events in the Balkans with alarm, the Bulgarians themselves were exhausted, out of supply, and suffering from both dysentery and cholera. The battle of Chatalja was over, and so was the triumphant Bulgarian march on Constantinople.

No discussion of the war would be complete without some mention of the siege of Adrianople. Like Port Arthur, Adrianople was not so much a walled city as it was a series of connected and mutually supporting strongpoints. Unlike Port Arthur, it had few armored or concrete fortifications. Also differentiating it from the bloody horrors of the earlier siege was the lack of truly heavy artillery. The heaviest guns in the Bulgarian arsenal during the Adrianople operation were 120-mm and 150-mm pieces, and not many at that, just seventy-seven guns all told. Ivanov's 2nd Army invested the town early in the war, made a failed and bloody attempt to storm it on October 22 to 24, then settled down to a sporadic bombardment. At the beginning of November, the Serbian 2nd Army (Stepanovic) arrived, 47,000 men strong, and eventually took over approximately twenty out of the forty-seven kilometers of the lines of investment.

The war ended in December, with Great Power intervention and an armistice. With both sides trying to take advantage of its terms to seek some battlefield advantage, however, fighting continued into 1913. In the early spring, all three besieged Ottoman fortresses fell to the enemy: Janina to the Greeks (March 3), Adrianople to a bloody assault by the Bulgarians and Serbs (March 25–26), and Scutari to the Montenegrins (April 22). Especially important to the fall of Adrianople was the February 1913 arrival of the Serbian siege artillery to augment the Bulgarian guns already in place: seventeen additional batteries, with a total of fifty-eight guns, among them twenty-four modern howitzers of 120 mm and 150 mm just purchased from the firm of Schneider in France. The victorious powers soon fell out over the spoils, leading to the Second Balkan War.[35] Bulgaria, the power that emerged from the war with the highest reputation for martial valor, and perhaps seduced by that reputation, launched an attack on its neighbors. Their combined forces were far too much for Bulgaria to handle, however, and the situation became acute as Romania entered the war and began to march on a totally undefended Sofia. Turkey also launched an assault out of the Chatalja lines and forced back the Bulgarians, eventually recapturing Adrianople. All these events are so inextricably linked with the international political situation that they offer few lessons on the strictly military plane.

POSTMORTEM

Most of the contemporary analysis focused on the Bulgarian campaign in Thrace. From the Turkish side, Mahmud Mukhtar argued that the Bulgarian victory resulted not from any true superiority but from Turkish mistakes. In 1877, the Turkish soldier had shown the world an example of true valor in defending Plevna from the Russians; now it was impossible not to be astonished at the turn of events. The only comparable historical example that came to his mind was the decline of the Prussian army between its great victory over the French at Rossbach in 1757 and its humiliation at the hands of Napoleon at Jena in 1806. "We weren't facing Napoleon, however, nor were our leaders completely ignorant of modern war."[36] The routs that repeatedly took place were moral failures, he felt, not material ones, and while many singled out the Christian soldiers in the Ottoman ranks for special criticism, he was not so sure. Since they had all deserted in the opening battles, they could hardly be held responsible for the later debacles. That is not to say that he laid the blame for the defeat on the men under him. They had not been well trained, the state was deficient in all areas of mobilization planning, and the overreliance on the territorial militia (the *redif* divisions) had been a disaster. Even the regular army *(nizam)*, although showing itself to be a bit more steadfast, had serious defects in training, supply, and equipment. All these problems he laid at the feet of the War Ministry in Constantinople. The real problem of the Turkish army in Thrace, however, was its officer corps. Too many young officers were political appointees, more interested in coups and intrigues than war, "Janissaries," he called them. Too many others were simply "civil servants in uniform," lacking the true military spirit. On paper, the army was huge, with twenty-four army corps of three divisions each. In reality, he argued, it was a shell, since there were no more than five good generals in the entire empire ready to command it.

Most contemporary observers agreed with his assessments, especially on the use of the militia. One American analyst, Major Edward Sigerfoos, wrote, "The principal lesson to be learned from this study is the utter uselessness and criminal folly of using militia or other ill-trained and ill-organized troops against a well-trained, well-organized and well-disciplined army, and that the nation that depends on them to stand between it and destruction and to save it in the hour of need, will sooner or later come to grief and suffer a great disaster."[37]

Those same observers disagreed with Mahmud Mukhtar, however, on the merits of the Bulgarians. The twentieth century has now played out, and it is clear that Bulgarian military power did not figure prominently in its history. One would not be able to predict that from reading a representative sampling of the professional military literature of 1913, however. Sigerfoos's analysis, for example, praised the boldness of the officers, singling out General Dimitriev, and the aggressiveness of the infantry. But the real secret to Bulgarian success was superior war planning and mobilization. For years before the war, the Bulgarian staff had poured out a stream of what would today be called "disinformation," to the effect that the main effort in case of war with Turkey would be in Macedonia. With the formation of the Balkan alliance, the Bulgarians had changed the point of main effort to Thrace but had carefully kept that fact a secret. As their mobilization unfolded, they made further efforts to disguise first the existence, then the location, of their 3rd Army. Consequently, the Turks went to war believing that the Bulgarians would invest Adrianople with all their forces. Their opening offensive of the war intended to march on Adrianople from the east, hit the open left wing of the Bulgarian armies descending on the fortress, and roll them up toward the west and north. Instead, it ran into an army whose very existence came as a shock to them. These meeting engagements in the opening days of the war—featuring a Turkish command structure shocked by the unknown and a Bulgarian one carrying out a well-formulated plan—set the tone for the entire war.

A French analyst writing in *Le Journal* echoed this argument. In the days just before the war, the Bulgarians let it be known that they intended to direct their effort toward storming Adrianople. Carefully orchestrated "leaks," such as General Savov's comment that he was ready to "sacrifice 50,000 men in the Japanese fashion" to take it, reinforced this belief. Many correspondents were surprised when the Bulgarian government gave them permission to publish the story. Operational plans also fell into the hands of the press. "The 1st and 2nd Armies were to invest Adrianople while the 3rd, to the *west* of the place, was to move first from north to south, then, having seized the railroad, was to take a resolute offensive toward the east, that is to say toward the principle army of the enemy. This was the famous Bulgarian plan."[38] Officers of the 3rd Army received identical orders just weeks before the opening of hostilities. But the General Staff was actually formulating a very different and extraordinary plan. With eastern Bulgaria under a press, mail, and telegraphic blackout, and with influential politicians, even former prime ministers, being kept in the dark, the Bulgarians sprung a surprise:

> Suddenly the 3rd Army, without leaving Bulgaria, made a sudden about face, moved no longer south but straight east and was concentrated upon Jamboli, that is in the southeast corner of the kingdom. A great part of its artillery had already, secretly, long before the declaration of war, been moved into that district. Then the 3rd Army moved forward still southeast through the very rough and theoretically impracticable country which forms the frontier of Turkey north of Lozengrad-Kirk Kilisse.[39]

Then, when hostilities opened, Bulgarian 1st Army, instead of marching on Adrianople, moved directly south through the Tundja River valley, appearing between Adrianople and Kirk Kilisse. Only one Bulgarian army, the 2nd, marched directly on the fortress.

The Turks, of course, knew nothing of this as yet. They marched due west, leaving the fortifications of Kirk Kilisse and expecting to encounter the dangling left flank of the Bulgarian 1st Army moving down on Adrianople.

Instead they ran headlong into not the flank but the main body of 1st Army at Seliolo and, even worse, into the onrushing columns of the 3rd Army that had just emerged from the Istrandja Dagh mountain range on the border. According to the French analyst, "The Ottomans had hardly begun their movement when they were themselves swept by shrapnel, counterattacked, beaten, swept back and pursued with bayonets at their backs." The Bulgarians did not have to storm Kirk Kilisse, although they later claimed that they did. The Turks simply abandoned it in their rout. It was a great triumph not only of fighting spirit but also of cleverness and deception: "Thanks to this secrecy the Bulgarians succeeded in seizing at the beginning of the campaign a fortified city which, though not as large as Adrianople, might, if rationally defended, have interfered with their offensive for a long time and have cost them great sacrifices."[40]

The discussion of the war also had its share of trivial aspects. This was most clearly evident in the discussion of artillery. Bulgarian guns, largely quick-firing 75-mm guns made by the French firm of Schneider-Creusot, had clearly outclassed the Turkish guns, generally older pieces of Krupp design. The French were not loathe to point this out, and German writers rushed to defend the honor of Krupp and to point out that both sides had used both French and German pieces. It was not at all unlike the later discussions of the relative merits of U.S. and Soviet tanks after one of the Arab-Israeli wars. The real issue appeared to be the age of the artillery, not the manufacturer, and whether or not it was of the quick-firing type.

In addition, the artillery lessons of Chatalja were quite different from those of earlier battles. The early encounters in the open field proved the worth of the French 75 mm, but the light weight of its shell and the flat trajectory of its fire made it nearly worthless in the assaults against the Turkish fortifications. At Chatalja, it was the heavier Turkish artillery and howitzers that ruled the battlefield, despite being old, slower-firing models. Of all the Great Powers, it was the Germans and Austrians who seemed to appreciate this lesson, equipping their forces with a large number of heavy field howitzers.[41]

Viewing the war from our modern perspective, the Turkish defeat certainly seems understandable, if only due to administrative and organizational failures on the part of the Turks. Only since the Young Turk revolution in 1908 had the empire set about creating a national army in the modern sense. The long years of lethargy that had preceded this development were not easily overcome. The *redif* divisions, in particular, both men and officers, were badly trained, and according to many period accounts often did not even know how to use their weapons. The German adviser to the Turkish army, von der Goltz, characterized the war this way: it was "an army of recruits facing an army that had been preparing for twenty-seven years for war."[42]

Only the Bulgarians themselves seemed unimpressed with their achievement. Their victory in the First Balkan War had turned into the disastrous decision to attack their former allies. But even if that had not happened, the Bulgarians seemed shocked that all their preparations, all their vigorous infantry attacks and pounding artillery bombardments, had not brought them to Constantinople itself. Their victory had been tactical and operational, but not strategic. In 1913, a very public quarrel exploded in the pages of the Sofia dailies between officers of the Bulgarian General Staff, on the one hand, and the generals commanding in the field, on the other.[43] Point men for the factions were General Ivan Fitchev, the chief of staff of the Army of Operations, and General Radko Dimitriev, the commander of the 3rd Army. At issue was the failure of the victorious armies to pursue the Turks after Kirk Kilisse and Lule Burgas–Bunarhissar. Each man accused the other of a lack of energy and boldness; both men produced wartime documents that they claimed proved the point. Both men were right, in one sense. Dimitriev clearly asked for permission to rest his men for one or two days after Lule Burgas; Fitchev had also clearly ordered him to hold up and wait for the 1st Army to clear itself of Adrianople so that the two armies could advance together on the Turks. But in a broader sense, both men were wrong. Their real argument, although neither they nor any other military professional of the day could recognize it, was with the incomplete and insufficient mechanisms for command and control of the mass army. A close reading of the First Balkan War will establish that there were not two more talented officers in all of Europe—Germany included. They had achieved all that flesh, blood, and the telegraph could achieve. The technology did not yet exist to allow them to demonstrate their true brilliance.

CONCLUSIONS: LESSONS OF THE LITTLE WARS

Are there any points in common that we can use to link these three "little wars"? Taken together, do they teach any lessons about the nature of war in the early twentieth century? The military professionals of the day certainly thought so. The only problem was that, as they attempted to read the tea leaves from the battles in South Africa, Manchuria, and Thrace, the lessons they derived seemed to be contradictory. Looking at the early battles of the Boer War, most observers felt that they proved the superiority of the defense in battle. The British response was to emphasize shooting, target practice, and marksmanship in future military training. As a result, the British army would enjoy a distinct advantage in those areas in the opening days of World War I. Examining the record of the Russo-Japanese and Balkan Wars, however, many of the same military analysts argued that they clearly proved the superiority of the offense and the necessity for training the entire army in the tactics of modern assault, imbuing the men with what was usually called "the offensive spirit" and a corresponding willingness to die in the service of the state.[44]

The contradiction is more apparent than real, however, and we can easily resolve it. To most European staff officers, the Boer War simply had too many unique characteristics to serve as a model. The Russo-Japanese and Balkan Wars were the sort of conflicts they expected to fight: Great Powers, big battalions, set-piece battles involving hundreds of thousands of men. They certainly did not expect to be hunting down armed farmers on the frontier. In Manchuria, Macedonia, and Thrace, the better-motivated, better-trained infantry was able to triumph, even in the teeth of overwhelming defensive fire. On numerous occasions, the Japanese and Bulgarians, the latter in particular, were able to get through the curtain of their opponent's fire and either drive him from his positions before contact or, on several celebrated instances, do what many had alleged was impossible—close with the bayonet and put him to flight.

In determining how this was possible, we must first look to the aggressive nature of Japanese and Bulgarian doctrine. Two weeks after the battle of the Yalu, the British attaché, General Ian Hamilton, was out for a morning ride when he came across a Japanese infantry company going through its drill near, of all places, a graveyard. About 1,500 yards away, there was a wooded hill, some 100 feet high, on which a Russian force was supposed to be entrenched. The first 200 yards in front of the Japanese force was undulating ground and offered a significant amount of cover. After that, however, the country was level, freshly plowed, tough to cross, and absolutely open, "as ugly a bit of terrain in fact as any soldier could desire not to have to cross under fire," he wrote. His description of what he saw is worth quoting at length:

> On a sharp word of command and the flourish of the captain's sword, a section, one-third of his company, darted out of the hollow, made a forward rush of about 100 to 150 yards, flung themselves down and opened fire. I jumped on my horse and cantered along with the section. The men ran with a rapidity which was positively startling.
>
> Intervals were about a yard, but as the attack progressed these intervals tended to decrease until, here and there, the men were shoulder to shoulder. Very little time was spent in firing, and in less than a minute another rush carried the section to within 1200 yards of the position. The first section was reinforced from the rear during its next advance by the

second section, which came up at a great pace and prolonged the line to the left. To my surprise, this reinforcing section covered the whole distance of 400 yards in one tremendous spurt. . . .

The advance then continued by 100 yards rushes of alternate sections, only one minute at the most being allowed for shooting at each halt. At about 800 yards from the enemy's position the line was reinforced by the remaining section of the company, which had meanwhile worked its way independently and without any firing, to the cover of a farmhouse just to the right of the general line of advance. This last reinforcement prolonged the line to the right, and thenceforth the rushes were made by alternate half companies until the final stage, which was reached at 350 yards from the supposed Russian position. Here the bugles sounded; the men fixed bayonets and charged in with a loud shout of "Wa-a-a!" dashing over and through the deep plough with marvelous swiftness, and not subsiding until they had got two-thirds of the way up the hill.

Hamilton was astonished. "Our men could not do this," he wrote, "nor could the men of any Continental, Asiatic, or American army I have seen." After congratulating the captain on the exercise, he asked him if the use of such a tight formation would not lead to useless casualties. He responded with "the stock German answer," wrote Hamilton: "You cannot have success without loss of life."[45] Hamilton did not argue the point. The Japanese dead piled up in front of the Mukden trenches would no doubt have had their own opinion.

The Bulgarians had attacked with even more reckless abandon than the Japanese, in fast-moving, dense formations. Virtually every account of the fighting, whether journalistic, military, or scholarly, makes mention of the incredible ferocity of the Bulgarian infantry in the assault. The preference for shock tactics had its roots in Bulgaria's overall strategic situation. With the budget strained to the limit by military spending, and with over 15 percent of the total Bulgarian population fighting in the war—an incredible figure— Bulgaria had to beat the Turks as quickly as possible. Long-drawn-out maneuvers before battle and tactical finesse during the encounter itself would not have been sufficient. The social composition of the Bulgarian army also played a part. With a force made up almost exclusively of sturdy peasants inured to the hard life (and, frankly, burning with a hatred for the Turks), trusting implicitly in their superiors, the Bulgarian staff was able to use tactics that most other European armies would have refused to carry out. Describing the attack at Lule Burgas, one Bulgarian officer stated, "We came up in waves."[46] Their casualties were enormous. A Turk taken prisoner at Kirk Kilisse said, "In the bayonet charge the Bulgarians are irresistible. Even if hundreds fell before the fire of our repeating rifles, hundreds more would

Some of the finest infantry in Europe. Bulgarian soldiers looking relaxed and confident after a hard march. Courtesy of the Imperial War Museum, London (Q 99860).

come rushing onward over the corpses."[47] Numerous Turkish accounts speak to the terror of the sudden onrushing wave, the shouts of "Hurrah!" and the panic that inevitably followed within Turkish ranks, the fear of the *nosche* (knife, or bayonet) that seemed to overcome all cohesion among the defenders. Even the Bulgarian cavalry got into the act, charging home against Turkish positions with abandon, with predictably high casualties. Perhaps the most perceptive comment on the war came from British correspondent Philip Gibbs, who wrote, "The history of this war would have been very different if the Bulgarians had set out to fight a nation less utterly demoralized than the Turks, for their bayonet charges when the peasant soldiers flung off their sheepskin coats and rushed forward in the full fire of the guns would have been checked by walls of dead."[48] In the end, the unwillingness or inability of the Turks to stand and fight anywhere outside of the Chatalja line made it a moot point.

There was another factor in the Japanese and Bulgarian success, however, that went well beyond their infantry's fierceness and contempt for losses. Nearly every battle in both these wars, from the Yalu to Chatalja, had begun as an artillery duel. In each battle of the First Balkan War, the Bulgarian guns established a clear superiority of fire over the Turks, who were often hampered by ammunition shortages. In several instances, airplanes and balloons helped to increase the accuracy by spotting for the guns. When the fire from the Turkish batteries had slowed, due either to Bulgarian action or to the lack of shells, the Bulgarian guns were free to concentrate on the Turkish infantry. "Our artillery mowed the enemy down mercilessly," said one Bulgarian officer.[49] Those infantry charges, as bloody as they were, would simply have been impossible if the Bulgarian guns had not first beat down their Turkish counterparts. Indeed, on the two sectors of the Thracian front where the Bulgarians did not gain such a clear fire ascendancy, at Adrianople and in front of Chatalja, the Turks managed to hold firm. Only after the Bulgarian guns had silenced the enemy's artillery and shifted fire to his infantry could the bayonet charge succeed. In fact, in full harmony with du Picq's conception of battle in the nineteenth century, the Turks almost always fled before the Bulgarian columns made contact with them. Bayonet casualties were extremely rare. It was the moral ascendancy provided by the guns, not the infantry shock, that destroyed the Turkish defenses. The guns had to fire before the attack and keep up their fire during the attack. According to one French officer who observed the fighting, "The artillery no longer prepares attacks, it supports them."[50] Fire had become an indispensable partner to movement; fire superiority had become indispensable to the assault.

Conversely, if the enemy force could ensconce itself in an entrenched and fortified position with unassailable flanks and artillery superiority, even the most determined infantry assault was bound to fail. That was the lesson of Chatalja. Most European staff officers and planners recognized, however, that there were few bottlenecks on the Continent as narrow and as easy to defend as Chatalja. They attributed the Turkish defensive victory and the blunting of the previously irresistible Bulgarian ferocity to the extremely unusual topography of the battlefield, a special case that did not obtain anywhere else in Europe. As they thought about the next war, they assumed one factor: there would always be room to maneuver and an opportunity to find the opponent's flank as the great Moltke had done. The situation from 1914 to 1917, in which all the world had become Chatalja—a solid phalanx of corps in entrenched, fortified, and unflankable positions from the North Sea to the Swiss border—was absolutely inconceivable to them.

The second great lesson of these wars, not as apparent at the time but no less real, was this: despite their ability to win battlefield victory, aggressive assault tactics no longer seemed able to win wars. Command problems, and the enormous supplies eaten up by the modern mass army, prevented swift maneuvers and all-out pursuits, as we have seen. As a result, in the Russo-Japanese War, there was only a tenuous link between one battle to the next.

Battles, as large and as bloody as they were, tended to be sterile and without result. After the Russian defenders retreated, the Japanese had to march up to their next position and do the same thing all over again. The Russian army that the Japanese fought at Mukden had not been worn down in the previous year of fighting. In fact, it was larger and better equipped than ever. The Bulgarian communications troops did yeoman's work in constructing telephone and telegraph lines in the course of the First Balkan War, laying over 2,100 miles of telegraph lines, for example. Still, the army commanders were rarely in close enough contact with the units at the front in this rapidly changing campaign. Ivanov himself wrote, "The conduct of hostilities was in the hands of the regimental and lower commanders."[51] The Turks had disintegrated after Kirk Kilisse but were able to re-form due to a lack of Bulgarian pursuit. They disintegrated again after Lule Burgas but again were able to revive in the lull before the encounter at Chatalja. The lack of pursuit meant that the *campaign*—defined here as a series of interconnected maneuvers and battles aiming at the defeat or destruction of the enemy field army—was in danger of becoming obsolete.

Much of the fault for the lack of pursuit lies with the continuing decline of horse cavalry as a military arm. In all three of these wars, the performance of cavalry had been disappointing, to say the least. No one's cavalry appeared particularly well trained or well mounted. One American analyst, however, came to the defense of the horse arm in curious terms. "Endeavoring to reach back from reasonably well-assured results to their causes," wrote General James N. Allison, "it would appear inevitable that many of the apparently hazardous and invariably successful movements of the allied forces were based on reliable information of dispositions in their front which could only have been secured by active and intelligent work of well trained and daring cavalry." He was just getting warmed up:

> The seizure and retention of important strategical points, the capture of trains and supplies, and the destruction of railroad bridges at widely separated points in advance of the main army, of which there is ample evidence, all point to the legitimate work of an energetic mobile force under competent leadership. And it will not be surprising to learn—if a waiting world ever does learn anything reliable of the course of events of past months in the Balkan states—that the tough and wiry little horses of the Servian [sic] and Bulgarian mountains have played no mean part in the brilliant campaigns of the Allied states.[52]

Nothing of the sort had happened in the course of the war, although the passage is highly instructive of the lengths to which military conservatives would go to defend the horse arm.[53]

All these cautionary words about fire, leadership, and pursuit would have fallen on deaf ears in the years before 1914. Instead, the talk was on the importance of the "offensive spirit." Since, with the benefit of hindsight, we know that a horrible war was just around the corner, one that would prove to everyone's satisfaction that "spirit" was not enough to overcome machine guns and rapid fire artillery, it is perhaps worth looking at this concept in more detail. As an idea, it had a very short life: a little over ten years if one dates it from the Russo-Japanese War and a little less than one year if one dates it from the period after the Balkan Wars. But in that very short time, it became the received wisdom of the professional military class: articles on every conceivable topic in the military journals argued that the offensive and the "will to win" were the keys to victory.

In September 1913, a pseudonymous article (authored by "Ubique") appeared in the British *United Service Magazine*.[54] Entitled "The Offensive Spirit in War," it defined its topic in terms that help to explain a great deal about what was to happen in the next war: "To all students of war the term 'offensive spirit' may be defined as the motive force that supplies to an army and its commander energy and determination to conceive, develop, and carry through a policy of attacking and ever attacking the foe until the supreme object is achieved, to attain which the army took the field." The record of the past few decades was clear: victory in war could never result from a defensive posture but only from "a combination of the strategical and tactical offensive." It was vitally important to imbue the entire nation with this spirit, from the political leadership all the way down to the ordinary citizen. Likewise, every man in the army from the supreme commander down to the rawest recruit had to share it.

The success of Prussia was the perfect example, based as it was on three factors: first, a careful and methodical planning, since modern inventions had transformed warfare into "an exact science"; second, the mobilization of the entire manhood of the nation for war, and the indoctrination of this "nation in arms" with a sense of duty and patriotic enthusiasm; and third, reliance on an offensive posture, embracing both strategy and tactics, once the fighting had started. Speaking of Prussian success in the war with France, the author went on to conclude, "The results of this careful forethought and preparation were that the army was enabled from the first to assume and maintain the offensive, that victory was hardly, if ever, in doubt, and that fewer mistakes were made in this campaign than in any that preceded it." While the modern historian, or anyone with even a passing familiarity with the campaign, may see this as an incredibly wrongheaded statement, it demonstrates once again the hold that the great Moltke had on the military professionals of the day.

The Japanese were another good example, argued our author. "Ten years ago few would have been found to predict that in a few months our great bugbear—the Russian menace—would be swept away by Japan." Like the Prussians, the Japanese had spent decades preparing for this war, cultivating "the virile national spirit that was the chief factor in their success. The nation shook off its medieval past, sent its soldiers to Germany and its sailors to Britain. When the great crisis came, the entire nation was prepared to gain victory by any means necessary: "No sacrifice of money, effort, or life was deemed too great in defense of the national honor." While the Russians had fought bravely, their national character was better suited to defense than attack; the battle of Borodino, where they fought Napoleon to a bloody draw outside of Moscow, was their finest historical hour. In the Manchurian war, "the Russians, defending alien territory to which they were bound by no tie, having no wrongs to avenge, conscious of unpreparedness, and lacking both enthusiasm for the war and confidence in their leaders, were not the formidable opponents that Napoleon the First found them." While modern readers may view the siege of Port Arthur as a bloody mess, our author from 1913 admired it as a symbol of the "ruthless determination on the part of the Japanese soldiery to win at all costs," combining the "fanaticism of the East with the bulldog tenacity of the British soldier." He makes similar observations on the field campaign. In virtually every battle from the Yalu to Mukden, the Russians not only had more men but also fought on ground of their own choosing. Yet the Japanese drove them from the field again and again. Why? It was a matter of lacking "the will to win." They trusted in their entrenchments and tried to fight a war of positions, "retiring always when pressed" and feeding in their reserves piecemeal, "instead of keeping them back for a great counterstroke." A certain inertia was the result. When moments arose in all these battles for the Russians to switch over from the defensive to the offensive, their troops were simply incapable of doing it.

The Bulgarians represented a third example of the "offensive spirit" in action. "It is not so long ago that Europe would have laughed at the idea of resistance being offered to Turkey by any states in the Balkan peninsula." Yet a campaign had taken place that "eclipsed the Hundred Days both in swiftness and decisiveness." The Turks had lacked all the prerequisites for modern war: they had done no careful planning, and they were, as a multinational state whose army was filled by sullen conscripts belonging to the subject races, incapable of any sort of Prussian-style "national training" and as a result had lacked the will to win. The Bulgarians, by contrast, had all these things. Although they were "hardly free from the taint of servitude," they had spent years in successfully preparing to topple their former overlords. While Bulgarian strategic skill had been evident in their bold move on to Kirk Kilisse, and the bravery of their infantry clear at Lule Burgas, it was "the spadework of the last few years" that was worthy of admiration, "the ungrudging submergence of the individual will, the molding of this semi-barbarous Slav into a disciplined soldier." Let us ponder this contemporary evaluation of the Bulgarian achievement: "It may well be that the strategy of Savoff [*sic*] will be found not unworthy to be compared with that of von Moltke, but one thing at least is certain—that Bulgaria won for herself the right to be numbered among the great military nations of the world."

In seeking to emulate Bulgaria, Britain needed to do three things, argued "Ubique." First, the government had to sponsor a comprehensive program to ready the nation for war. Statecraft and diplomacy had to serve the nation's strategic ends. There had to be plans to defend the nation's roads, railways, and seaports, and to see to it that they were sufficient to support an offensive posture in war. There had to be an education on patriotic lines for the young, tossing aside all questions of party affiliation and political benefit. Above all, "methods of false economy" must not be allowed to get in the way of preparedness.

Second, Britain needed something approaching the Prussian General Staff system. There had to be a "uniform system" in which officers of all grades imbibed the same general principles of war. This was the only way that the army could successfully navigate the confusion and sprawl of the modern battlefield. "In those parts of the field not under the eye of the supreme commander, the leader on the spot should act boldly in accordance with his commander's wishes, but having due regard to the altering situations. Then, if the training has been uniform, correct decisions in accordance with the ruling principles will be reached, and the wishes of the supreme commander will be rightly interpreted by his subordinates."

The most important task was the third: the entire army must be prepared to attack, attack, and attack. The principle of the offensive "must be driven home." Recent campaigns, as well as the opinions of the "masters of the art of war," agreed that decisive victory was only to be had by a vigorous offensive. "This principle must be kept always foremost, it must be emphasized at lectures, staff rides, and maneuvers, and, as it is the fundamental principle in our manuals, so it must form the basis of our operations in the field." It wasn't just a matter for the officers; superior numbers didn't matter half as much as "a firm determination in all ranks to conquer at all costs."

"To conquer at all costs"—these and similar phrases were on the lips of the vast majority of the Western world's military professionals as the year 1914 approached.[55] The problem that a modern analyst has in criticizing them is that they make so much sense, given the context of the times. The author bases his arguments solidly on recent events, and his analysis of recent wars seems quite reasonable. His specific points are well-taken: offensives win wars; troops must be imbued with an aggressive, attacking spirit; doing nothing but defending passively in a line of entrenchments is a guarantee of defeat. It is difficult to see how the wars before 1914 could have taught any contrary lessons.

Chapter 5

• • • • • • • • • • • • • • •

World War I:
The End of Decisive Operations

INTRODUCTION: THE MYTH OF THE GREAT WAR

As bad as World War I was, an exaggerated view of it arose in the post-war years and has seared its way into Western consciousness since then. World War I, it says, was the bloodiest, most hideous conflict of all time, in which an incompetent officer corps sacrificed millions of infantrymen in vain frontal assaults against fortified entrenchments.[1] The attacks went forward in thick waves, with officers brandishing sabers, and immediately collapsed in a hail of machine gun fire. It was four years of mud and blood and trenches: an orgy of senseless killing. It is the hell described in Erich Maria Remarque's *All Quiet on the Western Front,* to name the most famous novel on the war.[2] It was the "end of glory."

Scholars have been challenging this view in recent decades. They argue, without minimizing the horrors of the World War I battlefield, that the first year of the war featured mobile campaigns in open country, not trench warfare. They point out that mobility never departed on the eastern front, where the wide-open spaces and the smaller forces engaged allowed for just the sort of maneuver-based campaigns that staff officers had envisioned before 1914. During the last year of the war, trench warfare come to an end, as German *Stosstrupp* tactics and Allied tanks provided a solution for getting through the enemy's fortified positions and breaking into open country. Likewise, they point out that half the total casualties of the war occurred in the first fifteen months, before the fronts became hardened and the trenches dug. These were not battles between entrenched enemies but huge meeting engagements in the field between forces marching shoulder to shoulder. Taking into account the tremendously bloody nature of the final year's fighting, featuring the largest German offensive in the west since 1914 and the great Allied counteroffensive that drove the German army out of France, a surprisingly small share of casualties actually date from the classic "trench years" of 1915–17, about one-fourth of the total for the entire war. This belies the charge that officers on all sides spent the entire war ordering senseless, meat-grinding attacks into the teeth of impregnable defenses.[3]

In fact, battlefield conditions of the Great War were not radically new to military professionals of the day. They had seen them before, recently in fact, in Manchuria and Thrace. The key role of medium and heavy artillery, the invisibility of entrenched defenders, the heavy losses to be expected crossing the fire zone between the trenches: all these were part of the mental lexicon of trained officers in the years preceding the war.[4] This is not to argue that World War I was not so bad, or that the officer corps was brilliant. It does suggest that World War I was not as much of a break in military history as is often assumed.

In challenging old views, one must be careful not to discard the truth they contain. Clearly, something was different about World War I. For two years, the armies of the Great Powers, all of them without exception trained to fight mobile operations, hunkered down in their trenches hurling shells at one another. The stalemate ate away at their morale and turned the infantry on both sides into cannon fodder for artillery bombardment. Whatever a modern observer might say about the matter, the anguished diaries of both commanders and men, asking what had gone wrong and what could be done to restore some semblance of mobility to the front, indicate that there was something different about this conflict.

The first thing that was new about this war was the size of the armies. Armies had been growing dramatically since the nineteenth century, and how to control and direct these masses in combat had been a matter for a great deal of discussion. The armies of World War I, however, dwarfed anything previously seen. By 1914, approximately one in ten Frenchmen were trained and available for military service, and by the start of the war, France alone had over 3 million men in its trained reserve. Russia had almost 4 million. The "million-man army," that creature of the chronicler's mythology ever since Herodotus's day, was now a reality.[5] These numbers should stop anyone from minimizing the problems of battlefield command in 1914 and after. Think of the criticism Lord Raglan has received for his perceived loss of control over the relatively tiny British force on the Alma, and multiply the problems that he faced thirtyfold. It is ridiculous to expect armies of this size, consisting mainly of infantry, to maneuver nimbly across the countryside in the manner of a Napoleonic army containing 75,000 men.

The growth of the mass army caused headaches for the supply services. During the Russo-Japanese War, the Russian artillery expended an average of 87,000 rounds per month, seen then as an incredible figure. Less than a decade later, in the First Balkan War, the Bulgarian army's monthly rate had grown to 254,000 shells. By 1916, the French were averaging 4,500,000 rounds per month.[6] During the weeklong battle for Messines Ridge (June 3–10, 1917), the British guns fired 3,258,000 rounds.[7] Those figures are daunting enough, but it was not a problem of shells alone. The average daily food requirement of a Western army is two pounds of grain per day per man—in other words, 250 tons of grain per day for an army of 250,000 men. Modern armies cannot requisition such quantities from the local farmers. The daily task of the supply services was to find enough supplies, material, and transport to feed and arm a force the size of a good-sized city. The huge freight capacity of the modern railroad made it possible, of course, but the complexity of the problem grew geometrically with every march away from the railhead. All armies still relied on the horse-drawn wagon, with its slow speed and small capacity, to carry supplies to the forward troops. As a result, risky maneuvers that might endanger the moving force's supply lines, or that involved moving an unacceptable distance from the railroad, became increasingly unlikely.[8]

THE OPENING CAMPAIGN IN THE WEST: PLANNING AND ITS LIMITATIONS

Course of the Campaign

True to the spirit of the Russo-Japanese and Balkan Wars, the war opened in an aggressive spirit, with everyone invading everyone else. Each of these operations was the result of detailed prewar planning, and each failed miserably. The classic case is the German Schlieffen Plan, the work of the chief of the General Staff before 1906, Count Alfred von Schlieffen. The result of a lifetime of study on Schlieffen's part, polished and refined by his successors, the object of detailed study at annual maneuvers, the obsession of an entire generation of the world's most gifted staff officers, the plan was a test of the proposition that waging war could be a controlled activity subject to rational analysis and scientific laws.[9]

Schlieffen's basic assumption was that, in any conceivable future conflict, an encircled Germany would be facing a war on two fronts and would have to split its forces against France and Russia. Decisive victory, however, was only possible through concentration of effort; every staff officer of the day knew that. Schlieffen's solution to the two-front war was to split it into two one-front wars. At the start of the conflict, Germany would concentrate its forces against France and overrun its western neighbor in a rapid, six-week campaign. Using Germany's superb rail net, the entire force would then head east and turn on Russia.

Schlieffen also drew up the operational scheme in the west. The *Schwerpunkt* (point of main effort) would be on the German right wing. Heavy forces, three armies containing some fifty-three divisions in all, would be concentrated here, pass through Belgium and the Netherlands, make a great wheel to the west of Paris, then turn and bag the entire French army by coming up on its rear. It had to be a broad sweep, and in fact Schlieffen once stated that the last man on the right should brush his sleeve on the English Channel. By contrast, the left wing would be much weaker. Schlieffen hoped that this weakness might serve to lure the French on in what would ultimately be, for them, a disastrous direction. If they did attack the German left, they would simply be putting themselves deeper into the German sack.

It was a risky plan, requiring a gambler's nerve. What if a great French offensive succeeded in crashing through the weak German forces in Lorraine or Alsace? How would the German civilian population, not to mention the emperor, react? But all the great captains had taught that, in order to concentrate for a decisive blow, one had to risk weakness on some part of the front. To be strong everywhere is to be strong nowhere. The plan gave the Germans as good a chance for decisive victory as existed in 1914.

It is common to blame Schlieffen's successor, Helmuth von Moltke, the nephew of the great man, for having "watered down" *(verwässert)* the Schlieffen Plan. It is true that there was little of the gambler in Moltke the Younger. He removed the Netherlands from the plan for sound diplomatic reasons, meaning that the entire German right wing would now have to squeeze past the Belgian fortress of Liège. Of nine new divisions formed before 1914, he assigned six to strengthen his left, wasting them on a secondary sector and ignoring Schlieffen's reputed last words, "Keep the right wing strong!" Today, however, there are analysts who are willing to argue Moltke's brief. Given the problems the Germans had in supplying their right wing in the course of the campaign, cramming more divisions into it might have had disastrous consequences, without increasing its fighting efficiency.[10]

No army rode off to war better equipped, and that, too, took place on Moltke's watch. Staff studies of the Russo-Japanese and Balkan Wars had shown the importance of howitzers and heavy artillery. Both the Krupp works in Germany and Skoda in Austria-Hungary had conducted what one modern scholar has called "aggressive research and development programs in heavy artillery" before 1914. After 1909, each German division had its own battalion of light field howitzers (105 mm) and each corps its own battalion of heavy field howitzers (150 mm). The German army went to war in 1914 with 2,280 howitzers and larger guns in its arsenal, the largest number by far among the contending powers, and each division possessed the imposing figure of 72 organic guns and howitzers. The British had recognized the importance of the howitzer in the Boer War, and their 1914 division had 18 4.5-inch howitzers, as well as 4 heavy "60-pounders" (120 mm). But the British Expeditionary Force (BEF) went to France with a total of only 89 medium and heavy guns, a total that included 24 old siege guns.[11]

France's own plan for war was far simpler. Plan XVII, as it was called, was a crude, all-out offensive by all available French forces into the lost province of Lorraine.[12] Its very primitivism was a reaction to the debacle of the war with Prussia in 1870, when the French army had run for its fortresses. Now the French soldier would charge forward aggressively, relying on his fiery spirit and the support of the 75-mm field gun. The M 1897 was lightweight, easy to reload, and had a rate of fire of twenty to thirty rounds per minute, perhaps the finest field artillery piece then in existence. Heavy artillery was almost completely absent, since it would only slow down the pace of the advance. In 1914, there were 3,840 75 mm guns in the French army but only 308 guns of larger caliber. Officers who had observed the fighting in the Balkans argued that heavy artillery would be essential in a future conflict. Supporters of the 75 mm triumphed, however, and the French marched off to war outnumbered in heavy guns by seven to one.[13]

Under General Louis de Grandmaison, chief of the Third Bureau of the General Headquarters, the French army had made a virtual cult of offensive operations. Its war-fighting doctrine was the attack and nothing but the attack. This spirit was embodied in Grandmaison's "Regulations for the Conduct of Major Formations," issued in 1913. In ringing phrases, it declared, "The French Army, returning to its traditions, recognizes no law save that of the offensive,"[14] and heralded the bayonet as the supreme weapon of the infantryman. There was little thought given to tactical details. "It is more important to develop a conquering state of mind than to cavil about tactics," Grandmaison once proclaimed.[15] Historians, clear as to what was about to happen, typically offer a ritual denunciation of this doctrine, but in fact it was based on the proven experience of events in Manchuria and

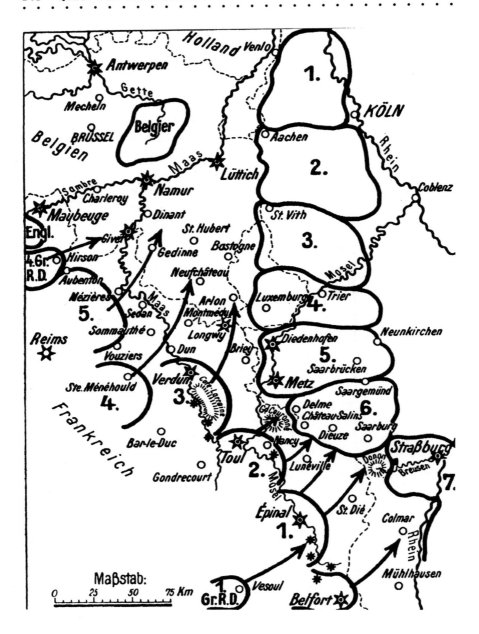

Opening moves of August 1914: the German view. Taken from an issue of the semiofficial journal, the *Militär-Wochenblatt,* this map emphasizes the aggressive nature of French operational plans. Map taken from the *Militär-Wochenblatt* 121, no. 1, July 4, 1936, p. 12.

the Balkans. Even the army's dress reflected its bold, aggressive doctrine: the bright red cap, or *képi;* the blue tunic; the bright red trousers. One thing was for sure—you would know they were coming. The supreme commander of the army was a perfect match for the plan. General Joseph Césaire Joffre was no intellectual, no brilliant theoretician of war, no great handler of mass formations of men. Plan XVII needed none of those things. It needed someone imperturbable, with a stomach for high casualties, and Joffre fit the bill.

After a two-week mobilization, German 1st Army (General Alexander von Kluck) and 2nd Army (General Bernard von Bülow) invaded Belgium.[16] The Germans had already struck Liège with a coup de main by a task force under General Erich Ludendorff. The outlying forts, constructed on modern principles and supposedly impregnable, were pulverized with gigantic 405-mm and 310-mm siege mortars. With Liège reduced, the path was clear for the passage of the German right wing. Entering the country on August 16, the German armies met light resistance from the Belgian army under King Albert.

On August 14, the French 1st Army (General Auguste DuBail) and 2nd Army (General Noël de Castelnau) implemented Plan XVII by invading Lorraine. By August 20 they had advanced ten miles, with 1st Army approaching the main German position at Sarrebourg, and 2nd Army doing the same at Morhange. In both places, aggressive French attacks came to naught, being roughly handled by German artillery and machine gun fire. A mythology has grown up around these encounters, however, that describes them as the slaughter of two entire French armies. This is far from the case. At Sarrebourg, the VII Corps of 1st Army attacked on a seven-mile front.[17] It failed on the right and in the center, coming to a halt at the foot of a long open slope, where the Germans had good fields of fire, but it made some progress on the left, where the terrain was more open. German counterattacks soon drove the French back but in so doing exposed German troops to the fire of French artillery and machine guns. Altogether, the total number of French troops engaged was about 24,000, with 8,000 casualties, an expensive bill, to be sure, but hardly out of line with recent wars. Morhange was on a larger scale, with all three French corps attacking abreast on a twenty-mile front. After an initial advance, with General Ferdinand Foch's XX Corps distinguishing itself, the Germans halted the French drive, then went over to the counterattack. As his center gave way, Castelnau had to retreat. The real culprit here for the French was not simply fire: they often gave as good as they got in that area. Instead, it was their system of organization. Each corps had two divisions, each division two brigades, and each brigade two regiments. In battle, a French commander had to choose: place only one half of his force in the line and the other in reserve, or place nearly everything in the front line with almost no reserve.

In Lorraine, the French had attacked with maximum strength in the front line and without a proper reserve. The disruption caused by combat found them without any fresh reserve to commit, and thus vulnerable to a German counterstroke.

Although Joffre was by now aware of the danger from Belgium, he underestimated the scale of the German sweep. He now ordered two full French armies (3rd and 4th) into the Ardennes forest in eastern Belgium. On August 22 they crashed head-on into the advancing German 4th and 5th Armies, the pivot of the German wheel. A confused battle now took place in the dark forest, in the midst of a thick fog. It was a true soldiers' battle, in which the French were forced back with heavy losses; 3rd Colonial Division, for example, lost 11,000 men and all three of its generals. In the aftermath, French 5th Army commander, General Lanrezac, detected activity west of the forest. To counter it, he advanced to Namur at the bend of the Meuse and Sambre Rivers.[18] On August 23 he found himself under heavy attack on both flanks, as German 2nd and 3rd Armies advanced on either side of him. They hit Lanrezac hard, and he was lucky to get out of it with much of his command intact. All these "battles of the frontiers" had been disasters for France, and Joffre was still unaware that one whole other German army was bearing down on him.

It was the British who would discover Kluck's 1st Army. On August 12 the BEF had arrived in France under Sir John French, coming up on Lanrezac's left. It was small, just 100,000 men formed into two corps, but it was a well-trained and well-drilled force of expert marksmen—the legacy of the Boer War. On August 23 the BEF and General Kluck blundered into each other at the Belgian town of Mons.[19] Sir John French did not know that there were Germans this far west. Kluck did not know that the British were in Belgium; clearly, the "fog of war" lay heavy. A daylong battle took place among the coal and slag heaps of Mons. Although the British, drawn up behind the Condé-Mons canal, inflicted heavy casualties on the attackers, German numbers eventually triumphed. The British withdrew, joining Lanrezac to the east. The "Great Retreat," two hard weeks of falling back before superior German forces, now began.

According to the Germans' prewar plans, their right wing was to be on the French border on the twenty-second day after mobilization, and this had been achieved. Now, however, three factors combined to wreck the German timetable. First, after crushing Plan XVII in the south, German 6th and 7th Armies launched a counterstroke of their own toward Nancy; 5th Army, in the center, did the same toward Verdun. In neither case did the army commanders inform Moltke beforehand. This is not entirely shocking, since the essence of *Auftragstaktik* was to allow army commanders latitude to seize favorable opportunities. On both occasions, however, they managed to talk Moltke into reinforcing their improvised attacks with fresh troops that had been slated for his right wing. Neither attack succeeded. The French, as inept as they had proved in the attack, proved to be tenacious defenders of their major cities.

Second, on August 12 the Russian army had invaded East Prussia, weeks ahead of Schlieffen's prediction. On August 20, Moltke received a request for reinforcements from General Max von Prittwitz, the jumpy commander of German 8th Army defending the province. Moltke dispatched two corps from the western front to East Prussia. With the fall of the fortress of Namur to Bülow's 2nd Army, XI Corps and the Guard Reserve Corps were now available for other duties. Along with the 8th Cavalry Division, they entrained and began the journey to the east. By the time they arrived, the German army had already won the great victory at Tannenberg.[20] These troops, nearly 100,000 men, were simply wasted.

Finally, as they drove into northern France, both Kluck and Bülow had become uneasy about the amount of resistance they were meeting. On August 29, for example, there had been a nearly suicidal attack by the French 5th Army at Guise. Lanrezac turned on Kluck and was in turn flanked by Bülow. The Germans drove him back with terrific losses, but he had made an impact. On September 1, Kluck decided that, for security reasons, he would remain closely aligned with Bülow. Rather than pass to the west of Paris, he would wheel to the northeast of the city, essentially abandoning the Schlieffen Plan.

Joffre had stayed calm during this month of catastrophe, sacking failed generals, including forty-two of his seventy-four divisional commanders, shifting troops by rail from his shattered right to his increasingly threatened left. With Kluck just fifteen miles away, the government decided to abandon Paris. Joffre insisted that it be held, however, declaring the city an entrenched camp under General Joseph Galliéni. Joffre also formed two new armies, the 6th in Paris (General Michel Maunoury) and the 9th under General Foch, who had proved himself in the fighting in Lorraine, the latter entering the line between the 4th and 5th Armies.

On September 3, French air patrols spotted Kluck's wheel to the northeast of Paris, military aviation's first great moment. Spotting an opportunity, Galliéni ordered 6th Army to attack Kluck's open right wing along the Marne River.[21] The attack began on September 6 as part of a general Allied offensive. This was France's last-ditch effort. Joffre threw in his final reserves, even requisitioning Paris taxis to rush units to the front. Kluck had to wheel again, this time to the southwest, to meet the thrust out of Paris by Maunoury, while attacks by French 5th Army (now under General Louis Franchet d'Esperey) forced Bülow back slightly to the northeast. A twenty-mile gap had opened between the two German armies of the right wing. Into this gap the three corps of the BEF now advanced: III Corps (General Pulteney) on the left, II Corps (General Sir Horace Smith-Dorrien) in the center, and I Corps (General Sir Douglas Haig) on the right. Although small pickets of German cavalry were there to delay them, and the British moved quite slowly, just twenty-five miles in three days, the entire German right wing was in danger of being cut off.

At this point, with the fate of the war in the balance, Moltke came unglued. He was far behind the line at Koblenz, over 100 miles from the fighting, and confused by a horde of conflicting reports and rumors, and his fears got the better of him. With the battle raging but still undecided, he sent an aide, Colonel Hentsch, to the front on September 8. A sort of "human telegram" who could not be taken back once dispatched, Hentsch was ordered to coordinate a general withdrawal of all five German armies if he deemed it necessary, with "full powers to give orders in the name of the Supreme Command."[22] On the evening of September 8, he spoke with a despondent Bülow at his headquarters at Montmort. Bülow felt certain that Kluck should retreat and told Hentsch that he was about to do so, at any rate. Early the next morning, Hentsch set out for Chézy, 1st Army headquarters, just twenty-five miles away. It was a depressing trip through the chaos that was the German rear area by this time, and it took him nearly five hours to cover the distance. Kluck was not in, so Hentsch spoke to his chief of staff, General von Kuhl. As they were conferring, a message came in that Bülow had ordered a retreat. Without consulting with Kluck directly, Hentsch gave his fateful orders: retreat. The exhausted German forces began withdrawing in good order back to the Aisne River. The "race to the sea," the digging of the trenches, and the years of stalemate were the result. The war was far from over, and over 500,000 men were dead.

The Schlieffen Plan Evaluated

A great deal has been written about the failure of the Schlieffen Plan. Critics have faulted the plan itself for failing to deal adequately with Paris, the railroad hub and the natural rallying point for French reserves. Passing to either side of the great city was a risk. Moltke has come in for his share of the blame, as well. According to the insightful critique of one German staff officer, Moltke was the "general against his will," lacking the blazing fire needed for command, failing to impose his will on his army commanders or on the campaign itself.[23] During the Marne, Moltke lost control of his battle, allowing a mere colonel to give the most fateful orders in all of German military history. Alone in his office, far away from the action, bearing the burden of the entire destiny of Germany on his slumped shoulders, his desk piled high with a mountain of daily dispatches that he had no time to read, let alone digest, Moltke was perhaps the first victim of a new twentieth-century problem: information overload.[24] The solution to the problem would have to wait for new technology, in this case the computer. Finally, it has become customary to mention the impact of new technology upon war. With new weapons like machine guns and rapid-fire artillery generating tremendous firepower, even successful attacks took huge losses, leaving the victor too weak to pursue and destroy the foe.

And yet, none of these supposedly "new" weapons were really new. Both machine guns and rapid-fire artillery had made their debut over ten years earlier, in the Russo-Japanese War. Military men had studied their use, analyzed their strengths and weaknesses, and argued about their impact, obsessively, for a whole decade. The literature available on the Balkan War alone was already voluminous by 1914. The firepower had been awesome, but its impact had not been surprising in the least to the professional soldier.

Once again, as in the great operational maneuvers in Manchuria and Thrace, the failure of the Schlieffen Plan was due more to software issues than to hardware. A German critique in 1936 argued that the campaign fell victim to a series of "preconceived ideas." Kluck held troops out of the fights at Mons and Namur because of his belief that the British were planning a landing in his rear at Dunkirk and Zeebrugge, even though the only real evidence to support his fear was a long-out-of-date intelligence report. In this way he squandered a chance at a strategic victory: destruction of the French 5th Army and the BEF at the same time. At the Marne, staff officers of both 1st Army and 2nd Army reported to Colonel Hentsch that their neighboring army was in trouble, when in fact both were actually winning their respective encounters.[25]

A closer look at the campaign shows that it was above all a failure of command and logistics. The problems of directing a mass army in the field and supplying it in enemy territory many miles away from its railheads led to the loss of German momentum after Mons. Supply difficulties were much more important than simplistic assertions about an impenetrable "storm of steel." It is true that no German unit ran out of supplies on the Marne. It is equally clear that shortages of all sorts, and the anxieties of the commanders as they marched ever farther from their railhead, were on the rise. It was hard enough to procure bread for the men; the memoirs of German supply officers also speak repeatedly of the difficulty of procuring oats for the hundreds of thousands of horses in the field. The Aachen-Landen line alone was responsible for 445,000 animals, requiring 2,700 tons of oats and 3,200 tons of hay per day. The supply services were simply overextended, with all three armies of the German right wing drawing supply from one single rail line. On September 4, the lead units of Kluck's 1st Army were at Coulommiers-Esternay, while the railhead was at Saint-Quentin, an astounding 85 miles away. Even worse, many of its stores were still gathered at Cambrai, the previous railhead, still farther to the rear. On the same day, Bülow's 2nd Army was in even worse shape, 105 miles from its railhead. Schlieffen himself had said on numerous occasions that 75 miles was the maximum distance that an army could advance away from its railhead, and that figure had to have been in Moltke's mind as he looked at the situation maps during the Marne. These unpleasant facts, in turn, probably helped to generate the aura of gloom that Colonel Hentsch detected during his visits to the various army headquarters. A modern authority on the topic has reached a judicious conclusion on the supply situation:

> Overburdened and at times close to collapse, as they were, there is no direct evidence to suggest that the failure of the railways to carry sufficient traffic, or to keep up with the pace of the advance, played any significant part in the German defeat on the Marne. Had that battle gone in their favor, however, there is every reason to believe that the state of the railway network would have prevented the Germans from following up their victory and penetrating further into France.[26]

In the final analysis, there was little that was completely new here, outside of the absolutely massive size of the forces engaged. The German offensive had met with success at the outset because it concentrated far greater force at the point of contact than the French did. As the operation unfolded, the Germans advanced farther and farther away from their supply sources, while the French and British retreated onto theirs. At a time when the energy of the footsore German columns was beginning to lag, the Allies were collecting their second wind. That almost imperceptible moment when the momentum swings from one side to the other, what Clausewitz called the "culmination point" of the campaign, had taken place on the Marne. A more determined commander than Moltke might have tried to rescue the situation, but it is highly doubtful that anyone could have solved the command and supply problems that had become endemic to modern war.

CATASTROPHE: THE RUSSIAN INVASION OF GERMANY, 1914

Russian war planning was in the hands of General Vladimir Sukhomlinov, since 1908 chief of the General Staff and war minister. Opinions on his abilities differ widely. According to one view, he was a hardworking and conscientious officer who had done a great deal to improve the army since 1908: overseeing a strategic railroad-building plan to improve transport to the western frontier; increasing the number of machine guns in Russian units; making great improvements in the food and clothing of the Russian soldier. His supporters grant that he had available to him large sums of money in the form of French loans (equivalent to 104 million British pounds in 1913 alone), but they argue that he invested them wisely in ammunition and supplies.[27] There is another view, however, exemplified in the reports of the French ambassador to St. Petersburg in 1914, Maurice Paléologue. Sukhomlinov, he wrote, had risen to the top of the army "by being at once obsequious and entertaining, by funny stories and acts of buffoonery, and by avoiding serious or unpleasant matters."[28] Rumors in the capital had him siphoning off money earmarked for defense to support his young wife's passion for glittering balls, gowns, and nightlife.[29] Whatever the truth about his character, Sukhomlinov's plans for war were certainly simple: the Russian army would attack both Germany and Austria-Hungary as soon as possible after the outbreak of war. Specifically, he promised France that he would field 800,000 men within fifteen days of mobilization, and then attack Germany with all available men.

By contrast, Russia's operational plans for war with Germany were quite complex—perhaps too much so. Two armies would launch a simultaneous invasion of the German province of East Prussia: 1st Army (General von Rennenkampf) would advance from the east; 2nd Army (General Samsonov) from the south. In the course of their concentric advance into the province, the two armies would catch the German forces between them in a gigantic pincer, surround and destroy them, then drive on the fortress and provincial capital of Königsberg. It was a sound plan, designed along Moltkean lines, but also a risky one. As the two armies advanced, they would be isolated from one another, separated by the fifty-mile chain of the Masurian Lakes, thickly forested and nearly impassable. Coordination between the two armies was the key, but it was also bound to be a problem. When the attack had last been war gamed, in April 1914, Rennenkampf had moved more quickly than Samsonov. If that happened in real life, the Germans would be able to use their superior railroad net to attack and destroy the invading armies one at a time. Defending East Prussia was just one German army, the 8th (General von Prittwitz), but it had at its disposal seventeen double-track rail lines, able to carry 500 troop trains per day (i.e., sixteen divisions). By contrast, the Russians had only six lines serving the entire Warsaw district (the zone of operations for Samsonov's 2nd Army), with a capacity of only 140 trains.

Rennenkampf crossed the border first, on August 12. Cossacks, the Russian light cavalry arm, sacked the German frontier village of Marggrabowa, leading to panic on the part of the East Prussian civilian population and a great deal of anguish in 8th Army headquarters. By August 17 all three corps of 1st Army were in the province. In the south, however, Samsonov was moving much more slowly. Before 1914, the Russians had deliberately left the roads and railroads in Poland in bad shape, as a hindrance to a German invasion. The roads, which were nothing more than sandy tracks through the pine forests, soon collapsed under the weight of men, horses, and wagons. The heat was stifling, and by August 19, Samsonov had barely crossed the border. The Russian plan had already begun to unravel.

Still, Rennenkampf was a force to be reckoned with. The 8th Army's gifted general staff officer I (operations), General Max von Hoffmann, drew up a plan to ambush 1st Army at Gumbinnen. Fortified positions were carefully prepared on the Angerapp River. Once Rennenkampf, whose reconnaissance effort appeared to the Germans to be feeble at best, had entered the fortified zone, a coordinated assault of three German corps (I, XVII, and I Reserve Corps) would pin and destroy him. It was a sound plan, squarely in the tradition of technical excellence for which the German General Staff was renowned. Unfortunately, it failed to take into account the commander of the German I Corps, General Hermann von François. He was an East Prussian native, as were most of the men in his force. He rejected any plan to surrender "the sacred soil of the Fatherland to the Cossack hordes."[30] On August 16, François ordered an advance to the east, telling an angry Prittwitz that "the nearer to Russia I engage the enemy the less the risk to German territory."[31] German territory, of course, was not the point. By August 17, he was at Stallupönen on the Russian border. Here he fought a brief, successful engagement against the lead units of 1st Army, capturing some 3,000 before retiring. Still, he had wrecked Hoffmann's plan, and in the end he had not stopped Rennenkampf, who now resumed his westward advance.

On August 19, Prittwitz learned that the 2nd Army was over the border. Facing its five infantry corps was just one German corps (XX Corps). With time running out, he decided to abandon the original plan of waiting for Rennenkampf to come to him and instead ordered an immediate attack on Rennenkampf at Gumbinnen for August 20. Due to the suddenness of the order, German troops had to make an overnight march followed by an attack in broad daylight. It went nowhere. The massed fire of the Russian artillery inflicted heavy casualties, and the Germans had to retreat. With his strategy in ruins, Prittwitz panicked, running to his office and telephoning

Moltke with news of the defeat. Moltke promised him reinforcements. Prittwitz now emerged from his office and announced to his astonished staff that East Prussia would have to be evacuated. All forces must retreat immediately behind the Vistula River. Hoffmann pulled out a compass to prove that the Russians were closer to the river than the Germans were. Prittwitz insisted that his order be obeyed. Although it is no doubt apocryphal that Hoffmann asked to be instructed on "the execution of a maneuver that was geographically impossible," other observers have him bursting into fits of tears and rage and tearing off his decorations in frustration and despair. All in all, it was a bad day in the headquarters of 8th Army.[32]

Moltke had also made another decision: to relieve Prittwitz as 8th Army commander. His replacement would be General Paul von Hindenburg, aged sixty-seven, who came out of retirement to accept the post. While it is true that he was chosen more for his calm demeanor than for any particular military brilliance, it is equally true that he had not risen so high in the command structure of the German army by accident. His chief of staff was the brilliant, prickly, and slightly unstable General Erich Ludendorff.

By the time Hindenburg and Ludendorff arrived in East Prussia, Hoffmann had already drawn up a new plan. Rennenkampf had halted after Gumbinnen, waiting for supplies to come up. His orders to his units had been intercepted by the Germans, an easy thing to do, since the Russians were transmitting en clair. Hoffmann now decided to turn to the south and smash poor Samsonov—advancing blindly into enemy territory with open flanks. Since he was known as a dawdler, there was a constant stream of messages from supreme headquarters *(Stavka)* telling him to hurry, messages that the Germans were reading.

By August 25, all three corps that had fought at Gumbinnen were arriving in the south: I Corps moving by rail onto the right of XX Corps, I Reserve and XVII Corps force-marching onto the left. Samsonov was unaware of all this, and on August 26 he gave orders to his units in the center to continue their advance against XX Corps. On the morning of August 27, François attacked and drove in Samsonov's left, I Reserve and XVII Corps his right. By evening, the Germans had encircled most of 2nd Army, 150,000 men at the start of the campaign, near the village of Tannenberg. Cut off from home, 2nd Army now dissolved into a panic-stricken mob. Herded by German machine gun fire into a smaller and smaller perimeter, over 90,000 surrendered. Tales of hordes of Russian soldiers blundering into swamps or lakes in their blind panic to escape the trap and drowning are surely fictitious. The reality had been bad enough, however. "The Emperor trusted me," Samsonov told an aide. "How can I face him again?"[33] He went off into the forest alone and shot himself.

DOUBLE DISASTER:
THE HABSBURG ARMY IN SERBIA AND GALICIA

Austrian plans for war were drawn up by General Franz Conrad von Hötzendorf. History has been kinder to him than he deserves. Despite the disastrous results of the campaigns he conducted, he is usually described as an able strategist, a man who devised clever plans but who lacked the army to carry them out.[34] The description begs the question of what to call a general who designs plans too complex for his own men to execute. He had divided his forces into three groups before 1914: A-Group (A-Staffel), twenty-seven infantry and nine cavalry divisions deployed against Russia; Minimum Group Balkans (Minimalgruppe Balkan), nine infantry divisions opposite Serbia; and B-Group (B-Staffel), a strategic reserve of eleven infantry and one cavalry divisions. Conrad's primary decision when the war began was what to do with B-Group. In case of a war with Serbia alone and Russia neutral, he would add B-Group to Minimum Group Balkans, that is, direct it against Serbia. Three Austrian armies would overwhelm the Serbs, while three more stood on the defensive in Galicia against possible Russian intervention. In case of a war against Russia and Serbia together, he would add B-Group to A-Group, that is, direct his reserve against Russia. Only two armies would face the Serbs, standing on the defensive or making holding attacks, while the other four would launch a grand offensive out of Galicia, driving across the base of the great Polish salient. In conjunction with a German drive to the south, something that he had often discussed with German staff officers before 1914, this offensive would cut off and destroy the great mass of Russian forces in the salient. On May 12, 1914, however, Conrad and Moltke had met at Carlsbad to discuss such combined operations in the event of war, and Moltke had warned him bluntly at that time not to expect any German help until six weeks after the start of operations, that is, until mid-September.

As the crisis unfolded, Conrad first gave orders for B-Group to mobilize against Serbia, apparently out of fear of provoking Russia. When it became clear that Germany was concentrating against France and could offer him no aid in the east for the foreseeable future, he changed plans. The troops of B-Group, almost on the Serbian frontier, had to scramble back onto their trains for the long ride to Galicia. One whole army, the 2nd, missed the fighting in Serbia and arrived in Galicia just in time to get caught up in a disaster.[35]

Despite its tiny population and resource base, Serbia was much more efficiently mobilized for war than the Habsburg Empire and, in fact, put more men in the field than the Austrian army did during this campaign.[36] The Austrians fielded two armies, 5th and 6th, 140,000 men in all, under the overall command of Field Marshal Oskar Potiorek, against a total force of some 185,000 Serbs, organized into three armies. Leading the Serbs was their *vojvoda* (roughly equivalent to "field marshal"), the hero of the Balkan Wars, Radomir Putnik. Seriously ill and commanding in the field from a stretcher, Putnik knew every inch of his land well enough that he was often able to dictate orders during the campaign without consulting a map.[37] Terrain would also aid the Serbs, consisting of a series of deep, unfordable rivers backed by rugged mountains.

Conrad's initial bungling also helped. The Austrian operational plans for war with Serbia alone had originally called for simultaneous thrusts by 2nd Army from the north and by 5th and 6th Armies from the northwest. The 2nd Army would cross the Danube River and advance on the capital, Belgrade, while 5th and 6th would cross the rugged country of the Drina and Sava Rivers in northwestern Serbia, drive into the Jadar River Valley, and cut the country in half. With 2nd Army gone, however, the plan for an attack into Serbia was completely unhinged and should have been scrapped altogether.

On August 12, both Austrian armies crossed the Drina and Sava Rivers into Serbia. Putnik had expected any Austrian offensive to come from the Danube (i.e., from the north), and the Serb armies were facing in that direction. In the opening days of the campaign, Putnik had to redeploy his forces a full ninety degrees, so that they were now facing to the west. It was a neat maneuver that his experienced staff handled with aplomb. Putnik let the Austrians advance, then launched a sharp counterattack on August 16 to 19 that sent them reeling back across the Drina. It was a well-planned attack, with 3rd Army stopping the Austrian drive along the Jadar toward Valjevo, while 2nd Army hit their left flank and rear near Mount Cer. It was the first Allied victory of the war.[38]

After an abortive Serb drive into Austrian Bosnia, Potiorek opened a second Austrian offensive on September 7. It succeeded in establishing two small bridgeheads in the Drina-Sava triangle. For the next ten days, both sides slugged it out along the river line. Attack and counterattack followed in rapid succession, just the sort of campaign that small Serbia could not sustain. Putnik was taking heavy losses that he could not replace, and the ammunition supply situation soon became dire. On September 18, he ordered a general retreat.

Although the weather was appalling, with snow and rain turning Serbia's dirt roads into muddy tracks, the Austrian 6th Army pushed some fifty miles into the Serbian interior. By November 5, it was on the Kolubara River, and over the next few weeks it pushed across the river, by then in its early flood stage. Putnik had to continue his retreat and swing his defenses away from Belgrade. The capital fell to Austrian 5th Army on December 2.

A situation map would have shown Putnik being caught in a nutcracker between two Austrian armies, but the wily Serbian commander was not yet finished. Reconnaissance told him that the Austrian columns had become seriously overextended as they crossed the Kolubara and entered the mountainous Serbian interior. In addition, the two invading armies were not really close enough to render each other mutual assistance. An ammunition shipment had finally arrived in Serbia on December 2, coming from France through neutral Greece. Rallying his exhausted troops one last time, he launched a furious counterattack the very next day, hitting the right wing of the Austrian 6th Army, dangling into the Rudnik Mountains. A projected counterattack from the Austrian 5th Army, intended to relieve the situation, never materialized, as a sudden thaw made the roads impassable. The Austrian 6th Army, exhausted, freezing, facing supply difficulties (with many men on one-third rations), and with a river in full flood stage at their back, simply came apart. They scurried back whence they had come, completely evacuating Serbia by December 15. The campaign was an utter disaster for the Austrians: losses amounted to 270,000 (of 450,000 men) and an incalculable amount of prestige. Serb losses had also been heavy, around 150,000 of the original 200,000.

While this disaster was brewing, Conrad launched his grand offensive versus the Russians in Galicia.[39] His embarrassing mobilization shuffle had left him with only three armies, instead of the projected four, which might have barely sufficed to defend Galicia while his main body snuffed out the Serbs. It was certainly not enough for a general offensive. The largest Austrian army was the 1st, under General Viktor von Dankl. Forming the left of the Austrian line, it had the most ambitious orders: march north, destroy whatever opposition he encountered, and occupy the rail line between Warsaw and Russian proper, cutting off all Russian forces in the great Polish salient. Dankl had most of the Austrian army's artillery for this purpose. The 4th Army, under General Moritz Ritter von Auffenberg, formed the Austrian center. It was to advance alongside and behind Dankl, echeloned to protect his right flank from any Russian forces in the area. Forming the Austrian right was the 3rd Army under General Rudolf von Brudermann. His orders were to defend against any Russian moves from the southeast. He interpreted those orders liberally, however, and the start of operations found him advancing to the northeast and east. Conrad's fumbling had already opened a considerable gap between Brudermann and the other two armies; Brudermann's own actions made the problem worse.

By contrast, the Russian army was large enough to undertake two great offensives at the same time. While the invasion of East Prussia was still under way, Russian plans called for an invasion of the Austrian province of Galicia.

If victorious, the Russians would advance through the Carpathian moun-
tain passes and into the fertile Hungarian plain, source of most of Austria-
Hungary's food supply. An advance into the very heartland of the Habsburg
Empire, it was hoped, would knock it out of the war. Under the command
of General Nikolai Ivanov, the Southwest Front consisted of four armies,
from left to right, 8th Army (General Alexei Brusilov); 3rd Army (General
N. V. Ruszky); 5th Army (General P. A. Plehve); and 4th Army (General
A. E. Zalts). Ivanov's plan was for the two armies on the left (8th and 3rd)
to attack into eastern Galicia, take the Austrian armies in western Galicia in
the flank and rear, and sweep the province clean of Austrian forces. Thus,
both forces planned to hold with their right and strike with their left: a battle
of the revolving door.

The Austrian advance opened on August 19. Over the next four days,
Dankl advanced without opposition some fifty miles inside Russian Poland.
Reading accounts of the offensive today, it seems like something out of a
dream. Every night his regiments would set up camp, the tents in perfect
rows, the orderlies providing linen and gourmet meals to the officers. There
was no attempt at scouting or reconnaissance. On August 23, he blundered
into Russian 4th Army (General Zalts) at Krasnik, and in a sharp three-day
battle, managed to get around the Russian right flank and force Zalts to
retreat. Zalts now had the distinction of being the first general in the war to
be sacked, replaced by A. E. Evert. Nervous about the encounter at Krasnik,
Ivanov responded by ordering 5th Army (Plehve) to swing down on Dankl
and to outflank and destroy him. As Plehve wheeled, however, he found
himself under heavy attack by Auffenberg. Coming up in echelon on Dankl's
right, he saw a sight that surely was not in the military textbooks: an entire
enemy army apparently unaware of his presence, turning and offering him
its flank. Auffenberg drove in Plehve's flanks and for a time threatened to
surround him completely. Conrad, surveying the situation, was ecstatic. The
anticipated decisive victory seemed within grasp. He even detached several
divisions from Brudermann, on the far Austrian right, to aid in the destruction of Russian 5th Army.

He was all the more shocked on August 26, when Ruszky and Brusilov
struck in the southeast, simply overwhelming Brudermann's weakened
army along the Gnila Lipa River. In four days of fighting (August 26–30),
3rd Army dissolved into a panicked horde of refugees. The provincial capital of Galicia, Lemberg, fell to the Russians on September 3. By now, lead
units of the Russian 3rd Army were actually behind Auffenberg. Conrad did
his best to stave off the collapse of his entire position, ordering Auffenberg
to march south to the assistance of 3rd Army, but this did not solve the basic
problem: Conrad was operating with an order of battle that was light by one

.ire army. A huge gap now opened between Auffenberg and Dankl. On .eptember 6, Plehve was ordered into the gap at Rava Russka. Over the next five days (September 6–10), he drove into Auffenberg's flank and rear. With the two armies on his right nearly surrounded, Conrad now ordered a general retreat. Under heavy Russian pressure, the retreat dissolved into a rout that did not end until it had reached the crest of the Carpathians. Galicia was evacuated. Only the fortress of Przemysl held out, though it was encircled and besieged by the Russians. It would fall in early 1915.

The Galician campaign was a disaster for Austria-Hungary. The Habsburg army suffered at least 400,000 casualties (300,000 killed or wounded, some 100,000 prisoners) and lost huge amounts of precious equipment. It never really recovered. Although it held its own on the defensive, it could never undertake offensive operations without the support of its German ally. In less than one month of fighting, Conrad had destroyed his own army. Before the war, he had repeatedly said that the army was strong enough to overwhelm Serbia, or to launch a great offensive out of Galicia against the Russians. When war came, however, he had tried to do both—with catastrophic results.

THE TRENCH YEARS: FROM DECISION TO ATTRITION

All the campaigns of 1914 shared one characteristic: they were highly mobile, not at all the stereotype commonly associated with World War I. In each of them, the opponents sought, and often found, the flank of their adversary. There were times when virtually every participant seemed to have decisive victory within his grasp, only to see some dramatic twist of fate, or incredible blunder, snatch it away. In the end, all of these operations came to naught, and the world would have to endure four full years of bloodletting before reaching a decision.

In the end, it was the inadequacies of the mass army that rendered a decisive victory impossible. They had far exceeded the maximum possible size for effective command and control and supply, given the primitive technology available in those areas in 1914. This helps to explain the seemingly inexplicable events in all of these campaigns: the mutual offering of army flanks in Galicia, Kluck's decision to wheel to the southeast and offer his army's flank to Paris, the complete lack of flank security on the part of Russian 2nd Army as it entered East Prussia. It also helps explain the incredibly poor reconnaissance that preceded all the major battles. While reconnaissance suffered greatly from the continuing decline of cavalry as a battlefield arm, the real problem was that these armies were so large, their maneuvers so lumbering, that rarely were they prepared to take advantage of a favorable opportunity divulged by reconnaissance. Consider the words of Schlieffen himself. Often accused of an overly simplistic view regarding command, he had written the following in 1901:

> According to current theory, modern means of communication have made the command of million-man armies as easy and sure as an earlier corps of 15,000 to 20,000 men. While this may be true in one's own land, the telegraph will not suffice in enemy territory; it has already proven itself unreliable in maneuvers. Wet weather and difficult roads stop the cyclist; automobiles are subject to endless difficulties; the thick woods of East Prussia stop the light rays of the optical telegraph and the electrical signals of the radio telegraph alike. It is to be hoped that improvements in these areas will make the distribution of orders easier and simpler. At present, however, the large armies consist of masses that are ever more difficult to control and ever less maneuverable.[40]

Indeed, you set these armies in motion and took your chances. Few of the commanding generals of 1914 were especially incompetent, despite the mountain of literature that argues that they were. It is surely no accident that the Germans—whose rail network and command system were the best that the world had ever seen—won their only decisive victory in the theater where their force commitment was the smallest: East Prussia.

The rest of the war would bear out Schlieffen's warning. The trench years were ahead, in which decisive victory on the battlefield seemed like an impossible dream. Attempts to achieve decisive victory, as at Gallipoli or the Somme, all pretty much played out the same way. The attackers planned for the offensive in the grand style, and those attacks went nowhere in operational terms, a combination of the same factors we have already seen in 1914: defensive firepower, supply, command, and the inability of the mass army to maneuver. The years 1915–17 have come to stand for military futility; for the mass slaughter of attacking infantry in a hail of enemy machine gun and artillery fire; for soldiers rotting in the mud and blood of the trenches, literally driven mad by the nonstop shelling, in which "gains" consisted of a few yards of shell-scarred, worthless earth.[41]

In contrast to the war's early years, this commonly held view is true, and there will never be a successful attempt to revise it. The war was not merely a graveyard of individual reputations, as this or that commander proved his incompetence, insensitivity to casualties, or both. It was almost the graveyard for the entire profession of arms. The trench years witnessed the collapse of the very concept of military operations as they had been traditionally defined: forces engaging in fire and movement in order to bring about a decisive battle against the enemy's main force. There was fire, all right—

more than enough to go around—but movement seemed to have disappeared, perhaps forever. In the end, all that would be left was attrition, hostile armies grinding one another to pieces. For the rest of the war, there was no such thing as an "operational objective," at least as those had been previously defined; the killing of the enemy had become the end in itself.[42]

The turn to attrition found its classic expression in the great German offensive against Verdun. In February 1916, the German supreme commander, Erich von Falkenhayn, launched Germany's largest offensive since the Marne. The target was Verdun, the great and historic French fortress city astride the Meuse River.[43] Operation Gericht marked a break with the classic Prussian-German tradition, in that it was intended from the start as an exercise in attrition, not as a decisive operation. He intended to attack on a narrow front against an objective "for the retention of which the French General Staff would be compelled to throw in every man they have." He did not intend to take Verdun, just threaten it so seriously the French would have to defend it. Pinned in front of Verdun, the French would be helpless targets for Germany's superior artillery. The guns would grind them up, "bleeding them dry," in Falkenhayn's grisly phrase. As to Verdun itself, using words that should be hung up on the wall of every military academy on the planet, Falkenhayn actually said that "it is immaterial whether we reach our goal." The force given this thankless task was a single German army, the 5th, under the command of Crown Prince August Wilhelm.

Gericht began with a stupendous artillery barrage, the heaviest ever seen in the history of war—1,400 guns on a front about eight miles wide, ranging from field guns to Germany's superheavy 305-mm and 420-mm siege mortars. It began at 7:15 A.M. and simply obliterated the French positions facing 5th Army. At 4:00 P.M., the bombardment reached its height, lasting for another forty-five minutes, and then ceased after having vaporized thousands of defenders, or in many cases buried them alive. The German infantry now went into the attack. It was not a full-scale infantry assault, involving as it did just six divisions along four and a half miles of front between Bois d'Haumont and Herbebois on the left bank of the Meuse. The few surviving groups of French soldiers were therefore able to delay the German advance out of all proportion to their numbers.

The contradictions in Falkenhayn's ill-conceived plan were already evident. Although taking Verdun was not on his list of priorities, Falkenhayn could hardly tell that to his troops. For everyone involved—from the foot soldiers of the 5th Army, to the crown prince commanding it, to the civilians at home—Verdun represented the great prize from the start, the only objective that could possibly justify the huge outlay of German blood and resources. Even Falkenhayn soon became blinded to the requirements of his original plan, if he had ever believed in it in the first place. He threw more and more men into the fray. Casualties rose into the hundreds of thousands by the onset of summer. Fifth Army crept closer to Verdun but never did take it. There were times when the French position in front of Verdun hung by the most slender of threads, but hold it did, amid scenes of carnage that had never been seen before and probably never will be again. While in terms of the actual operations, there is little to study here, there certainly was drama to spare. Verdun, in fact, became something larger than a key fortress town—it became a symbol of French will, a living, breathing manifestation of the French soul, enduring the terrible pounding of the best that modern German technology could throw at it.

Not that France was averse to using its own technology. During much of the battle, Verdun's lifeline to the outside world was the single paved road coming up to the city from Bar-le-Duc in the south, which became known as the "Sacred Way" (La Voie sacrée). And just as the airplane had played a key role in helping France at the Marne, now it was the automobile: a nearly constant stream of motor vehicles of all sorts coming up the Voie. They carried the supplies, the ammunition, and above all the warm bodies of fresh replacement troops to the cauldron at Verdun. Under constant shelling, these drivers became as much a part of the battle of Verdun as any poilu in his stinking trench at the front. Even the trucks were forced to be heroic; when one failed, crews simply pushed it off the road to make way for the next, sacrificing it so that France might live.

Despite the expenditure of so much high explosive, in the end the difference in this battle was leadership. While command (the ability to control a huge force under modern conditions) was a struggle for everyone in the war, leadership (the ability to size up a situation, act decisively, and inspire confidence among one's subordinates) was present in abundance. After initial scenes of panic, French defenses stiffened, especially after the appointment of General Philippe Pétain as commander of the Verdun sector. Two phrases of his have entered the political-military lexicon: "Ils ne passeront pas!" he said, when things looked bleakest for the French defenders. No, they would not pass. And second, when the French had received their second wind and the spirit of the German troops was beginning to lag, "On les aura!" (We'll get 'em!). Petain could see what was at stake if Verdun fell. France's morale, shaky after nearly two years of disaster in the field, might crack altogether. He succeeded in restoring the spirit of the French troops in front of Verdun at a critical moment and has a secure place in the pantheon of French heroes, despite the unfortunate role he played in World War II.

Falkenhayn, by contrast, lost control of the battle quite early. As the fighting intensified, in fact, the battlefield itself began to grow. At first, the Germans had limited their attack to the east bank of the Meuse.[44] Very soon, flanking fire from a small clump of woods on the west bank (nicknamed, of all things, "Mort Homme") necessitated an assault here as well. This was in March. Then, the assault on the Mort Homme began to take flanking fire from a small hill even farther to the left, Côte 304. Falkenhayn used an entire division, the 11th Bavarian, to assault it, trying to flank it from the west. As Falkenhayn strung out the operation farther to his right, he also had to pay attention to his extreme left. Here fire from a group of concrete fortifications, foremost among them Fort Vaux, was also hitting his infantry in the flank. He therefore assaulted Vaux, successfully, in June.

Operation Gericht dragged on until December. In one way, it fulfilled Falkenhayn's initial operational conception: it was a battle of attrition, the bloodiest and longest battle of attrition that had even been fought. It was like Mukden, if the Japanese and Russians had had unlimited resources. In the end it bled both sides dry, not just the French. In form it was mainly an artillery battle, a ghastly scene of foot soldiers sitting under a rain of shells twenty-four hours a day. The role of the infantry was to endure, to suffer, to be crushed under the weight of the shells.

Verdun must also stand as a cautionary tale about command problems in the Great War. Again, the commander himself was not necessarily at fault. Falkenhayn was a perfectly competent general and product of the German staff system. It was the under-developed state of the command mechanism, the system for controlling the mass army in contact with the enemy, that led to his undoing. From the start of the fighting at Verdun, the battle began to control itself. It started as a perhaps overclever attempt to launch a limited assault on one bank of the Meuse, designed to pin the French in place so they could be chewed up by heavy German guns. Such an operation requires a fine touch, especially in the planning of infantry attacks. After all, they did not have to break through; they merely had to be convincing to the French. There was no need to risk high casualties. But a fine touch is precisely what the 1916 mass army did not possess. It could only, as an entity, understand simple commands: advance, strike, retreat. Both sides came to see Verdun itself as the true object of the fight, and 5th Army was soon engaged in a general assault designed to take the city. In order to advance, it had to assault along both banks of the Meuse. This in turn required clearing opposition on the flanks: Mort Homme, Côte 304, and Fort Vaux.

Even viewed in that light (i.e., as an attempt to seize Verdun), the Germans had numerous opportunities to "win." The opening of the battle was one. The stupendous German barrage left the French demoralized and

ripe for a bold infantry stroke. The period immediately after the fall of Fort
Douaumont on February 25 was another, identified by many French observers as the darkest day in the entire battle for the French. Another crisis came
on June 23, as German attacks drove up the last ridge on the right bank, topped
by the forts of Souville and Froideterre. Seizing them would have rendered
Verdun untenable, since all the bridges over the Meuse would have been under
direct German observation. The French, in fact, were prepared at this point
to evacuate the city. But in none of these cases was the German command
system responsive enough to seize the opportunities that beckoned. Nor would
the command system of any contemporary army have done any better.

In the end, Verdun should be remembered for one thing alone, its casualty list: the French lost 542,000 men, the Germans 434,000. Never recognized as a particularly clever wordsmith, 5th Army commander August
Wilhelm called Verdun "the mill on the Meuse," grinding up its victims on
both sides.[45] It is entirely fitting that the French memorial to the battle should
be the Ossuarium, a huge, forbidding temple filled with the bones of those
who died on this grisly battlefield.

MOBILITY RESTORED: *STOSSTRUPPEN* AND TANKS

The year 1917 was the absolute low point for military operations in this
war, featuring a disastrous French offensive whose collapse actually led to
large-scale mutinies in the French army, and General Douglas Haig's "big
push" at the Third Battle of Ypres, which ended with his assault troops
wading forward in knee-deep mud, dodging German machine gun fire as
they struggled toward their objective at Passchendaele. But this terrible year
ended with two developments that finally returned mobility to the modern
battlefield. In September, a German offensive in the east easily crashed
through the Russian defensive positions in front of Riga and seized the city,
an event that helped take Russia out of the war by precipitating the fall of
the provisional government and the seizure of power by the Bolsheviks under
Vladimir Lenin. Then, in October, an Austro-German offensive at Caporetto
shredded the Italian line along the Isonzo River, inflicting 800,000 casualties on an army of 2 million and almost knocking Italy out of the war with a
single blow. These two battles marked the debut of a new German tactical
approach. The term most often used in the West to describe it, *infiltration
tactics,* is something of a misnomer. The Germans called their new approach
Stosstrupp (shock troop or storm troop) tactics.

In November, a British assault in front of Cambrai tore a great hole in
the German defensive positions, easily crossing no-man's-land and driving
away entire German units in panic. Spearheading the attack was a new,

ungainly mechanical vehicle that the British had been working on for over two years and had dubbed, for security reasons, "the tank." The penetration of a significant section of German trench—indeed, the prosecution of any sort of successful offensive action at all—was something that had eluded the Allies since 1914, and in London, the church bells rang out to celebrate the victory. While the success fell short of a complete breakthrough into the German rear, it was a clear sign that the times were changing on the western front. And as if to mark that notion with an exclamation point, the Germans then launched a riposte at Cambrai with their new *Stosstruppen,* shredding the British line and driving the enemy back to his starting positions. A new age in warfare had begun.

Breakthrough at Riga

No single explanation suffices for the transformation of German battlefield doctrine in the course of the war.[46] *Stosstrupp* tactics were not an innovation designed by Germany's military leadership. The General Staff, whose training had always emphasized operations over tactics, did not invent them, although it did encourage tactical progress by forming an experimental assault detachment *(Sturmabteilung)* in 1915. Neither were they the invention of a single great mind. They were not, as they are still often called, "Hutier tactics," after General Oskar Hutier, commander of the German 8th Army at Riga in 1917. He had nothing to do with their development, though he did use *Stosstruppen* in his great breakthrough victory. Instead, the humble German infantryman, faced with an impossible situation on the battlefield and saddled with old tactics that simply did not work, must share credit for instigating this tactical revolution.[47]

We may identify three salient characteristics of this new doctrine. First, contrary to past practice, preparations for the offensive were to be made in secret. Troop movements into the assault sector took place at night, and the forces were not to move up until the last possible moment. At Riga, Hutier assembled his ten attack divisions miles behind the front, trained and rehearsed them for ten solid days, and did not move them up to their jump-off positions until the night before.[48]

Second, like previous doctrines, *Stosstrupp* tactics laid heavy emphasis on the preparatory bombardment—with several crucial differences. Contrary to past practice, the assault was to be preceded by a short, violent bombardment featuring a combination of gas and high explosive. Just a few hours long—only five hours and ten minutes at Riga—the bombing was aimed at enemy headquarters and communications, not necessarily the men in the trenches. The key figure in this new scheme of fire was the German army's resident artillery expert, Colonel Georg Bruchmüller, who won the nickname

"Durchbruchmüller" from the men, a play on his name and the Ge: word for "breakthrough" (*Durchbruch*). At Riga, the Germans assembled 615 guns (including 251 heavy guns) and 544 trench mortars into a sector just six miles wide, stockpiling 650,000 rounds of ammunition.[49] There was no prebattle registration fire, of the sort that had always tipped off the defender in the past that an assault was on the way, and often gave away the positions of the firing batteries themselves.

Third, the assault itself was spearheaded by *Stosstruppen*, independent squads, highly trained and armed with a full variety of modern support weapons—light artillery (7.62-cm gun), light machine guns, grenades, flamethrowers. The details of their mission might vary with the terrain and the situation but in essence were always the same: they were to find and infiltrate through weak spots in the defense, bypassing all obstacles and leaving them for the follow-up waves of regular infantry, moving constantly forward. Each squad was to advance as rapidly as possible, and there was to be no attempt to keep contact with units on the flanks—another of the factors that had so often hindered attacking infantry in the past. Thus, *Stosstrupp* tactics broke up the assault into numerous "little battles." What had begun as a war of armies and corps had now "dissolved" into a war of squads. *Stosstrupp* tactics required the complete decentralization of command, the surrender of a higher commander's authority to the squads and fire teams that were actually making the assault. The German tradition of *Auftragstaktik,* in which the supreme command gave his army commanders a mission, then left the method of achieving it up to them, had now "infiltrated" its way down to the lowest possible level of command—the squad. One modern authority has described the doctrinal revolution that now took place as "the elevation of the squad to the rank of independent tactical unit."[50] In this new scheme, the main responsibility of higher command was to insert reinforcements where the attack succeeded, rather than the past practice of reinforcing points at which the assault had been held up, the misguided procedure that had turned the Somme from a one-day disaster into a six-month slaughterhouse.

The city of Riga sits on the Dvina River (the Düna to the Germans), which flows from east to west.[51] It was the right anchor of the entire Russian defensive line in the east, it contained the only modern road and railway bridges in the area, and it was an obvious target of a German assault. Rather than strike it directly, Hutier chose to launch his main effort at a spot twenty miles upriver. Near the village of Üxküll, the river bent out toward German lines, forming a small peninsula. Three islands lay just offshore, and once the assaulting troops had seized them, the engineers would erect three bridges over the river, enabling nine of Hutier's thirteen division to cross and envelop the left flank of the Russian forces in front of Riga. He would pin the Russians in place with a diversionary thrust by three divisions directly against Riga itself.[52]

The actual assault conformed closely to the script. At 4:00 A.M. on the morning of September 1, 1917, all 615 German guns opened up simultaneously, shattering the silence and catching the Russians completely unawares. The opening bombardment, 25 percent high explosive and 75 percent gas, was essentially a huge counterbattery mission, directed at the Russian guns. Only at the two-hour mark did the primary target switch to the Russian infantry. Now the trench mortars joined in to pound the Russian front line. This fire lasted for another three hours and ten minutes and was eventually joined by the guns that had still been firing counterbattery missions. The final twenty minutes featured saturation of the Russian front line, with all guns and mortars firing as rapidly as possible.

With the Russian position blanketed by German fire, three divisions of Hutier's LI Corps attacked across the river: 19th Reserve Division on the right, 14th Bavarian Infantry Division in the center, and 2nd Guards Infantry Division on the left. The Dvina is over 350 yards wide here, and the divisions had to use wooden assault boats to cross, a part of the operation that had been thoroughly rehearsed for days, with lakes far behind the line substituting for the river. The Bavarians in the center also had to worry about securing the largest of the three islands, heavily fortified Borkum, directly to their front. All three divisions got over the river and easily overran the first Russian position, aided immensely by the bombardment and the presence of forward observers who directed the German artillery. The Germans employed a "creeping barrage" here in order to lead their infantry into the Russian positions, not a new idea by this point in the war, but never before handled with such skill or organization: "The assault was preceded by a carefully orchestrated creeping barrage that had the unusual feature of being organized along six phase lines. The barrage moved on schedule until it reached each phase line. Then it halted and continued as a standing barrage. It started moving again to the next phase line on a signal (green flare) from the infantry."[53] The rate of German artillery fire demanded nearly superhuman exertion on the part of the gun crews. During the five hours of preparatory fire, the Germans fired 560,000 rounds, about 480 rounds per gun, or approximately three shots every two minutes.

It was worth it. German infantry formations had overwhelming fire support not only in the immediate assault but also as they broke into the depth of the Russian positions, the second and third lines behind the shoreline trenches on the Dvina. This had been one of the major problems of trench warfare: how to keep the infantry supported once it was out of communication and command. It could be done, the Germans now proved, but only through careful coordination and centralized control of the artillery.

Within a few minutes, the German infantry had passed through the first Russian position and was driving on the second. Pioneers were lashing together the pontoon bridges, and follow-on forces were crossing the river. By evening of the first day, six German divisions were over the Dvina, and the right hook that was to trap the Russian 12th Army in Riga was well under way. Interestingly enough, the direct German thrust toward Riga that was to act as the diversion had been crushed, with one of the divisions (3rd Reserve Infantry) unable even to leave its trenches in the face of Russian artillery fire. The Russian commander in Riga, General L. G. Kornilov, watched his army melting away around him and decided on a pell-mell retreat from the city before the trap could close. The next day, the Germans continued their drive against sporadic opposition, and on September 3, their lead units entered Riga. At a cost of only 4,200 men, the German 8th Army had taken a great city, inflicted 25,000 casualties on the Russians, and effectively driven Russia out of the war.

The battle of Riga needs to be evaluated carefully. While it appears that the German plan had worked to perfection, it ought to be pointed out that the Russians had not fought well at all. With the empire teetering on the brink of its second revolution in one year, units had abandoned their trenches, their machine guns, and even their artillery at the first whiff of the German assault; the Germans captured 262 Russian guns in the course of the battle. Hastily organized Russian counterattacks, often without any artillery support whatsoever, broke down without seriously disrupting the German timetable. In fact, recent analysis has pointed out that the Russians were already in the process of pulling out of the Riga line days before the attack. Other analysts have pointed out that the tactical approach in this battle was not all that different from what had gone before. Although the Germans crossed the Dvina as independent squads, they formed up into company-strength skirmish lines as soon as they reached the far bank.

Still, the German breakthrough at Riga, coming after three years of stalemate, opened a number of eyes in the west to the fact that the Germans had come up with something worth investigating. Whatever modern scholarship may eventually determine, military men alive at the time were shocked by what had happened. It appeared once again to be possible to carry out grand maneuvers on the enemy's flank and rear, traditional operations as they were conceived in the days before 1914. As always, people have to put a human face on such developments, and suddenly "Hutier tactics" were the subject of a great deal of interest, not least from the supreme commander of the German armies, General Erich Ludendorff.

The Tanks at Cambrai

The second great event of 1917 was the British attack at Cambrai. Here, the British used a newly developed weapon, variously called the "landship" or "armored machine gun destroyer." Produced in great secrecy, it eventually came to be known as the "tank." The tank was an armored vehicle mounted on caterpillar tracks, able to cross over the roughest terrain or trench. It was designed to cross no-man's-land, destroy the enemy's wire and machine guns, and open a path for the infantry. It was not intended for independent operations, and indeed with a top speed of four miles per hour that was not likely to happen.[54] Tanks came in two basic types: the male, equipped with a 6-lb gun, and the female, armed with machine guns, intended to protect the male from enemy infantry.

By 1917, the British had nine battalions of tanks, organized into a "tank corps" of three brigades. Each battalion consisted of three companies of sixteen tanks each, with the companies consisting of four four-tank platoons. The commander of the corps was Brigadier Hugh Elles, a smart, daring, and extremely charismatic soldier who fit the part perfectly. His brilliant, abrasive chief of staff would become the man most closely associated with the rise of British armor: Lieutenant Colonel J. F. C. Fuller.[55]

In September 1917, Fuller drew up a plan for a surprise attack by massed armored formations on ground especially chosen for the use of tanks. Searching a map of the western front, his eyes came to rest on the sector between Saint-Quentin and Cambrai, then held by 3rd Army under General Sir Julian Byng. It had been a quiet sector for some time. The ground was flat and relatively free of the tank's great nemesis, shell craters. German defenses were weak. Here, Fuller decided, the tanks would prove their worth once and for all, crashing through the German trenches before the defenders could even react. His original plan called for a lightning raid on Saint-Quentin. Elles changed it into a larger raid on Cambrai, and then Byng into an offensive by the whole 3rd Army. By the time it was finished, Operation GY called for a full-fledged breakthrough of the Hindenburg line. Once German defenses had been shredded, the way would be open for the reserves and cavalry to exploit. The victorious 3rd Army would sweep northeast and then north, "out of the mud and blood and into the green fields beyond." As the scope of the operation grew, so did the number of tanks involved. Fuller's plan had required only six battalions; Byng's called for all nine.

The offensive opened at 6:20 A.M. on November 20, 1917. Without any preparatory bombardment, artillery registration, or cutting of wire, a force of nearly 400 tanks that had been brought up to the front in secrecy suddenly came up out of the mist, heading for the German lines. Leading the first tank attack in history was the dashing Elles himself, in his personal tank *Hilda*, operating "unbuttoned," with his head sticking up out of the hatch for better visibility. Fuller had remonstrated with him before the battle not to lead the charge in person but in the end made a rare admission: "He was right, and I was wrong."

Surprise was almost total. The German defenders were stunned. This was not like past attacks by a handful of tanks. There seemed to be hundreds, thousands, in lines kilometers long! Face-to-face with this almost inconceivable armored onslaught, they did what virtually any troops of the day would have done: they threw down their weapons and surrendered, or tried to flee, or hid in a gully or shell crater. "What a joy it was," wrote one of the participants, "to be driving on good dry ground without having to crawl in bottom gear with mud up to your sponsons." They crossed the wire that had proved so invulnerable to shell fire in the past almost without noticing it. The lead tanks approached the first trench, raking it with fire as planned. The tanks of the main body then dropped their fascines and crossed the first and second lines. The first tanks passed the enemy's outpost line within nine minutes; within the first hour, they had torn a hole six miles wide and three miles deep in the Hindenburg line. To Fuller, messages from the observation post were "more like a railway timetable than a series of battle reports."[56]

Even in the euphoria of that first day, it was clear that success had not been total. General G. M. Harper of the 51st Highland Division, given the task of attacking the village of Flesquières in the center, kept his infantry well back and sent in the tanks line abreast, essentially unsupported. When they reached Flesquières, they received a bloody check from German artillery emplaced behind the ridge on which the village stood. Sixteen tanks were knocked out, giving rise to the legend of a lone German officer, the "gunner of Flesquières," who supposedly destroyed all sixteen after his men had either fled or been killed.[57]

By November 21, the tanks had shot their bolt. The British had no "armored reserve." With the German line shattered, and a second blow all that was needed to break clear through into open country, the British could launch only limited strikes involving forty tanks here, fifty there. Second, the tank's mechanical unreliability accounted for far more losses than German fire. Third, battlefield command and control continued to be poor, a situation exacerbated by the much faster pace of the operation. There were at times great gaps in the German line that could have been penetrated, such as that between Bourlon Wood and the village of Fontaine on the night of November 21. But recognizing them and exploiting them in time proved to be two different things. The arm to which that task had been assigned, the cavalry, stood behind the line, massed in great strength. And there it stood, for the duration of the battle—with its headquarters some six miles behind the lines in the village of Fins. Fuller blamed the commanders, but in fact cavalry had no more place in a tank battle than it had in a trench raid. Finally, German reinforcements began pouring into the sector. By November 27, the front had solidified. The British withdrew their tanks and put up barbed wire in front of their new positions.

In all the attention devoted to the debut of the tanks at Cambrai, it is easy to lose sight of the German counterattack. By now it was down to a well-prepared script. Early on the morning of November 30, a tremendous barrage hit the British lines, gas and high explosive on the batteries, shrapnel and high explosive on the trenches. Then the *Stosstruppen* attacked. Coming forward in squads, making no attempt to keep formation or to worry about their flanks, by noon they had overrun the British trenches and pushed forward some five miles. The British managed to reform a defensive line well to the rear over the next few days, but by the end of the German counteroffensive, on December 7, the line stood approximately where it had been on November 19, before the tank attack.

In terms of operational art, the Cambrai offensive was barren of any new approach. It had been a pure frontal assault, designed above all to test out the tanks on good flat ground. There was no plan to maneuver, to create or exploit a flank, and no real thought given to what to do after the tanks had achieved the breakthrough. During the *Stosstrupp* assault against the Italians at Caporetto, elements of the German 14th Army, foot soldiers all, had advanced nearly seventy-five miles. The tanks at Cambrai had barely made five. In that sense, Cambrai was nothing more than a traditional trench battle with new weapons.

1918: THE REBIRTH OF DECISIVE BATTLE?

The final battles of the war were mobile ones, up to a point. In March 1918, General Ludendorff launched the first of three great offensives in the west. Operation Michael began on March 21, 1918. The Germans called it the kaiser's battle *(Kaiserschlacht)*, the decisive battle of the war, Germany's last throw of the dice.[58] At 4:40 A.M., some 6,000 German guns began a furious hurricane bombardment, featuring gas. It shredded British headquarters and command facilities and reduced the target of the assault, British 5th Army (General Sir Hubert Gough), into small pockets of confused and frightened men. At 9:40 A.M., the German infantry emerged from its trenches, and, after three long years, the war of movement returned to the west. In a thick fog, behind a creeping barrage, sixty-three divisions of *Stosstruppen* slashed through the British wire, and then through the bewildered British defenders themselves. By 11:00 A.M., the lead units were through into open ground. It was a combined arm success. The assault battalions, controlled by the army commanders themselves, were divided into *Sturmblöcke,* company-sized task forces reinforced with machine guns, light trench mortars, and flamethrowers. By the second day, all three armies had broken through the British positions, with 2nd Army in the center making the fastest progress. At this point, Ludendorff ordered 2nd and 17th Armies to swing north, while 18th protected the left of this maneuver from any French interference. A fifty-mile gap had appeared in the British defenses, a nearly inconceivable idea given the past three years of trench warfare. "I cannot make out why the 5th Army has gone so far back without making some kind of a stand," said a bewildered General Haig.[59] By the end of the next day, the Germans had advanced thirty miles, taking over 90,000 prisoners.

But almost as soon as it had appeared, the crisis passed. Facing defeat, the Allies finally did something that they had steadfastly resisted up to that point and should have done much earlier: they agreed to coordinate their efforts and submit to a common command. French general Ferdinand Foch became supreme Allied commander on March 26. Having lost the element of surprise, the *Stosstruppen* were unable to sustain their momentum. There are numerous tales of advancing troops pausing to loot British depots, but they seem to grow in the telling, and could only have had a minor impact on the overall course of the battle.[60] One key factor in stopping the German drive was the increasing length of their lines of communication and consequent difficulty in supplying, feeding, and replacing their forward units. "One cannot go on victoriously forever without any ammunition or any sort of reinforcements," complained one German soldier."[61] A second, even more decisive, factor was the arrival in the sector of fresh British reinforcements, coming up by railroad. Nearly every day the British managed to throw some sort of thin khaki line in front of the Germans. The *Stosstruppen* would blow it away in the morning, but there would be another one in the afternoon, and another one the following morning. This was built-up terrain over which the Germans were advancing; the phrase "green fields beyond" is deceiving. There were villages and towns and woods, canals and rivers, and the British were able to make use of the covering terrain to hold up German attacks until the latter had dragged up artillery. By March 29, the line had stabilized. While the offensive had wrecked the British 5th Army, losses on both sides had been staggering: 212,000 Allied to 239,000 German casualties. The Germans now inhabited a great salient in the line; they were no closer to winning the war.

Ludendorff now launched a second drive against the British, this time to the north on the Lys River in Flanders. It was originally dubbed Operation

George, but the great effort required for Michael meant that only fifteen *Stosstrupp* divisions took part, and "George" therefore became "Georgette." It was perhaps an ill omen. The attack opened on April 9 with a short, violent bombardment, carefully planned to fall on a single Portuguese division that was manning a quiet stretch of the British sector. It simply dissolved under the blow. Many British units were in the area recovering from Michael, since this was reputed to be a quiet stretch of front. The initial German advance was swift: five miles the first day, five more the second. By April 12, the Germans were just five miles from the railroad junction at Hazebrouck, the principal British supply depot in Europe. Haig's barrel of reserves was empty, and with disaster staring him in the face, he was moved to issue the war's most famous order of the day: "There is no other course open to us but to fight it out. Every position must be held to the last man. There must be no retirement. With our backs to the wall and believing in the justice of our cause each one must fight on to the end."[62]

Once again, however, the *Stosstruppen* were unable to sustain their momentum. By April 18, the attack had stalled. Germany had conquered two large salients and had mauled two British armies (not to mention a division from Portugal). But once again, losses had been high. The totals for Georgette were 86,000 Germans and 100,000 Allies. Unlike the Allies, Germany could not afford these losses, not with U.S. troops pouring into Europe.

Ludendorff now decided to attack the French. The third offensive, Operation Blücher, was an offensive against the French positions in the Chemin des Dames. It opened on May 27, and had the greatest success of all, so great it suggests that Ludendorff should have hit the French first. Thirty *Stosstrupp* divisions shredded the French front line, advancing ten miles the first day, twenty miles by May 29, and another twelve miles on May 30, lunging once again to the Marne, just fifty miles from Paris. The gravity of this situation persuaded General Pershing to do something that *he* had steadfastly refused up to now: release American troops to French command. Two U.S. infantry divisions, the 2nd and 3rd, each the size of two European divisions, now hustled up to the front along the Marne. On June 4, the 3rd Division arrived just in time to blunt German attempts to cross the river at Château Thierry. Ludendorff now ordered a halt to resupply and regroup his worn-out units, suffering not only exhaustion from the punishing pace of the past four months but also from the increasing depredations of the influenza epidemic.

Ludendorff's offensives still attract a great deal of interest for their innovative tactics. They were the first use of *Stosstruppen* tactics on a grand scale in the west. As operations they are much less interesting. Ludendorff launched a three-army offensive, Germany's largest operation since 1914, without any real firm objectives in mind, save for "Amiens, Arras, and be-yond." It is a cliché that the "devil is in the details," but it might be argued that a verdict on Ludendorff's operational conception rests on our defini-tion of that simple word *beyond.* He knew that he would achieve a break-through, but just where it would take place was open to question. He left that decision to circumstance. While it might be argued that flexibility is exactly what modern command requires, Ludendorff had gone too far. His attempt to direct the maneuver of three armies, almost 800,000 men, by ad hoc orders issued on the second day of the Michael offensive—his orders to 2nd and 18th Armies to wheel north—was not simply ineffective. It was altogether irrelevant. By the time the order had filtered down the chain of command to the assault units, they were gorging themselves on captured British stores and rum. In fact, it is clear from Michael that *Stosstrupp* as-saults had a logic—perhaps a chaos—all their own: the success or failure of a given *Sturmblock* in a given area had much more impact on the subsequent direction of operations than all the decisions of the army commanders or Ludendorff combined. Far from solving the essential operational problem of the era—command and control over the mass army—*Stosstruppen* tactics had only made it worse.

SOISSONS, AMIENS, AND AFTER: THE END IN THE WEST

Ludendorff's pause was just the breathing space the Allies needed. On June 6, the U.S. 2nd Infantry Division, with a marine brigade attached, was moving up on the left of 3rd Infantry Division, when it ran smack into a German force moving south into the Belleau Wood. There was heavy fight-ing, which the marines, as they always do, seemed to relish. When a French officer advised Colonel Wendell C. Neville of the 5th Marine Regiment that a retreat might be in order, Neville answered with words that summed up the unique American attitude toward the 1918 fighting: "Retreat, hell! We just got here!"[63] By July 1, the marines had cleared the wood. American casualties in this fight were extremely heavy, 40 percent in many units, but they had managed to consume four German divisions.

With the Germans now stuck in front of the Marne, they occupied a sa-lient projecting deep into French territory. This gave Marshal Foch an op-portunity for a counterblow. On July 18 a French assault began toward Soissons on the western face of the salient. Carrying it out was French 10th Army (General Charles Mangin). Borrowing a leaf from the Germans, he assembled his assault force in secret, making skillful use of the impenetrable screen of the Villers-Cotterêts forest. Surprise, he said, was "perfectly pos-sible." There was to be a massive commitment of force. His spearhead would be over 300 tanks, mostly light Renault FT-17s. This new model was the first tank in the world with a fully rotating turret, carrying either a 37-mm gun or machine guns and a crew of two.[64]

Early on the morning of July 18, in the fog and mist, a bombardment by 2,000 guns opened up along a front of twenty-seven miles, the tanks got rolling, and French 10th Army crashed into the German lines. They had achieved surprise and were fighting not *Stosstruppen* but exhausted, demoralized German trench divisions. Progress was extremely rapid, three to four miles being covered in the first few hours, and thousands of German soldiers threw up their hands in surrender, a pretty rare sight in this war. Soon Soissons itself was under French fire. The railway station in town was now useless to the Germans, who had to detrain their reinforcements several miles to the north. Likewise, the key road south out of Soissons, the principal supply route for German troops lower down in the salient, was now cut. That evening the Germans began to evacuate the salient, once more retreating from the Marne River back to the Vesle. The "Second Battle of the Marne" was over. The French had taken 20,000 prisoners and captured 400 heavy guns. By August 1, further French attacks had driven the Germans out of all the gains of Operation Blücher. Ludendorff's strategy was in ruins. His losses now topped 600,000, and his irreplaceable elite divisions had been bled dry. Soissons was the turning point on the western front.[65]

On August 8, British 4th Army under General Henry Rawlinson launched a massive counteroffensive of its own at Amiens.[66] Spearheading it were two of the most effective corps in the Allied camp, the Canadian and Australian. Rawlinson had the entire Tank Corps at his disposal, 420 machines in all. Most of them, over 300, were heavy tanks of the new Mark V design. It was the first heavy tank that could be driven by one man, with a more powerful engine and greater obstacle-crossing ability than the old Mark IV. There were also 96 Medium A "Whippets." The Whippet was a three-man tank with a top speed of eight miles per hour and an impressive radius of eighty miles. Its mission was to exploit the breach created by its heavier counterparts.[67] Counting supply tanks and gun carriers, the total number of machines at Amiens was closer to 600. More than five hundred aircraft also took part. Opposing this formidable array of men and machines were seven weak and exhausted German divisions.

At 4:20 A.M., the tanks moved out behind a creeping barrage, covered by dark and mist, and headed for the German lines. Surprise was almost total. Everywhere terrified German soldiers threw up their hands and surrendered en masse. That first day, the tanks tore a gash some eleven miles wide in the German lines. The German 225th Division reported, "The entire divisional artillery was lost; of the front line and support battalions practically nothing had come back; and the resting battalions thrown in piecemeal had either been thrown back or had not got into action at all."[68] Command and control on the German side broke down quickly, a combination of the Whippet's speed and the low visibility. According to Hindenburg, "The thick mist made supervision and control very difficult." German gunners fired into the fog whenever they heard the sound of motors or the rattle of gears. "The wildest rumors began to spread in our lines," Hindenburg later wrote. "It was said that masses of English cavalry were already far in the rear of the foremost German infantry positions."[69] No place seemed safe, a lesson hammered home by the aerial bombardment on various rail junctions far behind the lines, such as Péronne.

That first day, the Allies advanced eight miles, taking 12,000 prisoners and capturing 400 guns. Over the next three days, 4th Army took 40,000 German prisoners of war. Although the Germans managed to re-form their lines, their will to fight seemed to have disappeared. Ludendorff himself called August 8 a "black day" for the German army. "Troops allowed themselves to be surprised . . . and lost all cohesion when the tanks suddenly appeared behind them," he wrote.[70] Fuller called Amiens "the strategical end of the war, a second Waterloo; the rest was minor tactics."[71]

For all of the obvious importance of Amiens on the tactical and strategic level, it is hardly interesting at all as an operation. An army, vastly outnumbering the weak screen facing it and enjoying material support beyond the wildest dreams of its opposition, crashed straight ahead, scooping up a large part of the demoralized hostile manpower in a fifty-square-mile area. There was no attempt to maneuver or to create the conditions for a successful flank attack, or even to seize a springboard for further operations. What it aimed to do, it did quite well. It did not aim for all that much, however.

CONCLUSION: OPERATIONAL ART IN WORLD WAR I

A study of World War I's final year should dispel its commonly held image as a sterile conflict of trenches, barbed wire, and mud. It had been a year of movement and drama. The Germans came within an ace of winning the war and fell just short; the Allies recovered from the depths of the summer to become the irresistible conquerors of the fall.[72] Military history records few similar changes of fortune in such a short period of time.

Still, trench warfare continues to dominate both the historiography and the popular image of this vast and varied conflict. Despite the tanks and the aircraft, despite the entire range of modern technology that came to dominate the battlefields, despite the repeated breakthroughs in the conflict's final year, this was a war of frontal assault. Amiens is a good example. It was a fascinating battle from a tactical standpoint, but decent undergraduate students can gain a perfectly sound understanding of it without recourse to a map or diagram. That is not the case with, say, the Chancellorsville campaign in the American Civil War. There is something inherently appealing in Lee's conduct of the battle: his bold decision to split his force in the face of a superior Union army; Stonewall Jackson's great flank march around the Union right; the assault on the unsuspecting Union troops as they were lining up for chow. Even the incomplete nature of the victory and Jackson's untimely death cannot dim the glory of Lee's finest hour. This is the operational level of war, or "operational art" in modern U.S. Army parlance, at its finest. In devising operations, the commander *is* an artist, painting a portrait with armies and corps as his medium and an entire province, region, or continent as his canvas. Like all art, his creations can be clever, even elegant; they can be mediocre; they can be so ugly and poorly done that they offend one's aesthetic sense. Whether one agrees that this should be so or not, it is on the operational level that one instinctively judges the commander. Note how often the phrase "He was a sound tactician" is used in describing a historical commander. It is usually not a compliment but comes under the heading "damning with faint praise." Even the successful generals of 1914–18 rarely went beyond the level of sound tactician. With a few celebrated exceptions, there was simply very little happening on the operational level in this war.[73]

Chapter 6

• • • • • • • • • • • • • • •

The Interwar Years: Doctrine and Innovation

The military history of the interwar period (1919–39) has centered on one development above all. Military professionals and scholars alike have tended to look to these two decades as the age in which was born a new doctrine of mechanized warfare known as *blitzkrieg*, from the German word for "lightning war." It is fitting, therefore, to begin by making a definitive statement about this ubiquitous term: it has no objective meaning. The German army did not invent it, rarely used it outside of quotation marks, and would never use it to describe either a general operational doctrine or a specific historical operation.[1] Its origins are obscure, but it apparently first appeared in Western journalistic usage in a 1939 issue of *Time* magazine to describe the lightning-quick German victories of the opening days of World War II. It is obvious to all thinking persons that the term should be discarded.

And yet, it is by now obvious that it never will be discarded. It has come into such general usage in the West that it no longer matters, frankly, who invented it. Like an old piece of gum, it has stuck, no matter how often the specialists warn against using it. Since we cannot get rid of it, we should make the best possible use of it. What, then, is blitzkrieg? Put simply, it has come to stand for a style of warfare that employs machines, tanks and aircraft above all, to restore mobility to the conduct of war, and thus the possibility of decisive victory. It has become a kind of hero, especially in popular histories that describe it as a successful antidote to the horrors of trench warfare, a sort of "anti-Verdun" that has forever exorcised the evil prospects of another conflict like World War I.

Even reduced to that minimal meaning, however, blitzkrieg is a difficult concept to pin down. Tanks and aircraft arose in World War I, after all, and so did virtually every other "machine" that every respectable blitzkrieg-lover deems a necessary ingredient of the concept. By the end of the war, at Soissons and Amiens, French and British Commonwealth forces, respectively, drove through, over, and around their German adversaries with hordes of tanks and fleets of aircraft. German and Allied tanks even fought each other in the battle of Villers-Bretonneux, history's first tank-to-tank encounter.[2]

What we can say is this: the interwar years featured an intensive debate about the war that had just ended, about what the war of the future might look like, and about how modern armies could best prepare for it.[3] It was a

Armored behemoth. A German A7V tank, built and employed in small numbers in 1918. It carried a 57-mm cannon and six machine guns and had a crew of eighteen. Courtesy of James S. Corum.

time in which the military status quo came under attack, sometimes in logical terms and at other times stridently and even hysterically, by those who saw the previous war as a disaster that must never be repeated. At stake, they argued, was the future of civilization itself.

The central issue was the role that mechanization should play in the army of the future. Everywhere there were military men and civilians alike who argued that warfare as it had traditionally been known was obsolete. The next war, they said, would consist of great clashes between fleets of tanks and aircraft, with infantry greatly reduced in importance and cavalry abolished altogether. Warfare would return to the open fields, reclaiming its rightful legacy of mobility, decisive battles, and glory. Heinz Guderian in Germany, Basil Liddell Hart and J. F. C. Fuller in Great Britain, Charles de Gaulle in France, and M. N. Tukhachevsky in the Soviet Union were all "prophets" of this "new gospel" of mobile warfare, arguing that the future of warfare lay with mechanical vehicles, especially tanks.

Another school of prophets preached the virtues of airpower. Even the flimsy craft of the past war had been fearsome weapons, both to troops on the ground and to civilians. Now, officers like Hugh Trenchard in Great Britain and Giulio Douhet in Italy argued for a concept of strategic bombing—mass terror raids on enemy cities that would kill thousands and end the war in minutes, even before the armies mobilized. With antiaircraft measures still primitive, many enthusiasts argued that "the bomber will always get through." This terrifying theme caught the popular imagination, becoming a staple of contemporary fiction like H. G. Wells's 1933 novel, *The Shape of Things to Come.*

Facing these prophets were powerful forces: members of the high commands, old-style cavalry officers, and reactionaries of every description. It is a fictional figure, cartoonist David Low's "Colonel Blimp," who has come to represent this group in the popular imagination. The anecdotes about such fellows, many no doubt apocryphal, are legion. One officer actually exclaimed to Fuller on the afternoon of November 11, 1918, "Thank God we can now get back to real soldiering!" General Oldwig von Natzmer, Guderian's commander in the Inspectorate of Motor Troops, rejected plans to use trucks to transport troops into battle, allegedly shouting, "To hell with combat, they're supposed to carry flour!" General Archibald Montgomery-Massingberd once violently denounced a new book by Fuller, then admitted that he had not even read it, declaring, "It would only annoy me."[4]

Liddell Hart was more responsible than any other person for putting forth an "authorized version" of events in the interwar period.[5] Skillfully weaving together anecdotes such as those just noted, he constructed an attractive myth that still has the ring of received wisdom to many people. The "armor debate," it says, took place between a small but hardy band of brilliant, radical intellectuals on the one side, motivated only by their love of country and the belief that they were in the right, and the hidebound forces of reaction on the other, still clinging desperately to their pre-1914 notions of maneuver and battle. As their impassioned calls for change went unheeded, the radicals had to pay a heavy price, in terms of blocked career prospects and lost promotions, for challenging the powers that were. The result was that Britain entered World War II woefully unprepared for the sort of armored combat that it would have to fight. And, in a suitably ironic twist, while Liddell Hart's own military establishment rejected his ideas, the Germans spent the 1930s studying their brilliance and implementing them into their doctrine. In fact, these very ideas, mocked and rejected at home, formed the basis of blitzkrieg tactics and thus were responsible for the German army's incredible victories in the first two years of the war.

There is another story to be told, however. A great number of scholars have examined Liddell Hart's claims, and it is now clear that the climate for mechanization was not as unfavorable, in Britain and elsewhere, as he and his fellow prophets had alleged. First, the blind reactionaries who serve as the villains in his writings, as well as those of Fuller, Guderian, and the others, were actually quite rare. It would have been nearly impossible to find a responsible officer in any army who refused to accept the fact that tanks and aircraft had become important weapons on the modern battlefield. Legitimate debate could, and did, arise over how best to employ them. Second, not every word the prophets wrote was correct. They had their share of howlers, and many things they predicted were just wrong. Liddell Hart, especially, was an enthusiast, always arguing that whatever arcane fact he had learned the previous day was "the future of warfare." He went from being an advocate of mobile operations and the "indirect approach" to being a passionate supporter of strategic bombing, then a devotee of the "light tank"; on the eve of the next war in 1939, he was arguing that Great Britain should limit its liability on the Continent by sending only a small force to aid France. It is hard, to put it mildly, to argue that all of these positions were correct.

In Weimar Germany, a succession of commanders from Generals Hans von Seeckt to Kurt von Hammerstein were unanimous in their belief that tanks were indispensable to future warfare. German maneuvers, exercises, and war games grappled constantly with the issues of mechanization and armor.[6] Hardly a week went by without one or more articles on the subject appearing in the semiofficial journal, the *Militär-Wochenblatt*. There is no evidence that such ideas were imported from Britain in the form of Liddell Hart's writings. Even a quick glance at works published in interwar Germany shows the absurdity of such a claim.

Where, then, does that leave *blitzkrieg*? The present text will argue that the term still has some utility, whether or not the Germans actually used it, in describing an *operational doctrine* of the German army that was wildly successful in the opening days of World War II. The Allies would copy, learn, and employ the same doctrine with reasonable success, and use it to win the war. It still forms the basis of operational doctrine for every modern army in the world. Using the term in this way, we may define *blitzkrieg* as a doctrine of employing mechanized units (including air units) on a grand scale to defeat, pursue, and destroy sizable enemy forces within a two- to four-week span of time. With the old command problems solved, or at least eased, by the invention of the radio, the Germans were able to restore the *campaign*—an interconnected series of maneuvers and battles aimed at the defeat of the enemy's main field force—to its rightful place in military affairs. In so doing, they set a standard to which, consciously or unconsciously, every later army has aspired.

THE PROPHETS IN BRITAIN

J. F. C. Fuller was the original article. He was brilliant; he was obnoxious; he filled his copious writings with thought-provoking ideas, visionary predictions of future combat, and bitter personal attacks on anyone who dared to disagree with him. In his mental universe, every one of his foes in the debate was unimaginative, uncreative, or downright stupid, and he was not shy about letting them know it. He always presented his arguments at top volume, was profoundly disinterested in the feelings of his opponents, and often showed total disregard for the rules of fair intellectual play. That this actually hurt the cause he claimed to espouse did not seem to occur to him, or perhaps he simply did not care. For example, Fuller once described British cavalry officers as "this equine Tammany Hall, which would far rather have lost the war than have seen cavalry replaced by tanks."[7] Montgomery-Massingberd's quotation, given earlier, has permanently consigned the general to the list of history's "know-nothings." One rarely hears the rest of the passage: "Fuller's mode of writing and assumption of infallibility and mental superiority renders it impossible to take him seriously or derive any pleasure from reading what he writes." All of Fuller's books, he said, "are written with the intention of annoying someone."[8] Far from being a know-nothing, the general was actually a very perceptive man.

The quintessential military radical of the interwar period, Fuller called for nothing less than the total mechanization of the British army and the abolition of traditional infantry and cavalry.[9] In his book *The Reformation of War* (1923), he describes a meeting of two future armies.[10] Each has the traditional arms, plus light and heavy tanks (speeds of twenty-five and fifteen miles per hour, respectively). As the two forces maneuvered to contact, the tanks would engage first, due to their higher speed. Cavalry was too slow to keep up, and its vulnerability to fire would force it to the rear, awaiting a breakthrough. Infantry would be nothing but "an interested spectator" in such an encounter. Horse-drawn artillery would be far too late to lay down effective fire. The tanks belonging to one side or the other would gain the initiative, and the defeated tanks would have to retire. And who would be able to pursue them? Tanks. The defeated side would be helpless. "The only arm which will be able to save itself from destruction is the cavalry, not by charging the enemy, but by galloping off the field."

The only thing the traditional arms could do to avoid this distasteful scenario was full and immediate mechanization. Cavalry could still fill its time-honored role of reconnaissance by employing "light scout tanks." With a speed of 30 miles per hour, they could easily travel 150 miles in a single day. They could pass over all terrain, including many obstacles that would stop a horse. They could lie hidden for days, if necessary. In the pursuit, "cavalry tanks" could move twice as fast as a horse and could maintain the pursuit even at night, through the use of searchlights. Artillery was obsolete in its present configuration, helpless against new dangers like tank attack, aerial bombardment, and gas. The only solution was to mount it in a new gas-proof vehicle that could move at least 15 miles per hour. "If in the next war, the gunner wishes to pull his weight, then he also must get into a tank."

Fuller's most radical claim in *Reformation* was that leg-mobile infantry had no future at all. The present day resembled the Middle Ages, he argued, in that foot soldiers had become "mere pawns in the game." Just as armored knights ruled the battlefield then, so now the tank had achieved a position of dominance. If it continued to exist at all, infantry would do so "as police and the defenders of positions—railheads, bridgeheads, and supply magazines." And even for these secondary tasks, some sort of light armored personnel carrier would be required.

There is a tendency to link Basil Liddell Hart with Fuller, but in fact the two were far more different than alike. Liddell Hart's writings were calmer and more reasoned, had a much broader concern with strategy, and were much more readable in style. He may not have been Fuller's intellectual equal, but he certainly was more of a gentleman. His debates with his opponents were absent of the acrimony that Fuller generated. As a result, Liddell Hart's influence and achievements were greater.[11] As military correspondent for the *Daily Telegraph,* he was perhaps the best-known commentator in the world on military matters, read as much by interested civilians as by professional soldiers.

Liddell Hart spent a career preaching a new vision of warfare, in which highly mechanized armies backed by powerful air forces would forever abolish the deadlock of the trenches. In *Paris, or the Future of War* (1925), he offered a stinging critique of the conduct of World War I. Allied strategy had erred, he argued, in seeking to destroy the enemy's armed forces in the main theater of operations. The result had been the western front, the mud and blood and slaughter. Ordinary men had paid the price, "yoked like dumb, driven oxen to the chariot of Mars." What the Allies should have done was to find and exploit their opponent's weakest spot, like Paris striking at the heel of Achilles (hence the title). This was not the enemy's army but his will to fight. A modern industrial society was a delicate thing, highly vulnerable to shock and dislocation. A blow at the enemy's vulnerable cities and production centers, with massive air fleets dropping poison gas, would do the trick. Airpower had laid bare the nation's nerve system, and, just as with individuals, "the progress of civilization has rendered it far more sensitive than in earlier and more primitive times."[12] He described the possibilities with vivid imagery:

> Imagine for a moment London, Manchester, Birmingham, and half a dozen other great centers simultaneously attacked, the business localities and Fleet Street wrecked, Whitehall a heap of ruins, the slum districts maddened into the impulse to break loose and maraud, the railways cut, factories destroyed. Would not the general will to resist vanish, and what use would be the still determined fractions of the nation, without organization and central direction?

Ground forces, too, had to break the enemy's will to resist. Slow-moving infantry could no longer do this. The "new model army" should be fully mechanized, capable of demoralizing strikes and 100-mile daily advances into enemy territory. Tanks would be in the lead. They were the modern heavy cavalry, to be used in concentrated masses "for a decisive blow against the Achilles' heel of the enemy army, the communication and command centers which form its nerve system."[13]

Here we can see the origins of Liddell Hart's most famous concept, the "indirect approach," a strategy of avoiding an enemy's strength and hitting his weakness. In his book *The Decisive Wars of History* (1929), he analyzed some 240 military campaigns, from the Athenian victory at Marathon to the Allied triumph in 1918, and concluded that precisely 6 of them had been won by attacking an opponent directly ("moving along the line of natural expectation").

The aim of strategy, he argued, should always be victory at the lowest cost. The "indirect approach" meant landing a series of rapid blows where they were least expected, in order to dislocate and paralyze the opponent by upsetting his mental and physical equilibrium. It might mean a turning move that forced the enemy into a rapid change of front or separated one wing of his forces from the other. It might mean endangering his lines of communication back to his homeland or performing a series of advances that threatened him at more than one point. In the realm of the psychological, it might mean a sudden blow at the morale of the enemy commander. "The impression is strongly accentuated if his realization of being at a disadvantage is sudden, if he feels he is unable to counter the enemy's move." The indirect approach, he argued, meant following not only the path of least resistance but also the path of "least expectation," using surprise to discomfit and paralyze the enemy command structure.

In the present day, Liddell Hart argued, the potential for indirect approach had increased with the rise of tanks. Rapidly moving mechanized armies were the key. "Mechanized forces, by their combination of speed and flexibility, offered the means of pursuing this dual action far more effectively than any army could do in the past." Success lay

> partly in the tactical combination of tanks and aircraft, partly in the unexpectedness of the stroke in direction and time, *but above all* in the "follow through"—the way that a breakthrough (the tactical penetration of a front) is exploited by a deep strategic penetration, carried out by armored forces racing on ahead of the main army, and operating *independently*. [14]

Like Fuller, Liddell Hart had, and still has, numerous critics. They accused him of reductionism—bending and stretching the concept of the indirect approach in so many different directions that it ceased to have any real meaning. In a review essay on *The Decisive Wars of History* that appeared in the *Journal of the Royal United Service Institution* in November 1936, Colonel R. H. Beadon stated the case against Liddell Hart forcefully, while defending the position of the military professional. Liddell Hart's arguments were glib, he said, and were rarely questioned by a British public unschooled in military affairs:

> The critic for the most part remains uncriticized, except perhaps by such few professional soldiers who have time, inclination, and knowledge to give to the matter. And these latter can be effectively dismissed as hidebound, dull, and unimaginative, for it is part and parcel of the amateur critic's armament, both defensive and offensive, to decry what is commonly termed "the military mind."

While Beadon noted that Liddell Hart's arguments were cleverly stated, and that the "industry and ingenuity with which [he] builds up his case do, to

superficial examination, suffice to lend it a certain plausibility," no single
theory could account for two millennia of victory and defeat:

> For he is next concerned to enlarge the target itself by claiming as "indi-
> rect approach" or "true grand strategy"—for he makes the terms synony-
> mous—every instance when an army did not move straightaway and
> without ado to a frontal attack on its opponent—a procedure which he
> curiously remarks has always been the normal form of strategy. More-
> over, the method he employs to reach his deductions, which be it recalled
> hold good for a period of over two thousand years, is to argue the victory's
> "indirect approach," even when such is not very apparent, while ignor-
> ing or skating over the maneuvers of the vanquished even when the latter
> are more apparently "indirect."[15]

As with all controversial figures, the truth about Liddell Hart stands somewhere between the assessments of his detractors and his supporters. He was
a great and prolific writer on military affairs, and his influence stretches far
beyond the 1930s. The twin pillars of his thought, the "expanding torrent"
and the "indirect approach," are still an effective basis for understanding
modern mobile operations, even if they are not the eternally valid guaran-
tors of victory that he claimed. His call for deep penetrations by armored
spearheads, working in close cooperation with airpower, all within the context of a combined arms, mechanized force, is not at all out of date, nor is
his emphasis on the importance of the pursuit. He was at one and the same
time a skilled publicist for his ideas, a shameless self-promoter who often
made himself out to be more important than he was, and an enthusiast who
never met a new idea that he did not love.

THE FAILED DEVELOPMENT OF BRITISH ARMOR

In 1926, it appeared that the prophets had won the day, when the British
army announced the formation of the Experimental Mechanized Force
(EMF).[16] In May 1927, the EMF began a series of exercises on Salisbury
Plain. It was a milestone—the first totally mechanized formation in military
history, consisting of the 3rd Battalion Royal Tank Corps (two companies
of armored cars and a company of light, two-man "tankettes"); the 5th
Battalion Royal Tank Corps (three companies of Vickers medium tanks,
armed with 3-pounder guns, forty-eight tanks in all); the 2nd Battalion of
the Somerset Light Infantry (a machine gun battalion of three companies
mounted in half-tracks and trucks); and a large complement of artillery,
consisting of towed and self-propelled guns. It contained virtually all the
army's mechanized assets and even had its own Royal Air Force squadron.[17]

It was also the subject of a great deal of popular interest and controversy. Fuller was the original choice to command it, until he torpedoed his own appointment by engaging in a pointless argument over his subsidiary duties as commandant of the Tidworth garrison. He claimed that this additional assignment was an attempt to dilute his responsibilities and ensure the failure of the new unit. That was not true, but it struck many as typical of Fuller's arrogance, perhaps even paranoia.[18] During the trials themselves, Liddell Hart ran a series of articles criticizing the high command for "dropping the pilot" on the verge of armor's maiden voyage. He also pointed out the shortcomings of the unit's composition, as well as the tactical inadequacy of its new commander, Colonel R. J. Collins.[19] Liddell Hart called the EMF a "scratch collection" of many different types of vehicles, wrote sarcastically of the pace of the exercises ("ceremonial slow time," he called it), and mocked the amount of attention the force seemed to be paying to its own protection while on the move, comparing its spirit to that of the banker's motto "No advance without security."[20]

Certainly, criticisms were possible. The most serious was that the EMF was largely a tank and armored car force, not an all-arms mechanized formation. It had no real infantry component, a victory for Fuller and those Royal Tank Corps advocates who saw their unit as the model for the army of the future. It promoted the notion that the "all-tank" unit was the correct direction in which mechanization should proceed, a very different idea than that being followed in Germany, for example.[21] Colonel Collins seemed to recognize this problem and included the 2nd Battalion Cheshire Regiment, an ordinary infantry unit motorized with half-tracks, six-wheeled troop carriers, and trucks, in a number of trials. His decision, which most analysts would now recognize as correct, was roundly criticized by Liddell Hart at the time. He felt that infantry should be armored, or not appear at all in the exercises.

The trials were still a success, however, in that they stimulated a great deal of interest in armor both in Britain and abroad. The problems of maneuvering and supplying a mechanized force under battlefield conditions received a thorough examination for the first time. Lieutenant Colonel Charles Broad was able to incorporate the results of the trials into the so-called Purple Book, officially titled *Mechanized and Armored Formations,* the army's first handbook on armor.[22] A visit by Chief of the Imperial General Staff Sir George Milne near the end of the trials, during which he delivered a speech written by Broad and based on suggestions by Liddell Hart and Fuller, seemed to herald the dawning of a new age. He spoke of restoring "the art of generalship" through the petrol engine, tank, and aircraft and described armor as a unique force that, once concentrated in entire divisions, could carry out "a swinging blow to come round the flank" of the enemy. To employ such futuristic tactics, "a complete change of mental outlook" was necessary on the part of officers and men. He distributed a reading list to those present, in which the armor prophets were heavily represented.[23] As if to place an exclamation point on Milne's statement, the trials of the EMF came to an end a week later, with the experimental unit toying with and overrunning the 3rd Infantry Division and the 2nd Cavalry Brigade while they were still in march column.

One more innovation was on the horizon. By 1930, the British had carried out a number of experiments with radio equipment ("radio telephone," they called it, or "RT"). Though hardly recognized at the time amid all the hubbub about tanks, radio was the real breakthrough of the period. The days of the "runner," the unreliable telegraph, and the Morse code were over, replaced by direct voice messages from commander to subordinate and vice versa. It was not the result of a single invention but was instead a gradual process. The large and unwieldy "unquenched" sets of the wartime period gave way to smaller high-frequency sets, and manual tuning yielded to the crystal. Although technological advances in the field were international, the British were the first to make tactical use of them in their tanks. For the first time, a commander would be capable of real-time monitoring and direction of far-flung battlefield action.

In an exercise at Salisbury Plain in the summer of 1930, the radio played a key role. The 2nd and 5th Battalions Royal Tank Corps (RTC) were a "friendly" force, up against an enemy force consisting of the RTC's 3rd Battalion. At 8:00 A.M., three "enemy" columns—one of horsed cavalry, one of mechanized and one of leg infantry, all supported by artillery and the 3rd Battalion RTC—were advancing eastward to secure crossings over the river Avon. The 5th and 2nd Battalions RTC, concentrated near Tilshead, about ten miles to the east, had patrols out across the enemy's axis of advance. They kept friendly headquarters well-informed of the enemy's movements through radio messages.

As the three enemy columns appeared in strength, Brigadier Kenneth Laird, the friendly commander, sent most of his 5th Battalion to oppose them. The real enemy thrust then erupted not to his front but on his far left, when 3rd Battalion RTC, having detached itself from its infantry and cavalry, suddenly broke cover near Chitterne. Notified of this new threat by a blizzard of aerial and ground messages, Laird dictated a series of short, sharp orders over the radio and within minutes had dispatched 2nd Battalion RTC to cover the axis of the enemy advance. His own attempt to outflank the enemy's right wing, using the rest of 5th Battalion RTC, came to naught, however, as the enemy force was able to respond just as quickly as he had, and the exercise ended with the hostile armored column withdrawing in good order.[24] Compared with many exercises of the day, the German fall maneuvers of 1930, for example, it was the height of modernity. By the 1931 maneuvers, there were enough crystal sets for Broad to command an entire improvised Tank Brigade (three battalions of medium and light tanks) by radio from his command tank.

While it seemed as if Britain had an insurmountable lead in the theory and practice of mechanized war, it lost that lead in the course of the 1930s to its once and future foe, Germany. There were many reasons for the shift. The Great Depression was hard on the kind of research and development projects required for army mechanization. It also led to a loss of national consensus on military spending, with forces on the Left calling for more spending on "butter" as opposed to guns. Such pressures were absent in Germany, at least after 1933. Also troubling Britain was a great controversy over the strategy to be followed in any future war, much of it stemming from the fact that Britain had overseas responsibilities not shared by the other powers. During the 1930s, both the cabinet and the Chiefs of Staff were just as interested in defending the empire as they were in sending an army to the Continent in the event of war. They never did decide whether the British army should serve as an imperial constabulary or a Continental strike force.[25] A force configured for one mission might be useless for the other.

Liddell Hart's influence was again significant. In *The British War in Warfare* (1932), he praised the wisdom of Britain's past reliance on a maritime strategy and avoidance of Continental land conflict. The aberration of the Great War had shown how expensive it was to imitate the land powers. In the future, Britain should limit its Continental commitment to air forces alone. Liddell Hart was now a full-fledged advocate of strategic airpower, arguing that bombing alone could bring an enemy to its knees. "The air force," he wrote, "appears to be cast for the decisive role, as the heirs of Alexander's 'Companion' cavalry."[26] Reflecting the growing belief in a threat from the air, the War Office received orders in 1937 to place priority on antiaircraft defense.

Along with the problems of finance and the intricacies of strategic debate, there was also a great deal of tactical confusion. It was one of those times, now seen as cyclical in the history of armor, when antitank weaponry appeared to have eclipsed the power of the tank. The failure of armor to make any appreciable impact on the battlefields of the Spanish civil war and their high vulnerability to antitank fire had for the moment deflated the tank balloon.[27] Like many observers, Liddell Hart believed that modern defensive weapons had become strong enough to ward off tank attacks, no matter how heavy the vehicle or how thick the armor. He argued that the trend of the future was the miniature tankette, the Carden-Lloyd and the Morris-

Martel. Speed, not armor or weaponry, was the essential attribute of the armored unit. Under his influence, the British army became enamored of light tanks, the lighter the better.

One result of these arguments was that the army continued to form new armored units without a clear raison d'être. In 1931, the provisional 1st Tank Brigade was formed, under Brigadier Kenneth Laird, consisting of three of the RTC's four regiments.[28] It became a permanent part of the army in 1934, expanded into the Mobile Division in 1938, and had its name changed to Armoured Division in 1939. But the question of the correct battlefield role for this unit remained unanswered. The British failed to formulate a coherent armored doctrine. Cavalry officers favored the light tank, to ensure their arm's traditional hold on exploitation and pursuit. General Hugh Elles, now master general of ordnance, supported the "infantry tank," a slow but heavily armored vehicle immune to the standard 37-mm antitank weapon.[29] At the same time, under the influence of designers like Giffard le Quesne ("Q") Martel, there appeared a new line of "cruiser" tanks, designed with lighter armor for higher speed.[30] The division of the tanks into two main categories, cruiser and infantry tanks, plus light tanks besides, was unfortunate. The British had managed to separate the tank's two main attributes: mobility and armor. It would have been a better use of scarce resources to design one rugged, all-purpose tank.

An even more serious problem was the emphasis on the power of the tank at the expense of the other arms. Originating in the all-armor RTC and the fanatical writings of Fuller, it now seemed to have become widespread within the armored force. The successes at Cambrai and Amiens apparently weighed heavily. The talk was of tanks, tanks, tanks; they were rarely discussed as being part of a combined arms force. The fire-breathing commander of the 7th Armoured Division, General Percy Hobart, was a perfect example. He was a tank man through and through, the spiritual successor of Fuller, with a firm belief that tanks were all that mattered.[31] His Armoured Division was a disastrously tank-heavy force of six tank battalions, some 321 tanks in all, cruiser and light. Supporting them was precisely one motorized infantry battalion.

GERMANY: DOCTRINE AND DEVELOPMENTS

In Germany, events took a different, much more productive, course. The Treaty of Versailles told the Germans what sort of army they could have, how many divisions it could contain, how many of those divisions had to be cavalry, the total number of men and officers, and their terms of enlistment. As a result, Germany faced one of the most difficult strategic situations in its history: how to defend the Reich with an army of just 100,000 men, only about one-third the size of neighboring Poland's, smaller even than the armies of Belgium or Denmark. The treaty also forbade tanks. Before German officers or writers could begin to dream of tank fleets and raining down death and destruction on helpless enemy cities—the futuristic fantasies of the Fuller–Liddell Hart–Douhet school—they had to get down to basics.

Under the brilliant chief of the Army Command, General Hans von Seeckt, the army began a reassessment of its procedures, doctrines, and training.[32] He completely rewrote the army's manuals and field service regulations; he inaugurated research projects, sometimes in disguised facilities abroad, to keep abreast of new developments in technology; he did everything possible to ensure that his 100,000 men were the best-trained tiny army on the planet. But he also was wise enough not to topple the whole edifice and start over. A veteran of the war's eastern front, he was remarkably immune to the so-called lessons of World War I. To him, they were merely lessons of the aberration that was the western front: mass armies packed elbow to elbow across 400 miles of front.

Seeckt distrusted the mass army. Its immobility made it worthless. "The mass cannot maneuver," he wrote, "therefore it cannot win." New technology, armor and airpower above all, was increasingly capable of chewing up such immovable blocks of men, who became "cannon fodder for a small number of elite technicians on the other side."[33] A national army only needed to be large enough to fight off an enemy surprise attack. Its strength would lie in mobility, guaranteed by a large contingent of cavalry, a well-conditioned infantry, and a full complement of motorized or mechanized units. Superior mobility would enable this elite army to wage offensive warfare aiming at a decisive battle of annihilation against the enemy. "The goal of modern strategy will be to achieve a decision with highly mobile, highly capable forces, before the masses have even begun to move," he wrote.[34]

Although he was an ardent advocate of mobility, he was no tank fiend like Fuller. Like any German officer schooled in the staff system, he recognized that tanks were here to stay. He did not believe, however, that they had changed the nature of war or rewritten all its principles. He certainly did not see any sort of all-tank army as possible or even desirable. Tanks had strengths, such as firepower and mobility, but they had weaknesses as well: vulnerability to antitank weapons and artillery, and inability to hold the ground that they had taken in an assault. Only in harmony and close cooperation with the traditional arms did tanks have a future. From the start of their experiments with armor, the Germans thought about tanks only in the context of a combined arms force—never alone.[35]

Seeckt's great contribution to modern military thought was that, at the head of a "disarmed" military that was little more than a glorified police force, he continued to think in terms of a "war of movement" *(Bewegungskrieg)*. This was the term that German officers had used for generations to describe warfare in the open field, and we ought to use it today instead of the misnomer *blitzkrieg*. It was, above all, an operational concept: the use of tanks and other motorized and mechanized weapons not simply in the context of a tactical assault on a given stretch of the enemy's line but rather to allow the attacker to carry out large-scale enveloping operations around the flanks of the enemy army.

This is the crucial point: the Germans saw mechanization as a way to restore the operational possibilities that the elder Moltke had exploited so effectively but that had become increasingly difficult—perhaps even impossible—to achieve in the years since 1870. This was the real reason that Germany became the birthplace and test bed of mechanized warfare. It already had the operational doctrine in place: the concept of *Bewegungskrieg*, Moltke's concentric assaults by widely separated forces, his "operations on exterior lines," his search for the battle of encirclement *(Kesselschlacht)*. Magazine rifles, rapid-fire artillery, the inability of the telegraph to control and coordinate the movements of mass armies, and the difficulties of supplying them had made Moltke's operational conception obsolete. Mechanization of the army (tanks, personnel carriers, trucks, and the radio for communication) meant the rebirth of operational art. Once again, the attacking commander had access to the full palette: he could assault, penetrate, turn, perhaps even encircle, the foe. He could approach rapidly, attack audaciously, defeat and pursue, not simply seizing ground or forcing back the enemy but harrying him to his doom. All these achievements would be the work of one, very flexible, tool: the panzer division.

The development of the panzer division was the most important innovation in the interwar period, and it is curious that it is still so little understood. It is often said that the Germans concentrated their tanks in large units rather than parceling them out in "penny packets" among their infantry. One of the leading German military theorists of the era, Colonel (later General) Heinz Guderian, immortalized this doctrine in the untranslatable phrase "Klotzen, nicht kleckern," usually rendered in English as "Kick 'em, don't splatter 'em," but which really means "strike concentrated, not dispersed." Such phrases seem to give the mistaken impression that a panzer division was made up of nothing but tanks. Nothing could have been further from the truth. It was, in the well-chosen words of one armor historian, "a self-contained combined arms team, in which tanks were backed up by other arms brought up, as far as possible, to the tanks' standards of mobility."[36]

The Reichswehr at play. Despite the dummy tanks, the maneuvers had a highly realistic air. Note the smoke, as well as the machine gun deployed amid the vehicles. Courtesy of the Imperial War Museum, London (NYP 68044).

No one man invented it. Most people still tend to associate Guderian's name with the development, but that is a serious misconception. The evidence for this comes mainly from his own writings, especially his self-glorifying autobiography penned in the 1950s, *Panzer Leader*.[37] As with Liddell Hart, a careful reading of the sources indicates that Guderian was not as important as he later claimed. In the 1930s, his contributions to the professional military literature were few. He contributed a handful of signed articles to the *Militär-Wochenblatt* and two to the General Staff journal, the *Militärwissenschaftliche Rundschau*. The book he wrote in the late 1930s, *Achtung—Panzer!*, was a sound work but hardly distinguishable from the mass of German literature on tanks published in the 1930s.[38] It did not even appear until 1937, two years after the formation of the panzer divisions. Guderian led one of the first of Germany's panzer divisions, and he was a brilliant field commander in World War II. His fame will have to rest on those two substantial foundations.

Other figures were just as important to the development of German armor doctrine. Ernst Volckheim was probably the best-known tank writer of the period, author of an impressive body of literature on the role of tanks in both a historical and a contemporary context,[39] including over two dozen signed articles in the *Militär-Wochenblatt.* After 1937, he directed the writing of the tactical manuals for the panzer troops. Volckheim preached a moderate form of the armored gospel. A man whose vision was shaped in the Great War, he felt that tanks were primarily infantry support weapons operating in units of battalion or regimental size, and although he was influenced by Fuller in some areas, there are very few traces of the "all-tank" school in his writings. Success with tanks was a matter of combined arms. Infantry and armor had to work together for their mutual benefit, and tanks had to maintain close liai-

German officers gather at the Tannenberg Memorial: from left to right, Field Marshal August von Mackensen, adorned in the uniform of the Death's Head Hussars; Field Marshal Erich Ludendorff, quartermaster general of German forces in World War I; Field Marshal Paul von Hindenburg, president of the Weimar Republic from 1925 to 1934; and, on the extreme right, General Hans von Seeckt, the architect of the Reichswehr. Courtesy of the Imperial War Museum, London (Q 71364).

son with the artillery. He was also an advocate of strong antitank defenses. More than any other writer of the period, Volckheim emphasized the use of antitank weapons on the battlefield, the employment of artillery in the antitank role, and the role of the tank as a killer of other tanks.

Another writer of influence in the armor discussion, a figure hardly known at all today, was an Austrian general, Ludwig von Eimannsberger, who after the annexation of Austria would become a general in the Wehrmacht. In 1934, he published a book that gained a large audience in the German army, *Der Kampfwagenkrieg (The Tank War)*. A second edition would appear in 1938, updated to take into account the experiences in Ethiopia and Spain. He was also a regular contributor to the pages of the *Militär-Wochenblatt*, including a two-part feature article in December 1935 entitled "Panzertaktik" ("Armor Tactics").[40] He was Germany's best-known tank writer in the 1930s.

Combined arms was his gospel. The theme of "Armor Tactics" was that "the armored assault is not a tank attack, but an attack by a unit that has tanks at its disposal." While no country had any experience in the large-scale use of tanks or aircraft, the issue was becoming more pressing. Not only had the alarms of war sounded in Africa with the Italian invasion of Ethiopia, but German rearmament had fundamentally altered the balance of power. As in 1914, it seemed that developments in equipment were currently far ahead of doctrine.

Eimannsberger was no wild partisan; the spirit of fanaticism that animated many of the interwar tank prophets was far from him. It was silly, he wrote, to think that tanks could easily sail through enemy defenses and get at their headquarters and artillery; it was equally foolish to think that antitank weap-

Dummy tanks, 1928 maneuvers. Courtesy of the Imperial War Museum, London (Q 71388).

ons were capable of destroying every last tank. His mission, he wrote, and the task of all military professionals, was to seek a middle ground on the question of tanks. This was the only way to make sound decisions about their employment and, incidentally, how to defend against them.[41]

In the second part of "Armor Tactics," Eimannsberger discussed the attack.[42] He had no illusions. An attack against units equipped with modern weaponry was a difficult task. If it came down to a battle between tanks and shells, the tanks had already lost. It had always been so; the tank had never been able to defend itself against artillery. Against the formerly supreme machine gun, however, it was impervious. That had been the "original design justification for the tank," he argued, and still was. Yet it now faced more than machine guns—it faced antitank weapons of a wide variety. The prospects for attack were seemingly darker than ever. "New solutions are necessary," he argued, solutions that aimed above all at surprising the enemy. "The attacker must be as ingenious as life itself," he exhorted.[43]

The first and most important principle, he wrote, was that the tanks were never to attack alone but only in conjunction with the other weapons. Each had its own area of responsibility. The flier fought other aircraft, intervened tactically, and scouted; the artillery pinned the enemy; the infantry accompanied the tanks and occupied positions that had been overrun. "It is not just the tanks, but the entire unit that attacks."[44] This was, Eimannsberger believed, no longer open to argument or differences of opinion.

The second principle was that tanks had to attack in mass and with the greatest possible speed. Their worst enemy was hostile artillery; the longer those guns fired, the greater the danger to the tanks. If the tanks came on in waves on a broad front, it would be impossible for the defenders, in the short time available, to fire at every target. Surviving tanks would then pour through gaps in the defense, using the opportunity to attack on the flanks and rear of the enemy and thus achieve a complete breakthrough. It had to be rapid, even rash. A careful probing attack that first revealed the position of enemy weapons, then methodically beat them down had the disadvantage of taking too much time, and therefore robbing the attack of the factor of surprise that had made it powerful in the first place. Soon the defender's own tank units would be on the scene. Fighting enemy infantry and tanks alike would be "a very undesirable burden." Whether fighting enemy antitank positions or enemy tanks, speed was of the essence: "Speed means life." Speed meant surprise, and surprise was "the eternal advantage" in war. The tank alone made it possible to draw together superior force at a chosen point and launch a decisive attack.

Another important tank theorist of the era was Colonel Walter Spannenkrebs, author of *Angriff mit Kampfwagen (The Attack with Fighting Vehicles)*.[45]

He considered the issue of whether the tanks were tactical weapons, useful for helping the infantry get forward, or whether their main use should be on the operational level, with concentrated armored units carrying out long-range missions.[46] Used as tactical weapons in a positional breakthrough battle, he wrote, the attacking tanks would be facing a defender who was expecting an attack, had sufficient weapons to meet it, and was already concentrated for battle. The attacker, too, was prepared, having done careful reconnaissance of the enemy and the terrain and having evaluated the most fruitful lines of attack.

When employing armor on the operational level, none of these preconditions were in evidence. Uncertainty regarding the enemy and the exact shape of the terrain excluded such methodical procedures. "The battle plays out in a large, free area, which often cannot be scouted sufficiently by either friend or foe."[47] Neither side knew with any assurance where the enemy was, which gave attacking armored units the possibility of surprise, while also increasing the probability of them crashing unawares into a strong enemy force. High mobility on the part of the force and decisiveness on the part of its commanders were prerequisites to success. Even a weak defender, by 1939, had enough antitank power to make life unpleasant for the tanks; rapid movement and surprise maneuvers made it less likely that he would have time to use his weapons. The goal was to maneuver so as to strike an unarmored foe who was still in march column and thus for all intents and purposes defenseless. In a positional battle, tanks had to attack the enemy where he was strongest and where he was expecting an attack; used operationally, they would be capable of carrying out the "complete and rapid destruction" of slower, unarmored forces.

Another difference between the tactical and operational use of tanks was the role of support weapons: in a positional battle, tanks cooperated with infantry, artillery, even pioneers. Used operationally, the other weapons were simply not fast enough to keep up. This was the reason for the development of the combined arms mechanized unit known as the panzer division: "A pure tank formation is not capable of conducting operational warfare; only a panzer division is." The only other arm capable of conducting operations side by side with the panzer division was the air force. "It is scarcely possible to overrate its importance." Principal tasks included the following:

1. Air reconnaissance, both before and during the battle, to keep the panzer leader well informed by radio of enemy concentrations and countermeasures.
2. Direct support, with the fighters and bombers substituting for friendly artillery, paying close attention to strongpoints, enemy movements, and concentration points.

3. Air supply of the panzer spearheads. With the armored units operating at such distance, their supply columns were natural targets for the action of the enemy, especially if he had any degree of operational mobility himself. Air supply was rapid and immune to a land enemy and could give the panzer division true operational independence.[48]

Airpower, Spannenkrebs added, might also be useful in carrying out landings in cooperation with the advance of the panzer forces.

Spannenkrebs discussed more thoroughly than any prewar author the operational tasks to be carried out by panzer units, a topic that was usually discussed in very general terms. "The missions and objectives can be set all the higher," he wrote, "the larger the concentration of units."[49] Panzer divisions were only capable of limited independent actions. An entire panzer corps was capable of more wide-ranging missions, and a panzer army could seek truly decisive results. In the next war, armor would have the following operational tasks: (1) an independent blow at the outset of a war, before the enemy had time to secure his lines of communication and complete his preparations; (2) a drive against the flank or rear of the enemy army, especially carried out in cooperation with a decisive attack against his front; and (3) the decisive exploitation of a successful breakthrough. In general, tank units in a future war would take the place of the battle cavalry of the nineteenth century, only much stronger and far-reaching. Germany would need more than one or two panzer divisions. The task involved required "masses of armor."[50]

Spannenkrebs ended *Der Angriff* by taking the longer view. The development of fire weapons in the twentieth century had led to "a crisis in conducting a decisive battle." The invention of the motor had seemingly sharpened the crisis, since it allowed the defender to counter any move by the attacker and rush forces to any threatened sector. Things had reached a crossroads on the modern battlefield: either tanks would be used in a dispersed manner and in small numbers or they would be used en masse at the right time, with the support and cooperation of every other weapon: the rifle, the gun, the airplane, and the most modern means of communication. Used in massive numbers, tanks would be able to overload the antitank defenses on a given, narrow sector and in this way effect a breakthrough. Some would fall victim to the enemy's antitank fire; many more would get through. "All or nothing!" he wrote. "Half-measures lead to failure."[51]

From this short survey of the writings of Volckheim, Eimannsberger, and Spannenkrebs, we can trace the progression in the German thoughts on armor. Volckheim saw tanks as an infantry support arm. Eimannsberger spoke of both tactical and operational tasks but stressed the former. By 1939 and the publication of Spannenkrebs's work, the German army was clearly thinking in terms of conducting operational warfare with its panzer divisions.

Beyond the theoretical work, the development of the panzer division was a result of numerous practical experiments in the field. Since the days of the elder Moltke, the German army had relied on exercises, war games, and maneuvers as a means of training its officers and testing its doctrine. So it was with General von Seeckt's Reichswehr. In October 1921, less than three years after the Armistice, the army conducted maneuvers of motorized units in the Harz Mountains. In the winter of 1923–24, maneuvers investigated the possibility of cooperation between motorized ground forces and air forces.[52]

As exercise followed exercise in the 1920s, tanks and "motorized infantry"—that is, loaded on trucks, not tracked vehicles—came to play a more prominent role. In the 1925 maneuvers of the 1st Infantry Division, stationed in Königsberg, both the "Blue" and the "Red" team had motorcycles, armored cars, and dummy tanks in their order of battle. An American observer described an armored counterattack during the exercise, making it clear the Germans were still groping their way forward through experimentation:

> The tanks were employed in three lines about one hundred yards apart, consisting of five, four, and three tanks respectively. This was the first maneuver in which the Germans had used these camouflaged tanks and the infantry did not seem to know what to do with them. In one company the platoons were formed up in platoon columns in rear of the tanks. In another they marched parallel with the tank and in another company they preceded it.[53]

In 1931–32, Colonel Oswald Lutz, the inspector of motor transport troops, directed a series of exercises involving dummy tank battalions.[54] From these exercises Lutz derived a series of lessons to be used as a basis for further training. First, tank units should receive *independent battle missions* that took into account their special qualities. Tying them down in infantry support robbed them of their principal advantage: mobility. Even using them in an attack with limited objectives contradicted common sense. Tanks were for the main effort only, too valuable to waste on a sideshow. *Mass* was the second principle. Using tanks in anything under battalion strength was a blunder. Even given the present, rather primitive, state of antitank weapons and training, an attack by a tank company would not achieve a decisive result. The use of small armored units represented a dispersion of the new queen of battle, violating the principle of concentration of force. Lutz's third principle was *surprise*. An attack at dawn was best, he felt. The assault should be "surprising, sudden, and on a broad front," in order to splinter the defense. It was also necessary to echelon that attack in enough depth to make it possible to switch the *Schwerpunkt* itself during the pursuit, as well as to crush any newly arriving targets or obstructions.[55]

The Germans continued their experiments at the great fall maneuvers of 1932. This exercise was the first to employ a corps-sized mobile formation, testing its ability to carry out rapid strikes deep into an enemy's flank and rear. The highlight was an attempt by the Motorized Cavalry Corps to force a crossing of the Oder River from the east.[56] An amalgamation of horse, dummy tanks, and motorized units, its two component divisions had a full array of auxiliary units: 1st Cavalry Division included a bicycle battalion and a motorized reconnaissance battalion, as well as a fully motorized divisional headquarters; 3rd Cavalry Division had a motorcycle battalion attached, along with its two brigades of cavalry (not regiments, as was the case with the 1st). Corps headquarters included a motorized antiaircraft battalion, a motorized heavy artillery battalion, and an observation squadron of six planes.

The maneuvers were also a field test of Germany's first true motorized unit, the Motorized Reconnaissance Detachment (MRD). It was an interesting mix of unit types. The battalion headquarters included a mounted signal platoon; an armored car platoon of four cars; an antitank platoon (two 37-mm guns); a bicycle company of three platoons; a machine gun troop, consisting of four heavy machine guns; and a cavalry troop. In accordance with the treaty restrictions, the antitank platoon was equipped with wooden dummies mounted on actual gun platforms. The organization of this headquarters unit shows a Reichswehr in the transitional stage of motorization, with horses, cars, and motorcycles all present. The MRD itself was likewise

Regimental signal platoon and messenger dogs, 1932 maneuvers. Courtesy of the Imperial War Museum, London (Q 71397).

a mixed bag of types, liberally equipped with radios: two armored car companies (armed with light cannon and machine gun), two motorcycle companies, a so-called heavy company (a motorized gun platoon, an antitank platoon, and a pioneer platoon), and a signal platoon.[57]

One lesson of the 1932 maneuvers was that horses and motors did not mix. The Motorized Cavalry Corps was so jam-packed with units of diverse types that giving it a simple march order was next to impossible; trying to get it across the Oder was a nightmare. It is hard to debate the pithy comment of President von Hindenburg, who observed, "In war, only what is simple can succeed. I visited the staff of the Cavalry Corps. What I saw there was not simple." The chief of the Army Command, General Kurt von Hammerstein, agreed, citing "the intense confusion" that had arisen in the river-crossing attempt.[58] It not only had delayed the operation but also caused unnecessary and fatiguing movement by large bodies of troops assembled along the riverbank.

Still, the 1932 maneuvers, undertaken just months before the advent of the Hitler regime, were a major step forward for the Germans. The High Command, although still tentative in its approach and wedded to an essentially unworkable combination of motor and horse, was beginning to devise operational doctrine to employ its new mobile forces. The "Red" Cavalry Corps' initial plan on September 19 to "attack the Blue forces fighting on the Oder deep in the flank and rear"[59] showed the Germans once again aiming at nothing less than decisive operational victory.

Although Adolf Hitler did not invent the new German doctrine of mobile warfare, it is fair to say that he recognized the potential of tank warfare more rapidly than some other national leaders of the day. In May 1935, Hitler declared that Germany would henceforth not feel itself restricted to the limitations on arms imposed by the Treaty of Versailles. The new army, known as the Wehrmacht, contained some thirty-six infantry divisions, in place of the Reichswehr's seven, and in October, the first three panzer divisions came into existence: 1st Panzer Division under General Maximilian Freiherr von Weichs (stationed at Weimar); 2nd Panzer Division under Guderian (Würzburg); and 3rd Panzer Division, under General Ernst Fessmann (Berlin). Each consisted of a tank brigade paired with a motorized infantry brigade. The panzer division had enough tanks to satisfy even the purist: two tank regiments of two battalions each, with a strength of 128 Mark Is per battalion. Counting command tanks, the division contained some 561 in all. But there was also a very strong infantry component, consisting of a two-battalion motorized infantry regiment, plus a motorcycle battalion. In addition, in what was the true mark of the panzer division, there was a complete cast of supporting arms: a motorized artillery regiment, a motorized antitank battal-

The humble origins of blitzkrieg. Tiny German PzKw. Is crossing a stream during maneuvers. Courtesy of the Imperial War Museum, London (HU 2690).

ion, and a motorized pioneer company, later expanded into a battalion. There was also a motorized reconnaissance detachment, the same one the Germans had been employing since the 1932 maneuvers, made up of armored cars and motorcycles.

The 1936 maneuvers were the first for the new Wehrmacht and once again featured the motorized reconnaissance detachment, described by one Brit-

PzKw. Is on parade before the Brandenberg Gate in Berlin. Courtesy of the Imperial War Museum, London (MH 8876).

PzKw. Is, converted to infantry carriers by the removal of their turrets, on maneuvers in 1936. Courtesy of the Imperial War Museum, London (STT 7356A).

ish observer as "a mechanized creation of the most modern type."[60] Tanks had also made an appearance, a regiment of Mark Is. They launched a successful attack against a strongly held hill on day one of the exercise, although they suffered such heavy losses that the regiment was ruled out of play on the second day. On the final day, they transferred to the other side, and the whole regiment—all 140 machines—carried out a spectacular attack on a line of entrenchments.

The 1937 maneuvers made the superiority of the panzer division clear to the vast majority of German officers.[61] This was the largest exercise held in Germany since the end of the war, attended by Hitler and Mussolini, the latter being in the midst of his triumphal tour of Nazi Germany. As always in German maneuvers, Blue faced Red in an imaginary theater of war, this one consisting of the rolling hills, lakes, and watercourses of Mecklenburg, what we often fancifully call the "North German Plain." Blue, in the east, held a bridgehead over the winding Peene River near Lake Malchin. Red, located in the west, had to attack the bridgehead and had the 3rd Panzer Division for that purpose. Moving up 100 kilometers from the army reserve to its assault position in a single day (September 19), the 3rd Panzer Division launched its assault on September 20. It sent its motorized infantry brigade forward to help the 30th Infantry Division (Motorized) engage the bridgehead frontally, while swinging its panzer brigade around Blue's extreme left in the south. Working in close liaison with airpower, the panzers broke through the Blue position here. Without pausing, they drove on the

Armored action during the great fall maneuvers of 1936. Courtesy of the Imperial War Museum, London (HU 54960).

town of Stavenhagen, well behind the defenders' position, reaching it and cutting off the principal supply road into Malchin. Having encircled the entire bridgehead, still without pausing, they now assaulted it successfully; Blue reinforcements were late in arriving due to a very successful air interdiction effort by Red. Thus, midway through day four of what was supposed to be a seven-day maneuver, Red had completely destroyed the Blue position. The chief of the General Staff, General Ludwig Beck, a man by no means as opposed to the incorporation of armor as the mythology would have us believe, was apparently so shocked at what he had seen that he did something unprecedented since the days of the kaiser: he lodged a complaint with the umpires, accusing them of underestimating the effect of defensive anti-tank fire. He also ordered 3rd Panzer Division out of the rest of the maneuver, which concluded as a fairly trite infantry-versus-infantry encounter.

The 1937 maneuvers showed the maturation of German armored doctrine. It included not only tanks but also aircraft, which were extremely effective in cooperation with the panzer units, used tactically to punch a hole through enemy lines, but also in an operational role, carrying out interdiction missions against Blue's reinforcements, preventing them from arriving in a timely fashion on the battlefield. But the panzer division had clearly been the star. It had established once and for all its suitability for independent operational-level missions. The "battle of Malchin" was the first successful armored operation in history.

The Germans also spent a great deal of time on questions of command and control of these new mechanized formations. German officers had been mightily impressed by the 1931 British maneuvers in which General Broad had led his entire Tank Brigade by radio, as well as the 1934 maneuvers in which some 230 tanks were commanded over shortwave. In an October 1935 article, "Communications Technology and the Leadership of Mechanized Units," Major Friedrich Bertkau argued that mechanized units could only be commanded with the help of modern technology. It was not simply a luxury:

> The assembly of motor vehicles in extraordinarily long march columns or widespread battle formations, the noise of the machinery, the difficulty of observation from inside the tank, the speed of movement, the sudden change of the battle situation, the special difficulty of undertaking action at night—all these make great demands for a technological solution to the functions of command.[62]

Communications within the unit were just as important as those between the various units, and it did not matter whether the force was on the march, pausing to rest, or in the midst of battle. Only the radio could provide an instantaneous way to report the situation back to the commander and to

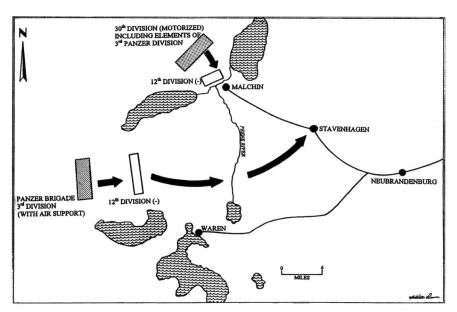

The assault of the 3rd Panzer Division: Wehrmacht maneuvers, Mecklenburg, September 1937.

Elements of the 15th Division crossing the Werra River during the great fall maneuvers of 1937. Courtesy of the Imperial War Museum, London (HU 54967).

send relevant orders to the troops. Problems might arise, such as crowding of frequencies, or interference both deliberate (enemy activity) and natural (weather conditions), and there was always the danger of the enemy intercepting the messages. "According to the experience gained in our exercises, it is clear that an army cannot move across country, broadcasting radio messages, without betraying its order of battle and its deployment to the enemy."[63] One could code one's messages, but that meant a waste of time on both the sending and receiving end, thus violating the prime advantage of radio, its instantaneous nature. New technology was necessary, perhaps nondetectable or nondirectional frequencies, to solve that thorny problem. From the start, the German principal for the new panzer force was a radio in each command station and each vehicle of the mechanized unit, from the smallest motorcycle to the heaviest tank, with specialized command vehicles designed to carry radio equipment, both senders and receivers. The motorcycle itself, with or without sidecar, also played a role in rapidly transmitting orders both within and between units.

The use of radio also influenced the rebirth of what had been a tradition in the Prussian-German army: short orders. The commander was supposed to devise a mission for his subordinate, frame the mission in a short, verbal order, and allow the subordinate a certain leeway in carrying it out. This was the essence of *Auftragstaktik*. The war had seen that tradition disappear, as trench warfare dictated ever longer orders for administration, attack, and especially bombardment. In addition, the switch from a two-brigade/four-regiment division to a three-regiment division, although it brought many tactical advantages to the Germans, also had the disadvantage of forcing a division commander to devise commands for three primary subunits instead of two. General von Seeckt had stressed over and again the need to shorten orders. But there were still complaints in the 1930s that "divisional orders today bear the imprint of positional warfare and the typewriter."[64] There would be no time for typewriters on the mechanized battlefield.

INTERWAR DOCTRINE: CONCLUSIONS

Compared with the numerous dead ends other countries reached, *Bewegungskrieg* and its tool, the panzer division, were no mean achievements. In Great Britain, doctrinal debate brought forth something called the "armoured division," an absurdly tank-heavy unit lacking in supporting arms, with tanks being divided by mission into cruiser and infantry types. In France, the armored force was likewise split between two kinds of units: the *division légère mécanique* (light mechanized division, or DLM), intended for the cavalry role, and the *division cuirassée* (armored division, or DCR), heavier and slower than the DLM, and intended for close support of attacking infantry. Although the French built some very fine equipment, the SOMUA S-35 medium tank and the Char B1 heavy, they never succeeded in making the doctrinal breakthrough that the Germans had. What the French needed was a unit with the speed of the DLM and the shock power of the DCR, something, in fact, like the German panzer division.

The interwar French army was torn on the question of military doctrine. How else could it have contained, at one and the same time, a contentious "armor prophet" in the form of Colonel Charles de Gaulle and a contradictory desire to plant itself behind a concrete fortification and fight a war of position? The latter strain of doctrinal thought eventually won out in the building of the Maginot line. While it was once fashionable to utter a series of accusations against the French commanders at this point, stressing their unwillingness to learn from the last war, their resistance to change, and their insistence on centralized command and control, many scholars today argue that the shift toward defensive doctrine made sense for the French army, a force composed of "overworked professionals, short-service conscripts, and badly prepared reservists." As badly as it served France in 1940, the resulting doctrine of "methodical battle" made sense for the Third Republic.[65]

The only country to come close to the German concept of armored operations was the Soviet Union. Here, too, there was an armor prophet. In the mid-1920s, the Red Army's gifted chief of staff, General Mikhail Tukhachevksy, formulated a concept that he called "deep battle."[66] As codified in the Field Regulations of 1936 *(PU-36)*, it called for "shock armies" to spearhead the assault, reinforced by extra artillery and infantry support tanks, as well as by "mobile groups" (one or two mechanized corps and a cavalry corps). The shock army's mission was to break through by delivering violent blows on a very narrow front. Once the enemy line had been breached, the exploitation phase would begin, carried out by the mobile groups, working in close cooperation with air strikes and even airborne assaults. The advance would be rapid, 40 to 50 kilometers per day, enabling the mobile groups to shred the enemy command and control network and simultaneously to seize "advantageous lines" for further operations. The exploiting force was to choose its axes of advance so as not merely to push back the enemy but to encircle and destroy him. Within two to three weeks, a 300- to 400-kilometer hole would be torn in the enemy line, and exploiting forces were expected to advance 200 to 300 kilometers. The brunt of "deep battle" would be borne by the mechanized corps, powerful formations containing up to 1,000 tanks. By 1936, Tukhachevsky had organized four of them, and he was planning more. German observers at the 1936 Soviet fall maneuvers were impressed with the commitment to mechanization:

Tanks were used in a meeting engagement, in a breakthrough, in a fight for an advanced position, in breaking off a combat, in a counterattack, in pursuit, in a powerful river-crossing assault, they were used tactically, in immediate cooperation with the infantry, they were also assembled into mechanized formations and given strategic assignments. Everything that could be asked of the tanks was demanded. We see a grand breadth of vision, a radical exhaustion of all possibilities, an almost boundless trust in the strength of armor.[67]

Actual battlefield developments lagged far behind the theory. The distrust of Josef Stalin for his bright, young chief of staff would culminate in Tukhachevsky's arrest, trial, and execution in 1938. The poor showing of Soviet armor in the Spanish civil war (1936–39) and during the occupation of eastern Poland in September 1939 also put his theories in disrepute, if there had been anyone brave enough to promote them. The four mechanized corps were disbanded in November 1939, replaced by fifteen motorized divisions and thirty-two tank brigades. These smaller formations were unsuited for the sort of strategic penetration envisioned in the 1936 field regulations, being designed instead for close infantry support. Germany's victories in the west in 1940 would cause the Soviets to rethink their move, and the invasion of 1941 would catch them in the midst of yet another reorganization, this time back to mechanized corps.[68]

Tukhachevsky's rediscovery by Western scholars at the height of the cold war righted a historical wrong and recognized a figure who had been consigned to the Stalinist "memory hole." Tukhachevsky had developed a form of the German recipe for mobile operations, if an inflexible and tightly choreographed version. It is easy, however, to overrate both his contribution and the ability of the forces he led actually to carry out a "deep battle." The historical record is mixed on whether it would have worked as he drew it up. There is little thought given in *PU-36* to the command and control problems inherent in deep battle, the same problems the Germans had been discussing publicly in the pages of the *Militär-Wochenblatt* for an entire decade. Command initiative was absolutely necessary for the kind of hard-driving warfare Tukhachevsky envisioned, and Stalin hardly seemed to encourage it by having him murdered.[69] Neither was National Socialism especially supportive of independent thought and action, of course, but as we have seen, the development of mobile operations doctrine predated Hitler by a good while. Tukhachevsky and the career he might have carved out in World War II will have to remain one of the great "what-ifs" of military history.[70]

In general, the German command managed to walk a middle path in evaluating the tank. The tank was neither the omnipotent wonder weapon that J. F. C. Fuller and, at times, Liddell Hart, claimed it was, nor simply an unfortunate and temporary interruption to soldiering as usual (what might be called the conservative view, present in every army of the day to some degree). Instead, the tank became thoroughly incorporated into a new version of something the Germans had always been very good at—in fact, it might be called a German tradition—combined arms warfare.

There was no "armor debate" in Germany. All German staff officers assumed the presence of tanks on any modern battlefield and subjected them to a rigorous series of war games, exercises, and maneuvers dwarfing anything done in any of the other nations with the possible exception of Soviet Russia. The findings of their experiments again walked a middle path: between seeing the tank as a mere tactical weapon (useful only as a means to help the infantry cross "no-man's-land" and break into a fortified position or trench line) and a strategic weapon (capable of winning the war by itself). Instead, in the organizational form of the panzer division, they designed the perfect weapon for winning decisive victory on the operational level, a way to fight and win not merely a battle but an entire campaign.

Despite the great changes since 1914, the Germans still clung to concepts that would have been familiar to Moltke and Schlieffen. They continued to recognize two types of war: *Stellungskrieg* (positional warfare), the very bloody kind that had characterized the western front from 1915 to 1917; and *Bewegungskrieg* (the war of movement), a series of hard blows by large units (corps and armies) in the open field, with the aim of destroying the enemy field force.[71] German officers had always regarded the former as an aberration, the latter as normative. The war of movement was the only path to a rapid, decisive victory, the only type of war suitable for a centrally located Continental power like Germany, whose enemies held larger reserves of manpower and thus would have the advantage in any long war of attrition.

The panzer division was a tool that the Germans designed for the restoration of the war of movement. Containing not just tanks but a full complement of supporting arms (motorized infantry, self-propelled artillery and antitank guns, even motorized pioneers and signal troops), a panzer division could maneuver, assault, and, most important, do what no army had been able to do effectively since the days of Napoleon—pursue the beaten foe and harry him to his destruction—all with equal dash and ability. As we have seen, this had been the problem of the Great War. Again and again, assaulting forces had made tactical penetrations. What had been lacking was the ability to widen the break-in (*Einbruch* in the German) into a breakthrough *(Durchbruch)* and then to follow it up with a pursuit—lacking, that is, until the advent of the radio-commanded panzer division.

Chapter 7

• • • • • • • • • • • • • •

Ethiopia and Spain

INTRODUCTION: THE "INTERWAR" ERA

Although most of the attention devoted to the interwar period focuses on the development of blitzkrieg, the era was an extremely violent one that witnessed conflict after conflict. They include the Russo-Polish War (1920–21), the little-known Chaco War between Paraguay and Bolivia (1932–35), the Italian invasion of Ethiopia (1935–36), and the Spanish civil war (1936–39).[1] The period also saw the beginning of Japanese aggression in China, the annexation of Manchuria in 1931 and the start of a full-scale invasion of China proper in 1937. It might have been "interwar," but it certainly was not peace.

The two wars that had the most impact on contemporaries were Ethiopia and Spain. Once again, as in the era before 1914, military professionals the world over examined them carefully to see what hints they might provide as to the future of warfare. Once again, the lessons they taught were incomplete and at times contradictory. Of particular interest to the armies of the Great Powers, engrossed as they were in their own doctrinal debate over this very issue, was the role that tanks and aircraft had played in the fighting. As we shall see, this approach turned out to be a distorting lens that often led observers to misconstrue the events they were trying to analyze.

THE CONFLICT IN ETHIOPIA: ANALYSIS AND LESSONS

The Italian campaign in Ethiopia can be described quickly. On October 3, 1935, with General Emilio de Bono in overall command, an Italian army of over 100,000 men invaded Ethiopia.[2] The force included nine divisions, supported both by tanks and by the modern aircraft of the Italian air force *(Regia Aeronautica)*. One thrust, under de Bono himself, came from the north, based on the Eritrean town of Asmara. A second, much smaller, came from the south under General Rodolfo Graziani, operating out of Somaliland, with Mogadishu as its base. The opponent was a feudal kingdom rich in manpower and valor but almost totally lacking in modern weapons.

The northern advance bogged down after crossing the border, due to de Bono's caution and the necessity to build supply roads back to his base. The Ethiopians took advantage of his hesitancy, and by December they were across the entire Italian front in force. They launched a series of powerful thrusts but never coordinated them into a general counterattack. After some dark moments in which it appeared that they might break through, superior Italian firepower routed them. With Marshal Pietro Badoglio having replaced de Bono in December, the Italians launched a series of multicorps assaults that crushed the Ethiopian main force. A conspicuous role was played by the Italian air force. From the first day of the war, it operated with total impunity, harrying Ethiopian ground troops, bombing rear areas, and, especially, completing the destruction of already defeated Ethiopian forces as they were attempting to retreat. It was "magnificent sport," in the words of Mussolini's nineteen-year-old son, and Italian air force pilot, Vittorio.[3] After the last great battle, at Mai Ceu (May 31–April 1, 1936), all that remained was the speedy occupation of the vast Ethiopian plateau. Badoglio entered Addis Ababa on May 5.

The campaign in the south was quite different. The Ogaden Desert was the theater, and here much smaller armies were in play. Italian commander Rodolfo Graziani led a much more mobile force than Badoglio's, organizing it into smaller task forces *(gruppi)* consisting of tanks, armored cars, and truck-borne infantry, along with considerable support from the air. Still, despite his mobility advantage, Graziani moved very slowly, an omen for his later career in the Western Desert during World War II. After destroying a clumsy and poorly supplied Ethiopian attack at Dolo, he sat for months. Not until April 18, two weeks after the destruction of the main Ethiopian army at Mai Ceu, did he resume his advance. Even then, he took ten full days to chew through the Ethiopian positions in front of Negelli. The spirit of mobile warfare was far from him.

Although it is largely neglected today, the Italian campaign in Ethiopia (or Abyssinia, as it was then known in Europe) was the subject of a great

deal of discussion at the time. This was not merely because of its significance to international relations but because of the military lessons allegedly
to be learned from it. At the time, the Ethiopians had a martial reputation
very different from their portrayal by modern writers. They were one of the
few colonial peoples in the last 100 years to inflict a defeat on a European
power—these same Italians—at the battle of Adowa in 1896. Their land was
remote, mountainous, and forbidding in the extreme. Much of the informed
military opinion of the day spoke of the upcoming campaign in terms of its
difficulties, not its alleged ease.

The Italians were faced with a tough operational task. Ethiopia, at a little
under 500,000 square miles, was about the size of France and Germany combined. The Italian force sent to overrun it was extremely heavy, featuring
motorized, mechanized, and air units with all their road, fuel, and supply requirements. Behind the fighting troops, the supply columns were almost fully
motorized. At the start of the campaign, the Italians had almost 5,000 trucks
in the theater of war; by the end of the war, there were 8,377 trucks in use on
the northern front alone, and the total for the entire Italian force was at least
10,000.[4] The use of machine forces in Ethiopia guaranteed that the logistical
burden of the campaign would be huge. The battle for supply far outstripped
the fighting in its intensity and in the amount of time and energy expended
on it. On the northern front, every crumb of food, drop of water, and can of
gasoline had to travel 2,500 miles from Italy to the Eritrean port of Massawa.
Despite the talk in Italian propaganda about Massawa being a "first-class
anchorage,"[5] it was barely more than a decent roadstead with a single pier in
1935. All that year, there were feverish preparations to improve the port, to
construct roads to the Ethiopian frontier, and to amass provisions for the tens
of thousands of men who were arriving monthly. In September 1935, 100,000
men, 1 million tons of stores and ammunition, 200 cannon, 6,000 mules, and
2,300 motor vehicles left Italy for Massawa.[6] At its height, the expeditionary
force consisted of 18,200 officers, 386,300 Italian soldiers, and 108,300 native soldiers, with 14,600 machine guns, 1,800 artillery pieces and trench
mortars, and tens of thousands of motor vehicles.

Once they had unloaded, men and supplies had a daunting journey just
to get to the Ethiopian border. It was over seventy miles as the crow flies
from Massawa to the frontier, although the road through Asmara, the capital of Eritrea, winds so sinuously that it is probably twice that distance on
the ground. Not only was it a daunting problem to supply 100,000 modern-
armed troops at such distances, but the insufficiency of the road net severely
hindered any sort of operational maneuver.

Much of the equipment was barely up to the challenge. The tanks were
quaint little vehicles. It was the heyday of the light tank in many nations.

The backbone of the Italian armored force in Ethiopia was the light CV-33 (for *carro veloce*), a two-man tankette.[7] Its main armament consisted of twin 8-mm machine guns in a limited traverse mounting, and its protection was just 5 to 15 mm of armor. Although it had a top road speed of twenty-six miles per hour, it was unlikely to find enough road anywhere in Ethiopia to keep up that speed for long. It had a great deal of difficulty with the heat and the rocky terrain, especially on the northern front, and an embarrassing number would break down in combat.

Command and control of the Italian force was a nightmare. The Fascist system had overseen the growth of a very confused military structure. The Italian army in East Africa was a bewildering mix of regular army divisions, in both the standard (three-regiment) and lighter "binary" (two-regiment) configuration; Blackshirt *(Camicie Nere)* Divisions, Fascist militia troops who were usually equipped with a larger proportion of motorized vehicles and whose training was long on lectures about "will" and "cold brutality" and short on actual field exercises; and, finally, a large number of native Eritreans, who would bear the brunt of the heaviest fighting in this campaign. They would also suffer most of the casualties.[8]

Although it is fashionable today to laugh at the Italian army, many people took it quite seriously in the 1930s. Many observers of this campaign, both civilian and military, were impressed with its efficiency, its drive, and its ability to improvise in such a difficult environment. Herbert Matthews of the *New York Times* called the conquest "a difficult job superbly done,"[9] and that would sum up the tone of much of the contemporary analysis.

There were some things to admire in the Italians' achievement. They displayed genius in areas of planning, organization, and supply. They were the first army in the world to operate large motorized and mechanized units in the field, after all the years of discussion. They had demonstrated that it was possible to keep them fed, supplied, and in command over vast distances—much larger than any European army was likely to have to face, and in much rougher country. They were the first to demonstrate the awesome power of the air arm, which had done something that no European force had done for 100 years: carry out a pursuit. Fighters and bombers had, apparently, replaced the cavalry, taking on a mission the horse could no longer perform. After Mai Ceu, 20,000 men of the Eritrean Corps had force-marched around the left flank of the disintegrating Ethiopian army to Dessie, cutting themselves loose from their supply lines on the ground. Italian aircraft supplied the vast column for the entire 200-mile length of the march, even to the point of dropping livestock by parachute. Supplied with over 113 tons of air-dropped supplies, the Eritreans made it to Dessie in less than a week, an average of over 30 miles per day.[10] Badoglio then transferred his headquarters to Dessie on April 20 by air—a true innovation. Twelve heavy Caproni-133 bombers brought the Marshal and his entire staff the 110 miles from Dessie in just ninety minutes.[11]

Nevertheless, it is difficult to say what lessons the campaign actually had to offer. The interwar "prophets" weighed in with more than their share of articles, delighted that their predictions of "machine war" had apparently been confirmed. But the analysis was often so general as to be worthless. An article by J. F. C. Fuller written just before the end of the fighting shows him at his worst, as he used the Ethiopian War to wax eloquent on his constant obsession, the uselessness of the traditional arms in modern combat, as well as his "obsession *du jour*," strategic airpower. The war, he argued, had been "one of the most remarkable ever fought," since it had proved the enormous power of modern weapons. In a war between "civilized nations," in whose ranks he did not include the Ethiopians, armaments would be more or less equal. Targets for air attack, however, would be abundant, because of the density of the population. If airpower could demoralize the tribesmen of a primitive land, its effects would be even worse on "overcrowded cities and industrial areas" of the civilized powers. "What does this then lead us to suppose? That in another European war the decisive weapon will be the airplane, and when it has defeated or mastered its like, the masses below are at its mercy, and that the larger they are, not only the more vulnerable will they become, but the greater will be the social upheaval following their catastrophe."[12] This is not an analysis of the Ethiopian War at all. Rather, it is an example of a writer using the war as an excuse to write the same things he had been writing for the previous twenty years. He could have written it without reference to Ethiopia at all. In fact, as eyewitness reports point out, the Italian use of bombing against targets behind the Ethiopian lines (i.e., in a strategic as opposed to a tactical role) had failed to make much of an impression on the Ethiopians. Towns and cities were simply not that prevalent in Ethiopia. The war said nothing one way or the other about the efficacy of bombing them.[13]

Liddell Hart was closer to the mark in his comments, although he, too, seemed more interested in his own personal obsession: proving that he was right.[14] In a chapter in *Europe in Arms* (1937) devoted to "The Abyssinian War and Its Bearing on Future Warfare," he reprinted much of an article he had written in the summer of 1935 in the *Times,* in which he had predicted that the Ethiopians, suffering from an "Adowa illusion," would probably launch a great attack and be crushed in the process by superior Italian firepower.[15] "Omdurman might be repeated," he had predicted at that time. He then went on to argue that his predictions about the campaign had been right all along: "The machine had triumphed—over the man.

The Lion of Judah had been crushed between the upper and nether jaws of Italy's mechanized forces."[16] No sane person would argue with this point. But Liddell Hart's simplistic analysis considerably understated the dangerous situation in which the Italians had found themselves in late December 1935, and it completely ignored the vast majority of the ground fighting—fighting in which the Ethiopians proved remarkably skilled at infiltrating into Italian positions and launching close assaults despite the incredible firepower disparity. Once again, he seemed to be trying to prove a point rather than analyze a war. He argued that it was the Ethiopian decision to attack, their attempt to land a knockout blow, that had been their undoing, since he still clung to the belief that no infantry assault was capable of succeeding under modern conditions. Despite all his modernism and enthusiasm for military novelty, the trench years of World War I were still Liddell Hart's touchstone.

Assessing the role of "the machine" in Ethiopia requires more nuance. Both Fuller and Liddell Hart had spent long, controversial careers championing the tank, and the public mind tended to associate them with it. The fact is, however, that tanks had performed disastrously in Ethiopia. The Ethiopians had destroyed nearly every one thrown into combat, even though they had no antitank weapons at all. The terrain was horrible, to be sure, and the tanks were extremely light, but events such as the following still were enough to give pause to armor advocates. As part of their motorized patrols across the Takkaze River in December 1935, a section of nine light tanks had reinforced the Italian forces on outpost at one of the fords. On December 15, a force of some 5,000 Ethiopians attacked them, part of Ras Imru's general offensive on the Italian right flank, discussed earlier. The Italians fled, making for the Dembeguina Pass, but found it occupied and had to force it:

> The action was so rapid and changed so fast that the tanks were unable to follow it and to support the infantry's tactical maneuvers. The glaring weakness of this type of light fast tank soon became apparent under these conditions of combat. The terrain was covered with large boulders which limited maneuver and made the twenty-five mile speed of the tanks useless. . . . The Ethiopians soon discovered that the tank's two machine guns could fire only to the front; they therefore climbed up on the tanks from the rear and sides and battered down the machine gun barrels with large rocks, rendering the tank useless. All nine tanks were lost and their crews killed.[17]

This was the face of "mechanized war" on the northern front in Ethiopia. In the Ogaden, likewise, Graziani had relied far more on trucks and armored cars than tanks. A contemporary U.S. Army intelligence report described the use of tanks in the Ogaden:

The light fast tanks, so widely heralded in the first months of the Abyssinian campaign, proved to be valueless in the Somaliland fighting. The high brush was an obstacle that could not be overcome. The tanks could not operate independently in advance of the fast troops. The Abyssinians soon found out about their limitations and would set fire to the brush and thus overcome the personnel with smoke. The lack of visibility from the tanks made it impossible to maintain direction, formation, or contact.

Usually, in fact, the infantry found itself protecting the tanks.[18]

Motorized (wheeled) units had played a much more important role in the campaign. Badoglio's lunge from Dessie to Addis in the last days of the war was the most celebrated example. Setting out from Dessie on April 26 with a gigantic motorized column, including some 1,700 trucks, the force made over 250 miles in just ten days, facing steep ascents, sudden plunging ravines, and everything in between. Badoglio called it, in the Fascist style, "the March of the Iron Will."[19] But this headline march took place after the collapse of Ethiopian resistance. The same U.S. intelligence report observed Badoglio's march on Addis was important mainly for "the steep grades, the hairpin turns, and great distances involved."[20]

When analysts discussed "machine power" in this war, the machine they were talking about was the airplane.[21] The unusual conditions of this war had allowed airpower to shine as it never had before. In early 1936, for example, an article appeared in the *Journal of the Royal United Service Institution* entitled "The Hare, the Tortoise, and the Eagle."[22] Written under the pseudonym "Solaire," it argued that modern war belonged not to the tortoise (the slow-moving traditional army), nor to the hare (the faster mechanized army). Instead, it was the eagle (airpower) who had proved itself master of the modern battlefield. It was virtually invulnerable, fast, "able to travel farther, to hit more frequently, and therefore harder." It was flexible, able to serve in a variety of roles: machine gun carrier, light or heavy bomber, smoke-layer; best of all, it was independent of the terrain over which it operated: "Let us take note of the lessons which the Italians are learning for us in Abyssinia and, this time, take two steps forward. Let us make every reasonable use of the advantages which mechanization on the ground has to offer us, but realizing its limitations, let us develop fully the possibilities held out to us by the air."[23]

The potential of the "eagle" was certainly much in evidence in the skies over East Africa. Aerial photography had been useful in mapping previously unknown tracts of the Ethiopian interior. Air supply of advancing columns was used on several occasions. The advance of Mariotti's column through Dankalia had benefited from an airdrop of rations and medical supplies on November 15, 1935; on December 27, a column of Eritrean troops in

Somaliland received ammunition, medicine, and food; from February 29 to March 3, 1936, Italian IV Corps received nineteen tons of air-dropped supplies during its flank march against Ras Imru during the battle of Shire. General Graziani had a plan to airlift troops to Dire Dawa in the last days of the war in Somaliland, but the Ethiopian collapse made it unnecessary.[24]

It was in a tactical role, however, that Italian airpower made the strongest impression on contemporaries. A White Russian military adviser to Ras Kassa, Colonel Theodore Konovaloff, described the reaction of Ethiopian troops to being strafed from the air:

> The moral effect of aviation in this was enormous. If the land space was unconquered yet, the aerial already belonged to the Italians. From the heights they penetrated our life, turned it upside down. They could intervene in all our movements. They prevented us from eating and warming ourselves after a heavy march round our camp fires, which we were afraid to light. They turned us into moles who dashed into their burrows at the slightest alarm.

"Each Ethiopian," he wrote, "thought that he was the special target of the bomb released."[25]

While Italian firepower on the ground had mauled the Ethiopian armies, it was airpower that had destroyed them, especially as they tried to retreat from battle. Military observers were unanimous in their agreement on that point. U.S. Army military intelligence described the pursuit as "the greatest service rendered by the air force" in Ethiopia:

> The air pursuit was pushed with the utmost vigor and caused heavy losses, both in men and morale. Due to the terrain and the road net the fleeing Ethiopians often crowded themselves in narrow defiles. In mass formations, the aviation gave the Ethiopians little respite and this vigorous exploitation of ground successes went far towards securing an early and successful termination of the campaign.[26]

Yet it is also possible to find roles in which airpower had failed during this campaign. In discussions of airpower in the 1930s, its ability to perform reconnaissance duties was mentioned again and again. In this campaign, however, aerial reconnaissance had been poor on both the strategic and the tactical level. The Ethiopians, moving at night, making good use of the ground, and quickly learning to scatter off the road at the first sound of an airplane motor, managed to surprise the Italians from the start of the campaign to its finish. Even so rudimentary a stratagem as digging dummy trenches often completely fooled the Italian aircrews. The Italians soon learned not to trust any air reconnaissance report that had not been verified by other sources. Tactical cooperation with the ground forces left a great deal to be desired, especially since every request for air support had to go through Badoglio, rather than from the ground troops directly to the fliers. Bombing raids against Ethiopian rear areas seemed to have had very little effect. A concerted Italian bombing effort against Addis Ababa was impossible because of the great distances involved for most of the campaign.

In highlighting the role of airpower, it is easy to lose sight of the most important Italian weapon: modern artillery. It delivered the vast majority of munitions in the Ethiopian War. Consider the following figures from U.S. Army intelligence on the battle of Enderta:

> The Italian air force is reported to have dropped 25,700 bombs of a total weight of about 192 tons during the period February 11th–17th. During a single day thirty tons of bombs were dropped in 140 flying hours. Converted into terms of artillery expenditure this latter is slightly in excess of the weight (28.7 tons) of the projectiles (95.5 lbs. each) comprising one day of fire (150 rounds per piece) of a single battery of 155 mm. howitzers.[27]

Put another way, the total amount of bombs dropped in the entire war (1,680 tons) was significantly less than the weight of shell delivered in a single day by U.S. Army artillery during the Meuse-Argonne campaign at the end of World War I. None of this is to argue for the "superiority" of artillery to aerial bombardment. The two have very different missions. These figures are, however, an effective argument against having aircraft bomb targets that are within artillery range.

The Ethiopian ground forces, almost totally devoid of antiaircraft artillery, had done a great deal of damage to Italian aircraft with small arms and machine gun fire. The planes came in extremely low to bomb and strafe reserves or fleeing columns, and virtually all of them reported having been hit by rifle or machine gun fire from the ground. Military professionals asked, would Italian tactics have been possible "against a determined, modern force, well trained and equipped with modern small arms and antiaircraft weapons? Would the probable losses in aircraft and personnel [have] been worth the possible losses inflicted upon the ground troops?"[28] Finally, any discussion of the Italian success in the air must include the fact that there was no competing enemy air force.

Perhaps nothing sums up the Italian effort in Ethiopia better than the use of the radio in the campaign. Its widespread employment was, seemingly, another innovation first field-tested on a large scale in this war, with over 1,000 sets in operation.[29] The equipment had functioned well; the altitude and thin air had made for clear, crisp connections. But within weeks of taking command, Badoglio had to issue directives about the misuse and overuse of the radio, as intense radio traffic was jamming the frequencies so badly that all echelons were having trouble getting their messages through. This problem, one foreign officer noted, would have been much worse if the Ethiopians had also had radio.

While this had been a "mobile war," featuring a full range of modern weapons, the lessons that it taught to the contemporary world were illusory. As the last large-scale colonial conquest, it belongs more to the nineteenth century than to the twentieth. In particular, it made the Italian army and air force look far better than they actually were. The unsung heroes were the Ethiopian and Eritrean infantry on both sides who did the vast majority of the fighting and dying.[30]

DRESS REHEARSAL? THE SPANISH CIVIL WAR

There is a traditional portrait of the Spanish civil war, and any analysis of the war must take it into account: Spain was the dress rehearsal for World War II. It was a conflict in which the Great Powers, especially Germany, became involved for the main purpose of testing out their new weapons, whose employment had been the subject of intense debate but heretofore had been consigned to the realm of the theoretical. No more talking about tanks—now, in the "Spanish laboratory," we could see how (or if) they really worked.[31] Other new items, such as antitank guns, modern single-wing aircraft, and antiaircraft guns, were also present. In addition to equipment, the powers also took advantage of the opportunity to put new doctrines to the test. The "war of movement" or "deep battle"? Try it out in Spain. "Strategic" or "terror" bombing? Here was a golden opportunity. Indeed, if there is one episode from this war that has become etched in the consciousness of non-Spaniards, it is the bombing of the town of Guernica by air units of the Condor Legion, a force of German pilots and aircraft allegedly fighting in Spain as "volunteers."

The portrait is true, up to a point. The war did feature the first large-scale use of many controversial modern weapons and doctrines. Occurring as it did in the midst of the fierce European debate on military doctrine, especially over the issue of mechanization, it was natural that all eyes would have been on Spain to see how their favorite (or least favorite) weapon system performed. But it is equally true that the war was not decided by those weapons, nor could it have been. It is also true that many facts alleged to have been true in Spain turned out to be false—the "terror bombing" of Guernica was in fact nothing of the kind.[32] When all was said and done, most of the "lessons" of the Spanish civil war, at least as they were enunciated and argued in the late 1930s, turned out to have been false.

The Early Fighting in Spain

On July 17, 1936, there was a military coup (in Spanish, a *pronunciamento*) against the government of the Spanish Republic, which soon erupted into a full-scale civil war.[33] The insurgent military forces (soon to be called the "Nationalists") held one-third of the country, including the important wheat-growing districts of Castile. The rest of the country, including Madrid and most of its industrial production, was in the hands of the Republican government. Madrid's communications with the rest of the country were tenuous, however, as there was only a single rail line linking it to the Mediterranean coast.[34]

The ringleaders of the uprising were Generals Emilio Mola, Queipo de Llano, and Francisco Franco. Franco was the youngest general in the Spanish army and had won a reputation during the 1920s by helping to organize and train an elite military force in Spanish Morocco, the Foreign Legion (Tercio Extranjero). They were probably the best-trained troops in Spain's military establishment, reasonably well equipped, and contemptuous of danger, with a dash of fanaticism. "Viva la Muerte!" ("Long live death!") was their motto.[35] Along with a contingent of Regulares, hardy Moorish infantry as handy with the curved knife as they were with the rifle, they formed the Army of Africa under Franco's command. The only problem was that both Franco, who had been stationed in the Canary Islands when he started the uprising, and the Army of Africa itself were stuck in Spanish Morocco, across the Straits of Gibraltar from mainland Spain. And since most of the navy had declared for the Republic, there was no apparent way that Franco could get his troops where they had to be. He turned to Hitler and Mussolini for assistance. They agreed to lend Franco transport aircraft to get his forces across the straits, as well as a few bombers. Germany sent twenty Junkers JU-52 transports to Morocco and Seville, and on July 29 regular flights began carrying Franco's Army of Africa to Europe. By August 5, 1,500 of Franco's men had arrived in Seville via airlift, and 500 per day arrived thereafter.[36] It was the first comprehensive airlift of a military force in history.

From its base in southern Spain, the Army of Africa now began its march to the north. While Franco was in overall command of the National Government in Seville and later in Burgos, Colonel Juan de Yagüe Blanco led the initial campaign in the field. This was the mobile phase of the Spanish civil war. Trained in the light infantry tactics of the desert, the Legionaries and the Moors were tough, all-terrain, all-weather troops who could subsist on the most meager of rations, and who seemed to live for battle. Not only were they fully motorized, speeding across the countryside in trucks commandeered in Seville by Queipo de Llano, they also had command of the air, in the form of nine JU-52s and eight SA-81s. From Seville, their columns drove on Merida and Badajoz, and thence toward Madrid. The advance during this triumphal march, which reduced stronghold after stronghold belonging to the government forces in southern Spain and brought the entire region under insurgent control in a matter of weeks, was the work of small columns, sometimes as few as 100 men apiece, other times as many as 500 to 1,000. Riding up to a village, they might dismount and enter it on foot, or bombard it from a distance with artillery and their small bomber fleet, or split up the column so that one section would pin the defenders in place while the other came around as a flanking force. In fact, they did whatever the situation seemed to call for, which in their eyes usually included the slaughter of anyone who had offered resistance.[37] On August 10, Yagüe reached Merida, after a 200-mile advance in less than a week. This rate of march compares quite favorably with Badoglio's "March of the Iron Will" at the end of the Ethiopian campaign, and Yagüe's columns actually saw fighting during their advance, unlike the Italians. On August 14 he stormed Badajoz.

From August to September 1936, the combination of Moors and Legionaries outmaneuvered and outfought every government force they met. The vast majority of their adversaries were nothing more than raw militia who, although they were numerous, tended to bunch up under fire, fire high, and panic. By September 2, Nationalist columns had reached Talavera de la Reina. Here they met a force of 10,000 militia supported by artillery and an armored train, drawn up in a fine defensive position on the high ground in front of the town. An assault by the insurgents soon put them to flight.

As he gazed northeast from Talavera, Franco must have felt that Madrid was within his grasp. The situation in the capital was still quite unsettled, and it seemed that he might take it by a coup de main. Instead, he diverted his victorious force toward Toledo. Here, in the fortress known as the Alcazar, an insurgent force had been holding out for weeks while besieged by government forces. The heroism of the defenders had become a staple of Nationalist propaganda, and Franco felt compelled to relieve the Alcazar before starting for Madrid.[38] The government used the respite of several weeks to prepare Madrid for battle.

In October, the insurgent forces began their drive on Madrid, converging on the city from a long arc to the west. But the momentum of their drive had begun to slacken. Casualties were wearing down the Army of Africa's cutting edge, and as it advanced toward Madrid, its spearheads came under flank attack from government forces north and south of the capital. Foreign aid had also begun to arrive on the Republican side, with Russian tanks already playing a key role. On October 29, Russian T-26 tanks spearheaded an attack on the Nationalists in Sesena, on the southern approaches to

Madrid, and that same day a squadron of Russian Katiuska bombers raided Seville.[39] In addition, the outbreak of the war had electrified an entire generation of Western leftists and intellectuals—writers, artists, teachers. They had already begun to flock to Spain, volunteering for action and forming International Battalions to fight for Spanish democracy.[40] Still, by early November, the ring had been drawn within fifteen miles of Madrid, and the government had moved to Valencia, deep in the loyalist interior.

An assault against a great city of over 1 million people should be an operation on a grand scale, but Franco's assault was a shoestring effort. Although the operation consisted of four converging columns (plus Franco's false boast that he had a "fifth column" of supporters within the city who would rise up at his approach), there were certainly fewer than 100,000 men on both sides. A great number of writers have described this battle, transforming it into some kind of epic, but in the end, the "assault" on Madrid amounted to a single thrust against the northwestern defenses near the university (University City). The defenders, a mixed bag of loyal army, militia, and international volunteers, managed, for the first time, to stand firm against the professional soldiers facing them. Although Franco's forces forced their way into University City, they were unable to widen their penetration beyond a pencil-thin toehold, much less effect a complete breakthrough. It was Franco's last bid for a rapid victory.[41]

Both sides now began to take stock, to consolidate their positions, and to beg for more outside aid. Mussolini led the way. By the spring of 1937, some 100,000 Italian troops were in Spain, organized into the Corps of Volunteer Troops (Corpo Truppe Volontarie, or CTV), under the command of General Mario Roatta.[42] Much of it was half-trained Fascist militia, the Blackshirt divisions whose performance had been so mediocre in Ethiopia, but it was well equipped with light tanks, motorized weapons, and transport. Nazi Germany sent specialist troops: light tanks (Pzkw. Mark Is, armed with machine guns only), antitank units, antiaircraft batteries, and a "volunteer" air force, the Condor Legion.[43]

The Republic, too, had a great deal of success. The Soviet Union sent a good deal of equipment, more than making up for Italian and German aid to Franco. Stalin sent a few men, mainly officers and specialists, but a large amount of equipment: 1,000 aircraft, almost 400 tanks, and 1,500 guns. Both Russian tanks in Spain, the T-26 and the BT-5, were armed with a 45-mm gun and were far superior to the German or Italian light tanks they faced.[44] The Republic also benefited from the presence of the International Battalions. Volunteers from the United States formed the Abraham Lincoln Battalion, anti-Nazi German refugees the Ernst Thälmann Battalion, Canadians the Mackenzie-Papineau Battalion (also known as "the Mac-Paps"), and many more.[45] These true believers played a key role in defending Madrid. Organized into International Brigades, they would serve as shock troops for the Republican cause for the next two years, thrown in wherever the fighting was hottest.

Stymied at Madrid, Franco launched a series of attacks to improve his position in front of the capital. On December 16, a Nationalist force of 12,000 men (more than twice the number that had assaulted Madrid) under General José Enrique Varela Iglesias mounted an attack designed to outflank the city to the north and west. Varela aimed his assault toward the Corunna Road along a stretch of front that extended east-west. After five days, the Nationalists had made only a small penetration, seizing the town of Boadilla.[46] German tanks spearheading the attack found themselves outclassed by their Soviet counterparts. On January 3, Varela reopened the assault, this time with 15,000 men and overwhelming superiority in firepower, including four batteries of 155-mm guns and a large complement of German 88-mm antiaircraft guns. The Republican forces defending here were so low on ammunition that the men were limited to twenty cartridges apiece. While Varela's men did reach the village of Las Rozas, seizing about seven miles of the highway, they never achieved a breakthrough. Losses had been heavy. Russian tanks operated with impunity, using the cover provided by a thick fog to drive into and through nationalist positions. But they seemed to know nothing of cooperating with their own infantry, which lagged behind and left the tanks unsupported. Although Republican forces had held the initial insurgent penetration, they were unable to roll it back. The "battle of Boadilla" ended in stalemate.

On February 6, 1937, the Nationalists made a second attempt to outflank Madrid, this time to the south. A force of 18,000—Moorish troops in the lead, German tanks and bombers supporting—attacked across the Jarama River aiming at the Valencia road.[47] Since the Republic had been planning an offensive of its own here, the bridges over the Jarama had not been destroyed. The Nationalists got over the river and quickly seized the high ground on the eastern bank. They now had the Valencia Road, Madrid's lifeline to the east, under observation. Russian tank crews had learned the dangers of coming under German artillery fire and spent most of the early part of the battle trying to stay out of the way. Once again, however, the Nationalists were halted short of a total breakthrough. By February 12, the addition of some forty Russian fighter planes gave the Republicans air superiority, and the international brigades had arrived. The British Battalion, part of the XV International Brigade, held what became known as "Suicide Hill" against greatly superior forces for the better part of February 12, the finger in the dike, as it were. The Abraham Lincoln Battalion also saw its first action in this battle, rushing in with impetuous enthusiasm and getting pretty badly shot up, suffering 120 killed and 175 wounded out of a total force of just 450 men. The real story was a homegrown one, however: the newly trained Republican army (Ejercito Popular, or Popular Army) gave a very good accounting of itself, first halting the Nationalist advance and then launching a counterattack on February 17 that put the Nationalists back onto the defensive. Once again the front stabilized. The Nationalists still had the road under artillery fire, but they had failed to achieve a breakthrough. The Republican forces had held but could not drive back their adversaries.

There was a last attempt to take Madrid in March 1937. This was an Italian show, spearheaded by the CTV. It involved five full divisions, over 50,000 men under the overall command of General Roatta: three Fascist Blackshirt divisions (the "Dio lo vuole" under General Silvio Rossi, the "Black Flames" under General Giovanni Coppi, and the "Black Arrows," under General Nuvolini), a division of the Italian regular army, the "Littorio" (General Annibale Bergonzoli), plus the Spanish "Soria" division (Colonel José Moscardó Ituarte commanding). This highly motorized force, supported by eighty tanks, over 200 pieces of mobile artillery, and 2,000 trucks, was concentrated near Siguenza, sixty miles northeast of Madrid. The plan was for the "Black Flames" and "Black Arrows" to pierce the Republican lines, hold open the breach, and allow the "Dio le Vuole" and "Littorio" to drive down the highway thirty miles to Guadalajara and thence to Madrid.[48]

The attack opened on March 8. It achieved initial surprise and tore a hole in the Republican lines, as the Italian spearhead advanced to Trijueque and Brihuega by March 13, about two-thirds of the way to Guadalajara. But things had already begun to go wrong. The weather soon turned ugly, with rain, sleet, ice, and fog, a grave problem, since much of the Italian force was in colonial uniforms more suited to the tropics. Bad weather grounded Italian aircraft operating from temporary fields established in the rear; Republican planes, flying from permanent fields near Madrid, were less affected. In addition, poor planning on the part of the Italian commander and staff was in evidence. Working from a 1:400,000 Michelin road map, Roatta was ignorant of the details of the terrain over which he was operating. There was apparently little thought given to either air cover or antiaircraft protection. One observer speculated that the Italians believed the attack would be nothing more than a triumphal march, a repeat of the "March of the Iron Will" on Addis Ababa.[49] Essentially, the Italians' plan was to drive forward in column and see what happened. Had they been facing militia, the sort of opposition the Republic had put up the previous fall, it might have worked anyway. But not only was the Popular Army more professional by this time; Russian advisers such as Major Alexander Rodimtsev (under his alias, "Captain Pablito"), Colonel Dimitri Pavlov, Colonel Rodion Malinovsky, and

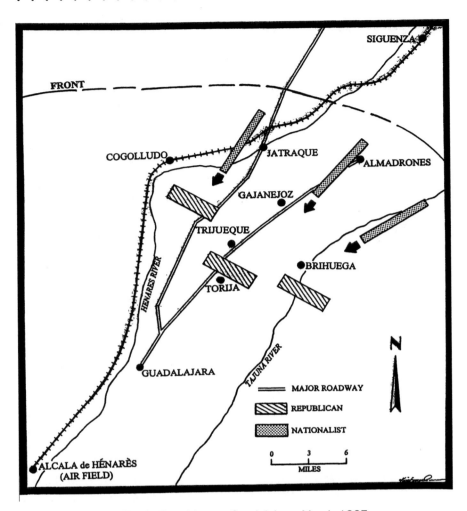

Motorized assault: The Italian drive on Guadalajara, March 1937.

Colonel Jakob Smushkevich (aka "General Douglas") played an important role in planning the Republican defense and counterattack.

As soon as the scope of the Italian offensive became known, the Republic rushed large reinforcements, both ground and air, to the front. International forces, including a large number of Russian tanks and aircraft, arrived on the scene, under the overall command of Pavlov and Smushkevich, respectively. On March 9, the new Republican commander, General Vincente Rojo Lluch, organized the best elements available into IV Corps and deployed it in the path of the Italian advance. Composed of the 11th Division under the communist commander "Lister" to the west of the Madrid-Saragossa highway and the 14th Division under anarchist Cipriano Mera to the east, with International Brigades attached in both cases, and with an entire division (the 12, under Colonel Andres Garcia Lacalle) in reserve, IV Corps stopped the Italian drive cold by March 12. One international unit made up of anti-Mussolini Italians, the Garibaldi Battalion, displayed conspicuous valor by a fierce struggle with advanced units of the CTV around a country house known as the Ibarra Palace, near the walled village of Brihuega.

With the Italian drive now halted, Rojo launched a counterattack against the point of the Italian penetration at Brihuega on March 18. Spearheading the Republican drive were the two divisions in the front line, Lister striking at the Italian right and Cipriano Mera at the left. Supported by seventy Soviet T-26 tanks and over 100 planes, plus a heavy concentration of artillery, the attack developed perfectly, landing nearly simultaneous blows against the Italians in Brihuega from two opposite directions and putting them to flight. Soviet aircraft continued to play a crucial role throughout this day and the next, bombing the dense columns of Italian tanks and trucks strung out along the congested road to Brihuega. The Italians now got a taste of the aerial punishment that they had dished out in Ethiopia.

The CTV did manage to re-form and to hold onto a considerable amount of the territory that it had seized at the outset of the offensive, and one modern historian has assessed the battle in modest terms: "A nationalist attempt to complete the encirclement of Madrid was thwarted at the cost of twelve miles."[50] Still, this badly named "battle of Guadalajara" was an utter humiliation for Mussolini's forces in Spain, beginning a process that would culminate in World War II and see the Italian army transformed into a laughingstock. The Popular Army captured sixty-five guns, thirteen mortars, 500 machine guns, 3,000 rifles, and ten tanks, all abandoned by the Italians in their hasty retreat. Finally, it marked one of the war's turning points. It was plain to the Nationalist side that Madrid would have to be left for another day. The action shifted to other fronts.

Spanish Civil War: The Static Phase

No longer believing in the quick knockout blow, Franco now turned to a series of careful operations designed to wipe out Republic resistance in Spain one region at a time.[51] While the static fronts might seem to recall the stalemate of World War I, that is an incorrect view. First of all, the fighting was much less intense. Both sides did indeed occupy a more or less "continuous front," making it difficult to find the opponent's flank, but the limited size of the forces on both sides meant that huge stretches of the front were held by outposts only. George Orwell, who fought for the Republic, described the front in Catalonia as a series of mountaintop positions too far away from one another for the exchange of fire:

> According to my ideas of trench warfare the Fascists would be fifty or a hundred yards away. I could see nothing—seemingly their trenches were very well-concealed. Then with a shock of dismay I saw where Benjamin was pointing; on the opposite hill-top, beyond the ravine, seven hundred meters away at the very least, the tiny outline of a parapet and a red-and-yellow flag—the Fascist position. I was indescribably disappointed. We were nowhere near them! At that range our rifles were completely useless.[52]

Under such conditions, it was always possible for one side to concentrate enough force to punch a hole through the line at virtually any point he desired. Widening the breach and following it up into a complete breakthrough proved to be beyond the forces and staffs on both sides, however. With motorized infantry and tanks proving to be much less effective than advertised, there was little hope of effecting any sort of dramatic breakthrough.

Still, there were some interesting operational lessons. The Nationalist attack into the Basque country, beginning in late March 1937, featured the newly organized Navarre Division. The men were members of the Carlist militia, the Requeté, fanatically devoted to defending the traditions of Catholic Spain. Along with the Moors and Legionaries, these Red Berets would be one of the elite forces on the Nationalist side.[53] Supported by 150 aircraft (80 of them German) and 200 guns, this well-trained light infantry proved quite skillful at infiltrating through the Basque positions while air attacks kept the defenders pinned. Once the bombardment lifted, Navarrese machine gun fire from their rear was often enough to make the Republic forces flee their shallow trenches.

To take pressure off the north, the Republic attempted a series of diversionary offensives. The greatest of these was the Brunete offensive, a mirror image of the Nationalist attack at Boadilla.[54] About fifteen miles west of the capital, the Nationalist-held town of Brunete was an important junction on the road to the capital. Thin lines on both sides faced each other here, facing generally north and south. If the Republicans could punch through Nationalist lines here and seize Brunete, the Nationalist armies in front of Madrid would be in danger of envelopment and have to retreat, removing the capital from the front lines. The Popular Army concentrated some 85,000 men here under the command of General Miaja, including Lister's veteran 11th Division, the 46th Division under the anarchist "El Campesino," and a number of International Brigades. Sources differ, as they often do in this war, on the amount of support weapons available, but one account gives figures of forty armored cars, 300 aircraft, 130 tanks, and over 200 field guns, plus over 100 modern Soviet aircraft providing air support.

The attack opened on July 6 and took the Nationalists, who had their eyes fixed to the north, completely by surprise. It began with a heavy artillery and aerial bombardment that lasted several hours. Leading the ground assault was Lister's division, moving forward in the early dawn hours and quickly punching a hole through a thinly held portion of the Nationalist lines chosen by Miaja. Lister's men advanced five miles within the first few hours, enveloping Brunete and then assaulting it successfully. They had created a bulge about ten miles wide by eight deep, but they failed to do much beyond that. The source of the Republican problem was command and control. Although Lister was as good a general as anyone in the war, there were too few trained officers to keep the assault units moving forward. Rather than bypass Nationalist strongpoints, all too often the attacking forces tried to attack them directly. The Nationalists managed to block attempts to widen the breach, holding the bases of the bulge near the villages of Quijorna (on the left) and Villanueva del Pardillo (on the right). The Republicans found it difficult, therefore, to insert their second wave of troops into the battle. Overcrowding of the bulge was a problem by noon on July 6. By midnight on the first day, the Nationalist commander in front of Madrid, Varela, could report to Franco that he had reestablished a solid front.

Nevertheless, the bulge threatened Nationalist supply lines in front of Madrid. Franco behaved in a way that would become his pattern, reacting to a local Republican advance, whatever threat it posed, by gathering as much force as he could to oppose it and drive it back to its start line. Within three days, 30,000 Nationalist reinforcements had arrived, and 20,000 more arrived over the next three. More important, he redeployed virtually the entire Condor Legion, along with the Italian air units operating in the north, to the Brunete front.

The battle turned into a struggle of attrition, a meat grinder with large air and artillery forces operating on a very tiny, very crowded piece of ground. It was high summer on the dusty Castilian plain, and the men on both sides suffered terribly in this "battle of Thirst."[55] On July 8, El Campesino took Quijorna, and Villanueva del Pardillo fell three days later. But with Nationalist reinforcements and aircraft arriving on the scene, the tide of battle turned. German aircraft like the Messerschmitt ME-109 fighter plane and the Heinkel HE-111 bomber appeared in the skies over Brunete and soon won control of the air. By July 13, the Republican offensive had spent itself. Now the Nationalists went over to the counteroffensive, and by July 26, they had driven the Republicans back to their start line.

It had been the bloodiest battle of the war so far. Republican losses topped 30,000 men and sixty-one tanks; Nationalist losses were 20,000 men. It had also been a fiasco for the Republic, compared by one modern Spanish officer to the battle of Kursk in World War II: "After Brunete the Popular Army was never again a coherent force capable of matching the Nationalists. From that stage of the conflict, their superior armored forces were unable to present a real threat to the technically inferior armored forces of General Franco."[56]

In August, the Republic launched another diversionary offensive, this one in Aragon along the Ebro River. Again, it opened well. Without preparatory bombardment, 80,000 men, over 100 tanks and 200 aircraft launched a series of thrusts north and south of Saragossa. Two fortified villages near the front, Quinto and Belchite, fell to Republican tank and infantry assaults, and the attackers made other gains here and there along the line. Franco immediately rushed all available reinforcements to the site, however. Led by the 13th and 150th Divisions from the Madrid sector, they soon stabilized the front.

The offensive, in which the Republic committed a great deal of its armored reserve, lasted well into the fall. The tiny village of Fuentes de Ebro became a focal point. Held by the Nationalists, it guarded the main crossing over the Ebro River on the way to Saragossa and was therefore a natural target of the Republican offensive. On October 13, 1937, the XV International Brigade received orders to storm the town. A member of the Canadian Mac-Pap battalion, Ronald Liversedge, described the defenders' position:

> The layout was formidable. We were on a plain gradually sloping up to the town almost a mile away. The town was perched on a high ridge, probably two hundred feet, and in front of the town was a deep arroyo. All it needed was water in the arroyo to make this a very very large medieval fortress, and we had almost a mile of open plain to cross to get there. . . . Below the town on the far side of the arroyo from us was a line of fascist trenches and from the town down to these trenches was a steep communication trench down which were coming troops.[57]

The Republican plans called for an initial aerial bombardment, followed by a strong thrust by over 100 tanks, with infantry following the armor across the field toward the village. The bombers came, fifty of them, and duly plastered the Nationalist trenches. But due to a mistake in timing, an hour-and-a-half pause ensued before the tanks came up. Whether they were late, or the bombers were early, or both, was never established. The Mac-Paps had to sit and wait, helpless and enraged, as the enemy crawled back into his defensive positions. It was noon when the tanks arrived, with elements of the Spanish 24th Battalion sprawled across their backs. According to Mac-Pap member Saul Wellman, someone had seen this maneuver in a film.[58]

The attack came to grief even before it had formally started. The tanks never really "formed up" for the assault. Instead, they simply drove directly over the XV Brigade's position, wrecking the friendly trenches and squashing the parapets. Some of the infantry passengers apparently thought that the assault had started and that they had reached the enemy front line. They opened fire on the startled Canadians. Once they had passed through the friendly line, the tanks trundled off across the field at twenty miles per hour. Although they had orders to walk the attacking infantry up to the Nationalist line, in best infantry-support fashion, they soon left the XV Brigade behind. The internationals had to rush out of their trenches and run pell-mell across the field, desperately trying to keep up with their own tanks. But the line near Fuentes de Ebro bent sharply to the southwest just to the left of the Canadian position, and the men now found themselves under heavy enfilade fire from machine guns that either had been untouched by the bombardment or had crept back into position during the lull before the assault. The battalion hit the dirt and tried hurriedly to dig into the hard soil of Aragon, using tin dinner plates as shovels. In solidarity with every infantryman ever lying out on a killing field, Corporal Lionel Edwards of the 3rd Company found himself thinking "how marvelous the earth was and why I had been so long in getting acquainted with it."[59] The tanks did little better. They took losses all the way to Fuentes de Ebro, and those that managed to get to the Nationalist position suffered further losses from antitank guns in the narrow lanes of the village. The pinned Mac-Paps could clearly hear the occasional explosion of tanks over the tapping of the machine gun fire. All day they lay out in the field. Toward evening, individual members of the battalion began to straggle back, and by the next morning they occupied a new position several hundred meters in advance of their start line. The battalion had suffered 60 killed and over 200 wounded, out of an original force of perhaps 700. It would remain in these hastily dug trenches for the next two weeks, enduring constant bombardment that raised the casualty total still higher.

The Nationalist experience at Fuentes de Ebro was far different. Just seven companies of infantry held the line of trenches in front of the village. One of the defenders, Lieutenant Antonio Duarte Alvarez, said that "the attack took us by surprise":

All at once we heard the sound of the tanks. The noise increased, coming from either side of the crest occupied by the enemy trenches, at about five hundred or seven hundred meters from our front. Then a column, which seemed endless, began to develop, issued from a breach which existed between the enemy trenches, and headed straight for the spot where I happened to be with my platoon.[60]

At about one hundred meters, the tanks executed a diagonal turn to the right and came up parallel to the trench. When the entire column had executed this maneuver, the lead tank hung out a red flag. At this signal, every tenth tank made a half turn to the left, pointing toward Duarte's position. Five or six others followed each one, and soon nine or ten columns, each of six tanks, were headed for the trench. The thirty or so remaining tanks maneuvered into a "battle line" and opened fire on the trenches with cannon and machine guns.

Duarte's platoon had no artillery batteries. There were three 37-mm antitank guns in the vicinity, but all were sited for fire to the left of the national highway to Saragossa, where four companies were defending the sector between the highway and the banks of the Ebro. Despite the momentary panic at the sudden onset of the attack, Duarte's platoon, along with the 19th Company on his right, managed to defeat it. Machine gun fire swept the accompanying infantry off the tanks, and grenades and cans filled with sulfur and gasoline tossed into the vulnerable tracks and ventilators of the attacking machines soon wrecked the order of the enemy columns. Some of them did indeed manage to get through Duarte's positions. "We left those tanks which had succeeded in passing our defense to the reserve companies, which were located in the ravines behind our trenches."[61] A few enemy tanks reached the village but there ran into the fire of the antitank guns. Soon, Duarte and his men saw two burning tanks coming from the village, withdrawing down the national highway. Other tanks came forward to help them escape, but they were destroyed by grenades. Another one fell prey to the fire of an 88-mm antiaircraft gun. This was the signal for a general retreat on the part of both enemy tanks and infantry. But Duarte's platoon was not yet done:

> We thereupon brought half of our men towards the rear to complete the destruction of the tanks which were still trying to retreat. We captured sixteen of them. Two had reached the village, but stone buildings and narrow winding streets do not constitute a favorable spot for tank evolutions. The personnel of the battalion command post, the supply details, and the cooks set fire to them.[62]

Months later, the burned-out hulks of the Popular Army's Soviet tanks still littered the battlefield and were part of the standard Nationalist tour for international correspondents.

One lesson of Fuentes de Ebro was, according to a Soviet analysis, that the location of antitank weapons was difficult to pinpoint, especially by a tank. "The discharge of these guns is usually barely noticeable. There have been various instances where antitank guns came back to life after it was supposed that they had been completely destroyed."[63] One Soviet tank commander involved in the battle described the action:

> Our artillery fire continued for forty-five minutes. It was getting dark. The infantry advanced to the attack. On the right flank two battalions came upon wire entanglements. Hostile fire died down. The government ranks were advancing over a depression, and were at a point where two buildings had stood a short time before and had been razed by our artillery. I noticed two points of fire on the spot, and proceeded against them. As soon as the tanks came near them the enemy suddenly opened intensive machine-gun fire, while six antitank guns opened fire upon us from the vicinity of some small buildings which had been demolished.[64]

Another Republican offensive began in December 1937, this time against the Nationalist-held town of Teruel.[65] The town sits in the mountains at the confluence of the Alfambra and Guadalquivir Rivers, at the end of a long, narrow salient sticking into Republican territory northeast of Madrid. The offensive began on December 15, 1937, once again opening well. Spearheaded by Lister's 11th Division, the Republican XXII Corps struck from the north, the XVIII Corps from the south. By the end of the first day, the two forces had effected a junction at La Muela de Teruel, the ridge on the western side of Teruel, thus surrounding the city. By Christmas, Republican forces had penetrated into the city.

Once again, Nationalist reaction was swift. Blessed with superior staff officers, Franco gathered every man, gun, plane, and tank that he could find to relieve Teruel. Since getting reinforcements to the remote area would take time, Franco sent repeated messages to the garrison commander, Colonel Domingo Rey d'Harcourt, to hold out, to "trust in Spain as Spain trusts in you."[66] Rey d'Harcourt managed to do just that, turning the governor's office, the Bank of Spain, the seminary, and the convent of Santa Clara, all clustered in the southern part of town, into small fortresses. On December 29, a Nationalist counteroffensive began to the west of Teruel. Troops under General Varela quickly reached La Muela but could not capture it. A race was now under way: Could the Republicans reduce the Teruel garrison before Varela managed to break through and relieve it? A bitter street-by-street struggle now began inside Teruel. The Republicans brought up machine guns and artillery for point-blank fire into enemy strongpoints, then sent in infantry assault teams, armed with grenades, to finish them off. The Nationalists, meanwhile, continued to hammer at the Republican lines in the high ground to the west of the city. The weather added its own touch:

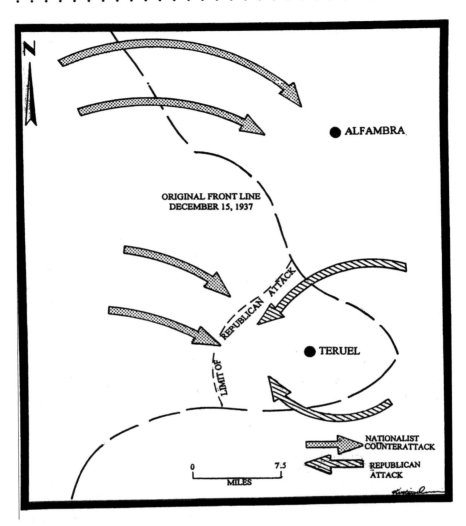

Mobile operations in Spain: Battle of Teruel, December 1937 to January 1938.

heavy, blinding snowstorms combined with temperatures of eighteen degrees below zero. By New Year's Day 1938, most of the garrison was dead, but not until January 8 did Rey d'Harcourt surrender, an act for which many in Nationalist Spain would, incredibly, condemn him as a traitor.

A second Nationalist counteroffensive began on January 17, 1938, in the mountainous region to the north of Teruel. Aided by Italian heavy artillery and aircraft, it broke through Republican lines in this sector. Along with a thrust south of Teruel, the Nationalists moved to surround the city, in a mirror image of the original Republican operation. In danger of being cut off, the Republican force now retreated from Teruel. On February 22nd, the last Republican forces in the city, including El Campesino's 46th Division, managed to fight their way out of the ever-tightening Nationalist ring. Most of them escaped, although over 10,000 prisoners did fall into enemy hands. The city fell that same day.

The battle of Teruel was the epic battle of the Spanish civil war and one of the great battles of the twentieth century. In the first phase, the Republicans had launched a well-crafted operation, turning both flanks of the Nationalist position in Teruel and enveloping the city. In the last phase, the Nationalists did the same thing to the Republicans. In between had come a tense, heroic struggle for mastery of the town itself. For all the foreign intervention in this war, all the new equipment and new doctrines, this battle had come down to the most old-fashioned of military virtues: the determination of the ordinary infantryman to overcome the freezing cold weather, the terrain, and the enemy—in that order. In the end, defeat at Teruel left the Republican forces in northeastern Spain exhausted, bled white, and low on supplies of every sort. On the other side, the victory had left the Nationalists confident and conscious of their growing superiority on land and in the air.

Franco now prepared his next offensive. He had over 100,000 men, with Moors, Carlists, and Italians in the lead, over 600 planes, some 200 tanks, and thousands of trucks. This massive force, organized into four corps with massive air and artillery support, would launch simultaneous thrusts in Aragon against the weakened Republican line between Saragossa and Teruel.[67] It began on March 9. For the first time in this war, the attackers made a complete breakthrough all along the front. Belchite and Quinto, the site of so much hard fighting of late, fell in a day to the Nationalists. The combination of air and artillery bombardment, spirited infantry assault, and, here and there, coordinated assaults by relatively large groups of tanks, proved overwhelming, routing the Republican forces and advancing sixty miles during the first week. The Popular Army was now disintegrating in many places. There were mutinies and desertions, which the Republican leaders opposed by court-martial and summary executions. Occasionally a unit would stand: El Campesino's division held Lérida for a week against vastly superior forces. But defections on one or both flanks usually forced a retreat anyway. The path to Barcelona lay open to Franco, and the seizure of Tremp, to the north, cut off the great city from its sources of hydroelectric power. Nonetheless, the ever-cautious Franco did not seize the opportunity, instead diverting his main thrust toward the Mediterranean sea to the south of Barcelona. This new "race to the sea" came to an end on April 15, as the

4th Navarrese Division under Colonel Camila Alonso Vega took Vinaroz. Franco now held a forty-mile strip of coast south of the Ebro River mouth. He had cut Republican Spain in two.

While the war appeared to be coming to a close, the Republic had one last gasp. The Popular Army's chief of staff, General Rojo, began planning a new offensive. Opposite the bend of the Ebro River between Fayon and Cherta, he concentrated 100,000 men, 100 heavy guns, twenty-seven anti-aircraft guns, plus newly assembled Soviet Rata fighter planes.[68] His plan called for a surprise crossing of the Ebro by troops on assault boats, the construction of pontoon bridges immediately after the crossing, and the establishment of a bridgehead over the river to use as a base for further operations. The mountainous terrain on the far side of the river would, Rojo felt, help to counteract the superiority in matériel that the Nationalists would bring to bear against the bridgehead. It was a complex plan and showed how far the Popular Army had come in its training, staff work, and supply services.

Just past midnight on the night of July 24, the Republic launched its offensive along the Ebro. Once again, as with every major Republican operation, it caught Franco completely by surprise. The Republican advance guard crossed the river in ninety assault boats at sixteen points and rapidly emplaced three pontoon bridges. Soon the rest of the force was crossing over to the bridgehead on the far side, including four companies of armored cars, although the T-26 tanks and heavy guns would have to wait for the construction of an iron bridge over the Ebro. The Nationalist defenders were confused, and their opposition was sporadic. The defenders managed to block some of the landings but soon found themselves under flank attack by columns that had crossed the river either farther up or farther down. In the center, the spearhead of Lister's division advanced almost twenty miles that first day. The Popular Army took 4,000 Nationalist prisoners and seized most of the observation points on the high ground west of the river.

Once the advantage of surprise had been lost, however, the Nationalists recovered their equilibrium. General Yagüe showed himself to be a skilled defender, reorganizing his shattered defenses, untangling intermingled units, improvising with the troops that he had at hand. The pace of the Republican operation began to slow, especially after the Nationalists wrecked the dams farther up the Ebro and washed away the pontoon bridges. By the beginning of August, against stiffening opposition, the Popular Army had crept up to the base of the salient created by the Ebro's bend and had created a small bulge of its own in the Nationalist lines to the north, across the Ebro between Mequinenza and Fayon. It had been a successful operation, but it had not led to any sort of strategic breakthrough.

Franco being Franco, there was no chance of this local success going unanswered. His staff—by now quite a professional organization—was soon in motion hurrying reinforcements to the Ebro. With a largely immobile Republican force entrenched in the bridgehead, the Nationalist superiority in artillery and airpower came to the fore. On the surface, it was akin to the western front in World War I: guns lined up hub to hub pounding entrenched Republic infantry in the bridgehead; Nationalist infantry assaults vanishing in a hail of fire from machine gun, artillery, and mortars, being followed by spirited Republican counterattacks; losses in men out of all proportion to the territorial gains.

In one way, however, this was a very modern battle: the use of airpower. The Condor Legion carried out an impressive series of missions in the course of the fighting on the Ebro. First of all, it seized control of the air soon after the outset of the fight, with the speedy new ME-109 fighters proving their worth. Once the skies had been cleared of Republican fighters, German bombers and JU-87 Stukas began an interdiction campaign, handing out a merciless pounding to Republican supply columns, the bridges over which they had to pass, reserves moving up to the front, and artillery batteries. Trapped inside a box—Nationalist ground troops to their front, hostile air forces hammering their rear—the Republicans suffered grievously in their bridgehead. Finally, as Franco's ground forces went back over to the attack, German aircraft were there to provide the close air support necessary to help drive the Republicans out of their entrenched positions. The battle ended on November 16, four months after it began, with the exhausted Popular Army back across the Ebro where it had started. It was as much a victory for German airpower as it was for Franco.

THE "LESSONS" OF SPAIN

The standard view of the Spanish civil war came from a series of interviews that General Wilhelm von Thoma gave to Liddell Hart after World War II. It was apparent soon after the war broke out, he said, that Spain would be "the European Aldershot," a proving ground for new equipment and doctrines. Thoma claimed a major share of the credit for the nationalist victory in the civil war:

> By a carefully organized dilution of the German personnel I was soon able to train a large number of Spanish tank crews. I found the Spanish quick to learn, though also quick to forget. By 1938 I had four tank battalions under my command—each of three companies, with fifteen tanks in a company. Four of the companies were equipped with Russian tanks. I also had thirty anti-tank companies, with six 37 mm. guns apiece.

General Franco wished to parcel out the tanks among the infantry—in the usual way of generals who belong to the old school. I had to fight this tendency constantly in the endeavor to use the tanks in a concentrated way. The Francoists' successes were largely due to this.

It is time to label this assessment for what it is: absolutely preposterous. The victorious armies of Nationalist Spain were made up overwhelmingly of infantry and artillery. Tanks played a role here and there, especially in the breakthrough battle in Aragon. But they never made the breakthroughs themselves; they were far too light for that. Instead, they had proved to be useful weapons in the exploitation phase, along with motorcycles, armored cars, and truck-borne infantry. It is difficult to see which battle Thoma could have meant when he spoke of "using the tanks in a concentrated way." He was, after all, speaking of a huge war in which there were never more than 200 German tanks present at a time.[69]

Another source for the notion that blitzkrieg was born in Spain was a Czech artillery officer named Ferdinand Miksche. He served with the Popular Army as a battery commander and in 1942 published *Attack: A Study of Blitzkrieg Tactics.* He argued that the Nationalists had triumphed in the war partly through superior use of their armor. Rather than parceling out their tanks, French-style, and using them primarily as infantry support weapons, they followed the German model of concentrating them and using them in mass on a single axis of attack against a single tactical thrust point *(Schwerpunkt).*[70]

Such notions persist to this day. Hugh Thomas's *Spanish Civil War,* a book that has gone through several editions since its first printing in 1961 and may be regarded as the "standard work" on the war, describes a Republican counterattack against Franco's forces in front of Madrid in October 1936:

> The attack took place at dawn on 29 October. Fifteen T-26 Russian tanks, driven by Russians, led by a Lithuanian tank specialist in the Russian army, Captain Paul Arman (known as "Greisser"), smashed into the nationalist cavalry. These tanks were used in the new *Blitzkrieg* style propagated in Germany by Colonel Guderian and admired in Russia; massed together for a shock attack rather than, as favored by the French, spread out in support of infantry, even though the lack of mechanized vehicles for the infantry to follow blunted the point.[71]

The passage begs the question of whether fifteen tanks can be considered a "concentrated assault." Historian Gabriel Jackson uses similar terms to describe the use of armor on the Nationalist side:

> The Germans insisted that their tanks, which were somewhat lighter and faster than the Soviet models, be used in groups to punch through the enemy front. Their tanks were accompanied by armored cars and mo-

torcycles but did not depend directly upon the infantry. The German tactic, which became world-famous as the *Blitzkrieg* of the Second World War, was more successful in Spain than that of the Russians.[72]

Again, we find the dubious notion that the German tanks in Spain operated in concentrated groups. If anything, it was the Russians who tried to use tanks alone to punch holes in the enemy front. Such a tactic on the Nationalist side would have been suicidal, given the extremely light nature of the German and Italian tanks in Spain. In general, modern historians of the war can argue that Spain was the proving ground for blitzkrieg only by leaving the definition of the term as vague as possible.

Any attempt to assess the lessons of the Spanish civil war must start with an unavoidable fact. This was a civil war, fought by Spaniards over issues of interest mainly to Spaniards. Although both Spains welcomed foreign aid, commanders on both sides could not have cared less for the experimental military doctrines of their foreign partners, except insofar as they led to victory. Complaints on the part of the Italians or Germans that Franco was not using their tanks correctly, for example, are meaningless. Franco was using them in the way that, in his opinion, best suited Spanish conditions, and it is difficult to say that he was wrong. He was more concerned with accomplishing his mission than he was in proving this or that theory of mechanized war.[73]

Ignorance of this factor has led to serious errors in interpreting what happened in the Spanish fighting. As always in the "lessons-learned" game, observers tended to mistake particular, perhaps even unique, cases for universal principles. They tended to perform a purely military analysis without thinking about the unusual political dynamics of a civil war. They forgot that Spain was not a proving ground, and that the Spaniards were not guinea pigs. No war led to a more inaccurate set of predictions than the Spanish civil war.

One lesson derived by many analysts was that the age of the tank was past, that antitank weapons had surpassed the tank in power, and that an aggressive tank attack under modern conditions had become impossible. At Brunete, to give just one example, the tanks had failed to sustain any sort of forward momentum. On the first day of the Republican offensive, twenty-four tanks took part in the attack on Quijorna, and although they managed to get themselves through the Nationalist lines, they lost contact with their infantry and barely fought their way back out. Likewise, on July 10, some sixty tanks were in the action against the Nationalist-held village of Castillo de Villafranca.[74] They came under fire from two antitank guns, which destroyed ten of them. In the course of the war, Nationalist forces captured sixty Soviet tanks, a sure sign that they had been operating without infantry support. The BT-5 had an incredible top speed of thirty-six miles per hour, but the rough terrain and poor quality of Spanish roads meant that it rarely had a chance to use it. Liddell Hart argued that the BT-5's high power-to-weight ratio made for inaccurate gunnery, and events seemed to bear out his contention. The after-action reports of the first commander of Soviet armor in Spain, Colonel Semyon M. Krivoshein, noted that the BT-5's guns were much more accurate firing from the halt than from on the move.[75] The German and Italians handled their tanks better, usually in groups of four or five, accompanied by armored cars and motorcycles. But both the German Mark I and the Italian CV-33 were already obsolete when they arrived in Spain.

The "demise of the tank" was an idea that had been bubbling up in the military consciousness for a while. In 1932, Liddell Hart published *The British Way in Warfare*, arguing on behalf of the advantages of Britain's traditional maritime strategy.[76] In the book he claimed that modern antitank weapons had become strong enough to ward off attacks by tanks, no matter how thick the armor or heavy the vehicle. The idea of building a "heavy tank" strong enough to resist antitank fire, a common notion at the time, was an illusion. Not only would developments in antitank guns and ammunition always catch up to them eventually, but they brought with them a host of problems: they were too heavy for most bridges and roads, their size made them huge targets, and they were too expensive to produce in mass.[77] He argued that the trend of the future was the "miniature tank," the Carden-Lloyds or Morris-Martels.[78] Speed was more important than protection or firepower. Such ideas were common throughout Europe.[79] Even the German tank proponent General von Eimannsberger had to admit: "One factor must not be overlooked: the battle between the shell and armor was lost by armor a long time ago."[80]

Spain gave support to those who were now arguing for the supremacy of antitank defenses. The battle of Guadalajara was the most carefully watched and analyzed battle of the Spanish civil war. To those still unsure of the ability of armored forces to carry out independent operations, it heralded the eclipse of the tank. To a smaller group of armor advocates, it proved that mobile units needed bold and aggressive command in order to succeed, and that the real danger of military reform was stopping at the doctrinal halfway house of motorization, as opposed to full-blown mechanization. To airpower advocates, it was proof that the airplane was the new queen of battle. In other words, as is often the case in parsing the "lessons" of a given battle or war, everyone saw what they wanted to see. The simple question of What happened at Guadalajara? generated a wide variety of answers.

We may first of all disregard the exaggerated, almost hysterical opinions of Republican sympathizers. Ernest Hemingway arrived in Spain just after the fighting and wrote: "I have been studying the battle for four days, going over the ground with the commanders who directed it, and I can state flatly that Brihuega will take its place in military history with the other decisive battles of the world."[81] Herbert Matthews, who had been enamored of Italian military prowess in Ethiopia, now dubbed Guadalajara "a symbol and a turning point for history in the years to come." It would be to Fascism, he said, what the battle of Bailen in the Peninsular War had been to Napoleon, the beginning of the end.[82]

The analysis provided by some military professionals was not much better. Typical of the genre was an article in the respected French journal *La Revue d'Infanterie* in which Major Wanty of the Belgian army noted that tanks had not played a decisive role in the battle: "In the first place, it is scarcely possible to make a worthwhile comparison between the disconnected engagements of tanks such as have taken place up to this time and the great battle of which the protagonists of this arm dream, but which remains to date in the realm of attractive speculation." But he followed those sensible words by using the battle of Guadalajara to establish four "definite points" about the use of modern tanks in combat: tanks could not occupy ground on their own; they required infantry to occupy the terrain they overran; they were highly vulnerable without infantry support; they could rarely make full use of their speed, since they usually had to maneuver slowly over a terrain scattered with obstacles and often had to stop to locate and battle opposition.[83] But it is difficult to see how Guadalajara proved any of these points. There were few tanks present at the battle, and most of the attacking force was motorized as opposed to mechanized.

Another curious view of Guadalajara appeared in 1938 in an article in the Soviet journal *Krasnaya Zvesda*.[84] The author, A. Shebanow, began by arguing that "Spain has refuted the fascist theories with regard to the gaining of swift and instantaneous victories solely with the aid of modern mechanical weapons," official Soviet doctrine in the wake of Tukhachevsky's purge and execution. He described the first Republican riposte at Trijueque and the second at Brihuega mainly in terms of superior tactics on the part of the "class-conscious" Republican infantry. Yet he is unable to bury altogether the crucial fact of artillery, tank, and air support in each of those actions—"aviation, fifty tanks, and an artillery group" at the former and "seventy planes, forty tanks, and an artillery group" at the latter. It is hard to read the article and be convinced that old-style "leg" infantry had played a major role either time.

A highly influential contemporary analysis was a 1938 article in *Wissen und Wehr,* in which Arthur Ehrhardt described Guadalajara as a "duel between the airplane and a combination of armor and ground motor." This was the first time that these two modern weapons, "whose capabilities and prospects for the future are being argued to this day," had faced off, and therefore the battle offered "valuable lessons" for modern operations.[85] He offers an interesting account of the battle that, as one might expect from his thesis, plays up the role of airpower at Guadalajara and vastly underrates the intensity of the ground fighting.

The operation got off to a quick start, Ehrhardt wrote. "The government defenders were completely taken by surprise; the thin screen of their outposts tore after hardly any resistance." The road to Madrid lay open. A French aviator who was flying for the Republic thought that the Nationalists could have cut through the defense "like a knife through butter." But Franco (whom Ehrhardt believed was in command of the operation) hesitated, failing to seize the opportunity. "To our surprise, we find that in the evening of March 9th, that is, thirty-six hours after the operation was launched, the forward elements of the attacking forces had advanced but twelve miles from their line of departure." It was not until March 10 that the Nationalists captured Brihuega. Four days after its start, the offensive had advanced just twenty-five miles. Causes for the delay included the broken terrain, with its thorny brush and walled villages, the fear of ambush, and above all the weather: "Shortly after the offensive was underway, it began to rain. The hilltops soon were shrouded by low-hanging wet clouds. The attacking infantry suffered greatly from the rain and cold; the men took cover in the trucks." Whatever the cause of the halt, the effect was disastrous. An immense motorized column, over a thousand vehicles forming a column twelve miles long, now sat immobilized on the congested highway.

At this moment, the Republican command decided to counterattack. Ehrhardt's description is of a pure air offensive. By March 10, General Miaja (again, Ehrhardt is an error as to the identity of the operational commander— he simply lists the general in overall charge of the Madrid sector) had concentrated about 100 planes for the counterattack. His force included 75 single-seater fighters, 10 bombers, and about 20 ground attack planes. The attack opened on March 10, "creating havoc among the long and crowded column of the Insurgent troops," and so disordered the Nationalist offensive that "a second devastating air attack, which followed the next day, completely wiped out the Insurgent columns." On March 11, General Miaja received another 30 Russian bombers and fighters, while his opponents were essentially operating without air cover at all.

Ehrhardt described more air attacks on March 12, as Republican aircraft continued to pound the Nationalist troops tied up along the highway. "A first wave of thirty airplanes, flying at a low altitude, took the column by surprise. A second wave followed and, by repeatedly swooping down upon the column, inflicted the heaviest losses upon the practically defenseless troops on the ground." Ehrhardt's account is written vividly, and one can see how convincing it might have been to a reader at the time:

> The divisions were unable to develop and so reduce the effect of the fire of the airplanes for the trucks could not give way to the sides and drive into the difficult terrain, but remained hopelessly stalled on the highway, the only road that was at all possible. In the general confusion, the drivers found it impossible to turn their vehicles around. Moreover, the crews lacked the strength to fire back at the airplanes. Burning vehicles blocked the highway; and piles of debris formed well-nigh impassable obstacles. . . . The infantrymen and the drivers deserted their trucks and ran aimlessly into the open country, trying to get away from their vehicles, the targets of the hostile bombs and machine gun fire. At that moment of utter confusion and demoralization, several battalions of governmentalist militia, supported by Russian tanks, launched an attack at Trijeque. The action of this militia completed the collapse of the Insurgent forces.

That night, he wrote, the Nationalists attempted to regroup, but "a new air attack, which took place the following day, made short work of whatever order there was left and completely routed the exhausted and demoralized soldiers—deserted guns, caissons, rifles, and trucks in large quantities stood and lay about in wild disorder."

That was the third time in this account that the Nationalist force had been destroyed. The next two days (March 14 and 15) "put an end to the fighting." Bad weather forced both air forces to the ground. The Republican forces had clearly won a victory but failed to exploit it. "Ground forces now should have taken up the pursuit to prevent the opponent from gaining a foothold." However, the Republican command "lacked the necessary troops." The Nationalists "took advantage of this breathing spell to reorganize and entrench for the defensive, strongly fortifying Brihuega, "which was still in their hands." It is difficult to reconcile this passage with what has gone before. How could a destroyed (let alone a thrice-destroyed) force still be holding territory beyond its original start line? Apparently the Nationalists would have to be "destroyed" a fourth time.

On March 16 and 17, Republican air and ground attacks cooperated to recapture Brihuega. This time the Republicans knew how to exploit their gains, with aircraft swooping down on the retreating Nationalist units without pause. Under constant bombardment, the retreating enemy found it "extremely difficult to bring up reinforcements, ammunition and food for the exhausted Insurgent troops." Although putting up a brave fight, the Nationalist force was "slowly disintegrating." On March 21, the fighting had ended in what Ehrhardt called "a temporary stalemate." The Nationalists still held about half of the originally captured territory, with the line standing about ten miles ahead of where it had been on March 8. Not bad for a force that had been "destroyed."

Ehrhardt's narrative of Guadalajara is confused. It contains much wrong information and barely mentions the Italians, and its emphasis on airpower alone leads the author into all sorts of distortions. The last factor, in particular, renders him unable to account for pauses and lulls in the operation. In fact, ground forces had halted the Nationalist drive; ground forces and air units working together had thrown it back; and while airpower had inflicted considerable hurt on the congested motorized columns on the Saragossa-Madrid highway, it had come nowhere near to "destroying" the Italian force.[86]

Liddell Hart offered his own critique of the battle, and at first it seems more sensible. He pointed out that, while many analysts described Guadalajara as a mechanized battle, it had been nothing of the kind. "The narratives showed that the bulk of the attacking force was composed of infantry, who were merely carried in lorries and had to dismount before attacking."

> Those who have studied the subject of mechanized warfare have long insisted on the importance of distinguishing between fully mechanized and merely motorized troops. They have pointed out that, to make the best of the former and diminish the dangers of air attack, the scale of manpower and consequently of superfluous vehicles should be much reduced; that the force should be composed of armored vehicles of high cross-country performance; that it should be trained to keep off the roads, to move on wide fronts, and to maintain a state of controlled dispersion.

Since the Italian force at Guadalajara had met none of these conditions, the battle could hardly be "a reliable guide to the value of mechanized forces."

As always, however, Liddell Hart's reference point was the western front in the last war: "Twenty years ago Passchendaele taught a lesson in the folly of using tanks in swamp-like conditions, if also of pursuing an offensive by any means in such conditions." This is a glib comparison, valid only if one equates the battlefield conditions at Passchendaele (where millions of shells fired over weeks churned up the earth and brought up the groundwater in low-lying Flanders, creating a sea of mud) to an ordinary day of bad weather in Spain.

Liddell Hart used Guadalajara to make a broader point about the nature of modern warfare, and because he was the most famous interwar military analyst, his words carried enormous weight with his contemporaries. Discussing the inability of either side to carry out a decisive offensive, the "captain who teaches generals" weighed in with this verdict on Spain:

> On land, the experience of the war has strongly supported the evidence of the World War that the defense is paramount at present. This has added significance because relatively small forces in vast areas offered the attack more scope, and a better chance, than it had on the closely packed Western Front. There have been few successes gained merely by maneuver. But offensives by either side have in general had small effect in proportion to their cost of life.[87]

Even when the attackers had made a breakthrough, he argued, "experience had again confirmed that of the World War in showing that conditions set a term to their powers of exploiting it." Drawing the broadest possible conclusion, events in Spain indicated "that the ultimate general effect of mechanization will be towards enhancing the power of the defense, through increasing rapidity of reinforcement and counter-move, rather than towards reviving the power of the offensive." Liddell Hart wrote this commentary in 1937, just one year into the war (but after the Italian debacle at Guadalajara). Less than two years later, the German army would demonstrate how totally wrong he had been in his prediction.[88]

The point of this exercise is not to single out Liddell Hart or to mock a wildly wrong prediction but to attempt, insofar as it is possible, to see *why* it was wrong. Like many contemporary analysts, he assumed that World War I and the Spanish civil war shared enough similarities to offer reasonable grounds of comparison. Liddell Hart had made a very successful career for himself by comparing conflicts that had taken place in widely separated times and places. His métier, in a sense, was comparing Scipio Africanus's ancient art of war to that of more modern figures like Napoleon or William Tecumseh Sherman, and contrasting their brilliance with the unimaginative British commanders of World War I. His book *Strategy* draws all sorts of fantastic allusions between Marathon, the War of the Spanish Succession, World War I, and every war in between. But are any of these comparisons valid? Does ancient war exhibit certain traits that are entirely missing from modern conflict, and vice versa? This is a controversial question worthy of serious debate. Liddell Hart's equation of World War I and the Spanish civil war may help to explain why his predictions turned out to be so incorrect for the war that was about to start.[89]

There was one organization that learned the lessons of Spain: the German Luftwaffe. The Condor Legion had fought during the entire war and had experienced virtually every mission a modern air force was likely to encounter: strategic bombing, interdiction, attacks on naval vessels, close air support, and air superiority. It had developed the ability to switch between these diverse missions at the drop of a hat, as it had demonstrated over the Ebro. During the latter phase of the war, it had gained considerable skill at flying in support of rapidly moving mobile formations. It had learned the difficulties of unescorted bombing missions; of night and bad-weather flying; of high-altitude horizontal bombing. The scale of its commitment was considerable: over 19,000 men served during the war in Spain. When a new war broke out in 1939, the Luftwaffe was the best-prepared air force in the world.[90]

Chapter 8

• • • • • • • • • • • • • • •

Operational Art Reborn:
The Opening Battles of World War II

INTRODUCTION: ON THE BRINK OF WAR

By 1939, European military doctrine was in a state of intense confusion. Neither twenty years of discussion and debate nor the wars in Ethiopia and Spain had been enough to settle the basic questions about the nature of modern warfare. When World War I ended, military reformers had come forth in all the warring countries with new ideas about how a future war could avoid the static trench lines and bloody slaughter of the western front. Two schools of reform emerged: one advocating the tank and another preaching the benefits of strategic airpower. As one surveys the military literature of the era, both civilian and professional, it is obvious that the ranks of the first had declined in favor of the second. By the late 1930s, the tank had shrunk in the estimation of most of those who had been its most ardent enthusiasts. The vision of the irresistible "land battleship" of World War I had given way, by 1939, to a belief that antitank weapons had risen to a position of dominance on the modern battlefield, and that tanks had best tread lightly, operating on the flanks or carrying out raids through poorly defended sectors of the enemy line.

By contrast, the ranks of those who preached strategic airpower were growing. For them, "the bomber will always get through" was an article of faith. They envisioned the next war being decided rapidly and decisively, within hours in fact, by massive aerial bombing raids over enemy cities, against which no known weapon would be effective. The Italian Giulio Douhet was the father of this school, but it embraced a number of other figures as well, such as Hugh Trenchard of the Royal Air Force and William "Billy" Mitchell in the United States.[1] The two most famous armor advocates of the interwar period, Fuller and Liddell Hart, both moved from the tank camp to the strategic air camp in the course of the 1930s, influenced by a misreading of events in Ethiopia and Spain. It is worth noting that strategic bombing never dominated the discussion in Germany, where interest in the operational level of war continued to hold sway, and where the principles of an "operational air war" had been developed by 1935 and then tested under live-fire conditions in the Spanish civil war.[2]

The faith in strategic airpower was so strong during the interwar period that it even gave birth to a characteristic literary form, a hybrid pulp novel–military analysis that described the devastating effect of air attack on the crowded modern cities of western Europe, written to warn the Western nations to increase spending on air defense. It could be truly awful. *War over England*, by Air Commodore L. E. O. Charlton, was a representative example. According to a contemporary review in a professional military journal, it was a "lurid picture of a war in the near future before we are prepared for it":

> If the reader has patience to bear kindly with this writer's *penchant* for lurid details, his ill-favored sneers at the older Services, and his obvious ignorance of their functions and capabilities, he will find that there is a very considerable sub-stratum of reality and truth in a work which the reviewer was sorely tempted at first to throw aside and ignore as being yet another contribution to that unbalanced treatment of the air menace which has been the worst enemy of the Royal Air Force and the air defenses of this country in general.

Charlton's novel ends with a world at peace, governed by a "Court of Equity" in Geneva, with an international air police force—"the only military force on earth"—to enforce the court's decrees. The reviewer concluded that Charlton's final vision "must be of another world than that in which we live," and while the modern reader is tempted to agree, it is interesting to note how strongly this vision still motivates international behavior.[3]

Ethiopia and Spain were central in the decline of the armor school and the rise of faith in air power. And yet, one cannot help but observe, what thin reeds were the Ethiopian and Spanish wars on which to base important doctrinal change! Neither war had proved much of anything about the massed use of armored formations, yet all sides in the debate quoted them repeatedly as support for their positions. Italian armor had had its troubles in both wars but had been used in such small numbers that it was impossible to deduce any sort of coherent conclusions. Likewise, General von Thoma had no empirical evidence for his contention that tanks had operated better in concentrated masses during the fighting in Spain.

The evidence for the efficacy of strategic airpower was even slimmer. It had helped to pursue and destroy Ethiopian forces who were totally devoid of antiaircraft weapons, and it had certainly played an important tactical and even operational role in Spain. But it had never come close to the grandiose predictions of many of its promoters. "The bomber will always get through" was a myth, a science fiction phrase that allowed those who uttered it to indulge in dark fantasies of mass destruction, social breakdown, and apocalypse.

The de-emphasis of the tank was a European-wide development. In the Soviet Union, for example, Tukhachevsky's concept of "deep battle" with gigantic mechanized corps disappeared, as did the man himself. Once again the tank became a pure infantry support weapon, with small tank brigades organized for that purpose. Although he had been the victim of a political purge and Stalin's paranoia, the failure of Soviet armor in Spain had convinced many Soviet officers that Tukhachevsky's ideas had simply been wrong. The change marked the end of a great period of Soviet experimentation in armored doctrine and equipment.

The French had never seen armor as an independent arm. The tank was an infantry support weapon, and the events of the interwar era gave them no reason to change their minds. The advent of the DLM (light mechanized division) had set some minds in the French army to thinking of long-range raids against the enemy's rear areas, but that notion had not yet gone beyond the paper stage. An article in *La France Militaire* by General Camon argued strongly in favor of such a deep raiding strategy. Counterarguments came forward almost immediately in both the professional and the civilian press. The DLM was too costly, its manpower too highly trained and specialized to use on such a risky venture. The division would have to rely on a very vulnerable supply network for fuel. Extricating it at the end of the raid would be a most hazardous operation.[4]

In Italy, doctrinal debate was at least based on real-life combat experience in Ethiopia and Spain, although here, too, there was a great deal of miscalculation. While the concepts explored by Italian officers like Colonel Enrico Maltese, General Ottavio Zoppi, and General Gervasio Bitossi had been as advanced as anything coming out of the Soviet Union or Germany, the army as a whole never adopted them, and at any rate the Italians never designed a tank good enough to carry them out.[5] And here, too, there was a disastrous doctrinal detour, one of the century's most spectacular failures: the "binary division" *(divisione binaria).*

Based on experience in Ethiopia and Spain, the Italians reduced the number of component regiments in their infantry divisions from three to two, exchanging the "two up, one back" regimental deployment in favor of a "two forward" arrangement. The binary division was smaller, and theoretically much more mobile, than any of its contemporaries. While discussion of it usually centers around Mussolini's desire to increase the number of divisions in his army for prestige purposes—divisions being the basic military currency of the day—there was legitimate theory behind the development.

In the modern age, so the argument ran, virtually all corps-level assets had already become motorized. These included artillery (two or three regiments for each corps), machine gun units (one regiment for each corps), tanks, pioneers, signal troops, even chemical units. The modern division was therefore capable of operating without a third regiment in reserve, since the corps commander could rapidly insert his motorized assets into the battle if one of his forward divisions reached the end of its strength.

According to a German analysis, the binary division was an attempt to make the corps commander the central figure of the battle, its "pillar and support." His task was to choose the point of main effort and insert his assets there, concentrating overwhelming strength at the designated point. The divisional commander was only a "skirmisher." His mission was merely to grab the enemy and hold him in place long enough for corps-level assets, including divisions of the second line, armored units, and airpower, to destroy him.[6] Dropping the unnecessary third infantry regiment made the division more mobile, the preeminent consideration in a decade obsessed with the question of mobility. It allowed the division to operate efficiently in road-poor areas, simplified supply and command arrangements, and made it a smaller target for attack from the air.

While the units performed worked well enough in Ethiopia, the Italian army found them troublesome as early as the 1938 maneuvers in the Abruzzi. Fully half of the units involved in the maneuver (the entire "Blue" team) were binary divisions, but their performance had been inconclusive. In fact, the directors had called off the maneuver at precisely the moment that the corps commander was inserting his assets to achieve the decisive victory—in other words, at that precise moment when the participants could have learned something about the possibility of warfare with binary units. What was clear, however, was that the division lacked staying power. Its weakness led the corps commander into a premature commitment of his assets, and the insertion of those assets—especially the second-line divisions—took longer than Italian theorists had predicted. A third regiment in reserve would have fit the bill nicely, enabling the division to hold the line solidly while the corps commander planned the most appropriate insertion of the tanks and heavy artillery.[7]

The Germans were largely immune from such enthusiasms. Whether it was a matter of "military culture" or "national character" or simply the lucky accident of having sober-minded individuals in important positions, German officers, both staff and line, tended simply to accept the presence of new weapons in the battlefield, while rejecting all calls for the abolition of the infantry, or the myth of a war between Great Powers decided in fifteen minutes, or any of the more esoteric doctrines being preached abroad. If there was one constant in the German military culture of the interwar period, and this dates back to the great Moltke, it was the rejection of any "schema" or formula for war. The notion that warfare could ever be reduced to a single proposition was repugnant to German military intellectuals.[8] Combined arms had been the secret of success in war from time immemorial—it would continue to be so in the future. How best to incorporate new weapons like the tank and the airplane, not to mention the truck, the motorcycle-sidecar combination, and the bicycle—this was the issue that most engaged German military professionals of the era. No one ever published an article in the *Militär-Wochenblatt*, the semiofficial voice of the German army, either before or after Spain, suggesting that tanks and tanks alone were capable of winning a victory all by themselves or of doing anything on the battlefield except to roll on to their destruction. Had anyone done so, he would have been accused of being one-sided, and overly rigid, and of departing from the firm ground—not open to debate in any real sense—of combined arms warfare.

An article from the *Journal of the Royal United Service Institution* illustrates the gulf between Germany and other nations in evaluating the tank. Describing the two schools of thought on the employment of the tank, Major J. K. Edwards, wrote: "First, there are those who favor independent tank action unrestricted by close cooperation with the less mobile arms; secondly, those who contend that the primary role of the tank still lies in the close support of infantry to assist the latter by fire and shock action against machine guns."[9] These and similar phrases show up so frequently in the military literature of the period that we can say they had become proverbial. But that does not mean they were correct.

In fact, these are *not* the only two alternatives. Unmentioned here is a third solution to the problem of the tank, the one that the Germans eventually devised: tanks working in close cooperation with the other arms whose standards of mobility had, as far as possible, been brought up to that of the tanks, in other words, the panzer division. Such a conception integrated the mobility of the internal combustion engine into the bedrock principle of combined arms warfare. This was the secret to restoring mobility, not merely to the tactical "battlefield" but to the operational campaign. Divisions, corps, and armies would use their armored spearheads to create opportunities for warfare on the operational level, in order to achieve the maneuver onto the enemy's flank and rear, leading to the envelopment and destruction of his entire military force.

THE POLISH CAMPAIGN

The first year of World War II saw the German army rewrite the book on modern warfare with a pair of impressive victories. This was a new style of warfare, highly mechanized, with tanks and aircraft working in close cooperation to cut their way through the enemy line, doing the work that had formerly belonged to the infantry, and forever banishing the specter of positional warfare. It was fast-paced and furious, and it left Germany's slower-moving adversaries stunned. It changed the face of warfare forever, and its principles are used today by all modern armies.

The war began on September 1, 1939, as the Wehrmacht invaded Poland in an operation code-named Case White.[10] An article in *Time* magazine on September 25 described it as a blitzkrieg, a term that had been used occasionally during the 1930s in both England and Germany to describe a war that ends in rapid victory.[11] It featured violent assault by massed panzer columns, closely supported by tactical airpower, especially the dive-bombing Stuka; deep penetration by the tanks; and then exploitation by reserves of tanks and motorized infantry deep into the rear of the Polish positions, preventing the Poles from re-forming the line or bringing up their reserves. The Luftwaffe played a key role, launching massive air raids on Polish airfields, hitting the Polish air force on the ground in the opening minutes of the campaign. While the Polish air force was not "destroyed on the ground," as most popular histories of this campaign claim, it certainly was mauled and its infrastructure—spare parts, fuel, repair facilities—essentially ruined. Air attacks on Polish rail lines also played an important role in disrupting Polish mobilization.

The geographic situation was ideal for this new "war of movement," with German or German-occupied territory reaching around three of Poland's four sides—not just Germany proper in the west, but East Prussia in the north and occupied Slovakia in the south. The Wehrmacht deployed in two "army groups": Army Group North (General Fedor von Bock) and Army

Group South (General Gerd von Rundstedt). Their drives resulted in the formation of two great pincers: 4th Army advancing from Pomerania and 8th and 10th Armies advancing from Silesia (8th/10th) forming one; 3rd Army from East Prussia and 14th Army from Slovakia forming another. The entire Polish army was caught in a fantastic *Kesselschlacht,* losing 65,000 killed in action, 144,000 wounded, and 587,000 prisoners of war. The advance was incredibly rapid, with the German panzer forces reaching the outskirts of Warsaw on September 8. By September 19, only the capital held out—the Germans, in fact, spoke of the "Eighteen Days' Campaign."[12] Surrounded and under constant aerial bombardment, Warsaw fell on the twenty-seventh.

The Poles were simply outmatched. Tactically, they relied on cavalry brigades as their strike force, an anachronism in the armor age. On the strategic level, faced with a list of bad options, the Polish commander, General Eduard Rydz-Smigly, and his staff probably chose the worst: a linear defense of the entire national border, rather than some system of defense in depth around Warsaw, or the lines of the Narew, Vistula, and San Rivers in the east. This even extended to the deployment of large forces in the district of Poznan (in 1914 the German province of Posen), a territory that formed an extensive salient jutting into German-held territory—seemingly daring the Germans to encircle it. They did. The result, overall, was a thin crust of defenders spread out over 875 miles of front, the approximate length of the Polish border with greater Germany and Slovakia.[13]

The Luftwaffe played a crucial role in aiding the revival of German operational mobility. It not only struck hard at Polish airfields in the opening days of the war but also successfully disrupted Polish mobilization and transportation facilities throughout the campaign. The Stukas, in particular, proved their effectiveness. Massed into a "close battle division" of 160 aircraft, they had displayed their worth by attacking and destroying the Modlin fortifications outside of Warsaw, cracking what would have been a tough nut indeed for ground forces alone.[14] No longer did armies have to pause interminably while the heavy siege guns rolled up; German bombers did the job just as effectively. Moreover, as the panzers advanced, highly mobile Luftwaffe airfield and logistics units moved up behind, opening up rough airfields in a day and allowing short-range German aircraft to fly close air support and interdiction missions almost immediately. This campaign marked the true birth of "Air-Land battle."[15]

Three comments are necessary in order to put this rapid German victory into perspective. First, in the absence of Western intervention, there really was no strategy that could have saved Poland. The attitude of the Western nations during the Polish campaign was shameful. Having gone to war to defend the country, they now sat back and watched the Wehrmacht carve it up. German forces in the west were a scratch collection of second-line divisions, with no tanks or air. There is no doubt that a French offensive could have easily penetrated to the Rhine, and perhaps beyond. But the French did not move. The commander of the French army, General Maurice Gamelin, was thinking almost purely in terms of a war of defense, in which the French army would sit behind the massive fortifications of the Maginot line and wait for the Germans to come to them. Upon mobilization, the French had some eighty-five divisions facing the German frontier, against just eight regular German divisions and twenty-five reserve divisions. The French had over 3,000 tanks and 1,500 aircraft; the Germans zero and zero. In fact, there was a small French advance. Starting on September 7, lead elements of two French armies crossed the border into the German Saar. In six days they advanced some ten miles, came to the main German defensive position (the so-called Siegfried line or Westwall), then retreated. The British did nothing at all of any note. They had spent a fortune building a bomber fleet in the interwar period. Over 800 bombers of the Royal Air Force were available to undertake missions against industrial targets in western Germany: and they did, dropping propaganda leaflets. Observers soon began to speak of a "phony war," and the Germans matched that clever turn of phrase with one of their own: *Sitzkrieg* (the "sitting war").

Second, while the huge body of literature on this campaign virtually ignores the Polish defenders, the Poles fought very bravely in what they call the "September campaign." They even launched a counterattack along the Bzura River west of Warsaw, on September 9 to 12. Units of the Polish Poznan Army under General Tadeusz Kutrzeba (the 14th, 17th, and 25th Infantry Divisions and the Podolska and Wielkopolska Cavalry Brigades) hit the overextended German 24th and 30th Infantry Divisions strung out along the Bzura, where they were serving as the northern flank guard for the advance of German 8th Army (General Johannes Blaskowitz). The attack achieved total surprise and made good progress at first, capturing some 1,500 German prisoners from 30th Division alone. It certainly caused anxious moments at German headquarters, on both the army and the army group level. Nevertheless, superior operational mobility on the part of the Germans turned the tables dramatically. German reinforcements were soon on the way, including large amounts of armor diverted from the drive on Warsaw, while the insufficient Polish radio net meant essentially that the Polish attackers were acting in isolation, without support from forces in the rest of Poland—who were having their own troubles, in any event. Faced with concentric attacks from all four points of the compass, the mass of the Polish attackers was soon hemmed into a small pocket, along with remnants of Army Pomorze that had retreated from the northwest under the hammer blows of Army Group North. Subjected to unremitting attack by the Luftwaffe and punished heavily by mobile German artillery, in a hopeless strategic situation, over 100,000 men surrendered by September 21.[16]

Also, the first German attempt to break into Warsaw, by 4th Panzer Division on September 8, received a bloody nose. The German tanks came on in a rush but took punishing fire from Polish antitank guns and artillery at point-blank range. The 4th Panzer repeated its error the next morning but again came under heavy fire from 37-mm antitank guns and 75-mm field artillery positioned at key street corners and supported by infantry. Thus ended the German attempt to "storm" Warsaw. The tanks soon redeployed to the west, to help beat back the Polish offensive on the Bzura.[17]

Third, and finally, there is a one common myth to dispel: tales of Polish cavalry charging German tanks are sheer nonsense. The Poles had cavalry, as did every other army of the day, and it did sometimes happen that Polish cavalry forces came under armor attack; like the infantry, they often found themselves surrounded and had to maneuver in order to escape the tanks. But it is a disservice to historical truth, not to mention the many brave men and officers of the Polish army, to suggest that using horses to attack tanks was somehow part of Polish military doctrine.

The final blow to Poland came on September 17, when, according to the terms of the Nazi-Soviet Pact, Soviet forces invaded Poland from the east. Two army groups (Byelorussian Front in the north and Ukrainian Front in the south) crossed the border against minimal opposition, taking some 200,000 prisoners of their own. Having spent a great deal of energy in the 1930s analyzing Soviet tank production and mechanized doctrine, the Germans were amazed at the primitive nature of the Soviet forces that invaded Poland, horse-drawn wagons being much in evidence. As the spearheads of the two invading forces met, what was left of the Polish army dissolved, although some 100,000 ragged survivors did manage to make it to neutral Romania. The campaign ended with a German-Soviet partition of Poland. German casualties in this first campaign of the war were astonishingly light, less than 50,000 all told, although equipment losses were fairly high. German tank losses, for example, were about 25 percent of those employed.

PLANNING FOR FRANCE, 1940: THE BATTLE FOR CASE YELLOW

The Wehrmacht's most stunning victory—in France and the Low Countries—came after nearly eight months of debate over the shape of the plan. In many ways, the battle over Case Yellow—the German operational plan for an offensive in the west—was more interesting than the campaign itself, and certainly more hard-fought. It pitted Hitler against the General Staff; junior against senior officers; and officers of the line against the planners. The main issue, how best to use the panzer formations, was not new. They had passed the test in Poland, certainly. But just as in the outside world, many German officers could and did explain away the Polish campaign as a result of inferior Polish weaponry, training, and doctrine. The Western powers, with their huge modern armies and air forces, would be a far stronger test. Despite all the postcampaign testimony, no one in the German army considered an attack in the west to be any sort of foregone conclusion.

If Hitler had had his way, the offensive would have immediately followed the victory in Poland. On October 9, he told his generals that the operation would begin on November 25. General Franz Halder, chief of staff of the Army High Command (OKH), duly prepared a plan by October 19. This early version of Case Yellow betrayed the lack of enthusiasm with which Halder and his generals viewed a face-off with the French and British armies. Though often labeled a rehash of the Schlieffen Plan, the "Halder plan" was in fact a great deal less. Three army groups would carry out separate thrusts into Holland, central Belgium, and the Ardennes forest. The central thrust, by General Fedor von Bock's Army Group B, would be the main one, driving west and northwest across central Belgium, north of Namur, to the sea.[18] It was a conservative plan that would push the Allied forces back but which, even if it succeeded, held out no prospects for any sort of decisive victory. An unsatisfied Hitler made his displeasure with the plan known and almost immediately began peppering army headquarters in Zossen with suggestions, urging redeployment of the panzer divisions and the use of airborne troops and, in a conference on October 25, suggesting a surprise assault on the upper Meuse to "cut off and annihilate the enemy." He also shocked his generals by announcing that he had decided to advance the starting date of the offensive to November 12, a not-so-subtle attempt to goad them into action.[19]

Hitler's ideas were in substantial harmony with those being put forth by General Erich von Manstein, chief of staff to General Gerd von Rundstedt, commander of Army Group A. In the Halder plan, Rundstedt had the inglorious task of holding the Ardennes front while Bock raced through Belgium to the north. Manstein objected to the plan, seeing it as a mere copy of the Schlieffen Plan, a "humiliating" admission of intellectual bankruptcy on the part of the General Staff on the verge of the most important offensive in German military history. It was, he said, a plan that "our opponents had already rehearsed with us once before."[20]

Further study only reinforced his first impression. Unlike the Schlieffen Plan, the Halder plan offered no chance of strategic surprise, no attempt to lure the French into an offensive in order to weaken resistance in front of the main German thrust. Since Bock's attack was likely to run head-on into the main Allied force, its chances of achieving a decisive victory were nil. Army Group B's forty-three divisions would first meet twenty Belgian and ten Dutch divisions. However weak their fighting strength, they would be fighting at home, with the benefit of strong fortifications (such as the Belgian fortress complex of Liège) and a great deal of favorable defensive terrain (the canals and dikes in Holland, for instance). It would be no easy task to destroy them all. In a few days, they would be reinforced by the French and British armies, complete with tanks and mechanized infantry, already waiting at the border, ready to move into Belgium at the first sign of a German attack. Thus, the German forces would find themselves face-to-face with the main body of their foe, and committed to a frontal attack at that.

Most annoying was the final aim of the plan. What Schlieffen had in mind was the encirclement and annihilation of the French army. The Halder plan "contained no clear-cut intention of fighting the campaign to a victorious conclusion. Its object was, quite clearly, *partial victory* (defeat of the Allied forces in northern Belgium) and *territorial gains* (possession of the Channel coast as a basis for future operations)."[21] Since there would be no strategic advantage such as surprise, German forces would have to rely on superior tactics, and it seemed to Manstein that the best they could hope for was a tactical victory. In fact, given the plan's lack of imagination, the Allies might well be victorious. Even if forced out of the fortified line from Antwerp-Liege-Meuse, Allied forces could retreat behind the Somme in good order. Powerful reserves would be available to form a new defensive front. By the time it reached the new Allied line, the German offensive would be losing its steam and would probably not be strong enough to lever the Allies out of their new positions. A continuous front from the Maginot line to the sea would be the result.

Manstein now began to consider a much more radical, and risky, plan. Instead of a thrust by the right wing into Belgium straight into the teeth of the Allied defenses, why not a blow from the unexpected left? A surprise attack in the south by Army Group A, through the rugged Ardennes, where the enemy would not be expecting an attack due to the difficulties of the terrain, would offer the possibility of destroying the enemy's entire northern wing in Belgium and set the stage for final victory in France. Manstein was taking a calculated risk, however. A dense, hilly forest, with winding paths and few good roads, the Ardennes was hardly good "tank country." That very difficulty could work to German advantage, however, since it was unlikely to be heavily defended by the enemy.

While Manstein pondered his plan, OKH brought out a revised plan on October 29.[22] Responding to Hitler's criticisms, it shifted the axis of the attack slightly to the south. The Panzer divisions would now cross the Meuse north and south of Namur. But the main assault was still in the hands of Bock's Army Group B, which included the vast preponderance of German military force, including all ten panzer divisions.

Two days later, Rundstedt sent an outline of Manstein's plan to OKH, beginning months of "paper warfare" on the best way to proceed in the west. Halder and his staff were not enthused, although the similarity of the Manstein plan to Hitler's own ideas forced OKH to treat it seriously. Above all, the staff questioned the feasibility of passing tanks through the Ardennes. Generals Wilhelm Keitel and Alfred Jodl consulted with General Guderian on this question, and Manstein approached him with the same concerns a short time later. Guderian had fought in the Ardennes in 1914 and taken part in a staff course at Sedan in 1918. He knew the terrain and expressed confidence that the tanks could get through.[23]

It soon became obvious that there would be no offensive in the fall. On November 7, Hitler postponed the date due to unfavorable weather conditions. The delay was to be temporary, he said, a matter of a few days until the weather cleared up. But then winter came, and offensive operations became impossible. From now until May 1940, there would be no less than twenty-nine cancellations and reschedulings of Case Yellow, as Hitler tried to keep the pressure on his recalcitrant generals to come up with a suitable plan for the offensive. This gave Manstein time not only to perfect his plan but also to lobby for its acceptance. In January, Rundstedt conducted a war game at Army Group A headquarters that convinced both him and Manstein that the alternative plan was both feasible and infinitely preferable to the OKH plan.

Manstein's plan would probably never have been accepted were it not for two fortuitous events in early 1940. First, in January, a German staff plane had to make a forced landing at Mechelen-sur-Meuse in Belgium.[24] On board were several staff officers who were carrying copies of the OKH plan for the western offensive. The original plan had never had surprise on its side, of course, but now its details were presumably in the hands of the Allies. Hitler was now even more insistent that an alternate plan, based on surprise and daring, be devised. Second, Manstein was assigned to command an infantry corps in the upcoming offensive. In February, he was invited along with all the other corps commanders to a reception with Hitler. After the luncheon, Hitler asked Manstein to meet with him privately and outline his views on how to handle an offensive in the west. Manstein found Hitler "surprisingly quick," by which he meant that the Führer agreed with everything he said.

A few days after their meeting, Hitler issued a new operational plan that adopted the Manstein plan in all its particulars. The new plan called for a concentration of strength on the left, or southern, wing of the German army. Army Group A, still under Rundstedt, would include three armies: the 12th, 4th, and 16th, plus a panzer group *(Panzergruppe)* under General Ewald von Kleist, made up of General Guderian's and General Reinhardt's panzer corps. Another panzer corps, under General Hermann Hoth, was also made available for operations in this sector, meaning that seven of Germany's ten panzer divisions were now assigned to Army Group A. In addition, most of the heavier tanks (Pzkw. IIIs and IVs) in the German inventory were transferred from Army Group B to the panzer group. Because the panzer group was the decisive element in the offensive, the question of who would command it was of the utmost importance. The fact that it went to Kleist, a rather conservative former cavalry general, created a certain amount of tension within the command, as he constantly tried to fight off the more aggressive suggestions of his corps commanders, especially Guderian.

Bock's command was now reduced to just two armies, the 18th and the 6th, plus three panzer divisions. His orders were to advance into Holland and Belgium, overrun the former as soon as possible, and engage any Allied forces he might encounter in Belgium. Described after the fact by Liddell Hart as "the Matador's cloak," Bock's real task was to fix the attention of the Allied forces in Belgium toward the north so that they would be oblivious to the real danger facing them.[25]

With Bock noisily invading the Low Countries, Army Group A would be passing through the Ardennes in the south. The *Schwerpunkt* of its attack would be at Sedan, on the Meuse River. Here Guderian's corps, backed by the elite Grossdeutschland Regiment of motorized infantry, and by an entire motorized infantry corps (the XIV, under Gustav von Wietersheim), would crash over the river. To the north, Reinhardt would head for Monthermé, while Hoth's corps would cover Guderian's flank by crossing the Meuse at Dinant. Once over the river, the panzers were to drive for the sea, cutting across the rear of the Allied forces engaged in Belgium and trapping them there. Winston Churchill would later liken the panzer thrust to a "scythe-cut," mowing down the unsuspecting enemy.[26]

It was a daring plan, laden with risk. If the Belgian defenses in the Ardennes were tougher than expected, if the Allies managed to recognize the German plan as it was developing and launched a counterstroke against the panzer spearheads when they were strung out and disorganized, if Bock was unable to deal with the main body of the Allied armies in Belgium— any or all of these possibilities could have made Case Yellow a disaster. Bock, perhaps unhappy that the new plan weakened his force at the expense of

Rundstedt's, was the most vocal opponent, although he was merely voicing the doubts of many:

> You will be creeping by ten miles from the Maginot Line with the flank of your breakthrough and hope that the French will watch inertly! You are cramming the mass of the tank units together into the sparse roads of the Ardennes mountain country, as if there were no such thing as air power! And you then hope to be able to lead an operation as far as the coast with an open southern flank two hundred miles long, where stands the mass of the French Army![27]

He need not have worried. Not only was the Allied plan no threat to Case Yellow; it actually helped it. General Gamelin was still leading the French armies. While his own failings as a commander were many, he merely represented the cautious, perhaps even defeatist, generation of officers in the French high command. He had vivid memories of the slaughter on the western front in the previous war and was determined to avoid any repeat. While the Germans had been carving up Poland in September 1939, he had sat tight in the west, even with a decisive superiority in manpower, planes, and tanks. German forces facing him, in fact, amounted to little more than a police force. Virtually the entire German army, all its tanks, planes, and heavy weapons, was engaged in Poland. Yet after a few insignificant probes, described in the Allied press grandiloquently as the "Saar offensive," Gamelin had ordered his troops to retreat.[28]

Since then, the "western front" had seen no fighting at all. Now that this "phoney war" seemed about to end, and a German invasion seemed imminent, Gamelin's strategic insight showed little improvement. He had decided on "Plan D." When the Germans launched their invasion, Franco-British forces in northern France would advance into central Belgium. There they would establish a main line of resistance along the river Dyle (hence "D"), where they would prepare to meet, and hopefully defeat, the German assault. It was a pedestrian strategy, perhaps even less imaginative (if that were possible) than 1914's Plan XVII. It handed the initiative to the enemy, and even Gamelin recognized that it offered no real chance for a decisive victory. It showed that while the French may have had tanks, they were not yet thinking in terms of mobile warfare. Allied tanks would drive into Belgium and . . . wait for the Germans! Perhaps its only advantage was that it would keep the fighting off of French soil, hardly a cause for celebration, of course, if you happened to be Belgian.[29]

Worst of all, Plan D fit perfectly into Manstein's scheme for a panzer thrust through the Ardennes. The Allies would be preparing to stop the advance of Bock, now commanding what was in fact a diversionary operation. Sitting in Belgium, immobilized on the Dyle, the Allies would be helpless to prevent the armored blow against Sedan and the subsequent race to the Channel. The only mobile units in the Allied forces (the one armored brigade, two light armored reconnaissance brigades, and three divisional cavalry regiments of the British Expeditionary Force and the three DCRs and three DLMs of the French army) would be engaged and pinned in Belgium while the German panzers would be sealing their doom to the south.

CASE YELLOW IN OPERATION

When finally unleashed, on May 10, 1940, Case Yellow played out exactly as Manstein had drawn it up on the board, a rare—perhaps unique—occurrence in military history.[30] The offensive opened in the north, with a thrust by Bock's Army Group B against the Netherlands and central Belgium. It was a noisy operation designed to draw maximum attention from the Allies. In Holland, a combination of tanks, strong air attacks, and paratroopers carried the main burden of attack, the last being the key element. In a series of widely scattered drops, German paratroopers *(Fallschirmjägern)* secured airfields, ground installations, and bridges over the land's numerous rivers and canals. Bock breached the main Dutch defensive positions by the fourth day, May 13. The Dutch army, 400,000 men strong at the start of the campaign, surrendered on May 15, following a massive Luftwaffe bombing strike against Rotterdam (May 14) that destroyed a major portion of the city center.[31]

Bock had similar success in central Belgium, kicking off operations with a spectacular assault by glider-borne infantry on Fort Eben Emael, the modern and supposedly impregnable Belgian fortress guarding the left bank of the Albert Canal. As all European armies had learned in the last fifty years from the fighting at Port Arthur, Adrianople, and Verdun, assaulting a fortress under modern conditions of warfare inevitably meant a long, drawn-out, and very bloody affair. Since fortresses had no flank, any operation against them inevitably turned into a series of frontal assaults against prepared defenses. The operation against Eben Emael proved that fortresses do indeed have a flank: from the air. Such operations were successful in convincing the Allied commanders that the main German thrust was occurring in the north. The Allied armies dutifully put Plan D into effect at dawn on May 10, rolling into Belgium without incident and moving up to the line of the Dyle, while the Belgian army withdrew from its advanced positions to join them. Some sharp fighting resulted as the spearheads of Bock's Army Group B made contact with French armor near Gembloux in central Belgium, the first tank versus tank encounter of the war.[32]

A triumphant—and smiling—Heinz Guderian, France, 1940. Courtesy of the Imperial War Museum, London (MH 9404).

The principal German thrust was actually taking place in the south. Here a massive force, Rundstedt's Army Group A, including seven of Germany's ten panzer divisions, had entered the Ardennes. A tremendous column of mechanized and motorized vehicles some fifty miles long began to wind its way through the dark forest. The problem of traffic control alone was a prodigious one, and there was a great deal of concern on the part of the Germans as to what might happen if the Allied air forces suddenly showed up. But the passage of the Ardennes went without incident. Brushing aside small units of Belgian motorized cavalry (the *chasseurs ardennais*), the head of the snake emerged into the open on the third day of the offensive, May 12, between Sedan and Dinant.

The Germans had won the campaign, and France was headed for an early exit in World War II. The mass of the German armor, seven divisions organized into three panzer corps, was about to smash into a neglected, weakly defended point in the French lines, while the main strength of the Allied armies, and virtually all of their mechanized and motorized formations, was engaged in a strategically pointless defensive battle far to the north. The "scythe-cut" had worked perfectly. German relief that the gamble had indeed paid off was palpable. "I could have wept for joy," Hitler later recalled. "They had fallen into the trap."

By 11:00 P.M. on May 12, all three panzer corps had arrived on the Meuse. In the north (on the right wing of the panzer forces), XV Corps under General Hermann Hoth was concentrated between Namur and Dinant; in the center, XLI Corps under General Reinhardt was at Monthermé; and on the left, XIX Corps under General Guderian formed the *Schwerpunkt* of the river-crossing operation, massed in front of Sedan. He had three panzer divisions to the two apiece allotted to Hoth and Reinhardt, as well as most of the Luftwaffe in support. But in fact, honors for crossing the Meuse went to a figure who was at this time little known to the outside world: General Erwin Rommel, who had received command of 7th Panzer Division exactly two months previously, on February 12, 1940. Moving faster than their neighbors, the division's forward elements, including its motorcycle battalion, reached the river near Houx late on the afternoon of May 12. Finding a weir linking both banks of the river, they tried to cross, were repulsed by the defenders, then crossed successfully under cover of darkness.[33] During the evening, elements of Rommel's 6th Motorized Rifle Regiment managed to join the motorcycle patrol across the river, coming across in ones and twos. No tanks had yet played a role; this was a panzer division, not a mere tank formation.

Seizing the opportunity, Rommel ordered a full-scale crossing by the entire division for first light on May 13. The first attempts to cross, carried out by infantry in rubber assault boats, were shot up by the French defenders. In a

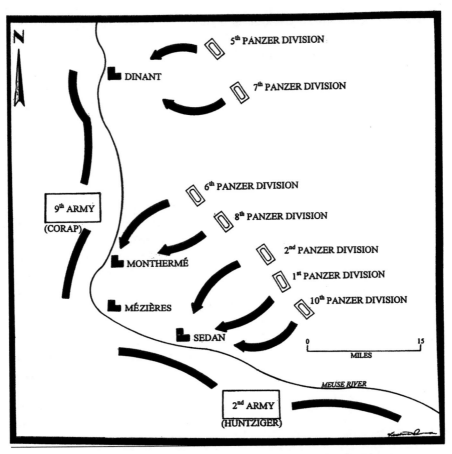

The chariot of Mars: The panzers approach the Meuse, May 1940.

day of hard fighting, Rommel tried desperately to reinforce his precarious foothold, rallying his shaken troops, getting them back into their boats and across the river, and directing artillery fire against French positions. Eventually, the division managed to carve out a bridgehead two miles deep and three miles wide, at a cost of 60 dead and 122 wounded. By the end of May 13, 7th Panzer was ferrying its tanks across the Meuse; fifteen were across the river by the morning of May 14.

And just what were these elite panzer forces up against? The portion of the Meuse selected for the breakthrough stood at the junction between the French 9th Army (on the left) and 2nd Army (on the right). Both had a large share of static fortress divisions and formations of older reservists classified as "Series B" ("definitely inferior, badly armed, over-aged and under-trained").

The 9th Army, under General André-Georges Corap, possessed seven infantry divisions: two regular, four reservist (of which two, the 53rd and 61st Divisions, were B-series); the remaining unit, the 102nd, was a static fortress division.[34] This force had to hold sixty miles of the Meuse riverbank. Likewise, 2nd Army (General Charles Huntziger) was predominantly a reservist army: two Series B divisions (the 71st and the 55th), with an average age over thirty and without a great deal of training or modern equipment. After all, this was a quiet sector of the front; the real soldiers in the French army were all on the Dyle. On the junction of their two armies, the commanders placed their four weakest divisions: reading left to right, the French defensive line along the Meuse consisted of 61st (B) Division, 102 Garrison Division, 55th (B) Division, and 71st (B) Division.

And what a sight greeted them on the morning of May 13. Across the Meuse, in plain sight of the French defenders, a wall-to-wall phalanx of every sort of motor vehicle imaginable—not just tanks but trucks, motorized gun carriages, motorcycles—had materialized on the far side of the river. If a concentration of French artillery or Allied aircraft could have come over at this moment, Case Yellow would have ended in disaster. "What a chance to acquire imperishable glory," wrote one French officer after the war, "by smothering at birth the German offensive and transforming all these mechanized and armored units into scraps of burnt and twisted metal."[35] Such talk was fantasy, unfortunately. The masses of French artillery and Allied airpower were farther north, along the Dyle.

Guderian planned a crossing of the river at 4:00 P.M., to be prefaced by seven straight hours of aerial bombardment. While there was urgency on the German side of the river, there was a high degree of efficiency and very little disorder. The crossing had been war-gamed at Koblenz two months previously, and Guderian's chief of staff, Colonel Walther Nehring, merely dusted off the orders used in the game, crossed out the dates, changed an item here and there, and used them almost verbatim.[36] The first Stukas began to arrive at 9:00 A.M. These ungainly craft, hurtling out of the sky in nearly vertical dives with their screeching sirens, dropping their bombs with pinpoint precision, systematically destroyed the French defenses, wrecking artillery batteries and reducing the French reservists to a state of numb resignation. As with the Ethiopians after Mai Ceu, each man seemed to feel that the bombs were aimed directly at him. One staff officer described the fear that the Stukas inspired: "When the dive-bombers came down on them they stood the noise—there were hardly any casualties—for only two hours, and then they bolted out with their hands over their ears."[37] Guderian's artillery arrived in the course of the day, as well, and now four groups of 105-mm and four of 150-mm guns joined in, deployed across just one and a half miles of front.

The French fought about as well as might be expected. Although they were deployed behind the wide Meuse, backed by their own artillery, and protected by concrete pillboxes, trenches, and antitank guns, these reservists were no match for the cream of the German army in 1940. With bombs raining down on their positions, German infantry crossing the Meuse in assault boats, and massed columns of tanks preparing to bear down on them, the 55th and 71st Divisions behaved predictably: they broke and ran in a panicky flight that tied up the roads and carried everything in its path. The stampede seems to have begun with a false report that German tanks had crossed the Meuse, showing the power of the mere threat of the German panzer. It was a rout, a "debacle," not the first time this sort of thing had happened to the French at Sedan. By late afternoon, Guderian's tanks were over the Meuse and by nightfall had a bridgehead some four miles wide and four to six deep. Between the corps of Guderian and Hoth, the 6th and 8th Panzer Divisions of Reinhardt's XLI Corps launched their own assault at 3:00 P.M. near Monthermé. Although his promised Luftwaffe support failed to materialize, Reinhardt's divisions got across the river with the aid of point-blank artillery fire that gutted much of the town.

By the end of May 13, elements of all three corps were across the river. They had ripped a hole some fifty miles wide in the French front. Even the Allies had to realize that something important was happening to the south. Attempts to stem the tide proved unsuccessful. All day on May 14, Allied bombers hit the pontoon bridge that the Germans had hastily constructed over the Meuse, the supply lifeline of their panzers. They failed to knock it out, taking heavy losses in the process.[38] Newly arriving French forces, like the 3rd DCR, were wasted by being detailed to hold static defensive positions, rather than launching concentrated assaults on the flanks of German forces heading west out of their bridgeheads. Other units received orders to move to positions that had already been overrun by the German panzers. Civilian refugees carrying all their possessions in wagons clogged the road behind the French lines, making the deployment of reserves a nightmare. The 1st DCR, ordered to Flavion in the path of the German advance, took fourteen hours to make a twenty-three mile journey over roads jammed with military traffic and civilian refugees. The hard-charging 5th and 7th Panzer Divisions caught it with empty fuel tanks and uncharged radio batteries before it had even deployed and destroyed it in an afternoon.[39] Repeated Luftwaffe raids heightened the chaos, not only causing a great deal of physical damage but also unleashing panic among troops and civilians alike.

The Germans began the "breakout" from their bridgeheads on May 15, though that is perhaps a misleading term for what was from the start the pursuit of a beaten enemy. Never pausing, never letting the foe regroup, the panzer forces raced across the open country of northern France to the sea. Here is a description that appeared soon after the fact in the normally staid and sober German military journal, the *Militär-Wochenblatt:*

> Deep into Belgium and France, the German army and air force began the pursuit of the enemy. In the north as in the south, everywhere, the enemy's air forces were beaten down in successful air battles and by flak, his lines of communication destroyed. German armor followed hard on the heels of the enemy and inflicted heavy losses on him. German infantry did super-human deeds in the assault as well as in the pursuit. German artillery and pioneers paved the way untiringly for the forward-driving army.[40]

None of this was particularly exaggerated. This was the first great armored drive of the war, a victory of tanks, to be sure, but tanks matched with supporting arms of equal mobility, commanded by men who understood the operational potential of their new mobile units, and who communicated with them, with each other, and with higher headquarters through the instantaneous medium of radio. Hardware was important, certainly, but only in that it allowed the Germans to bring concepts of leadership and command that had been simmering for decades to near-perfect fruition.

For many years German doctrine had stressed short, crisp orders that allowed subordinates some leeway in choosing the means to carry them out. The pace of armored operations meant that its commanders had to devise a new language, a sort of panzer shorthand. A recent operational study of Rommel's 7th Panzer Division in the campaign has reproduced some of the radio traffic in the armored spearhead. To call these messages "short" is to understate the case considerably. The 5th Panzer Division radioed Rommel on May 13, 1940: "Angriff 0430" ("Our attack is going in at 0430"). At 0550 that morning, Rommel requested a situation report from his own 7th Infantry Regiment with a two-word message: "Wie Lage?" ("How situation?"). Its response: "0600 S.R. 7 Fluss Maas überschritten" ("7th Infantry Regiment crossed the Meuse at 0600"). When Rommel wanted his division to pursue the beaten French on May 14, his orders consisted of a terse "Rommel 1930 Verfolgung mit allem Waffen" ("Rommel at 1930: Pursuit with all weapons"); and when he wanted his pioneers brought up to help repair the bridges near Arras, his message to the divisional staff was "Rommel Pioniere nach vorne" ("Rommel: Pioneers to the front"). This was the new language of mobile warfare—crisp, concise, and stripped down to essentials.

This is not to say that there was no confusion on the German side. On May 13, Rommel received a radio message that his 7th Motorized Regiment was *eingeschlossen* (surrounded). Showing his characteristic "bias for action," he gathered up every man and vehicle that he could find and rode off to relieve his encircled men. It turned out that the message had been that the regiment was *eingetroffen* (struck) by an attack by French armor around Onhaye and was handling the situation quite well on its own. The "fog of war" increases with the speed of the operation.[41]

While the panzers were practically unmolested during their historic ride across northern France, they did encounter some opposition from their own high command. Fearful that the armored columns were going too far, too fast, that they might be attacked and cut off from the rest of the army by reserves of Allied armor, Chief of Staff Halder actually ordered the panzer divisions to halt to allow the infantry divisions to catch up in support. There is debate today over how much of the pressure to halt came from Hitler. One staff officer later stated that "the Führer was nervous about the risk that the main French armies might strike westward, and wanted to wait until a large number of infantry divisions had been brought up to provide flank cover along the Aisne [the southern flank of the advance]."[42] On May 16, Halder wrote in his diary: "Rather an unpleasant day. The Führer is terribly nervous. Frightened by his own success, he is afraid to take any chance and so would rather pull the reins on us."[43] Guderian demanded, however, to be allowed to conduct a "reconnaissance in force" to the west, and he used that concession to continue the advance of his entire corps.[44] When further friction developed, Guderian actually threatened to resign, but he never did stop his advance. He later recalled bitterly that "the High Command's influence on my actions was merely restrictive throughout." It soon became clear that there were no Allied armored reserves to speak of, nor was the Allied command capable of marshaling such a large-scale operation on short notice.

All the Allies could muster were three local counterattacks. The first two came up from the south, carried out by the newly formed 4th DCR under the command of General Charles de Gaulle, based at Laon. But neither his first toward Montcornet (May 17) nor his second toward Crécy-sur-Serre (May 19), succeeded in doing much more than shooting up some German transport before the tanks of the panzer divisions drove them back. French tanks, with their one-man turrets in which the commander also had to load and fire the gun, as well as their primitive radio control systems, were no match for the panzers in terms of flexibility or maneuver. They had never been intended for tank-to-tank combat, but for infantry support. The last Allied counterthrust came from within the pocket, an attack by two British armored columns near Arras on May 21. It overran the flank screen of General Rommel's 7th Panzer Division, advanced ten miles, and took more than 400 German prisoners. Rommel once again showed his penchant for personal leadership, concentrating his divisional artillery, antitank guns, and 88-mm antiaircraft guns into a deadly screen against the advancing British tanks. They were Matilda Is and Matilda IIs for the most part, slow, heavily armored infantry tanks that were impervious to the main guns of his tanks. By evening, he had organized a counterattack with his tanks northwest of Arras that broke the back of the British attack.[45]

Once again, German airpower made a key contribution to this phase of the campaign. The Luftwaffe had been ranging widely and deeply since the start of the fighting in the west, flying close air support and, as in Poland, carrying out a very successful campaign against the French railway system. But it was in the breakout from the Meuse that German airpower really shone. Although the mobile formations of Panzergruppe Kleist far outstripped their accompanying infantry during their "race to sea," they were never truly isolated: protecting their flanks was the VIII Air Corps under General von Richtofen. This it did in style, keeping a close watch on French divisions moving up to the front, smashing concentrations of French troops

The German Stuka was as indispensable to blitzkrieg as the tank. Courtesy of James S. Corum.

and armor, and effectively defeating their attacks before they could get started. With German fighters flying four sorties per day, and the Stukas even more than that, airpower played a crucial role in blunting de Gaulle's two attacks. The Allied inability to counter the German thrust, often attributed to command paralysis, was due just as much to the strength of German airpower, demonstrating here that the Germans had given just as much thought to the "operational air war" as they had to operations on the ground. It was a revolutionary development in military affairs.[46]

None of the Allied counterattacks succeeded in achieving a breakthrough, or even disrupting the German advance in the slightest. On May 20, the armored spearheads of Guderian's corps reached Abbeville at the mouth of the Somme River, and at midnight on May 20–21, the first German tanks reached the Atlantic Ocean. The Allied armies in Belgium were trapped in a gigantic pocket, facing Bock from the north and northeast, Rundstedt from the south and southeast. The Belgians surrendered on May 27, making defense of the pocket impossible, although it would have been difficult enough anyway. While the British did manage to retreat to Dunkirk and to evacuate the continent by June, the cream of the French army was destroyed.

The citadel at Calais was heavily damaged by Stukas during the assault on the French city in June 1940. Courtesy of James S. Corum.

The French did attempt to re-form a position along the Somme, the so-called Weygand line, but the Germans crashed through it at numerous points in late May, entered Paris, and overran nearly the entire country before an armistice ended the fighting in June.

CONCLUSION: THE RETURN OF DECISIVE VICTORY

The German victory in 1940 was one of the most improbable in the history of war. The German army had done what virtually every military observer had deemed to be impossible since the Boer War. It had launched an offensive against a modern, well-armed foe from a position of numerical parity and won a rapid, decisive victory with minuscule casualties. The numbers do not cease to amaze more than sixty years later. In the course of the campaign, the Wehrmacht had inflicted over 1.2 million casualties at a cost of just 65,000 men and within six weeks had taken the surrender of three enemy armies. The fourth, the British, got away only by abandoning all its equipment.

To understand the importance of this campaign, we must go beyond its impact on World War II. It is often argued that Case Yellow restored mobility to warfare, but in fact it did a great deal more than that: it resurrected the possibility of decision. Mobility was merely a means to achieving a decisive result, something that had been noticeably absent from every war of the previous fifty years. All over the world, military staffs suddenly discovered the necessity for mechanization. Officers in the Red Army began reforming large-scale mechanized corps, rediscovering "deep battle," and rereading Tukhachevsky. The American army discovered the virtue of large armored formations and began arming itself for the involvement that President Franklin Roosevelt felt was all but inevitable.[47]

Less obvious at the time, but full of implications for the future, was the German victory in Norway in April and May, just prior to Case Yellow. It was the first campaign in history in which all three services—land, sea, and air—played an equal role, a classic example of a "combined operation."[48] On the morning of April 9, the Germans carried out simultaneous seaborne landings at Narvik, Trondheim, Bergen, and Kristiansand, slipping them past British naval patrols; a landing by paratroopers (a wartime first) at Stavanger; and a combined air-sea landing at Oslo. It was an epic achievement, a triumph of planning that required split-second timing, and, with German forces spread out over 900 miles of rugged terrain, an acid test of German command and control. With German forces pressing inland from all points on the compass, and with the Luftwaffe in total control of the air, the bewildered defenders never did form a cohesive resistance. The Allies tried to help, landing brigades at Narvik (April 15), Namsos (April 16), and

Andalsnes (April 18), but their command and control was a nightmare, with all these various forces actually reporting back to London. Under constant air attack, they soon had to withdraw. Meanwhile, the Germans rapidly built up their forces in Norway by air transport, demonstrating the tremendous potential of the air arm for future operations. Britain's superior naval strength, by contrast, had proved incapable of operating in the face of German air superiority.

The events in France soon stole the spotlight from Norway, and here the star of the show had been Germany's armored formations. Despite what was said at the time by many Allied observers, the Germans did not possess more tanks. They did not even have better tanks. What they did have was an operational vision for using not only the tank but also the highly mobile armored formation, to restore their ability to wage war on the operational level. The panzers did not merely "blast through" or "overrun" the opposition. Instead, they were used in rapier-like thrusts to cut through a designated section of enemy line, making a breach wide enough for entire divisions and corps to follow, so that these follow-on forces could seize favorable opportunities to launch attacks on the opponent's flanks and rear. In other words, they had allowed the German army to return to its Moltkean tradition of the *Kesselschlacht,* the "cauldron battle" or battle of encirclement. And the Germans had achieved this operational revolution with precisely 10 panzer divisions out of the more than 100 divisions mobilized for the offensive.[49]

The initial analysis of Case Yellow, as in all the other wars studied here, was often grossly in error. The French and British blamed German numerical superiority, claiming that the Germans had 7,500 tanks, for example, when the true number was 2,400, or 5,000 planes, when the true number was half of that.[50] A bit later, analysts would point to the qualitative advantages of German tanks, a notion that remained unchallenged until well after the campaign.[51]

There was one exception. Marc Bloch, a French officer, noted historian, and later member of the French resistance until his arrest, torture, and death at the hands of the gestapo in 1941, fashioned a much more profound critique. As a good social historian, he presented a blistering indictment of France's economic, political, and cultural structures, all of which shared the blame for having led the nation into disaster. The resulting book, *Strange Defeat,* is not an operational study in any sense, but it does contain several revealing passages about the new German method of waging war. "The whole rhythm of modern warfare had changed its tempo," he wrote. In the course of the campaign, he observed the following amazing encounter in the town of Landrecies, where he was administering a fuel depot:

One fine morning in May, the officer in charge ran into a column of tanks in the main street. They were, he thought, painted a very odd color, but that did not worry him overmuch, because he could not possibly know all the various types in use in the French Army. But what did upset him considerably was the very curious route that they seemed to be taking! They were moving in the direction of Cambrai; in other words, *away* from the front. But that, too, could be explained without much difficulty, since it was only natural that in the winding streets of a little town the guides might go wrong. He was just about to run after the commander of the convoy in order to put him right, when a casual passer-by, better informed than he was, shouted—"Look out! They're Germans!"[52]

The war, he said, was "a constant succession of surprises."

The German sense of swagger in the wake of Case Yellow was palpable and may in fact have sown the seeds of the Wehrmacht's future demise. Officers spoke of "the greatest battlefield success of all time,"[53] "a modern Austerlitz."[54] Defining the nature and essence of that success, however, proved to be difficult. Lieutenant Colonel Köhn, writing in August 1940, noted that already the outside world was coining catchwords like *blitzkrieg* and "the new tactics" to describe something that it only dimly understood. The German victories in Poland and France were no miracle, no mystery, he argued, but the result of brilliant leadership and well-trained infantry. His analysis started at the top, with Hitler: "If leadership that is brilliant, flexible in its decisions, and willing to accept responsibility unites all the political forces in one hand and uses them to the full," then victory was assured. "This is not new in world history and has many precedents." While there were few examples in the past as incredible as the military and political success of the 1940 campaign, there was no mystery involved. Rather, it was "the victory of a strong people united under one will against democratic, disunited, and decadent peoples."[55] Foreign leaders had jumped on the term *blitzkrieg* as a means of concealing their own failure and inability. Professional soldiers had a clearer view of things, however, and would not let themselves be fooled by such muddy thinking. They knew that, as always, victory went to the side that had the best training, that had the most complete understanding of combined arms, and that inserted every last unit and ounce of its strength into the struggle. As in all ages, there were two essential tactical principles: first, the goal of all weapons was to help the infantry get at the enemy with both fire and shock; second, the beaten enemy had to be pursued ruthlessly and to the end:

> As to point one, the prominence of our infantry rests on a full recognition of principles that are based on a good, old, German ideal: it's the man, not the weapon. Infantry is the main arm; all other arms support it

in order to bring it into close quarters with the enemy in as unmolested a condition as possible. If in this war, aircraft and tanks have fulfilled this tactical principle so completely that the infantry actually struck a broken enemy, that is only confirmation of the correctness of the way we train all the arms and not a diminishing of the role of the infantry.[56]

The infantry's cooperation with the artillery was evident both in Poland and in both phases of the battle in France. These campaigns showed repeatedly that, even in the age of armor, it was still the task of the infantry to break the resistance of the enemy, and in the "last one hundred meters," do it alone, with its own weapons only. The German infantry of 1940 had done the same thing that the infantry of 1914 and 1918 had done—driven forward motivated by the spirit of the attack—only this time there were new operational techniques to exploit the victory to the full and to conduct an energetic pursuit.

The pursuit was the key to the victory, with airpower, tanks, and mobile troops of all sorts widening a tactical victory into an operational one. But infantry, too, played a role here, storming forward relentlessly to prevent the enemy from re-forming his lines, and in the process forgoing the close contact with neighboring units that had been typical of World War I. This requires resolute and bold activity on the part of the lower officers, and their qualities, Köhn argued, were probably Germany's greatest advantage in this war.

There was nothing really new here, he concluded, although it might have looked new to Germany's enemies. The supporting weapons helped the infantry get forward so well that it achieved its mission—subduing the enemy—with "improbably small losses," especially in comparison with World War I: "If the German command managed with lightning speed to broaden early successes into operational victories and then carried out a pursuit that is unprecedented in perhaps all of military history by inserting all of its weapons and every available unit, then that perhaps is new to our foes. They call it *Blitzkrieg* and speak of mysteries." In the end, however, it was the infantry that had triumphed, with good training and the assistance of the new support weapons. The foot soldier, fighting man on man, "triumphs not only over the enemy but over technology itself."

Another officer writing at about the same time, Rittmeister F. Kronberger, argued that it was not tanks or infantry per se but the army's spirit of daring that had led to victory. He used Clausewitz's formula that "there are cases where the greatest daring is the highest wisdom."[57] Every officer in the army, he argued, was imbued with a sense of independence and freedom in engaging the enemy, tempered by willing obedience and military insight. The army's field service regulations, *Truppenführung*, made the point by instructing the officer that "omission and neglect are worse than a mistake in the choice of means." The pace of modern battle was so rapid, a matter of hours and minutes, that a commander could not possibly instruct his subordinates in the details of every battle situation. His drive for excellence allowed energy, responsibility, and enterprise to flourish among his men. Armed with these qualities, the German army had beaten larger opponents who lacked its spirit of initiative. Men and officers alike faced the tough task with hope and with full consciousness of their superiority—and that made them irresistible. "Our offensives in Poland and Norway, Holland and Belgium hit the enemy like a thunderclap, throwing him into terror and disorder." German operations in the war had been risky, but their "lively spirit of attack" seemed to rob the enemy of his power of decision. This was especially evident in the activities of the tank and air arms, giving German operations a level of "strength, mobility, and persistence" that would not have been possible in a previous era. Alone among the contending powers, the Germans had recognized that "a strategy of temporizing and delay could never lead to a lasting victory":

> Great successes only flourish where a bold, vigorous offensive strives for the decision. "The entire strength of our troops lies in the attack. We would have to be fools to give it up for no reason at all." (Frederick the Great) From the beginning, German commanders had the destruction of the enemy army in mind, although geography and the situation with the enemy would give that thought different forms.[58]

In the end, the quality of the commander rested on the capabilities of his troops. The Western powers sat by and watched the German army swallow up Poland. They renounced any sort of relief attack against Germany's western border in favor of a defensive posture in the Maginot line. They did this not so much because they feared a German counterblow but because their own armies were still only "hastily mobilized and loosely assembled." Their commanders saw no other choice but to go on the defensive. By contrast, the Germans immediately went on the attack in Poland. The German command counted on the indecision of the Western powers, and this view proved correct. Every attack was a step toward the destruction of the enemy. A series of concentric maneuvers ended with the capitulation of the entire Polish army.

The same thing happened in the west. The better the army, the higher the thoughts of its commanders could soar. The campaign proved that in the German army, the supreme command had "an instrument that justifies the boldest plans. After what our troops have achieved, it is as if difficult terrain and unassailable positions no longer exist." The air and sea landings in Norway had been daring, "but they were as nothing compared to the offensive in Holland and Belgium, the greatest military operation of modern times, that led to a series of flanking maneuvers and annihilation battles on the soil of Flanders and France." While a cool and sober reckoning of forces lay at the base of the German plan, the operation itself combined great energy with a bold decision to emphasize the destruction of the enemy over Germany's own security. It was, in that sense, an expression of the "racial character" of the German people *(Volkscharakter)*, which honored devotion to duty above all.

Others discussed the most obvious aspect of the German victory: the role of the tank. Colonel Rudolf Theiss, writing in October 1940, began with Hitler's statement that "German armor has, with this war, introduced itself into world history."[59] Theiss traced the wartime history of the German panzer, starting with its first appearance in the blitzkrieg in Poland. The entire world took notice of its appearance, he wrote, but denied its general validity. "There were even voices that described the campaign in Poland as a colonial war. The outside world did not want to accept that the type of warfare conducted by the German panzer arm was also feasible in the west."[60] Case Yellow put an end to such nonsense. Both the breakthrough of the strongly fortified line between Maubeuge and Sedan and the immediately following lightning-quick drive on Abbeville and the Channel coast were the work of the tanks. It was also the panzer divisions that hindered the enemy's attempts to break out of the encirclement, that drew the noose even tighter, that chopped up the isolated armies and finally destroyed them or took them prisoner.

Theiss argued that one had to go well back in time to find the true ancestor of the panzer force. He noted that many writers during the interwar period had made efforts to create a history (or even a prehistory) of the tank. Looking back at the Middle Ages, for instance, battering rams, Hussite wagons, and sickle wagons had all received mention. But he would go even further back, to the classical world: the battle of Marathon, in fact. It was here that the Athenians had used the correct combination of speed and armor that was the essence of the modern panzer arm.

At Marathon Miltiades devised a new method of battle. The prerequisite for it was the outstanding physical training of his Athenians, especially well-trained as long-distance runners. Instead of a slow advance by the heavy attack formation of the phalanx, Miltiades had his army run through the 1.8-kilometer-wide "no-man's-land." Thus, his Athenians only exposed themselves to fire from the enemy archers for a short time, allowed them to bring their weapons (pike and sword) rapidly into use, and brought them into contact with the Persians before the latter were ready for battle and before their cavalry was even mounted. The Persians saw this gang of madmen apparently running to their own doom, and by the time they realized how serious it was, it was too late. In the battle that now started, the armored Athenians were superior to the non-armored Persians, despite the tenfold superiority in number of the latter, and Miltiades drove the Persians back to their ships with heavy losses.[61]

Other legitimate ancestors of the tank were the war elephants of Hannibal, as well as the heavy cavalry of the Macedonians.

The immediate forebears of the modern panzer arm were the English tanks of World War I, which had earned their place in history as "machine gun destroyers" and had played an important role in the "so-called victory of 1918," Theiss admitted. In fact, Germany's enemies attributed the decision to "'General Tank,' rather than admitting that they had merely starved Germany to death over four long years."[62] They had never been anything more than a support weapon for the infantry, however, not an independent and separate arm. Since the war, technological developments had taken the three attributes of the World War I tank (armor, tracks, and firepower) and added a fourth: speed. This was the key to creating a new form of warfare, since it allowed the operational use of tanks in large, independent formations. The British had made a start with their "Plan 1919," as well as in published works and military regulations. "But the word and the deed are two different things." For years, the British claimed that they were eager for a chance to fight the German panzer force. Then the great day came in Belgium, and the Royal Tank Corps did nothing but showed its back in "the greatest retreat of all times," in Theiss's mocking phrase. "Belgium, Artois, and Flanders became the graveyard of the 'tanks' and the 'chars,'" he wrote. "The German Panzer has entered world history."[63]

The difficulty in defining *blitzkrieg* has already been discussed, and the best proof of the vagueness of the term is this: even the Germans were not clear as to what exactly had happened in France in 1940. While Theiss presented a reasonable argument that Germany's success was due to the use of its panzer divisions on the operational level, his characterization of Marathon as an "armored assault" is dubious at best, and he fails to make clear its exact relationship to Case Yellow. Other attempts to explain the victory bordered on the ludicrous, as in an article from September 1941 that likened the German panzer arm to the mounted horde of Genghis Khan—the same rapidity of action, the same spirit of the attack, the same reliance on a general staff for planning, and the same "tactical and operational conceptions" as the Germans had used in France.[64] The *Militär-Wochenblatt* ran articles interpreting the campaign—and the new doctrine that underlay it—in every conceivable way: it was an illustration of Clausewitz's two precepts "to act in the most concentrated way possible" and "to act as rapidly as possible."[65]

It was a classic application of Moltke's concept of "operations on exterior lines."[66] It was an example of the overwhelming significance of success in the initial encounters of a campaign,[67] or a manifestation of the continuing importance of surprise in war, with Hitler receiving credit as the "the master of Surprise-War."[68] There was no lack of officers, like company commander Hans Wolf Rode, who argued that "National Socialism was the key" to understanding the victory, whose foundation was the "unity of the Reich and the people" under Hitler.[69] Other German officers analyzing the victory stressed the "predominant role that the motor had conquered among implements of war";[70] the elevation of the battle of encirclement *(Einkesselung)* into "the characteristic form of the German conduct of war";[71] the flexible nature of German operational planning, which could change its overall form as circumstances dictated without losing sight of the main aim of battle— destruction of the enemy field force;[72] or the individual initiative of German officers and soldiers alike, which allowed them to seize favorable opportunities in battle without having to wait for orders as other armies did.[73]

The confusion evinced by the Germans in the wake of their stunning victories has continued into the present day, as some historians seek to define *blitzkrieg* and others to abolish the term altogether. It is clear that some fundamental change occurred on the battlefield in 1940, but what? Military historian Dennis Showalter said it well in 1996:

> Revisionism must not be taken to extremes. German operational successes in the early years of World War II were by no means the product of sheer good fortune. But neither did they reflect a coherent, planned approach to the diplomatic, economic, and military challenges that after 1918 confronted a state unwilling to accept the consequences of its defeat in World War I. What are commonly called blitzkrieg operations developed out of experiences gained on the field between 1939–1941. In that sense blitzkrieg is best understood as a post facto construction for explaining a complex structure of events and ideas.[74]

But we can go one step further. If there was anything truly different about 1940, it was this: the secret to German success in the first years of the war, the development that restored mobility and the possibility of decision to the conduct of war, was the Wehrmacht's use of large armored (not merely tank) units on the operational level. More important than tactical weapons, and nowhere near powerful enough to serve as war-winning strategic weapons all by themselves, the tanks proved most effective when integrated into highly mobile formations of all arms—panzer divisions—that could approach rapidly and under conditions of surprise, assault, penetrate, and break through enemy defenses, and then do what no one had been able to do successfully since the end of the age of cavalry: pursue and destroy the beaten foe. Colonel Theiss, who deserves more recognition as one of Germany's great writers on mobile warfare, came closest to the mark. In his article "From Tank to Armored Force," he traced the transformation of the "tank force" of World War I (tanks only, working in infantry support) into the "armored force" of 1940, with tanks and supporting arms grouped together into "large mechano-motorized units" and used operationally.[75]

While it is true that the Germans did go "zero for two" in the great wars of this century,[76] they are still responsible for the greatest battlefield revolution in the history of modern warfare: the restoration of true operational mobility in the firepower-intensive environment created by machine weapons, and the return of decision to military operations. Winning a campaign was the role of the panzer division, and it played it so well that the entire world was soon copying the concept. Winning a war was something else again, requiring sensible (or at least sane) political leadership, skilled diplomacy, and efficient mobilization of national resources—all of which the Nazi state lacked. The Wehrmacht's great achievement was to make decisive battlefield victory possible once again, through use of a doctrine that we can still call "blitzkrieg." Poland and France were the first victims. Germany, whose political leadership had unwisely picked a fight with a "Grand Alliance" of Great Britain, the Soviet Union, and the United States, would soon join the losers' club.

NOTES

Preface

1. The passage is found in 1 Maccabees 3:23–27. The translation is the *New Revised Standard Version, Catholic Edition* (Oxford: Oxford University Press, 1999).

2. See the article by Captain Stentzler, "Gedanken über die Tätigkeit der Fliegertruppe bei der Verfolgung einer im Rückzug befindlichen Erdtruppe," *Militär-Wochenblatt* 122, no. 47, May 20, 1938, p. 3009.

3. Lieutenant Colonel Alfred Baentsch, "Der Motor in der Durchbruchsschlacht," *Militärwissenschaftliche Rundschau* 3, no. 1, 1938, p. 83.

4. Book review of Major-General H. Rowan Robinson, *The Infantry Experiment* (London: William Clowes and Sons, 1935), in *Journal of the Royal United Service Institution* 80, no. 517, February 1935, p. 218.

5. Quoted in Heinz-Ludger Borgert, "Grundzüge der Landkriegführung von Schlieffen bis Guderian," *Handbuch zur deutschen Militärgeschichte 1648–1939*, vol. 9, *Grundzüge der militärischen Kriegführung* (Munich: Bernard & Graefe, 1979), p. 543.

Chapter 1. Nineteenth-Century Warfare

1. See, for example, the book by the noted British "armor prophet" of the interwar period, J. F. C. Fuller, *Grant and Lee: A Study in Personality and Generalship* (Bloomington: Indiana University Press, 1957), especially "The Two Tactics," pp. 43–50.

2. Ibid., p. 46, speaks of "a '1914' battle fought in 1863."

· ·

3. The work offering what may be described as the paradigmatic view of World War I is B. H. Liddell Hart, *The Real War, 1914–1918* (Boston: Little, Brown, 1930). For the Somme, see Martin Middlebrook, *The First Day on the Somme: 1 July 1916* (New York: Norton, 1971); for Verdun, see Alistair Horne, *The Price of Glory: Verdun 1916* (New York: Penguin, 1964). Third Ypres (also known as Passchendaele) has become an obsession of sorts for British historians in the last twenty-five years. See John Terraine, *The Road to Passchendaele: The Flanders Offensive of 1917: A Study in Inevitability* (London: Leo Cooper, 1977); Robin Prior and Trevor Wilson, *Passchendaele: The Untold Story* (New Haven, Conn.: Yale University Press, 1996); and Peter H. Liddle, ed., *Passchendaele in Perspective: The Third Battle of Ypres* (London: Leo Cooper, 1997). Denis Winter, *Death's Men: Soldiers of the Great War* (New York: Penguin, 1978), describes the trench experience in detail.

4. For a comprehensive survey of the military history of "the long nineteenth century," incorporating a great deal of recent research and vivid writing, see Geoffrey Wawro, *Warfare and Society in Europe, 1792–1914* (London: Routledge, 2000).

5. The best analysis of the dramatic impact of Napoleon on European history is still Robert Holtman, *The Napoleonic Revolution* (New York: Lippincott, 1967).

6. See, first of all, David G. Chandler, *The Campaigns of Napoleon* (New York: Macmillan, 1966), pp. 131–201, supplemented by Rory Muir's more recent work, *Tactics and the Experience of Battle in the Age of Napoleon* (New Haven, Conn.: Yale University Press, 1998), which focuses on the British army in the Peninsular Campaign. Other helpful works include Gunther E. Rothenberg, *The Art of Warfare in the Age of Napoleon* (Bloomington: Indiana University Press, 1978) and *Napoleon's Great Adversaries: The Archduke Charles and the Austrian Army, 1792–1814* (Bloomington: Indiana University Press, 1982); Albert A. Nofi, ed., *Napoleon at War: Selected Writings of F. Loraine Petre* (New York: Hippocrene, 1984); J. F. C. Fuller, *The Conduct of War, 1789–1961* (New York: Da Capo, 1992), especially chapter 3, "Napoleonic Warfare," pp. 42–58; and Larry H. Addington, *The Patterns of War Since the Eighteenth Century* (Bloomington: Indiana University Press, 1994), pp. 1–42. An extremely important work on the change in infantry tactics is Steven S. Ross, *From Flintlock to Rifle: Infantry Tactics, 1740–1866* (London: Frank Cass, 1996).

7. Martin van Creveld, *Supplying War: Logistics from Wallenstein to Patton* (Cambridge: Cambridge University Press, 1977), pp. 40–74.

8. See the article by Robert M. Epstein, "Patterns of Change and Continuity in Nineteenth-Century Warfare," *Journal of Military History* 56, no. 3, July 1992, pp. 375–388. Epstein calls them "victories of flexible tactics and superior command and control" (p. 378). The argument is further developed in his *Napoleon's Last Victory and the Emergence of Modern War* (Lawrence: University Press of Kansas, 1994).

9. For the corps system, the *bataillon carré,* and the *manoeuvre sur les derrières,* see Chandler, *Campaigns of Napoleon*, pp. 161–178; Nofi, *Napoleon at War*, pp. 28–29; Rothenberg, *Age of Napoleon*, p. 148.

10. For Napoleonic tactics, see Ross, *From Flintlock to Rifle;* Chandler, *Campaigns of Napoleon*, pp. 332–367; Nofi, *Napoleon at War*, pp. 43–51; Rothenberg, *Age of Napoleon*, pp. 149–156.

11. Rothenberg, *Age of Napoleon*, p. 64 includes drawings of the various muskets.

12. For the most well written account of the battle in English, see chapter 37, "The Battle of the Three Emperors—Austerlitz," in Chandler, *Campaigns of Napoleon*, pp. 413–433.

13. Davout would end his Napoleonic career, deservedly, as "duke of Auerstädt" and "Prince of Eckmühl."

14. See, for example, John Lynn, *The Bayonets of the Republic: Motivation and Tactics in the Army of Revolutionary France, 1791–94* (Chicago: University of Illinois Press, 1984), which focuses on the Armée du Nord. Brent Nosworthy, *The Anatomy of Victory: Battle Tactics, 1689–1763* (New York: Hippocrene, 1990), p. 352, argues that Napoleonic warfare grew from an "amalgamation of the French grand tactical aspirations as displayed during the Seven Years' War with the Prussian tactical systems that had evolved between 1748 and 1756."

15. The best analysis of this important military thinker is John Shy, "Jomini," in *Makers of Modern Strategy from Machiavelli to the Nuclear Age*, ed. Peter Paret, (Princeton, N.J.: Princeton University Press, 1986), pp. 143–185.

16. The *Précis* has been translated into English as *The Art of War* (1862; reprint, Westport, Conn.: Greenwood Press, 1971). The maxims are taken from p. 63.

17. Michael Howard, "Jomini and the Classical Tradition in Military Thought," in *The Theory and Practice of War*, ed. Michael Howard (Bloomington: Indiana University Press, 1965), p. 16.

18. Jomini, *Art of War*, pp. 112–115. See the article by General of Artillery Ludwig, "Die Operation auf der inneren und der äußeren Linie im Lichte unserer Zeit," *Militär-Wochenblatt* 126, no. 1, July 4, 1941, pp. 7–10.

19. The most useful modern edition is the one edited and translated by Michael Howard and Peter Paret: Carl von Clausewitz, *On War* (Princeton, N.J.: Princeton University Press, 1984). On Clausewitz, see two articles by Peter Paret: "Clausewitz and the Nineteenth Century," in *The Theory and Practice of War*, ed. Michael Howard (Bloomington: Indiana University Press, 1965), pp. 21–42; and "Clausewitz," in *Makers of Modern Strategy from Machiavelli to the Nuclear Age*, ed. Peter Paret (Princeton, N.J.: Princeton University Press, 1986), pp. 186–213.

20. All quotations are from Howard and Paret's translation of *On War:* "An act of force . . . ," p. 75; "No other human activity . . . ," p. 85; "the continuation of policy . . . ," p. 87; "In the rules and regulations . . . ," p. 136; "what genius does is the best rule . . . ," p. 136.

21. On the Crimean War, see the official British history, Alexander William Kinglake, *The Invasion of the Crimea: Its Origin, and an Account of Its Progress Down to the Death of Lord Raglan*, 6 vols. (New York: Harper, 1863–88); Edward Hamley, *The War in the Crimea* (London: Seeley, 1910); Alan Palmer, *The Crimean War* (New York: Dorset Press, 1987). The most recent entry into the field is Trevor Royle, *Crimea: The Great Crimean War, 1854–1856* (New York: St. Martin's Press, 2000), which has the virtue of discussing operations outside the Crimea: the landing at Varna, naval battles in the Baltic Sea, and skirmishes on the Armenian border.

22. For the origins of the war, Barbara Jelavich, *St. Petersburg and Moscow: Tsarist*

and Soviet Foreign Policy, 1814–1974 (Bloomington: Indiana University Press, 1974), is still the standard, although recent works offer new perspectives and mine new materials. See, for example, Ann Pottinger Saab, *The Origins of the Crimean Alliance* (Charlottesville: University Press of Virginia, 1977); and Norman Rich, *Why the Crimean War? A Cautionary Tale* (Hanover, N.H.: University Press of New England, 1985).

23. See Peter Gibbs, *The Battle of the Alma* (Philadelphia: Lippincott, 1963).

24. Hamley, *War in the Crimea*, p. 62.

25. For the organization of British supply and medical services during the winter, see John Sweetman, "'Ad Hoc' Support Services During the Crimean War, 1854–6: Temporary, Ill-Planned, and Largely Unsuccessful," *Military Affairs* 52, no. 3, July 1988, pp. 135–140.

26. See Cyril Falls, *The Art of War: From the Age of Napoleon to the Present Day* (New York: Oxford University Press, 1961), pp. 66–67, for a description of the five-mile railway that the British ran from Balaclava to their battery positions.

27. The body of work by Dennis Showalter has been essential to our understanding of the period and Prussia's role within it. His monograph *Railroads and Rifles: Soldiers, Technology, and the Unification of Germany* (Hamden, Conn.: Archon, 1976) restored respectability to what many disparaged at the time as "drum and trumpet" military history by demonstrating the key role that hardware, doctrine, and military planning had played in German unification. See also "Manifestation of Reform: The Rearmament of the Prussian Infantry, 1806–1813," *Journal of Modern History* 44, no. 3, September 1972, pp. 364–380, which places tactics and weaponry squarely within the broader problematic of the overhaul of the Prussian state in the aftermath of Jena; "Mass Multiplied by Impulsion: The Influence of Railroads on Prussia Planning for the Seven Weeks' War," *Military Affairs* 38, no. 2, April 1974, pp. 62–67; and "The Retaming of Bellona: Prussia and the Institutionalization of the Napoleonic Legacy, 1815–1876," *Military Affairs* 44, no. 2, April 1980, pp. 57–63. For a diagram of the needle gun, along with an analysis of its advantages and disadvantages, see Paul Dangel, "Blood and Iron," *Command* 21, March–April 1993, p. 16.

28. Martin van Creveld, *Command in War* (Cambridge, Mass.: Harvard University Press, 1985), p. 107.

29. Martin van Creveld, *Technology and War: From 2000 B.C. to the Present* (New York: Free Press, 1991), p. 169; Creveld, *Command in War*, p. 105.

30. The phrase comes from John A. English and Bruce I. Gudmundsson, *On Infantry* (Westport, Conn.: Praeger, 1994), pp. 1–14.

31. The Italian War has not received the scholarly attention it deserves. Wawro, *Warfare and Society*, pp. 65–72 is an exception. For the campaign, see Richard Brooks, "The Italian Campaign of 1859," the cover story in *Military History* 16, no. 2, June 1999. For Magenta, see, in the same issue, Andrew Uffindell, "Soldiers' Victory at Magenta," pp. 62–66. John Laffin, *High Command* (New York: Barnes and Noble, 1995), pp. 213–228, offers a solid account of the climactic battle of Solferino. For a general discussion set in the context of mid-nineteenth-century warfare, see William McElwee, *The Art of War: Waterloo to Mons* (Bloomington: Indiana University Press, 1974), pp. 33–69.

32. McElwee, *Art of War,* p. 41.

33. See the brutal portrayal of the Austrian army at war in 1859 by Geoffrey Wawro, "'An Army of Pigs': The Technical, Social, and Political Bases of Austrian Shock Tactics, 1859–1866," *Journal of Military History* 59, no. 3, July 1995, pp. 414–415.

34. See Laffin, *High Command,* pp. 227–228, for Dunant's reaction to Solferino.

35. Moltke's complete writings are found in the fourteen-volume collection edited by the Great General Staff, *Militärische Werke,* 14 vols. (Berlin: E. S. Mittler and Son, 1892–1912). Daniel J. Hughes, ed., *Moltke on the Art of War: Selected Writings* (Novato, Calif.: Presidio, 1993), is indispensable, combining a judicious selection of Moltke's most important works, solid translation, and insightful commentary. The professional journals of the German military are the source of literally hundreds of articles on Moltke. See, for example, the piece by General of Artillery Ludwig, "Moltke als Erzieher," and the unsigned article, "Generalfeldmarschall Graf von Schlieffen über den großen Feldherrn der preußisch-deutschen Armee," both in *Militär-Wochenblatt* 125, no. 17, October 25, 1940, pp. 802–804, 805–807; as well as Lieutenant Colonel Obkircher, "Moltke, der 'unbekannte' General von Königgrätz: Zur Errinerung an den 75. Gedenktag der Schlacht bei Königgrätz am 3. Juli 1866," *Militär-Wochenblatt* 125, no. 52, June 27, 1941, pp. 1994–1997.

36. For Moltke's views on maneuvers, war games, and exercises, see Arden Bucholz, *Moltke, Schlieffen, and Prussian War Planning* (Providence, R.I.: Berg, 1991), pp. 31–43.

37. The standard work in English is Michael Howard, *The Franco-Prussian War* (New York: Macmillan, 1962). Emile Zola, *The Debacle* (New York: Penguin, 1972), is still an important literary source.

38. For analysis of the *Kesselschlacht* doctrine, and the role it would play in twentieth-century German war-making, see Larry H. Addington, *The Blitzkrieg Era and the German General Staff, 1865–1941* (New Brunswick, N.J.: Rutgers University Press, 1971).

39. "Getrennt marschieren, vereint schlagen"; Ludwig, "Moltke als Erzieher," p. 803.

40. General Ernst Kabisch, "Systemlose Strategie," *Militär-Wochenblatt* 125, no. 26, December 27, 1940, p. 1235.

41. For the derivation of the term *Auftragstaktik,* see Antulio J. Echevarria II, *After Clausewitz: German Military Thinkers Before the Great War* (Lawrence: University Press of Kansas, 2000), pp. 32–42, 94–103. Arising in a post-Moltkean debate over infantry tactics, *Auftragstaktik* stood for a flexible system of organization, with units and doctrines being formed for specific missions in battle; it was opposed to *Normaltaktik,* the use of standardized formations and procedures in battle. The debate, raging from 1879 to the mid-1890s, featured some of the most developed military minds in the German officer corps: Sigismund von Schlichting (for *Auftragstaktik*) against Albrecht von Boguslawski and Wilhelm von Scherff (for *Normaltaktik*). In the course of the debate, the two terms expanded, gradually coming to stand for specific methods of commanding and controlling troops in modern combat, the former aiming toward

flexibility, the latter toward greater centralization. The later chief of the General Staff, Alfred von Schlieffen, was a proponent of *Normaltaktik* and tight centralization, for the most part. Echevarria warns that "the term *Auftragstaktik* has been greatly abused in military publications in recent years" (p. 38) and argues successfully that the Germans managed a synthesis of contending concepts in the years before 1914: with a stress on proper planning at the small-unit level and more openness and flexibility for the higher commanders. On the debate, see Daniel J. Hughes, "Schlichting, Schlieffen, and the Prussian Theory of War in 1914," *Journal of Military History* 59, no. 2, April 1995, pp. 257–277; and, for Schlieffen, Bucholz, *Moltke, Schlieffen, and Prussian War Planning*, especially pp. 109–157, 213.

42. Wawro, "Austrian Shock Tactics," pp. 415–424, argues that the Austrian army's turn toward shock from 1859 to 1864 was due to the motley quality of the rank and file, a lack of experienced noncommissioned officers, and, above all, the government's refusal to spend the necessary sums on rifle drill and training. It was "not only a simple way to coordinate multinational regiments in battle; it was also a means to fight a modern war 'on the cheap'" (p. 409). Vast sums flowed to "overfunded bureaucrats, pensioners, and supernumeraries," while troops of the line went without even the most basic kinds of training (p. 431).

43. See Showalter, *Railroads and Rifles*, pt. 3 (entitled "Cannon"), pp. 141–212.

44. See Geoffrey Wawro, *The Austro-Prussian War: Austria's War with Prussia and Italy in 1866* (Cambridge: Cambridge University Press, 1996), a meticulously researched account that presents the Austrian view of the conflict, including the campaign in northern Italy that culminated in Austria's victory at Custoza. Wawro is especially hard on Benedek, whose "irresolution was probably the single greatest defect in Austria's war effort" (p. 62).

45. See Gordon A. Craig, *The Battle of Königgrätz* (Philadelphia: Lippincott, 1964); and Creveld, *Command in War*, pp. 132–140. Dangel, "Blood and Iron," contains a cogent account of the campaign and the battle, along with very useful maps.

46. Creveld, *Command in War*, pp. 137–138; Craig, *Battle of Königgrätz*, p. 111.

47. For events in the Swiepwald, or Svib Forest, see Wawro, *Austro-Prussian War*, pp. 221–227, which credits it with success in threatening the Prussian left and argues that it might have yielded victory to the Austrians if Benedek had been willing to support it with his reserve. According to Showalter, *Railroads and Rifles*, pp. 130–134, the fighting in Swiepwald sucked up forty-nine Austrian battalions and destroyed twenty-eight of them.

48. Creveld, *Command in War*, p. 137–138. Even at the height of the battle, Frederick Charles still did not comprehend his role of "anvil" against which the Austrians were to be crushed by the "hammer" of 2nd Army; he was about to order his reserve into the senseless and bloody attacks on the Austrian position on the Chlum Heights when Moltke intervened.

49. Echevarria, *After Clausewitz*, pp. 4–5, offers reasoned counterarguments to ritualistic denunciations of pre-1914 generals. Armed with a vast amount of evidence in both the primary and the secondary literature, he faults modern historians, rightly, for preaching a "cult of the defensive" and for arguing that "Europe's

armies should have recognized the inherent superiority of the defensive and simply waited behind their trenchworks for their opponents to attack: no attack equals no war equals no problem."

50. For the impact of the breech-loading rifle on command and control, see Russell Gilmore, "'The New Courage': Rifles and Soldier Individualism, 1876–1918," *Military Affairs* 40, no. 3, October 1976, pp. 97–102.

51. The primary source is Charles-Ardant du Picq, *Battle Studies: Ancient and Modern Battle* (New York: Macmillan, 1921). The quoted passages are from Stefan T. Possony and Etienne Mantoux, "Du Picq and Foch: The French School," in *Makers of Modern Strategy: Military Thought from Machiavelli to Hitler*, ed. Edward Mead Earle (New York: Atheneum, 1966), pp. 206–233.

52. See the discussion in Jehuda L. Wallach, *The Dogma of the Battle of Annihilation: The Theories of Clausewitz and Schlieffen and Their Impact on the German Conduct of Two World Wars* (Westport, Conn.: Greenwood Press, 1986), pp. 165–166.

53. The literature on Chancellorsville is copious. Start with two recent works, Daniel E. Sutherland, *Fredericksburg and Chancellorsville: The Dare Mark Campaign* (Lincoln: University of Nebraska Press, 1998); and Stephen W. Sears, *Chancellorsville* (Boston: Houghton Mifflin, 1996). The standard work for many years, recently reissued and still worth consulting, is Theodore Ayrault Dodge, *The Campaign of Chancellorsville* (New York: Da Capo, 1999). Jay Luvaas and Harold W. Nelson, eds., *The U.S. Army War College Guide to the Battles of Chancellorsville and Fredericksburg* (Lawrence: University Press of Kansas, 1994), is extremely useful, especially when combined with a walking tour of the battlefields.

Chapter 2. Firepower Triumphant

1. For the huge literature on the war in South Africa, see Fred R. van Hartesveldt, *The Boer War: Historiography and Annotated Bibliography* (Westport, Conn.: Greenwood Press, 2000). The best general work is Bill Nasson, *The South African War, 1899–1902* (Oxford: Oxford University Press, 2000). Useful in part are Thomas Pakenham, *The Boer War* (New York: Random House, 1979), which makes more claims to originality than it can sustain; Byron Farwell, *The Great Anglo-Boer War* (New York: Norton, 1976), which has all the advantages and disadvantages of popular history; Michael Barthorp, *The Anglo-Boer Wars: The British and the Afrikaners, 1815–1902* (New York: Blandford Press, 1987), which marries crisp writing to wonderful photographs and has the advantage of covering the entire nineteenth century, albeit sketchily; and Edgar Holt, *The Boer War* (London: Putnam, 1958). William McElwee, *The Art of War: Waterloo to Mons* (Bloomington: Indiana University Press, 1974), places the war in the context of pre-1914 doctrinal and technological change. The best account of operations in the war, and still an impressive achievement, is W. Baring Pemberton, *Battles of the Boer War* (London: Batsford, 1964). In general, all these works focus on the British role in the fighting, British doctrine, and British problems in employing the new technology of war, to the general detriment of the Afrikaner view. There is a large literature in Afrikaans, of course,

but the language barrier makes it unavailable to most Western scholars. There is a need for a synthesis: a general history of the war incorporating both English and Afrikaans sources.

2. One of the most revealing primary sources on the war is Christiaan De Wet, *Three Years' War* (New York: Scribner's, 1903); see p. 8.

3. Ibid., p. 16.

4. Frederick Hoppin Howland, *The Chase of De Wet* (Providence, R.I.: Preston and Rounds, 1901), pp. 45–46.

5. Sir Ian Hamilton, *A Staff Officer's Scrap-Book* (London: Edward Arnold, 1912), p. 6.

6. For the battle of the Modder River, see Pemberton, *Battles of the Boer War,* pp. 55–78; Pakenham, *Boer War,* pp. 197–207; Farwell, *Anglo-Boer War,* pp. 91–101; and Barthorp, *Anglo-Boer Wars,* pp. 72–74. See also Stephen M. Miller, *Lord Methuen and the British Army* (London: Frank Cass, 1999), for a well-reasoned defense of Methuen's generalship.

7. Pemberton, *Battles of the Boer War,* p. 66.

8. Quoted, disapprovingly, in Admiral Alfred T. Mahan, *The Story of the War in South Africa, 1899–1900* (London: Samson Low, Marston, and Company, 1901), pp. 159–160.

9. For the battle of Magersfontein, see Pemberton, *Battles of the Boer War,* pp. 79–118; Pakenham, *Boer War,* pp. 208–214; Farwell, *Anglo-Boer War,* pp. 101–113; and Barthorp, *Anglo-Boer Wars,* pp. 75–80. See also Miller, *Lord Methuen,* pp. 123–159.

10. The orders for the attack on Magersfontein are reprinted in the British official history, Frederick Maurice, *History of the War in South Africa, 1899–1902* (London: Hurst and Blackett, 1906), 1:312–315. For the last-second changes in the order of deployment, see pp. 317–318.

11. For a discussion of the exchange between Wauchope and Colonel C. W. H. Douglas, see Miller, *Lord Methuen,* pp. 136–137. Wauchope's objection did make it into the official history; Maurice, *War in South Africa,* 1:311.

12. Miller, *Lord Methuen,* p. 140.

13. Ibid., p. 142.

14. Maurice, *War in South Africa,* 1:328.

15. Pemberton, *Battles of the Boer War,* p. 106.

16. Richard Harding Davis, *With Both Armies in South Africa* (New York: Scribner's, 1900), p. 5.

17. For the battle of Colenso, see Pakenham, *Boer War,* pp. 233–251; Pemberton, *Battles of the Boer War,* pp. 119–153; and Farwell, *Anglo-Boer War,* pp. 127–139. See also the pseudonymous work "Linesman," *Words by an Eyewitness: The Struggle in Natal* (London: William Blackwood, 1901), pp. 27–34, for the aftermath of Colenso.

18. Pemberton, *Battles of the Boer War,* pp. 129–130.

19. Ibid., p. 133.

20. Ibid., p. 148.

21. Quoted in Farwell, *Anglo-Boer War*, p. 139.

22. A recent volume combines two of Churchill's articles written during the war, "London to Ladysmith via Pretoria" and "Ian Hamilton's March." See Winston Churchill, *The Boer War* (New York: Dorset Press, 1991), p. 48.

23. Davis, *With Both Armies*, pp. 46–47.

24. Quotations in Farwell, *Anglo-Boer War*, p. 72. One of the British officers present described it as "most excellent pig-sticking"; Pakenham, *Boer War*, p. 143. See also G. W. Steevens, *From Cape Town to Ladysmith* (New York: Dodd, Mead, 1900), pp. 48–62.

25. McElwee, *Art of War*, pp. 226–227.

26. De Wet, *Three Years' War*, pp. 13–18.

27. For De Wet at Paardeberg, see Hugo von Freytag–Loringhoven, *The Power of Personality in War*, Roots of Strategy 3 (Harrisburg, Pa.: Stackpole Books, 1991), pp. 282–283. See also De Wet, *Three Year's War*, pp. 39–48.

28. For Sanna's Post, see De Wet, *Three Years' War*, pp. 61–68.

29. For Reddersburg, see ibid., pp. 71–76.

30. For Roodewal Station, De Wet, *Three Years' War*, pp. 96–107. The quotation is from p. 106.

31. Farwell, *Anglo-Boer War*, p. 312.

32. Howland, *Chase of De Wet*, pp. 122–126.

33. Ibid., p. 174.

34. Ibid., p. 178.

35. For the march into Cape Colony, see Pakenham, *Boer War*, pp. 550–556; and Farwell, *Anglo-Boer War*, pp. 336–348. For an extremely informative account by a primary source, see O. J. O. Ferreira, ed., *Memoirs of General Ben Bouwer* (Pretoria: Human Sciences Research Council, 1980).

36. De Wet, *Three Years' War*, p. 228.

37. Ben Viljoen, *My Reminiscences of the Anglo-Boer War* (Cape Town: C. Struik, 1972), p. 160.

38. De Wet, *Three Years' War*, pp. 281–282.

39. For an extremely interesting rumination on the "lessons learned" phenomenon and its relationship to military culture, see Gary P. Cox, "Of Aphorisms, Lessons, and Paradigms: Comparing the British and German Official Histories of the Russo-Japanese War," *Journal of Military History* 56, no. 3, July 1992, pp. 389–401.

40. For the German fascination with "Boer tactics," see the discussion in Bruce I. Gudmundsson, *Stormtroop Tactics: Innovation in the German Army, 1914–1918* (Westport, Conn.: Praeger, 1989), pp. 20–21.

41. For discussion of Bloch and his monumental, six-volume work, *Is War Now Impossible?*, see Tim Travers, "Technology, Tactics, and Morale: Jean de Bloch, the Boer War, and British Military Theory," *Journal of Modern History* 51, no. 2, June 1979, pp. 264–286; Geoffrey Wawro, *Warfare and Society in Europe, 1792–1914* (London: Routledge, 2000), p. 145; and, especially, Antulio J. Echevarria II, *After Clausewitz: German Military Thinkers Before the Great War* (Lawrence: University Press of Kansas, 2000), pp. 85–93.

42. See Joseph C. Arnold, "French Tactical Doctrine, 1870–1914," *Military Affairs* 42, no. 2 (April 1978), pp. 63–64. For the previous French regulations, those of 1904, see Michael Howard, "Men Against Fire: The Doctrine of the Offensive in 1914," in *Makers of Modern Strategy from Machiavelli to the Nuclear Age,* ed. Peter Paret (Princeton, N.J.: Princeton University Press, 1986), p. 516.

43. Mahan, *War in South Africa,* pp. 159–160.

44. Deneys Reitz, *Boer Commando: An Afrikaner Journal of the Boer War* (New York: Sarpedon, 1993), pp. 67, 69.

45. Viljoen, *Reminiscences,* pp. 163, 164.

46. Davis, *With Both Armies,* p. 15.

47. Ibid., pp. 40–42.

48. Reitz, *Boer Commando,* p. 70.

49. Howland, *Chase of De Wet,* pp. 65–67.

50. Ibid., p. 80.

51. There is an immense body of wartime literature testifying to the difficulties the British faced as they tried to chase down their foe. See, for example, Erskine Childers, *In the Ranks of the C.I.V.* (London: Smith, Elder, 1901). A driver with the City Imperial Volunteers Artillery, he wrote that the Boers "laugh at our feeble scouting a mile or two ahead, while their own men are ranging round in twos and threes, often fifteen miles from their commando, and at night venturing right up to our camps. In speed of movement, too, they can beat us; in spite of their heavy bullock transport they can travel at least a third quicker than we." He also described his surprise at finding out that there were actually *two* de Wets: Piet and Christiaan. "The whole thing is distracting," he wrote, "like constructing history out of myths and legends" (pp. 176–177).

52. J. F. C. Fuller, *The Last of the Gentlemen's Wars* (London: Faber and Faber, 1937), p. 150.

53. J. F. C. Fuller, *Memoirs of an Unconventional Soldier* (London: Ivor Nicholson and Watson, 1936), p. 11.

54. F. M. Crum, *With the Mounted Rifles in South Africa* (Cambridge: Macmillan, 1903). For Uitkyk, see pp. 100–106; for Piet Retief, see p. 155.

55. Ernest Swinton, "The Defence of Duffer's Drift" (Ft. Leavenworth, Kans.: U.S. Army Command and General Staff College, 1905).

Chapter 3. The Russo-Japanese War

1. For the Russo-Japanese War, see two recent scholarly works: Bruce Menning, *Bayonets Before Bullets: The Imperial Russian Army, 1861–1914* (Bloomington: Indiana University Press, 1992), includes a solid history of the war (pp. 152–199) in the context of an analysis of doctrine, training, and organization in the Russian army throughout the period. Richard W. Harrison, *The Russian Way of War: Operational Art, 1904–1940* (Lawrence: University Press of Kansas, 2001), pp. 7–23, looks carefully at operations and is extremely hard on Kuropatkin, who for much of the war

"behaved like a division commander" preoccupied with "the minutiae of battle" rather than a theater commander seeking an operational decision (p. 23). Beyond these two, the war has not been well served by English-language historians. The two major works devoted solely to it are R. M. Connaughton, *The War of the Rising Sun and Tumbling Bear: A Military History of the Russo-Japanese War* (London: Routledge, 1988); and Reginald Hargreaves, *Red Sun Rising: The Siege of Port Arthur* (Philadelphia: Lippincott, 1962). Connaughton's work has the virtue of breadth, but it references little recent research and contains a barely minimal scholarly apparatus. One reviewer called it a "readable military primer" on the conflict (James J. Bloom, *Journal of Military History* 55, no. 1, January 1991, pp. 114–115). William McElwee, *The Art of War: Waterloo to Mons* (Bloomington: Indiana University Press, 1974), pp. 241–255, offers an insightful discussion, centered around doctrine and technology. See also the pertinent sections in J. F. C. Fuller, *A Military History of the Western World*, vol. 3, *From the American Civil War to the End of World War II* (New York: Da Capo, 1956), pp. 141–181. Beyond these few works, one must consult the observers' reports, which are often quite informative. See, for example, the U.S. Army's *Reports of Military Observers Attached to the Armies in Manchuria During the Russo-Japanese War* (Washington, D.C.: Government Printing Office, 1906); and its *Epitome of the Russo-Japanese War* (Washington, D.C.: Government Printing Office, 1907); as well as the British series *The Russo-Japanese War: Reports from British Officers Attached to the Japanese Forces in the Field*, 3 vols. (London: General Staff, 1907). *The War in the Far East by the Military Correspondent of* The Times (New York: Dutton, 1905) is very useful, as is Major-General W. D. Bird, *Lectures on the Strategy of the Russo-Japanese War* (London: Hugh Rees, 1911). The new edition of Tadayoshi Sakurai, *Human Bullets: A Soldier's Story of the Russo-Japanese War* (Lincoln: University of Nebraska Press, 1999), is indispensable for the experience of the Japanese foot soldier.

2. Sir Ian Hamilton, *A Staff Officer's Scrap-Book* (London: Edward Arnold, 1912), pp. 53–54.

3. Ibid., p. 61.

4. For the battle of the Yalu, see Connaughton, *Rising Sun and Tumbling Bear*, pp. 46–65; Hargreaves, *Red Sun Rising*, pp. 36–39; Hamilton, *Staff Officer's Scrap-Book*, pp. 65–92; Major J. M. Home, "Historical Narrative from the Outbreak of the War to the 15th August 1904," in *Reports from British Officers Attached to the Japanese Forces in the Field*, 3:7–9; U.S. Army, *Epitome*, pp. 7–12; *Military Correspondent of* The Times, pp. 151–160. The article by Ron Bell, "The Russo-Japanese War, 1904–1905: The Land Campaigns," *Command* 19, November–December 1992, pp. 12–13, features incisive text and an excellent map typical of the magazine.

5. Hamilton, *Staff Officer's Scrap-Book*, p. 76. A German officer who was with the Japanese army during the war remarked, however, that his hosts would not let him near the front line in his "silver greatcoat" for fear of drawing Russian fire. See the editor's comment in General D. E. Fleck's article "Die Leere des Schlachtfelds," *Militär-Wochenblatt* 116, no. 25, January 4, 1932, p. 900.

6. Hamilton, *Staff Officer's Scrap-Book,* pp. 84–85.

7. Ibid., p. 78. For a discussion of the lack of pursuit in the Russo-Japanese War, see Lieutenant C. Ravenhill, "Tactics Employed by the Japanese Army in the War of 1904–5," *Journal of the Royal United Service Institution* 82, no. 527, August 1937, pp. 561–562.

8. For Nanshan, see Connaughton, *Rising Sun and Tumbling Bear,* pp. 66–78; Hamilton, *Staff Officer's Scrap-Book,* pp. 406–408; *Military Correspondent of* The Times, pp. 196–212; and Menning, *Bayonets Before Bullets,* pp. 158–160. Bell, "Russo-Japanese War," pp. 13–14, again offers sound analysis and a very useful map.

9. *Military Correspondent of* The Times, p. 199.

10. Ibid., p. 200.

11. Connaughton, *Rising Sun and Tumbling Bear,* p. 26.

12. For Telissu, see ibid., pp. 80–98; Hamilton, *Staff Officer's Scrap-Book,* pp. 410–425; Colonel W. H.-H. Waters, "The Battle of Tel-li-ssu (Wa-fang-kou), the 14th and 15th June 1904," in *Reports from British Officers Attached to the Japanese Forces in the Field,* 3:83–88; *Military Correspondent of* The Times, pp. 239–244; and Bell, "The Russo-Japanese War," p. 18.

13. Hargreaves, *Red Sun Rising,* in the best single volume on the siege of Port Arthur. See also Connaughton, *Rising Sun and Tumbling Bear,* pp. 168–207; Bell, "Russo-Japanese War," pp. 15–17; Fuller, *Military History of the Western World,* 3:152–163; and Menning, *Bayonets Before Bullets,* pp. 160–171. Also, see the series of eleven reports in *Reports from British Officers Attached to the Japanese Forces in the Field,* 3:348–473, especially Major C. M. Crawford, "Diary of the Officers Attached to the Third Japanese Army from 29th July 1904 to the Fall of the Fortress," pp. 370–415. The report by Major Joseph E. Kuhn, U.S. Army, on engineering aspects of the Port Arthur operation is well worth reading; *Reports of Military Observers,* pt. 3, pp. 115–191. Also, two works by contemporary journalists give vivid accounts combined with important details of the operation: David H. James, *The Siege of Port Arthur* (London: T. Fisher Unwin, 1905); and E. K. Nojine [Nozhin], *The Truth About Port Arthur* (London: John Murray, 1908).

14. For a discussion of the siege of Plevna, see Menning, *Bayonets Before Bullets,* pp. 60–64; McElwee, *Art of War,* pp. 199–205; as well as Paddy Griffith, *Forward into Battle: Fighting Tactics from Waterloo to the Near Future* (Novato, Calif.: Presidio, 1990), pp. 69–76.

15. James, *Siege of Port Arthur,* p. 49.

16. For the lack of preparedness in Port Arthur at the war's outset, see Nojine, *Truth About Port Arthur,* pp. 24–26.

17. James, *Siege of Port Arthur,* pp. 62–63.

18. Ibid., pp. 58–59.

19. Ibid., pp. 70–71.

20. Fuller, *Military History of the Western World,* 3:158.

21. James, *Siege of Port Arthur,* pp. 96–97.

22. For the battle of Liaoyang, see Connaughton, *Rising Sun and Tumbling Bear,* pp. 124–167; Hargreaves, *Red Sun Rising,* pp. 100–103; Hamilton, *Staff Officer's*

Scrap-Book, pp. 239–303; Menning, *Bayonets Before Bullets*, pp. 175–179; "Reports of Captain Peyton C. March, General Staff, Observer with the Japanese Army," in *Reports of Military Observers*, pt. 1, pp. 22–43; "Report of Captain Carl Reichmann, Seventeenth Infantry, Observer with the Russian Forces," in *Reports of Military Observers*, pt. 1, pp. 208–229; Colonel H.-H. Waters, "The Battle of Liao-Yang, the 30th August to the 5th September 1904," *Reports from British Officers Attached to the Japanese Forces in the Field*, 3:89–97; Major-General W. D. Bird, *An Account of the Battle of Liao-yang* (Aldershot: Gale and Polden, n.d.); and Bell, "Russo-Japanese War," pp. 18–19.

23. *Military Correspondent of* The Times, p. 305.

24. Hamilton, *Staff Officer's Scrap-Book*, pp. 290–291.

25. Ibid., p. 292.

26. Ibid., pp. 295–296.

27. Ibid., p. 306 and n.

28. For the battle of the Sha-Ho, see Connaughton, *Rising Sun and Tumbling Bear*, pp. 208–222; Hargreaves, *Red Sun Rising*, pp. 120–123; Menning, *Bayonets Before Bullets*, pp. 179–184; Hamilton, *Staff Officer's Scrap-Book*, pp. 311–376; "Reports of Captain Peyton C. March, General Staff, Observer with the Japanese Army," in *Reports of Military Observers*, pt. 1, pp. 43–56; "Report of Captain John F. Morrison, Twentieth Infantry (Now Major Thirteenth Infantry), Observer with the Japanese Army," in *Reports of Military Observers*, pt. 1, pp. 57–99; "Report of Lieutenant Colonel Walter S. Schuyler, General Staff, Observer with the Russian Army," in *Reports of Military Observers*, pt. 1, pp. 168–171; *Military Correspondent of* The Times, pp. 386–408; and Bell, "Russo-Japanese War," pp. 19–20.

29. Hamilton, *Staff Officer's Scrap-Book*, pp. 356–358; Connaughton, *Rising Sun and Tumbling Bear*, p. 217.

30. Hamilton, *Staff Officer's Scrap-Book*, p. 317.

31. R. G. Cherry, "Synopsis of the Battle of the Sha-Ho, October 1904," *Journal of the Royal Artillery* 40, no. 9, December 1913, p. 399.

32. Connaughton, *Rising Sun and Tumbling Bear*, p. 212.

33. Nojine, *Truth About Port Arthur*, p. 220.

34. James, *Siege of Port Arthur*, pp. 150, 153.

35. For the third assault on the fortress, see Hargreaves, *Red Sun Rising*, pp. 140–143; and James, *Siege of Port Arthur*, pp. 184–193.

36. For this climactic event of the siege of Port Arthur, see Hargreaves, *Red Sun Rising*, pp. 143–148; Connaughton, *Rising Sun and Tumbling Bear*, pp. 196–202; James, *Siege of Port Arthur*, pp. 194–210; and Nojine, *Truth About Port Arthur*, pp. 252–258. Major Joseph E. Kuhn, in *Reports of Military Observers*, pt. 3, pp. 118–120, has a series of photographs both facing and from 203 Meter Hill.

37. James, *Siege of Port Arthur*, p. 202.

38. Geoffrey Wawro, *Warfare and Society in Europe, 1792–1914* (London: Routledge, 2000), p. 156.

39. James, *Siege of Port Arthur*, pp. 194–195.

40. Quoted in Connaughton, *Rising Sun and Tumbling Bear*, p. 207.

41. For the Mishchenko raid, see Lieutenant-Colonel A. L. Haldane, "Second Japanese Army—Operations from 20th October 1904 to 29th January 1905, Including General Mishchenko's Raid and the Battle of Hei-kou-tai," in *The Russo-Japanese War: Reports from British Officers Attached to the Japanese Forces in the Field,* vol. 2 (London: General Staff, 1907), pp. 23–28, Connaughton, *Rising Sun and Tumbling Bear,* pp. 222–224; and Menning, *Bayonets Before Bullets,* pp. 184–185.

42. For Mukden, see Connaughton, *Rising Sun and Tumbling Bear,* pp. 227–236; Menning, *Bayonets Before Bullets,* pp. 186–195; *Military Correspondent of* The Times, pp. 517–535; Bell, "Russo-Japanese War," pp. 19–22; plus eight reports in *Reports from British Officers Attached to the Japanese Forces in the Field,* 2:83–347. See two reports by Colonel W. H. Birkbeck, "The Battle of Mukden: Operations of the Third Japanese Army," pp. 219–230, and "The Battle of Mukden: Action of the Cavalry of the Third Army," pp. 231–233; as well as Lieutenant-Colonel A. L. Haldane, "The Battle of Mukden: Operations of the Second Japanese Army," pp. 83–147.

43. Connaughton, *Rising Sun and Tumbling Bear,* p. 233.

44. *Military Correspondent of* The Times, pp. 405–406.

45. Major J. M. Home, "General Report on the Russo-Japanese War up to the 15th August 1904," in *Reports from British Officers Attached to the Japanese Forces in the Field,* 3:209. For German views of the artillery's role in the war, see the discussion in Antulio J. Echevarria II, *After Clausewitz: German Military Thinkers Before the Great War* (Lawrence: University Press of Kansas, 2000), pp. 140–146.

46. David T. Zabecki, "The Guns of Manchuria," *Field Artillery,* April 1988, p. 21.

47. David T. Zabecki, *Steel Wind: Colonel Georg Bruchmüller and the Birth of Modern Artillery* (Westport, Conn.: Praeger, 1994), p. 8.

48. For the indirect fire debate, the writings of the Russian Karl G. Guk and the German Prince Kraft zu Hohenlohe-Ingelfingen, see Boyd L. Dastrup, *The Field Artillery: History and Sourcebook* (Westport, Conn.: Greenwood Press, 1994), pp. 42–45.

49. Home, "General Report on the Russo-Japanese War," pp. 220. For the German view of cavalry in the war, see Echevarria, *After Clausewitz,* pp. 128–133.

50. Marshal Alexei N. Kuropatkin, *The Russian Army and the Japanese War,* vol. 2 (Wesport, Conn.: Hyperion Press, 1977), p. 169.

Chapter 4. *The Balkan Wars*

1. Any historical inquiry into the Balkan Wars must still base itself on the primary sources and period accounts. Lieutenant Hermenegild Wagner, *With the Victorious Bulgarians* (Boston: Houghton Mifflin, 1913), is a very useful analysis of the Bulgarian war effort by the German correspondent of the *Reichspost,* although rival correspondents often attacked his veracity. The other side of the hill receives attention in Ellis Ashmead-Bartlett, *With the Turks in Thrace* (New York: George H. Doran, 1913), an account by the special correspondent of the *London Daily Telegraph.* Philip Gibbs and Bernard Grant cover both sides in *The Balkan War: Adven-*

tures of War with Cross and Crescent (Boston: Small, Maynard, and Company, 1913). *The Balkan War Drama* (London: Andrew Melrose, 1913) is an anonymous account, mainly of Serbian operations, by "A Special Correspondent." N. E. Noel-Buxton, *With the Bulgarian Staff* (New York: Macmillan, 1913), is a very general account written by a member of the British Parliament. Jean Pélissier, *Dix mois de guerre dans les Balkans, Octobre 1912–Aout 1913* (Paris: Perrin, 1914), is a collection of articles by a French journalist first published in *La Dépêche*. Three extremely useful works are Lieutenant-Colonel Boucabeille, *La Guerre Turco-Balkanique 1912–1913: Thrace—Macédoine—Albanie—Epire* (Paris: Librairie Chapelot, 1914); A. Kutschbach, *Die Serben im Balkankrieg 1912–1913 und im Kriege gegen die Bulgaren* (Stuttgart: Frank'sche Verlagshandlung, 1913); and the German translation of the memoirs of Turkish III Corps commander Mahmud Mukhtar Pasha, *Meine Führung im Balkankriege 1912* (Berlin: E. S. Mittler and Son, 1913).

2. Wagner, *With the Victorious Bulgarians*, p. 122.

3. Gibbs and Grant, *Balkan War*, p. 62.

4. Since the Turks never formally completed their mobilization, any numbers for them have to rely on educated guesswork. Barbara Jelavich, *History of the Balkans*, vol. 2, *Twentieth Century* (Cambridge: Cambridge University Press, 1983), p. 97, gives a figure of 320,000 for the Turks; Captain Richard Lechowich, "Balkan Wars: Prelude to Disaster, 1912–1913," *Strategy and Tactics* 164, November 1993, pp. 5–23, gives figures of almost 900,000 for the allies and only 300,000 for the Turks, although he qualifies the latter figure "with an undetermined number of other reservists, militia, etc."

5. Lechowich, "Balkan Wars," p. 12; Wagner, *With the Victorious Bulgarians*, p. 88, gives a figure of half a million. See also Major L. L. Durfee, "Mobilization and Concentration of the Bulgarian Army in 1912," a report made for the Army War College in 1914–15. The original is in the U.S. Army Military History Institute (hereinafter MHI), at Carlisle Barracks in Carlisle, Pennsylvania.

6. Kutschbach, *Serben im Balkankrieg*, p. 27.

7. Savo Skoko, "An Analysis of the Strategy of *Vojvoda* Putnik During the Balkan Wars," in *War and Society in East Central Europe*, vol. 18, *East Central European Society and the Balkan Wars*, ed. Béla K. Király and Dimitrije Djordjevic (Boulder, Colo.: Social Science Monographs, 1987), pp. 17–18.

8. Kutschbach, *Serben im Balkankrieg*, pp. 66–67, "Die Operationen der III. Armee."

9. Brigadier General James N. Allison, "Notes on the War in the Balkans," *Journal of the Military Service Institution* 3, no. 182, March–April 1913, p. 256.

10. General of Artillery Ludwig, "Die Operation auf der inneren und der äußeren Linie im Lichte unserer Zeit," *Militär-Wochenblatt* 126, no. 1, July 4, 1941, pp. 7–10.

11. Wagner, *With the Victorious Bulgarians*, pp. 103–105.

12. For the battle of Kumanovo, see Kutschbach, *Serben im Balkankrieg*, especially his translation of telegraphic exchanges between the Turkish commanders (pp. 41–43). See also Boucabeille, *Guerre Turco-Balkanique*, pp. 100–108. Also quite helpful is General Otto Schulz, "Die serbische Armee in der Schlacht bei Kumanovo

am 10. und 11. Oktober 1912," *Militär-Wochenblatt* 123, no. 15, October 7th, 1938, pp. 931–935.

13. Kutschbach, *Serben im Balkankrieg,* pp. 103–105.

14. Ibid., p. 38.

15. Skoko, "Analysis of the Strategy of *Vojvode* Putnik," p. 19.

16. Ibid., p. 17.

17. Boucabeille, *Guerre Turco-Balkanique,* pp. 116–123.

18. For artillery in the war, see David T. Zabecki, "The Dress Rehearsal: Lost Artillery Lessons of the 1912–1913 Balkan Wars," *Field Artillery,* August 1988, pp. 18–23.

19. *Balkan War Drama,* p. 150.

20. Ljudmil Petrov, "The Training of Bulgarian Officers, 1878–1918," in *War and Society in East Central Europe,* vol. 24, *The East Central European Officer Corps 1740–1920s: Social Origins, Selection, Education, and Training,* ed. Béla K. Király and Walter Scott Dillard (Boulder, Colo.: Social Science Monographs, 1988), pp. 114–115.

21. See Petar Stoilov, "General of Infantry Nikola Ivanov," in *War and Society in East Central Europe,* vol. 25, *East Central European War Leaders: Civilian and Military,* ed. Béla K. Király and Albert A. Nofi (Boulder, Colo.: Social Science Monographs, 1988), pp. 249–272. Based on the holdings of the Central Military Archives in Sofia, it is a model for further research.

22. This narrative is based on several different accounts of Kirk Kilisse: Mahmud Mukhtar, *Meine Führung im Balkankriege,* pp. 11–34; Major Edward Sigerfoos, "The Campaign of Kirk Kilisse," the original typescript of which is in the MHI; Ludovic Naudeau, "Battles of Which One Never Heard," a translation of an article that appeared in *Le Journal* in Paris on December 25, 1912, also in the MHI; and Major R. A. Brown, "Why the Bulgarians Did Not Enter Constantinople: Bulgarian Operations Ending with the Battle of Tchataldja, November 17 and 18, 1912," *Journal of the Military Service Institution* 53, no. 185, September–October 1913, pp. 240–252, which includes a translation of an extended version of Naudeau's article.

23. Mahmud Mukhtar, *Meine Führung im Balkankriege,* pp. 4–5.

24. Ibid., p. 26.

25. Ibid., p. 29.

26. For the battle of Lule Burgas–Bunarhissar, see Wagner, *With the Victorious Bulgarians,* pp. 157–177; Mahmud Mukhtar, *Meine Führung im Balkankriege,* pp. 44–124.

27. Mahmud Mukhtar, *Meine Führung im Balkankriege,* p. 45.

28. Ibid., pp. 50–51.

29. Ibid., p. 54. For analysis of this short-lived Turkish victory, see Zabecki, "Dress Rehearsal," pp. 20–21.

30. Ashmead-Bartlett, *With the Turks in Thrace,* p. 145.

31. Boucabeille, *Guerre Turco-Balkanique,* pp. 162–164.

32. Ashmead-Bartlett, *With the Turks in Thrace,* pp. 160–161, 177–178, 174.

33. On Chatalja, see Wagner, *With the Victorious Bulgarians,* pp. 178–188; Brown,

"Why the Bulgarians Did Not Enter Constantinople," pp. 245–252; Bouca̲ ̲ ̲ ̲ ̲
Guerre Turco-Balkanique, pp. 181–193; Mahmud Mukhtar, *Meine Führung im Balkankriege,* pp. 149–161; Ashmead-Bartlett, *With the Turks in Thrace,* pp. 263–291; Lieutenant Colonel Brückner, "Der Durchbruchsangriff vor dem Weltkriege in Anwendung und Theorie," *Militärwissenschaftliche Rundschau* 3, no. 6, 1938, pp. 728–730; and Momchil Yonov, "Bulgarian Military Operations in the Balkan Wars," in *War and Society in East Central Europe,* vol. 18, *East Central European Society and the Balkan Wars,* ed. Béla K. Király and Dimitrije Djordjevic (Boulder, Colo.: Social Science Monographs, 1987), pp. 73–76.

34. Mahmud Mukhtar, *Meine Führung im Balkankriege,* pp. 154–155.

35. See Kutschbach, *Serben im Balkankrieg,* pp. 106–111, for a solid analysis of operations in the lopsided struggle.

36. Mahmud Mukhtar, *Meine Führung im Balkankriege,* pp. 163.

37. Sigerfoos, "Campaign of Kirk Kilissé," p. 36.

38. Naudeau, "Battles of Which One Never Heard," p. 2.

39. Ibid., p. 3.

40. Ibid., pp. 6–7.

41. Zabecki, "Dress Rehearsal," p. 22. See also his *Steel Wind: Colonel Georg Bruchmüller and the Birth of Modern Artillery* (Westport, Conn.: Praeger, 1994), p. 11.

42. Quoted in Colonel C. B. Mayne, "The Balkan War and Some of Its Lessons," *Journal of the Royal United Service Institution* 57, no. 423, May 1913, p. 643.

43. "Controversy Between Generals Fitcheff and Dimitrieff on the Conduct of Affairs in the Bulgarian Army During the Recent Balkan Wars," *Journal of the Military Service Institution* 55, no. 191, September–October 1914, pp. 293–326.

44. See Tim Travers, "Technology, Tactics, and Morale: Jean de Bloch, the Boer War, and British Military Theory," *Journal of Modern History* 51, no. 2, June 1979, pp. 280–281, which finds the following phrase in Lieutenant-General R. S. S. Baden-Powell's Boy Scout handbook: "BE PREPARED to die for your country . . . , so that when the time comes you may charge home with confidence, not caring whether you are to be killed or not."

45. Sir Ian Hamilton, *A Staff Officer's Scrap-Book* (London: Edward Arnold, 1912), pp. 94–95.

46. Gibbs and Grant, *Balkan War,* p. 65.

47. Wagner, *With the Victorious Bulgarians,* p. 143.

48. Gibbs and Grant, *Balkan War,* p. 49.

49. Quoted in Wagner, *With the Victorious Bulgarians,* p. 154.

50. Zabecki, "Dress Rehearsal," p. 22. For the French view on artillery in the Balkan Wars, see Robert M. Ripperger, "The Development of the French Artillery for the Offensive, 1890–1914," *Journal of Military History* 59, no. 4, October 1995, pp. 613–614. The French believed that the war proved the superiority of light guns: they were less cumbersome, were better suited for direct fire support of the infantry, and required less ammunition.

51. Petrov, "Training of Bulgarian Officers," p. 118.

52. Allison, "Notes on the War in the Balkans," p. 254.

53. See William A. Taylor, "The Debate over Changing Cavalry Tactics and Weapons, 1900–1914," *Military Affairs* 28, no. 4, winter 1964–65, pp. 173–183.

54. [Ubique], "The Offensive Spirit in War," *United Service Magazine* 47, no. 1018, September 1913, pp. 637–643.

55. This was a powerful idea that lived long and died hard. A British officer, writing about the Russo-Japanese War, argued that "it was the will-to-win, the indomitable courage, endurance, self-sacrifice, and energy of the fighting personnel which outweighed all other factors in deciding the issue." He was writing in 1937. Lieutenant C. Ravenhill, "Tactics Employed by the Japanese Army in the War of 1904–5," *Journal of the Royal United Service Institution* 82, no. 527, August 1937, p. 563. Antulio J. Echevarria II, *After Clausewitz: German Military Thinkers Before the Great War* (Lawrence: University Press of Kansas, 2000), p. 118, describes such language as "part of the military's campaign to reaffirm and regenerate its warrior identity" in an era of rapid technological and doctrinal change. "To remain cohesive, an organization must have a code, motto, or ethos to bind its members both psychologically and spiritually; and military organizations are no exception." In that sense, the emphasis on will, courage, and self-sacrifice was "both logical and necessary."

Chapter 5. *World War I*

1. See Gary P. Cox, "Of Aphorisms, Lessons, and Paradigms: Comparing the British and German Official Histories of the Russo-Japanese War," *Journal of Military History* 56, no. 3, July 1992, pp. 389–401, who argues that this view of the war, "the Fuller–Lloyd George–Liddell Hart interpretation, has become a paradigm," and adds that "it is built upon a particularly British view of the Great War, that of an essentially pointless struggle controlled by prototypical 'Colonel Blimps' who, in failing to take into account over fifty years of military history, condemned the 'flower' of British youth to the hecatombs of the Somme and Passchendaele" (p. 391). The literature on World War I is copious and keeps growing. The oldest one-volume operational histories are still useful: B. H. Liddell Hart, *The Real War, 1914–1918* (Boston: Little, Brown, 1930); and C. R. M. F. Crutwell, *A History of the Great War, 1914–1918* (Chicago: Academy Chicago, 1991). The former, written by one of the great "armor prophets" of the interwar period, is interesting but too often tendentious. It is hard to argue with T. H. Thomas's review, published in 1935: Liddell Hart's "critical attitude is not only permanent but universal, and with a loftiness of view unparalleled in military historians he condemns as incompetent a whole generation of soldiers" (*American Historical Review* 41, no. 1, October 1935, pp. 145–147). Crutwell's history, a reprint of the work originally published in 1934, is comprehensive and judicious throughout. Other one-volume histories are Cyril Falls, *The Great War* (New York: Capricorn, 1959); Hanson Baldwin, *World War I: An Outline History* (New York: Harper and Row, 1962); James L. Stokesbury, *A Short History of World War I* (New York: William Morrow, 1981), the best-written work on the topic, part of a series of works by Stokesbury, including short histories of World War II and Korea; and, most recently, John Keegan, *The First World War*

(London: Hutchinson, 1998). Daniel David, *The 1914 Campaign* (New York: Wieser and Wieser, 1987), is a very useful collection of text, period photographs, maps, and orders of battle for the opening year of the war.

2. Erich Maria Remarque, *All Quiet on the Western Front* (New York: Grosset and Dunlap, 1929). For similar images of the war as senseless, see Robert Graves, *Good-Bye to All That: An Autobiography* (London: J. Cape, 1929); and Henri Barbusse, *Le Feu: Journal d'une Escouade* (Paris: E. Flammarion, 1916).

3. For a powerfully argued presentation of these revisionist arguments, see two works by Paddy Griffith: *Forward into Battle: Fighting Tactics from Waterloo to the Near Future* (Novato, Calif.: Presidio, 1990); and *Battle Tactics of the Western Front: The British Army's Art of Attack, 1916–1918* (New Haven, Conn.: Yale University Press, 1994). The latter book's testy style brought forth a testy review by John Ferris in *Journal of Military History* 59, no. 3, July 1995, pp. 540–542. Griffith is one of many historians dedicated to revising our view of the British army's role in the war, especially the final victories of 1918. See Shelford Bidwell and Dominick Graham, *Fire-Power: British Army Weapons and Theories of War, 1904–1945* (London: Allen and Unwin, 1982); the large body of work by Tim Travers, *The Killing Ground: The British Army, the Western Front, and the Emergence of Modern Warfare, 1900–1918* (London: Allen and Unwin, 1987); "The Evolution of British Strategy and Tactics on the Western Front in 1918: GHQ, Manpower, and Technology," *Journal of Military History* 54, no. 2, April 1990, pp. 173–200, "Could the Tanks of 1918 Have Been War-Winners for the British Expeditionary Force?" *Journal of Contemporary History* 27, no. 3, July 1992, pp. 389–406; and *How the War Was Won: Command and Technology in the British Army on the Western Front, 1917–1918* (New York: Routledge, 1992). Even General Douglas Haig's reputation, the victim of the Liddell Hart–Fuller school in the interwar era, is in the process of revision, especially on the question of his openness to the tank and other new technology. See Brian Bond and Nigel Cave, eds., *Haig: A Reappraisal 70 Years On* (London: Leo Cooper, 1999).

4. Griffith, *Forward into Battle,* p. 50, uses the phrase "the alleged novelty of the 'empty battlefield' in World War I."

5. Martin van Creveld, *Command in War* (Cambridge, Mass.: Harvard University Press, 1985), pp. 148–149.

6. David T. Zabecki, *Steel Wind: Colonel Georg Bruchmüller and the Birth of Modern Artillery* (Westport, Conn.: Praeger, 1994), p. 8.

7. Colonel Terence Cave, "Foreword," in Ralph G. A. Hamilton, *The War Diary of the Master of Belhaven (Ralph Hamilton), 1914–1918* (Barnsley: Wharncliffe, 1990), p. i. Often seen merely as the great "mine explosion," the successful offensive at Messines owed much to a three-to-one British superiority in artillery. See Ian Passingham, *Pillars of Fire: The Battle of Messines Ridge, June 1917* (Stroud: Sutton Publishing, 1999).

8. The only book to deal solely with the critical issue of logistics in modern warfare is Martin van Creveld, *Supplying War: Logistics from Wallenstein to Patton* (Cambridge: Cambridge University Press, 1977). It has not pleased everyone. See, for example, the negative critique by John Lynn, "The History of Logistics and *Sup-*

plying War," in *Feeding Mars: Logistics in Western Warfare from the Middle Ages to the Present*, ed. John Lynn (Boulder, Colo.: Westview Press, 1993), pp. 9–27, which faults Creveld on both conceptual and statistical grounds. The critique is focused on Creveld's analysis of warfare in the early modern period, however, especially his contention that armies were not dependent upon magazines as is commonly assumed but were usually able to forage for their supplies. See also the review of *Feeding Mars* by Charles R. Shrader, *Journal of Military History* 58, no. 2, April 1994, pp. 316–317.

9. For the Schlieffen Plan, first see Gerhard Ritter, *Der Schlieffenplan: Kritik eines Mythos* (Munich: R. Oldenbourg, 1956), which included the plan itself, the first time that it had appeared in published form. Ritter's verdict (the plan "was never a sound formula for victory," being instead "a daring, indeed an over daring, gamble whose success depended on many lucky chances") has stood the test of time. Virtually every book or article written on the war offers its own critique of the plan. Especially worthwhile expositions are to be found in Cyril Falls, *The Art of War: From the Age of Napoleon to the Present Day* (New York: Oxford University Press, 1961), pp. 102–104; Creveld, *Command in War*, pp. 148–155; Arden Bucholz, *Moltke, Schlieffen, and Prussian War Planning* (Providence, R.I.: Berg, 1991), pp. 158–213; Brian Bond, *The Pursuit of Victory: From Napoleon to Saddam Hussein* (Oxford: Oxford University Press, 1996); Holger Herwig, "Strategic Uncertainties of a Nation-State: Prussia-Germany, 1871–1918," in *The Making of Strategy: Rulers, States, and War*, ed. Williamson Murray, MacGregor Knox, and Alvin Bernstein (Cambridge: Cambridge University Press, 1994), pp. 242–277; and Herwig, *The First World War: Germany and Austria-Hungary, 1914–1918* (London: Arnold, 1997), pp. 56–62. Most recently, Terence Zuber has constructed a strong argument, based on a great deal of archival research, that the "Schlieffen Plan" is a postwar construction, and that Schlieffen himself simply planned to win the opening battle along the frontiers, thereby positioning German forces for a second-stage advance deep into France. See Zuber, "The Schlieffen Plan Reconsidered," *War in History* 6, no. 3, 1999, pp. 262–305. Dennis E. Showalter, "For Deterrence to Doomsday Machine: The German Way of War, 1890–1914," *Journal of Military History* 64, 3, July 2000, pp. 679–710, contains a synthesis of the current state of research into the plan.

10. For a representative example of the case against Moltke, see, J. F. C. Fuller, *A Military History of the Western World*, vol. 3, *From the American Civil War to the End of World War II* (New York: Da Capo, 1956), pp. 196–198.

11. Zabecki, *Steel Wind*, pp. 11, 166; Boyd L. Dastrup, *The Field Artillery: History and Sourcebook* (Westport, Conn.: Greenwood Press, 1994), pp. 44–45.

12. For Plan XVII, see Liddell Hart, *Real War*, pp. 49–50; and Cruttwell, *History of the Great War*, pp. 9–10, both of whom use the adjective *notorious*. Still the most useful piece by far is a short article by R. L. Dinardo, "French Military Planning, 1871–1914" *Strategy and Tactics* 118, March–April 1988, pp. 10–13. It includes diagrams of Plans XI, XIV, XV, XV (modified), XVI (1905), XVI (modified), and XVII.

13. See Robert M. Ripperger, "The Development of the French Artillery for the Offensive, 1890–1914," *Journal of Military History* 59, no. 4, October 1995, pp. 599–

618, who argues that "the French Army had not sought heavy field artillery prior to 1914 because heavy field guns did not fit its strategy and doctrine" (p. 599); and Douglas Porch, *The March to the Marne: The French Army, 1871–1914* (Cambridge: Cambridge University Press, 1981), pp. 232–245.

14. Quoted in Michael Howard, "Men Against Fire: The Doctrine of the Offensive in 1914," in *Makers of Modern Strategy from Machiavelli to the Nuclear Age*, ed. Peter Paret (Princeton, N.J.: Princeton University Press, 1986), p. 520. A thorough discussion of the "spirit of the offensive" in French doctrine is found in Porch, *March to the Marne*, pp. 213–231.

15. Porch, *March to the Marne*, p. 228.

16. Still the most readable account of German operations in 1914 is Correlli Barnett, *The Swordbearers: Supreme Command in the First World War* (Bloomington: Indiana University Press, 1963), pp. 1–98.

17. This account of the opening battles in Lorraine follows Griffith, *Forward into Battle*, pp. 90–94. For the traditional view of the battle, replete with the French "advancing as if at Waterloo," moving to the attack "in long lines in perfect order," only to be slaughtered en masse by German machine guns, see Stokesbury, *Short History of World War I*, 40–41.

18. For the battle of Namur ("Meuse et Sambre," to the French), see Liddell Hart, *Real War*, pp. 57–59; Fuller, *Military History of the Western World*, 3:201; and Keegan, *First World War*, pp. 104–107.

19. There is disagreement on the aftermath of the battle. Stephen Badsey, "Cavalry and the Development of Breakthrough Doctrine," in *British Fighting Methods in the Great War*, ed. Paddy Griffith (London: Frank Cass, 1996), p. 147, maintains that "the ability of the cavalry to dominate its enemies in scouting and patrol work prevented the Germans from pressing the BEF during the retreat from Mons." Nikolas Gardner, "Command and Control in the 'Great Retreat' of 1914: The Disintegration of the British Cavalry Division," *Journal of Military History* 63, no. 1, January 1999, pp. 29–54, tells a different story, describing the divisional commander's complete loss of control over his brigades.

20. The preeminent book on the Tannenberg campaign is Dennis Showalter, *Tannenberg: Clash of Empires* (Hamden, Conn.: Archon, 1991). For Moltke's decision to send what proved to be unnecessary reinforcements to the east, see pp. 193–196. Norman Stone, *The Eastern Front, 1914–1917* (London: Hodder and Stoughton, 1975), is indispensable for any inquiry into the war between the Central Powers and Russia; see pp. 44–69 for the Tannenberg campaign. Still quite useful is Sir Edmund Ironside, *Tannenberg: The First Thirty Days in East Prussia* (Edinburgh: William Blackwood, 1933). A detailed account of operations, with essential maps, is to be found in an article by Lieutenant Colonel Ponath, "Die Schlacht bei Tannenberg 1914 in kriegsgeschichtlicher, taktischer, und erzieherischer Auswertung," *Militär-Wochenblatt* 124, no. 8, August 18, 1939, pp. 476–482.

21. Two still-useful books on the battle of the Marne are Robert B. Asprey, *The First Battle of the Marne* (Philadelphia: Lippincott, 1962); and Georges Blond, *The Marne* (London: Macdonald, 1965).

22. The "Hentsch mission" was and still remains the most controversial aspect of the opening campaign in the west. See Liddell Hart, *Real War*, pp. 83–84; Crutwell, *History of the Great War*, p. 34; Falls, *Great War*, pp. 68–69; Fuller, *Military History of the Western World*, 3:225–227; Keegan, *First World War*, pp. 130–133.

23. See Wilhelm Groener, last quartermaster-general of the old army and later defense minister during the Weimar period, *Der Feldherr wider Willen: Operative Studien über den Weltkrieg* (Berlin: E. S. Mittler und Sohn, 1927). See also the verdict in Herwig, *Germany and Austria-Hungary*, pp. 105–106.

24. For a discussion of the problem in a modern context, see Robert L. Bateman III, "Avoiding Information Overload," *Military Review* 78, no. 4, July 1998, pp. 53–58.

25. These thoughts on the 1914 campaign are found in General Georg Wetzell, "Gedanken zum X. Band des Weltkriegswerkes über das Kriegsjahr 1916," *Militär-Wochenblatt* 121, no. 8, August 25, 1936, p. 377.

26. Creveld, *Supplying War*, p. 134. See also the very informative, two-part article focusing on the logistics of the Schlieffen Plan: Colonel von Mantey, "Nachschub und Operationsplan," pt. 1, *Militär-Wochenblatt* 124, no. 1, July 1, 1939, pp. 1–6 and pt. 2, *Militär-Wochenblatt* 124, no. 2, July 7, 1939, pp. 76–81.

27. The positive view of Sukhomlinov is ably presented in Winston Churchill, *The Unknown War: The Eastern Front* (New York: Scribner's, 1932), pp. 91–92. See also Stone, *Eastern Front*, pp. 24–33, for a thoughtful rehabilitation of this maligned character.

28. Quoted in Alan Clark, *Suicide of the Empires: The Battles on the Eastern Front, 1914–18* (New York: American Heritage Press, 1971), pp. 19–20. Crutwell, *History of the Great War*, p. 40, describes Sukhomlinov as "a chocking mixture of corruption and cynical inefficiency."

29. W. Bruce Lincoln, *Passage Through Armageddon: The Russians in War and Revolution, 1914–1918* (New York: Simon and Schuster, 1986), pp. 23–24.

30. Churchill, *Unknown War*, p. 177. François deserves a military biography. See Randy R. Talbot, "General Hermann von François and Corps-Level Operations During the Tannenberg Campaign, August 1914" (master's thesis, Eastern Michigan University, 1999).

31. Quoted in Clark, *Suicide of the Empires*, p. 29.

32. Who said what, to whom, and in what tone of voice has been a matter of controversy since the day it happened. The sources even contradict one another on the exact day of Prittwitz's phone call to Moltke. See Showalter, *Tannenberg*, pp. 193–94, as well as his article "Even Generals Wet Their Pants: The First Three Weeks in East Prussia, August 1914," *War and Society* 2, no. 2, 1984, pp. 61–86, which assesses the "psychological effects of the telephone" and its impact on operations.

33. Quoted in Keegan, *First World War*, p. 162.

34. See, for example, Gunther Rothenberg, *The Army of Francis Joseph* (West Lafayette, Ind.: Purdue University Press, 1976), p. 178, who argues that "on paper, Conrad's plans always had an almost Napoleonic sweep, though he often lacked the instruments to execute them." For the Austrian army since Königgrätz, see Scott

W. Lackey, *The Rebirth of the Habsburg Army: Friedrich Beck and the Rise of the General Staff* (Westport, Conn.: Greenwood Press, 1995). The evidence for such a "rebirth," however, seems scanty.

35. See Herwig, *Germany and Austria-Hungary,* especially pp. 45–56, for the Central Powers' plans in the east, as well as Stone, *Eastern Front,* pp. 72–74. Ted S. Raicer, "When Eagles Fight: The Eastern Front in World War I," *Command* 25, November–December 1993, pp. 14–37, combines lucid text with magnificent maps, as well as a very interesting simulation game (also entitled "When Eagles Fight") of the conflict on the eastern front.

36. For the Austrian invasion of Serbia, see Gunther E. Rothenberg, "The Austro-Hungarian Campaign Against Serbia in 1914," *Journal of Military History* 53, no. 2, April 1989, pp. 127–146. See also James B. Lyon, "Serbia and the Balkan Front, 1914" (Ph.D. diss., University of California, Los Angeles, 1995); and Lyon, "'A Peasant Mob': The Serbian Army on the Eve of the Great War," *Journal of Military History* 61, no. 3, July 1997, pp. 481–502.

37. For the figure of Putnik, see Dimitrije Djordjevic, "*Vojvoda* Radomir Putnik," in *War and Society in East Central Europe,* vol. 25, *East Central European War Leaders: Civilian and Military,* ed. Béla K. Király and Albert A. Nofi (Boulder, Colo.: Social Science Monographs, 1988), pp. 223–248.

38. Ibid., pp. 235–236.

39. For the immense battles in Galicia, see Stone, *Eastern Front,* pp. 70–91; Churchill, *Unknown War,* pp. 144–173; Clark, *Suicide of the Empires,* pp. 49–59; Stokesbury, *Short History of World War I,* pp. 69–71; Herwig, *Germany and Austria-Hungary,* pp. 89–95; and Keegan, *First World War,* pp. 168–174. For an interesting analysis by a former member of the Austro-Hungarian General Staff, see Max Freiherr von Pitreich, "Osterreich-Ungarns Kriegsbeginn gegen Russland und das Siedlecproblem," *Militär-Wochenblatt* 122, no. 8, August 20, 1937, pp. 441–446.

40. Quoted in Colonel Fuppe, "Neuzeitliches Nachrichtenverbindungswesen als Führungsmittel im Kriege," *Militärwissenschaftliche Rundschau* 3, no. 6, 1938, p. 750.

41. The plight of the foot soldier in the trench fighting of World War I is the subject of Denis Winter, *Death's Men: Soldiers of the Great War* (New York: Penguin, 1978).

42. See the argument put forth by Michael Howard, "World War One: The Crisis in European History, the Role of the Military Historian," *Journal of Military History* 57, no. 1, October 1993, p. 136.

43. Alistair Horne, *The Price of Glory: Verdun, 1916* (New York: Penguin, 1964), is a highly readable and interesting account of the battle, but it lacks source notes. Herwig, *Germany and Austria-Hungary,* contains a solid, scholarly account on pp. 183–196.

44. Falkenhayn was the subject of intense criticism for this decision. See, for example, the work by a German staff officer, Colonel Max Bauer, *Der grosse Krieg in Feld und Heimat* (Tübingen: Osiander'sche Buchhandlung, 1921), pp. 101–102, who claims that he advised an offensive on both banks of the Meuse from the beginning but was ignored. For a defense of Falkenhayn's decision, see General Georg

Wetzell, "Verdun in der kriegswissenschaftlichen Kritik," *Militär-Wochenblatt* 121, no. 9, September 4, 1936, p. 427.

45. The quotation is found in Holger Herwig, *Hammer or Anvil: Modern Germany, 1648–Present* (Lexington, Mass.: Heath, 1994), pp. 208–209.

46. For the rise of *Stosstrupp* tactics, see Bruce I. Gudmundsson, *Stormtroop Tactics: Innovation in the German Army, 1914–1918* (Westport, Conn.: Praeger, 1989), which in turn builds upon a previous work by Timothy S. Lupfer, *The Dynamics of Doctrine: The Changes in German Tactical Doctrine During the First World War* (Ft. Leavenworth, Kans.: U.S. Army Command and General Staff College, 1981). For a discussion of *Stosstrupp* tactics as a combined arms doctrine featuring artillery as well as infantry, see Zabecki, *Steel Wind*. Finally, for the relationship of this tactical innovation to later trends in operational warfare, see Stephen W. Richey, "Auftragstaktik, Schwerpunkt, Aufrollen: The Philosophical Basis of the AirLand Battle," *Military Review* 64, no. 5, May 1984, 48–53.

47. Gudmundsson, *Stormtroop Tactics*, pp. 47–51.

48. Zabecki, *Steel Wind*, p. 23; Gudmundsson, *Stormtroop Tactics*, pp. 116–117.

49. Zabecki, *Steel Wind*, p. 24.

50. Gudmundsson, *Stormtroop Tactics*, p. 151.

51. For the assault on Riga, see Zabecki, *Steel Wind*, pp. 21–25; Gudmundsson, *Stormtroop Tactics*, pp. 114–121. For a battle with such crucial tactical, operational, and strategic implications, it has received scant attention in general histories of the war, from a single mention in Liddell Hart, *Real War*, p. 304, to two short references in Keegan, *First World War*, pp. 365, 405–406.

52. Gudmundsson, *Stormtroop Tactics*, p. 115.

53. Zabecki, *Steel Wind*, pp. 24–25.

54. See David J. Childs, *A Peripheral Weapon: The Production and Employment of British Tanks in the First World War* (Westport, Conn.: Greenwood Press, 1999).

55. See the account by Fuller in two of his own books: *Tanks in the Great War, 1914–1918* (New York: Dutton, 1920), and *Memoirs of an Unconventional Soldier* (London: Ivor Nicholson and Watson, 1936). D. J. Fletcher, "The Origins of Armour," in *Armoured Warfare*, ed. J. P. Harris and F. H. Toase (London: B. T. Batsford, 1990), p. 8, calls Fuller "the Mahan of the Tank Corps."

56. Fuller, *Memoirs*, p. 212.

57. The myth of the "gunner of Flesquières" was first given widespread credence by its appearance in Sir Douglas Haig's dispatch on the battle. See Clough Williams-Ellis and A. Williams-Ellis, *The Tank Corps* (New York: George H. Doran, 1919), p. 177. It is no longer credible. See Heinz Guderian, *Achtung—Panzer! The Development of Armored Forces, Their Tactics, and Operational Potential* (London: Arms and Armor, 1992), pp. 82–83, who credits skillful tactics on the part of the German defenders; and Chandler, "Cambrai," pp. 110, 116, who is rather more inclined to blame the faulty manner in which General Harper handled the assault in this sector. Lieutenant Colonel Büdingen, "Flak gegen Tanks im Weltkriege," *Militär-Wochenblatt* 125, no. 11, September 13, 1941, pp. 421–423, offers a solid account of the use of antiaircraft guns against the British tanks at Cambrai.

58. For the Ludendorff offensives, see Barnett, *The Swordbearers*, pp. 269–361. The quotation is taken from p. 285. For an account of the discussion between Ludendorff and the army chiefs of staff at the "Mons conference" of November 11, 1917, where the decision to attack the British at Saint-Quentin was made, see Dr. Arthur Kühn, "Raum und Gelände in den deutschen und gegnerischen Operationsplänen Frühjahr 1918," *Militär-Wochenblatt* 123, no. 4, July 22, 1938, pp. 194–198. For Operation Michael, see Gudmundsson, *Stormtroop Tactics*, pp. 162–168; and Herwig, *Germany and Austria-Hungary*, pp. 400–408.

59. Quoted in Hubert C. Johnson, *Breakthrough: Tactics, Technology, and the Search for Victory on the Western Front in World War I* (Novato, Calif.: Presidio, 1994), p. 228.

60. Herwig, *Germany and Austria-Hungary*, p. 410.

61. The soldier is Rudolf Binding, quoted in Johnson, *Breakthrough*, p. 229.

62. Quoted in Crutwell, *History of the Great War*, pp. 518–519.

63. For the end of the war on the western front, see Rod Paschall, *The Defeat of Imperial Germany, 1917–1918* (Chapel Hill, N.C.: Algonquin, 1989), pp. 128–232. The quotation, attributed here to an anonymous marine officer, is from p. 56.

64. For the FT-17, see Pierre Touzin and Christian Gurtner, "Renault F.T.," in *AFVs of World War One*, vol. 1, ed. Duncan Crow (Windsor, Ontario: Profile Publications, 1970), pp. 77–88, especially the illustrations on pp. 86–87.

65. A point made in the most recent work on the battle: Douglas V. Johnston II and Rolfe Hillman Jr., *Soissons 1918* (College Station: Texas A&M University Press, 1999). Despite the title, the work deals only with the AEF divisions attached to the French army, and not the French effort itself. For a look at the French offensive, see Robert J. Sinnema, "General Mangin and the Tenth Army, 1918" (master's thesis, University of Calgary, 1996).

66. Fuller, *Tanks in the Great War*, pp. 217–229, is still the classic rendering of the battle of Amiens. See also Kenneth Macksey, *Tank Warfare: A History of Tanks in Battle* (New York: Stein and Day, 1972), pp. 59–62; H. C. B. Rogers, *Tanks in Battle* (London: Seeley Service, 1965), pp. 72–74; Williams-Ellis and Williams-Ellis, *Tank Corps*, pp. 288–323; and Fletcher, "Origins of Armour," pp. 22–24. Douglas Orgill, *The Tank: Studies in the Development and Use of a Weapon* (London: Heinemann, 1970), pp. 41–55, offers an interesting portrait of the commander of the Australian Corps, Lieutenant General John Monash, as a "new model general."

67. Liddell Hart discusses the origins of the Whippet in B. H. Liddell Hart, *The Tanks*, vol. 1 (London: Cassell, 1959), pp. 155–157. See Chris Ellis and Peter Chamberlain, "Medium Tanks Marks A to D," in *AFVs of World War One*, 1:89–108, especially the illustrations on pp. 98–99; Fuller, *Tanks in the Great War*, pp. 44–47; Kenneth Macksey, "Tank Development," in *Tanks and Weapons of World War I*, ed. Bernard Fitzsimons (London: Phoebus, 1973), p. 134; and Macksey, *Tank Versus Tank: The Illustrated Story of Armored Battlefield Conflict in the Twentieth Century* (New York: Barnes and Noble, 1999), pp. 30–31; Rogers, *Tanks in Battle*, pp. 63, 66–68; Orgill, *The Tank*, pp. 61–62.

68. Quoted in Macksey, *Tank Warfare*, p. 60.

69. Field Marshal Paul von Hindenburg, *Out of My Life* (New York: Harper and Brothers, 1921), 2:214.

70. Quoted in Macksey, *Tank Warfare*, p. 61.

71. Fuller, *Memoirs*, p. 317.

72. It is worth remembering the tremendous cost in blood the Allies paid to flatten their already beaten foe. The South African Deneys Reitz commanded a battalion for a short time in 1918. On October 7, he published his one and only battalion order, a casualty list for a two-week period: 36 killed and 139 wounded, losses of over 20 percent. Deneys Reitz, *Trekking On* (Prescott, Ariz.: Wolfe, 1994), pp. 286–289.

73. Michael Howard has gone so far as to say that he does not know of a "single satisfactory operational account" of the war, since "it is extraordinarily difficult to treat the military aspects of this war in the discrete fashion that traditional military historians prefer and their readers expect." Howard, "The Crisis in European History," p. 129.

Chapter 6. *The Interwar Years*

1. See, for example, Lieutenant Colonel Köhn, "Die Infanterie im 'Blitzkrieg,'" *Militär-Wochenblatt* 125, no. 5, August 2, 1940, pp. 165–166, in which *Blitzkrieg* is used only in quotation marks and is described as a "catchphrase" *(Schlagwort)*; as well as Colonel Rudolf Theiss, "Der Panzer in der Weltgeschichte," *Militär-Wochenblatt* 125, no. 15, October 11, 1940, pp. 705–708, which likewise uses the term in quotes. By 1941, German usage in the professional literature had dropped the quotes, although the word was still not being used in any sort of precise technical sense. See Lieutenant Colonel Gaul, "Der Blitzkrieg in Frankreich," *Militär-Wochenblatt* 125, no. 35, February 28, 1941, pp. 1513–1517.

2. For Villers-Bretonneux, see Kenneth Macksey, *Tank Versus Tank: The Illustrated Story of Armored Battlefield Conflict in the Twentieth Century* (New York: Barnes and Noble, 1999), pp. 30–40. Often forgotten in this context is Heinz Guderian, *Achtung—Panzer! The Development of Armored Forces, Their Tactics, and Operational Potential* (London: Arms and Armour, 1992). Not merely a doctrinal handbook, it is also a fine operational history of armored combat in World War I. For Villers-Bretonneux, see pp. 184–186.

3. The interwar period has attracted intense study of late, seen by scholars and military professionals alike as a laboratory of change in doctrine, training, and weaponry, in which some succeeded (the Germans), others failed (the French), and still others squandered rich opportunities (the British). Two essential works give an overview: Williamson Murray and Allan R. Millett, eds., *Military Innovation in the Interwar Period* (Cambridge: Cambridge University Press, 1996); and Harold R. Winton and David R. Mets, *The Challenge of Change: Military Institutions and New Realities, 1918–1941* (Lincoln: University of Nebraska Press, 2000). Both gather together essays from leading scholars in the area. The former is arranged topically, with chapters dealing with armored warfare, assault from the sea, strategic bomb-

ing, and more; the latter is arranged by country, with chapters on France, Germany, Great Britain, the Soviet Union, and the United States, tied together by a concluding essay by Dennis E. Showalter. The list of publications dealing with this era is long and getting longer. See, among others, Robert M. Citino, *The Evolution of Blitzkrieg Tactics: Germany Defends Itself Against Poland, 1918–1933* (Westport, Conn.: Greenwood Press, 1987); Citino, *The Path to Blitzkrieg: Doctrine and Training in the German Army, 1920–1939* (Boulder, Colo.: Lynne Rienner, 1998); Citino, "The Weimar Roots of German Military Planning," in *Military Planning and the Origins of the Second World War in Europe,* ed. B. J. C. McKercher and Roch Legault (Westport, Conn.: Praeger, 2001), pp. 59–87; James S. Corum, *The Roots of Blitzkrieg: Hans von Seeckt and German Military Reform* (Lawrence: University Press of Kansas, 1992); Eugenia C. Kiesling, *Arming Against Hitler: France and the Limits of Military Planning* (Lawrence: University Press of Kansas, 1996); David E. Johnson, *Fast Tanks and Heavy Bombers: Innovation in the U.S. Army, 1917–1945* (Ithaca, N.Y.: Cornell University Press, 1998); William O. Odom, *After the Trenches: The Transformation of U.S. Army Doctrine, 1918–1939* (College Station: Texas A&M University Press, 1999); Harold R. Winton, *To Change an Army: General Sir John Burnett-Stuart and British Armored Doctrine, 1927–1938* (Lawrence: University Press of Kansas, 1988). Larry Addington, *The Blitzkrieg Era and the German General Staff, 1865–1941* (New Brunswick, N.J.: Rutgers University Press, 1971), continues to be useful in reminding us that the German Army of World War II was often operating on a shoestring, spearheaded by a handful of panzer divisions and consisting mainly of old-style infantry divisions relying on horse transport. For a detailed view of the question, see R. L. DiNardo, *Mechanized Juggernaut or Military Anachronism? Horses and the German Army of World War II* (Westport, Conn.: Greenwood Press, 1991). A recent entry, tying blitzkrieg and machine-age warfare to fascism, is Azar Gat, *Fascist and Liberal Visions of War: Fuller, Liddell Hart, Douhet, and Other Modernists* (Oxford: Oxford University Press, 1998). It is a provocative, though flawed, argument; see Harold R. Winton's review in *Journal of Military History* 64, no. 3, July 2000, pp. 871–873.

4. J. F. C. Fuller, *Tanks in the Great War, 1914–1918* (New York: Dutton, 1920), p. xix; Heinz Guderian, *Panzer Leader* (New York: Ballantine, 1957), pp. 10–11; B. H. Liddell Hart, *Memoirs* (London: Cassell, 1965), 1:102.

5. The primary source for this "authorized version" is B. H. Liddell Hart, *The Tanks,* vol. 1 (London: Cassell, 1959). For a corrective, see J. P. Harris, "British Armour 1918–1940: Doctrine and Development," in *Armoured Warfare,* ed. J. P. Harris and F. H. Toase (London: B. T. Batsford, 1990), p. 28; also see pp. 27–50. For a mildly revisionist view on Liddell Hart, see Robert H. Larson, *The British Army and the Theory of Armored Warfare* (Newark: University of Delaware Press, 1984); or Brian Bond, *British Military Policy Between the Two World Wars* (Oxford: Clarendon Press, 1980). For a much more brutal critique, see John J. Mearsheimer, *Liddell Hart and the Weight of History* (Ithaca, N.Y.: Cornell University Press, 1988).

6. The three principal works on the modernization of the German army in the 1920s are Citino, *Evolution of Blitzkrieg Tactics;* Corum, *Roots of Blitzkrieg;* and

• •

Citino, *Path to Blitzkrieg*. See also R. L. DiNardo, *Germany's Panzer Arm* (Westport, Conn.: Greenwood Press, 1997), especially chap. 4, "Doctrine: Correcting the Myths," pp. 73–94.

7. J. F. C. Fuller, *Memoirs of an Unconventional Soldier* (London: Ivor Nicholson and Watson, 1936), p. 363.

8. Larson, *British Army and the Theory of Armored Warfare*, pp. 75–76.

9. Fuller has a strong defender among contemporary scholars. See Brian Holden Reid, "Colonel J. F. C. Fuller and the Revival of Classical Military Thinking in Britain, 1918–1926," *Military Affairs* 49, no. 4, October 1985, pp. 192–197; Reid, *J. F. C. Fuller: Military Thinker* (New York: St. Martin's Press, 1987); and Reid, *Studies in British Military Thought: Debates with Fuller and Liddell Hart* (Lincoln: University of Nebraska Press, 1998).

10. J. F. C. Fuller, *The Reformation of War* (London: Hutchinson, 1923), pp. 152–169.

11. For a sympathetic account, see Brian Bond, *Liddell Hart: A Study of His Military Thought* (New Brunswick, N.J.: Rutgers University Press, 1977); Larson, *British Army and the Theory of Armored Warfare*, pp. 76–84; and Alex Danchev, "Liddell Hart and the Indirect Approach," *Journal of Military History* 63, no. 2, April 1999, pp. 313–337.

12. Here Liddell Hart echoes Ivan S. Bloch, the great civilian analyst writing before World War I, who argued that "the modern European feels more keenly and is much more excitable and impressionable than his forefathers. Upon this highly excitable, sensitive population you are going to inflict the miseries of hunger and all the horrors of war." See Tim Travers, "Technology, Tactics, and Morale: Jean de Bloch, the Boer War, and British Military Theory," *Journal of Modern History* 51, no. 2, June 1979, pp. 266–267.

13. B. H. Liddell Hart, *Paris, or the Future of War* (London: Kegan Paul, 1925), pp. 46–48, quoted in Bond, *Liddell Hart*, pp. 40–42. See also Liddell Hart, *A Greater Than Napoleon: Scipio Africanus* (London: Blackwood, 1926); Liddell Hart, *Sherman: Soldier, Realist, American* (London: Eyre and Spottiswoode, 1930); and Liddell Hart, *The Remaking of Modern Armies* (Boston: Little, Brown, 1927).

14. B. H. Liddell Hart, *The Decisive Wars of History* (London: G. Bell, 1929). See also the quotations in *Memoirs*, pp. 162–165.

15. Colonel R. H. Beadon, "Some Strategical Theories of Captain Liddell Hart," *Journal of the Royal United Service Institution* 81, no. 524, November 1936, p. 748–749.

16. For the best scholarly discussion of the Experimental Mechanized Force, see Winton, *To Change an Army*, pp. 72–94. Larson, *British Army and the Theory of Armored Warfare*, pp. 133–147; and J. P. Harris, *Men, Ideas, and Tanks: British Military Thought and Armoured Forces, 1903–1939* (Manchester: Manchester University Press, 1995), pp. 217–219, continue to be useful.

17. Liddell Hart, *The Tanks*, 1:247. See also Eric Morris, *Tanks* (London: Octopus Books, 1975), pp. 42–43; Harris, *Men, Ideas, and Tanks*, p. 217.

18. Fuller told the story in his inimitable way in *Memoirs*, pp. 434–441. For a more balanced view, see Harris, *Men, Ideas, and Tanks*, pp. 215–217.

19. Harris, "British Armour 1918–1940," pp. 36–37.

20. Liddell Hart, *The Tanks,* 1:249.

21. See the arguments put forth by Larson, *The British Army and the Theory of Armored Warfare,* pp. 146–147; Ogorkiewicz, *Armoured Warfare,* pp. 16–17, 56–58; and Harris, *Men, Ideas, and Tanks,* pp. 225–229, 289–290.

22. Liddell Hart, *The Tanks,* 1:268–271; Harris, "British Armour 1918–1940," pp. 37–38; Harris, *Men, Ideas, and Tanks,* pp. 222–225; and Larson, *British Army and the Theory of Armored Warfare,* pp. 150–151.

23. Three of the twelve books on the list were Liddell Hart's. *The Tanks,* 1:251–253, quotes extensively from Milne's speech.

24. For the "battle of Tilshead," replete with diagrams and maps, see Macksey, *Tank Versus Tank,* pp. 49–53.

25. See Winton, *To Change an Army,* pp. 220–244; Harris, "British Armour 1918–1940," pp. 42–44; Harris, *Men, Ideas, and Tanks,* pp. 273–274; Larson, *British Army and the Theory of Armored Warfare,* pp. 185–187.

26. Liddell Hart, *The British Way in Warfare* (London: Faber and Faber, 1932), p. 136. German analysts, for obvious reasons, were vocal in their praise of Liddell Hart's resistance to committing the British army to the Continent. See, for example, General Georg Wetzell's review essay on the book in "Britische Strategie," *Militär-Wochenblatt* 121, no. 48, June 11, 1937, pp. 3037–3041.

27. For a discussion of the topic of tank versus antitank, see John Weeks, *Men Against Tanks: A History of Antitank Warfare* (New York: Mason/Charter, 1975). For the German view of the matter, see Rittmeister Gerhard, "Oberstleutnant Perré, Hauptmann Liddell Hart—und wir," *Militär-Wochenblatt* 120, no. 3, July 18, 1935, pp. 105–107.

28. Liddell Hart's arguments in favor of the light tank are to be found in *The British Way in Warfare,* pp. 128–131. The formation of the First Tank Brigade is discussed in Winton, *To Change an Army,* pp. 116–118; Larson, *British Army and the Theory of Armored Warfare,* pp. 163–167; and Harris, *Men, Ideas, and Tanks,* pp. 245–249, 289–290.

29. On Elles, see Liddell Hart, *Memoirs,* pp. 388–389; Harris, *Men, Ideas, and Tanks,* pp. 240–241. On the infantry tank, see Major G. B. J. Kellie, "The Support of Infantry Tanks in the Attack," *Journal of the Royal United Service Institution* 83, no. 531, August 1938, pp. 592–598.

30. On the split of the British armored force into cruiser and infantry tanks, see Ogorkiewicz, *Armoured Forces,* pp. 155–157; and Rogers, *Tanks in Battle,* pp. 96–100.

31. Harris, "British Armour 1918–1940," p. 48, calls him "one of the rudest men in the Army, a fanatic for his own conception of armoured forces, full of prejudices and exceptionally intolerant." The standard biography is Kenneth Macksey, *Armoured Crusader* (London: Hutchinson, 1967).

32. For the role of General von Seeckt in the reformation of German training and doctrine, see Citino, *Evolution of Blitzkrieg Tactics,* pp. 40–98; Corum, *Roots of Blitzkrieg,* pp. 25–50; and Citino, *Path to Blitzkrieg,* pp. 7–42. For an overview, see also

Robert M. Citino, *Armored Forces: History and Sourcebook* (Westport, Conn.: Greenwood Press, 1994), pp. 50–57.

33. General Hans von Seeckt, "Modernes Heer," in *Gedanken eines Soldaten* (Leipzig: K. F. Koehler, 1935), pp. 51–61. For the quotation on "cannon fodder," see p. 56; the quotation on the poor maneuverability of mass armies is on p. 54.

34. General Hans von Seeckt, "Grundsätze moderner Landesverteidigung," in *Gedanken eines Soldaten* (Leipzig: K. F. Koehler, 1935), pp. 62–85. The quotation is from p. 77.

35. Virtually the entire body of interwar German writings about armor stresses the importance of the cooperation of all arms with the tanks. To give just one example of hundreds from the pages of the *Militär-Wochenblatt,* see Helmut Burckhardt, "Grosstanks oder Massenangriff mit unzureichend gepanzerten Tanks?" *Militär-Wochenblatt* 122, no. 3, July 16, 1937, pp. 143–144: "Schließlich kämpfen die Panzer ja nicht allein . . . , sondern werden von allen möglichen Waffen unterstützt" (p. 143). For a representative sample of German writing on *Bewegungskrieg* in the interwar period—again, one of hundreds of possible examples—see General of Artillery Ludwig, "Gedanken über den Angriff im Bewegungskriege," *Militärwissenschaftliche Rundschau* 1, no. 2, 1936, pp. 153–164.

36. Ogorkiewicz, *Armoured Forces,* p. 73.

37. Guderian, *Panzer Leader.*

38. See Guderian, "Kraftfahrtruppen," *Militärwissenschaftliche Rundschau* 1, no. 1, 1936, pp. 52–77; and Guderian, "Die Panzertruppen und ihr Zusammenwirken mit den anderen Waffen," *Militärwissenschaftliche Rundschau* 1, no. 5, 1936, pp. 607–626. The two articles formed the basis for *Achtung—Panzer!*

39. For Volckheim, see Citino, *Armored Forces,* pp. 277–278.

40. General Ludwig von Eimannsberger, "Panzertaktik," pt. 1, *Militär-Wochenblatt* 120, no. 23, December 18, 1935, pp. 981–985.

41. Ibid., p. 981.

42. General Ludwig von Eimannsberger, "Panzertaktik," pt. 2, *Militär-Wochenblatt* 120, no. 24, December 25, 1935, pp. 1027–1030.

43. "Der Angreifer muß erfinderich sein wie das Leben." Ibid., p. 1028.

44. "Es greift also nicht der Panzer an, sondern die betreffende Heereseinheit." Ibid., p. 1029.

45. Colonel Walter Spannenkrebs, *Angriff mit Kampfwagen* (Oldenburg: Gerhard Stalling, 1939).

46. See ibid., "Operative Verwendung von Panzerverbände," pp. 350–358.

47. "Die Kämpfe spielen sich im größeren und freieren Räumen ab, welche oftmals weder durch den Freund noch durch den Feind ausreichend erkundet werdern konnten." Ibid., p. 351.

48. Ibid., pp. 352–353.

49. "Die Aufgaben und Ziele können um so weiter gesteckt werden, je größen die zusammengefaßte Anzahl dieser Verbände ist." Ibid., p. 354.

50. Ibid., p. 358.

51. "Alles oder nichts! Jede Halbheit führt zum Mißerfolg!" Ibid., p. 375. For the importance of mass in the armored assault, see another article by Spannenkrebs, "Infanterie und Panzer," *Militär-Wochenblatt* 123, no. 7, August 12, 1938, pp. 402–404.

52. Gordon A. Craig, *The Politics of the Prussian Army, 1640–1945* (Oxford: Oxford University Press, 1955), p. 396.

53. Colonel A. L. Conger, U.S. Military Attaché, "Maneuvers: First Division," in *United States Military Intelligence Reports: Germany, 1919–1941* (Frederick, Md.: University Publications of America, 1983), microfilm reel XIV, frame 189. In shorthand notation, this document would be labeled USMI, XIV, 149.

54. Citino, *Path to Blitzkrieg*, pp. 202–204.

55. Colonel Oswald Lutz, "Anregungen und Lehren aus dem unter Leitung der Inspektion der Kraftfahrtruppen abgehaltenen Übungen der Kampfwagen-Nachbildungs-Bataillone zusammen mit Infanterie und Artillerie auf den Truppenübungsplätzen Grafenwöhr und Jüterbog," found in "Records of the German Army High Command" (Oberkommando des Heeres, or OKH, the post-1935 designation of the Heeresleitung). A microfilmed copy of these records is on file in the U.S. National Archives in Washington, D.C., Microcopy T-78, serial H25/24, reel 300, frames 6250579–6250595. See, especially, "Taktik der Kampfwagen," frames 6250581–6250586. Lutz specified a breadth of 800 to 1,500 meters for the attack of a tank battalion.

56. For the 1932 fall maneuvers, see Citino, *Path to Blitzkrieg*, pp. 212–215.

57. Oswald Lutz, "Beispiel für die Gliederung einer Aufklärungsabteilung," Berlin, 1 December 1932, OKH, serial H25/24, reel 300, frames 6250656–6250657.

58. Guderian, *Panzer Leader*, p. 18.

59. Lieutenant Colonel Jacob Wuest, "The German Maneuvers, September 19–22, 1932," USMI, XIX, 847–874, especially "September 19th," frame 854.

60. Lieutenant-Colonel H. de Watteville, "The German Army Maneuvers, 1936," *Journal of the Royal United Service Institution* 81, no. 524, November 1936, p. 783.

61. For the 1937 fall maneuvers, see Citino, *Path to Blitzkrieg*, pp. 236–242.

62. Major Friedrich Bertkau, "Die nachrichtentechnische Führung mechanisierter Verbände," *Militär-Wochenblatt* 120, no. 15, October 18, 1935, p. 611.

63. Ibid., p. 615.

64. See the unsigned article "Divisionsführung und Befehlstechnik," *Militär-Wochenblatt* 126, no. 44, May 18, 1932, pp. 1540–1542.

65. For a fine discussion of French army mechanization and the evolution of France's "very careful doctrine," see Kiesling, *Arming Against Hitler*, pp. 136–172. Still important is Charles de Gaulle, *Vers l'armée de métier* (Paris: Librairie Plon, 1971). The English translation is *The Army of the Future* (London: Hutchinson, 1940).

66. Concepts like "deep battle," and "Soviet operational art" became a staple of professional military literature in the 1980s. Generated by a desire to unlock the military secrets of the West's chief adversary in the cold war, virtually all of this literature is now badly dated. Even at the time, however, there were perceptive voices

claiming that authors were "inventing history" in order to find a Soviet military genius that did not in fact exist. See the argument over Bryan Fugate, *Operation Barbarossa* (Novato, Calif.: Presidio, 1984), in Barry D. Watts and Williamson Murray, "Inventing History: Soviet Military Genius Revealed," *Air University Review* 26, no. 3, March–April 1985: 102–104; Fugate's rebuttal, "On Inventing History," *Air University Review* 26, no. 6, September–October 1985: 121–125; and the discussion of the controversy in Jacob W. Kipp, "Barbarossa, Soviet Covering Forces and the Initial Period of War: Military History and AirLand Battle," *Journal of Soviet Military Studies* 1, no. 2, June 1988, p. 188–212. For "deep battle," see Richard E. Simpkin, *Deep Battle: The Brainchild of Marshal Tukhachevskii* (New York: Pergamon, 1987). See also Paddy Griffith, *Forward into Battle: Fighting Tactics from Waterloo to the Near Future* (Novato, Calif.: Presidio, 1990), p. 131. Bruce Menning, "The Deep Strike in Russian and Soviet Military History," *Journal of Soviet Military Studies* 1, no. 1, April 1988, pp. 9–28, contributes a historical context by pointing to the long Russian-Soviet tradition of the deep cavalry raid and the *corps volant.*

67. Major M. Braun, "Gedanken über Kampfwagen- und Fliegerverwendung bei den russischen Herbstmanövern 1936," *Militär-Wochenblatt* 121, no. 28, January 22, 1937, pp. 1589–1592. See also the report on the U.S. military attaché in Moscow, Lieutenant Colonel Philip R. Faymonville, on the 1935 Kiev maneuvers, which featured an airborne landing by 500 men and an attack on the paratroopers by a "strong detachment of fast tanks." In David M. Glantz, "Observing the Soviets: U.S. Army Attachés in Eastern Europe During the 1930s," *Journal of Military History* 55, no. 2, April 1991, pp. 153–183, especially pp. 163–165.

68. For the shuffle between large and small armored units, see Michael Parrish, "Formation and Leadership of the Soviet Mechanized Corps in 1941," *Military Affairs* 47, no. 2, April 1983, pp. 63–66.

69. Simpkin, "Comments," in *Deep Battle*, pp. 49–52.

70. Shimon Naveh, *In Pursuit of Excellence: The Evolution of Operational Theory* (London: Frank Cass, 1997), might be the high-water mark in Tukhachevsky's apotheosis, although the author's insistence on applying "systems theory" to his analysis of operations makes his argument extremely opaque. His definition of *blitzkrieg,* for example, as "a mechanized manipulation of tactical patterns" raises more questions than it answers, and his declaration that the German manual *Truppenführung* is "the best evidence confirming the existence of operational cognition prior to the year 1938," is simply puzzling; it would certainly have surprised an entire generation of German officers from Moltke to Seeckt. For a better presentation on Tukhachevksy, see Roman Johann Jarymowycz, "Jedi Knights in the Kremlin: The Soviet Military in the 1930s and the Genesis of Deep Battle," in *Military Planning and the Origins of the Second World War in Europe,* pp. 122–124, who argues that "the proper study of American doctrine begins in the Kremlin and centers on Marshal Tukhachevsky and his Bonapartist fraternity" (p. 122). The marshal continues to arouse a great deal of interest among younger scholars. See Sally Webb Stoecker, *Forging Stalin's Army: Marshal Tukhachevsky and the Politics of Military Innovation* (Boulder, Colo.: Westview Press, 1998); Mary Ruth Habeck, "Imagin-

ing War: The Development of Armored Doctrine in Germany and the Soviet Union, 1919–1939" (Ph.D. diss., Yale University, 1996); and Frederick Carleton Turner, "The Genesis of the Soviet 'Deep Operation': The Stalin-Era Doctrine for Large-Scale Offensive Maneuver Warfare" (Ph.D. diss., Duke University, 1988). A useful corrective to this tendency to center on one man is found in Richard W. Harrison, *The Russian Way of War: Operational Art, 1904–1940* (Lawrence: University Press of Kansas, 2001), pp. 169–217, which analyzes the contributions of numerous other Soviet contributors to "deep battle," especially G. S. Isserson.

71. See S. J. Lewis, *Forgotten Legions: German Infantry Policy, 1918–1941* (Westport, Conn.: Praeger, 1985), pp. 45–46. Looking back on his Reichswehr service, Adolf Reinicke described the training of the officers as focusing on two principles: "*Bewegungskrieg* and the close cooperation of the arms." Adolf Reinicke, *Das Reichsheer 1921–1934: Ziele, Methoden der Ausbildung und Erziehung sowie der Dienstgestaltung* (Osnabrück: Biblio Verlag, 1986), p. 220.

Chapter 7. Ethiopia and Spain

1. For the Russo-Polish War, see Norman Davies, *White Eagle—Red Star* (London: Macdonald, 1972); Adam Zamoyski, *The Battle for the Marchlands* (Boulder, Colo.: East European Monographs, 1981); Jozef Pilsudksi, *Year 1920* (London: Pilsudski Institute of London, 1972), which also contains Soviet Marshal M. N. Tukhachevsky's lectures to the Soviet Military Academy, entitled "The March Beyond the Vistula"; and the extremely cogent account in Richard W. Harrison, *The Russian Way of War: Operational Art, 1904–1940* (Lawrence: University Press of Kansas, 2001), pp. 107–118. For the Chaco War, see David Zook, *The Conduct of the Chaco War* (New York: Bookman Associates, 1961); and Bruce W. Farcau, *The Chaco War: Bolivia and Paraguay, 1932–1935* (Westport, Conn.: Praeger, 1996). Two contemporary articles are worth consulting: Lieutenant E. E. Farnsworth, "The War in the Chaco," *Infantry Journal* 42, no. 3, May–June 1935, pp. 195–203; and, by a German officer who served with the Bolivian army, Major Wim Brandt, "Die Tankerfahrungen des Chacokrieges," *Militär-Wochenblatt* 120, no. 35, March 18, 1936, pp. 1562–1565.

2. The Italians have not published an official history of the Ethiopian War. The best scholarly account in English is still Brian R. Sullivan, "A Thirst for Glory: Mussolini, the Italian Military and the Fascist Regime, 1922–1936" (Ph.D. diss., Columbia University, 1984), pp. 441–545; see its distilled essence in his article "The Italian-Ethiopian War, October 1935–November 1941: Causes, Conduct, and Consequences," in *Great Powers and Little Wars: The Limits of Power*, ed. A. Hamish Ion and E. J. Errington (Westport, Conn.: Praeger, 1993), pp. 167–201. Two works by Angelo del Boca continue to be indispensable: *The Ethiopian War, 1935–1941* (Chicago: University of Chicago Press, 1965), and *I gas di Mussolini: Il Fascismo e la Guerra d'Etiopia* (Rome: Editori Riuniti, 1996), the former a solid operational history spiced with interviews with various Ethiopian principals, and the latter a work that marked the culmination of del Boca's long struggle to get the Italian armed

forces to admit to the use of poison gas in Ethiopia, a fact they had consistently denied. Giorgio Rochat has long been the leading Italian scholar in the field, author of the standard biography of Marshal Pietro Badoglio. His *Guerre Italiane in Libia e in Etiopia: Studi Militari, 1921–1939* (Paese: Pagus Edizioni, 1991) contains a particularly illuminating chapter, "Badoglio e le Operazioni contro L'Etiopia, 1935–1936." Other important works, especially on the war's diplomatic background, are P. M. H. Bell, *The Origins of the Second World War in Europe* (London: Longman, 1986); and two works by Denis Mack Smith: *Mussolini* (New York: Knopf, 1982), especially pp. 188–196, and *Mussolini's Roman Empire* (New York: Viking, 1976). A. J. Barker, *The Rape of Ethiopia, 1936* (New York: Ballantine, 1971), is a popular history, competent and well written, as are Thomas M. Coffey, *Lion by the Tail: The Story of the Italian-Ethiopian War* (London: Hamish Hamilton, 1974); and Anthony Mockler, *Haile Selassie's War: The Italian-Ethiopian Campaign, 1935–1941* (New York: Random House, 1984). Contemporary accounts are both packed with relevant detail and passionate about a war we have almost forgotten. See George Martelli, *Italy Against the World* (New York: Harcourt, Brace, 1938); and Major E. W. Polson Newman, *Italy's Conquest of Ethiopia* (London: Thornton Butterworth, 1937), both extremely pro-Italian; Geoffrey T. Garratt, *Mussolini's Roman Empire* (New York: Bobbs-Merrill, 1938), violently anti-Italian (and anti-Catholic, as well); Herbert Matthews, *Two Wars and More to Come* (New York: Carrick and Evans, 1938), pp. 13–173; and J. F. C. Fuller, "The Italo-Ethiopian War: Military Analysis by an Eyewitness Observer," *Army Ordnance* 16, no. 96, May–June 1936.

3. Quoted in Garratt, *Mussolini's Roman Empire*, p. 123 n.

4. See the U.S. Army "special report" prepared by the Military Intelligence Division of the War Department, March 15, 1937, "Subject: Certain Studies on and Deductions from Operations of Italian Army in East Africa, October 1935–May 1936" (hereafter "Operations of Italian Army in East Africa"), on file in the U.S. Army Military History Institute at Carlisle Barracks in Carlisle, Pa. (hereafter MHI), p. 2. Rochat, *Guerre Italiane in Libia e in Etiopia*, p. 105, gives a round figure of 14,000.

5. Del Boca, *Ethiopian War*, p. 3; Fuller, "Italo-Ethiopian War," p. 341.

6. Del Boca, *Ethiopian War*, p. 21. See also Colonel Rudolf von Xylander, "Military Problems in Ethiopia," an English translation of an article that appeared in the December 1935 issue of *Wissen und Wehr*, p. 12ff. Prepared by the Translation Section of the U.S. Army War College, the document is on file at the MHI.

7. For the CV-33 tankette, see David Miller, *Illustrated Directory of Tanks of the World: From World War I to the Present Day* (London: Salamander Books, 2000), pp. 164–167. For the use of tank units in the campaign, see General Otto Schulz, "Die italienische Denkschrift über die Verwendung der grossen Einheiten in Abessinien," *Militär-Wochenblatt* 122, no. 10, September 3, 1937, pp. 588–591: "Light and heavy tanks, capable of overcoming anything, even the greatest terrain difficulties, can achieve great success if well-led" (p. 590). See also Michael Duffield, "Ethiopia: The Unconquered Lion of Africa," *Command* 4, May–June 1990, p. 17, especially interesting on Graziani's "proto-Blitzkrieg" in the Ogaden.

8. For orders of battle, extremely useful maps, and incredible levels of obfuscation and unconvincing self-exculpatory testimony, see Marshal Pietro Badoglio, *The War in Abyssinia* (London: Methuen, 1937), the English translation of his *La Guerra d'Etiopia*. For operations, see Lieutenant Colonel A. C. Arnold, "The Italo-Abyssinian Campaign, 1935–36," *Journal of the Royal United Service Institution* 82, no. 525, February 1937, pp. 71–88, and a lecture by the Italian military attaché in London, Colonel Count Ruggeri Laderchi, "Tactical and Administrative Lessons of the War in Abyssinia," *Journal of the Royal United Service Institution* 83, no. 530, May 1938, pp. 233–246.

9. Matthews, *Two Wars and More to Come,* p. 18.

10. "Operations of Italian Army in East Africa," pp. 46–47.

11. Ibid., p. 30.

12. Fuller, "Italo-Ethiopian War," p. 348.

13. Fuller's book on the Ethiopian War, *The First of the League Wars: Its Lessons and Omens* (London: Eyre and Spottiswoode, 1936), came under similar criticism in a review in the *Journal of the United Service Institution* 82, no. 525, February 1937, pp. 236–237. "General Fuller," the reviewer writes, "is inclined to twist facts to suit his purpose" (p. 237).

14. See Alex Danchev, "Liddell Hart and the Indirect Approach," *Journal of Military History* 63, no. 2, April 1999, pp. 313–337: "Liddell Hart wrote to be fed and to be famous. But he also wrote to be right, and to demonstrate his rightness to others."

15. B. H. Liddell Hart, *Europe in Arms* (London: Faber and Faber, 1937), pp. 304–320.

16. Ibid., p. 319.

17. "Operations of Italian Army in East Africa," p. 19.

18. Ibid., p. 24.

19. Herbert Matthews captured it better; it was "the last mad dash." *Two Wars and More to Come,* pp. 151–165.

20. "Operations of Italian Army in East Africa," p. 24.

21. For the Italian air force, see James J. Sadkovich, "The Development of the Italian Air Force Prior to World War II," *Military Affairs* 51, no. 3, July 1987, pp. 128–136.

22. [Solaire], "The Hare, the Tortoise, and the Eagle," *Journal of the Royal United Service Institution* 81, no. 521, February 1936, pp. 126–134.

23. Ibid., p. 134.

24. "Operations of Italian Army in East Africa," p. 46. See also Major Schüttel, "Die Mitwirkung der italienischen Luftwaffe am Niederbruch Abessiniens," *Militärwissenschaftliche Rundschau* 1, no. 4, 1936, pp. 546–548, for an evaluation of the reconnaissance and supply activity of Italian air units.

25. Quoted in Martelli, *Italy Against the World,* p. 269.

26. "Operations of Italian Army in East Africa," pp. 39–40.

27. Ibid., p. 39.

28. Ibid.

29. See the concluding remarks by Major General R. H. Haining in Arnold, "Italo-Abyssinian Campaign," p. 88.

30. Opinion on this subject among professional Italian soldiers was clear: native soldiers were far more useful in the African environment. "Native troops were superior to whites," wrote Italian major G. Caproni in the May 1936 edition of the *Rivista di artigleria e genio*. "They were capable of thirty to forty kilometers per day on the march, several days in a row, with scarcely any fatigue. Individual soldiers such as messengers sometimes traveled the incredible distance of eighty kilometers within twenty-four hours." Quoted in Lieutenant Colonel M. Braun, "Kriegseindrücke von der Somalifront," *Militär-Wochenblatt* 121, no. 5, August 4, 1936, pp. 220. See also "Erfahrungen Badoglios mit den einzelnen Waffengattungen," *Militär-Wochenblatt* 121, no. 19, November 18, 1936, pp. 990–992.

31. The genesis of the phrase "Spanish laboratory" is found in Ferdinand O. Miksche, *Attack: A Study of Blitzkrieg Tactics* (New York: Random House, 1942), pp. vi, 9, 11. Miksche was a Czech artillery officer who served in the Spanish Republican Army, the Ejercito Popular. For an analysis of Spain as a laboratory for weapons and doctrine, see two articles by John L. S. Daley: "An Experiment Reconsidered: The Theory and Practice of Armored Warfare in Spain: October 1936–February 1937," *Armor* 108, no. 2, March–April 1999, pp. 30, 39–43; and "Soviet and German Advisors Put Doctrine to the Test: Tanks in the Siege of Madrid," *Armor* 103, no. 3, May 1999, pp. 33–37.

32. The best single work on the Condor Legion is Raymond L. Proctor, *Hitler's Luftwaffe in the Spanish Civil War* (Westport, Conn.: Greenwood Press, 1983). See also Jesus Salas Larrazabal, *Air War over Spain* (London: Ian Allen, 1969); Karl Ries and Hans Ring, *The Legion Condor: A History of the Luftwaffe in the Spanish Civil War, 1939–1939* (West Chester, Pa.: Schiffer Military History, 1992); Gerald Howson, *Aircraft in the Spanish Civil War* (Washington, D.C.: Smithsonian Institution Press, 1990); Wilfred von Oven, *Hitler und der spanische Bürgerkrieg: Mission und Schicksal der Legion Condor* (Tübingen: Grabert, 1978); and James P. Werbaneth, "Fletching the Arrows: The Luftwaffe in Spain," *Command* 1, November–December 1989, pp. 52–53. For the most recent discussion of the Condor Legion, incorporating a number of new German sources, see James S. Corum, *The Luftwaffe: Creating the Operational Air War, 1918–1940* (Lawrence: University Press of Kansas, 1997), pp. 182–223. After a careful survey of the German documents, Corum argues, "There is no evidence that the German air attack on Guernica was a 'terror bombing' or that Guernica was carefully targeted to break the morale of the Basque populace." Rather, the raid was an attempt to cut off the "two major roads needed for the retreat of much of the twenty-three Basque battalions east of Bilbao," both of which intersected at Guernica (p. 199). In other words, the Condor Legion targeted it for legitimate operational reasons, although Corum does point out that the German air commander in Spain, Wolfram von Richtofen, "was a ruthless commander who never expressed any sympathy or concern for civilians who might be located in the vicinity of the military target" (p. 200). For the air war over Spain in general, see Corum, "The Spanish Civil War: Lessons Learned and Not Learned

by the Great Powers," *Journal of Military History* 62, no. 2, April 1998, pp. 313–334. On Guernica, see also Gordon Thomas and Max Morgan Witts, *Guernica: The Crucible of World War II* (New York: Stein and Day, 1975); and Herbert Southworth, *Guernica, Guernica: A Study of Journalism, Diplomacy, Propaganda, and History* (Berkeley: University of California Press, 1977). For an indication of how entrenched the old view still is, see Joe Zentner, "The Destruction of a Basque Town Served as a Model for Terror Bombing and Inspired an Anti-war Masterpiece," *Military History* 14, no. 2, June 1997, pp. 10–12.

33. The literature on the Spanish civil war is immense. For the origins of the *pronunciamento,* its failure, and the revolutionary uprising that it triggered, see the most recent edition of the standard work by Hugh Thomas, *The Spanish Civil War* (New York: Touchstone, 1986), pp. 1–196; Gabriel Jackson, *The Spanish Republic and the Civil War* (Princeton, N.J.: Princeton University Press, 1965), pp. 231–246; and Jackson, *A Concise History of the Spanish Civil War* (New York: John Day, 1974), pp. 11–25. Other important works include Hellmuth Dahms, *Der spanische Bürgerkrieg 1936–1939* (Tübingen: R. Wunderlich, 1962); Laurence Ernest Snellgrove, *Franco and the Spanish Civil War* (New York: McGraw-Hill, 1968); Frank Jellinek, *The Civil War in Spain* (New York: H. Fertig, 1969); Raymond Carr, *The Republic and the Civil War in Spain* (New York: St. Martin's Press, 1971); Jack Gibbs, *The Spanish Civil War* (London: E. Benn, 1973); Raymond Carr, *The Spanish Tragedy: The Civil War in Perspective* (London: Weidenfeld and Nicolson, 1977); Ronald Fraser, *Blood of Spain: An Oral History of the Spanish Civil War* (New York: Pantheon, 1979); Antony Beevor, *The Spanish Civil War* (London: Orbis, 1982); Burnett Bolloten, *The Spanish Civil War: Revolution and Counterrevolution* (Chapel Hill: University of North Carolina Press, 1991); Michael Alpert, *A New International History of the Spanish Civil War* (New York: St. Martin's Press, 1994); George Esenwein and Adrian Schubert, *Spain at War: The Spanish Civil War in Context, 1931–1939* (London: Longman, 1995); Paul Preston and Ann L. Mackenzie, eds., *The Republic Besieged: Civil War in Spain 1936–1939* (Edinburgh: Edinburgh University Press, 1996); and Harry Browne, *Spain's Civil War* (London: Longman, 1996). For a detailed account of military operations on the ground, see the series of weekly articles, spanning the entire war, published by German Colonel Rudolf von Xylander under the title *Vom spanischen Krieg.* For the origins of the war, see pt. 1, "Anlaß zum Bürgerkrieg," and pt. 2, "Der Ausbruch des Aufstandes," *Militär-Wochenblatt* 121, no. 19, November 18, 1936, pp. 942–946.

34. Jackson, *Spanish Republic,* pp. 245–246; Xylander, *Vom spanischen Krieg,* pt. 3, "Ausgangslage bei Beginn der Operationen," *Militär-Wochenblatt* 121, no. 20, November 25, 1936, pp. 1063–1068.

35. See Thomas, *Spanish Civil War,* pp. 501–502. For an account of the Legion, its origins, and its character, see the unsigned article "Die spanische Legionen," *Militär-Wochenblatt* 121, no. 46, May 28, 1937, pp. 2903–2905.

36. Jackson, *Spanish Republic,* pp. 248–249, mentions a figure of 15,000, but that is an evident misprint, based on the other figures he presents; Xylander, *Vom spanischen Krieg,* pt. 4, "Vorgänge bis Ende September 1936," *Militär-Wochenblatt*

121, no. 20, November 25, 1936, pp. 1063–1068, mentions nothing of the foreign aerial assistance but does admit that "the [Republican] ships had to show ever greater respect for Franco's superior airpower" in their efforts to close the straits to Nationalist shipping. For naval aspects of the war, see Vice-Admiral C. V. Usborne, "The Influence of Sea Power on the Fighting in Spain," *Journal of the Royal United Service Institution* 83, no. 529, February 1938, pp. 22–43.

37. For an operational-level analysis of this period, see Xylander, "Vorgänge bis Ende September 1936," which is particularly informative on General Mola's much slower advance from the north.

38. The best account of the Alcazar is Cecil D. Eby, *The Siege of the Alcazar* (New York: Random House, 1965). See also Jackson, *Spanish Republic*, pp. 271–273.

39. See Steven J. Zaloga, "Soviet Tank Operations in the Spanish Civil War," *Journal of Slavic Military Studies* 12, no. 3 (September 1999): 134–162.

40. The best account of American volunteers in the war is still Cecil D. Eby, *Between the Bullet and the Lie: American Volunteers in the Spanish Civil War* (New York: Holt, Rinehart and Winston, 1969).

41. For the battle of Madrid, centering on the storming of University City, see R. Dan Richardson, "The Defense of Madrid: Mysterious Generals, Red Front Fighters, and the International Brigades," *Military Affairs* 43, no. 4 (December 1979), pp. 178–185; Xylander, *Vom spanischen Krieg*, pt. 7, "Der Einbruch in Madrid," *Militär-Wochenblatt* 121, no. 29, January 29, 1937, pp. 1652–1657; Robert Garland Colodny, *The Struggle for Madrid: The Central Epic of the Spanish Conflict, 1936–37* (New York: Paine-Whitman, 1958); and Dan Kurzman, *Miracle of November: Madrid's Epic Stand, 1936* (New York: Putnam, 1980).

42. See the article by Brian R. Sullivan, "Fascist Italy's Military Involvement in the Spanish Civil War," *Journal of Military History* 59, no. 4, October 1995, pp. 697–727. In 1992–93, all three Italian services finally published official histories of their participation in the Spanish civil war.

43. See Robert H. Whealey, *Hitler and Spain: The Nazi Role in the Spanish Civil War, 1936–1939* (Lexington: University Press of Kentucky, 1989); Gerald Howson, *Arms for Spain: The Untold Story of the Spanish Civil War* (New York St. Martin's Press, 1999); and Corum, *Luftwaffe*, pp. 182–223.

44. See Colonel Antonio J. Candil, "Soviet Armor in Spain: Aid Mission to the Republicans Tested Doctrine and Equipment," *Armor* 108, no. 2, March–April 1999, pp. 31–38; and Daley, "Theory and Practice of Armored Warfare in Spain," p. 41. The amount of Soviet aid to the Republic is being revised down by new research. Thomas, *Spanish Civil War*, gives a figure of 900 Soviet tanks; Howson, *Arms for Spain,* gives 280 T-26s and 50 BT-5s.

45. For the Abraham Lincoln Battalion (later enlarged to a brigade), see Eby, *Bullet and the Lie;* Robert A. Rosenstone, *Crusade of the Left: The Lincoln Battalion in the Spanish Civil War* (New York: Pegasus, 1969); Carl Geiser, *Prisoners of the Good Fight: The Spanish Civil War, 1936–1939* (Westport, Conn.: L. Hill, 1986); John Gerassi, *The Premature Antifascists: North American Volunteers in the Spanish Civil War, 1936–39, an Oral History* (New York: Praeger, 1986); and Peter N. Carroll, *The Odyssey of*

the *Abraham Lincoln Brigade: Americans in the Spanish Civil War* (Stanford, Calif.: Stanford University Press, 1994). For Canadian volunteers in the war, see Victor Howard with Mac Reynolds, *The Mackenzie-Papineau Battalion: The Canadian Contingent in the Spanish Civil War* (Ottawa: Carleton University Press, 1986).

46. For the battle of Boadilla (or "the battle of the Coruña road"), see Esmond Romilly, *Boadilla* (London: Macdonald, 1971); Jackson, *Spanish Republic,* p. 333; Thomas, *Spanish Civil War,* pp. 487–491; Xylander, *Vom spanischen Krieg,* pt. 14, "Die Januarschlacht nordwestlich Madrid," *Militär-Wochenblatt* 121, no. 33, February 26, 1937, pp. 1941–1944.

47. For the battle of the Jarama, see Thomas, *Spanish Civil War,* pp. 588–594; Jackson, *Spanish Republic,* pp. 345–348; Jackson, *Spanish Civil War,* pp. 99–100; Xylander, *Vom spanischen Krieg,* pt. 16, "Varelas Vorstoß südostwärts Madrid," *Militär-Wochenblatt* 121, no. 36, March 19, 1937, pp. 2153–2155.

48. For the battle of Guadalajara, see Thomas, *Spanish Civil War,* pp. 596–605; Jackson, *Spanish Republic,* pp. 349–354; Jackson, *Spanish Civil War,* pp. 101–104; Xylander, *Vom spanischen Krieg,* pt. 19, "Die Schlacht von Guadalajara," *Militär-Wochenblatt* 121, no. 37, March 26, 1937, pp. 2237–2239; and pt. 20, "Der Rückschlag von Madrid," *Militär-Wochenblatt* 121, no. 42, April 30, 1937, pp. 2604–2607; Candil, "Soviet Armor in Spain," pp. 36–37.

49. A point made explicitly by Major Wanty, "A Year of War in Spain: Facts and Lessons," p. 17. Originally published in *La Revue d'Infanterie,* Paris in April 1938, it was translated into English by the Translation Section of the U.S. Army War College and is on file at the MHI. Citations are from the English translation.

50. Thomas, *Spanish Civil War,* p. 603.

51. The war was not mobile, in other words, in part because Franco did not wish it to be. He wanted to cleanse Spain in a bloodbath, one region at a time. See the appropriate sections in Paul Preston, *Franco: A Biography* (New York: Basic Books, 1994), and the comments by Sullivan, "Fascist Italy's Military Involvement in the Spanish Civil War," p. 726, which characterizes Franco's strategy as a "merciless war of attrition" against his ideological enemies.

52. George Orwell, *Homage to Catalonia* (New York: Harcourt, Brace, 1952), p. 21.

53. For the northern offensive, see Xylander, *Vom spanischen Krieg,* pt. 23, "Molas Angriff gegen Bilbao" *Militär-Wochenblatt* 121, no. 43, May 7, 1937, pp. 2674–2676; pt. 25, "Fortsetzung des Angriffs auf Bilbao," *Militär-Wochenblatt* 121, no. 45, May 21, 1937, pp. 2825–2828; pt. 29, "Vorbereitung der Eroberung Bilbaos," *Militär-Wochenblatt* 121, no. 43, May 7, 1937, pp. 2674–2676; pt. 25, "Fortsetzung des Angriffs auf Bilbao," *Militär-Wochenblatt* 122, no. 3, July 16, 1937, pp. 148–149; and pt. 20, "Die Einnahme von Bilbao," *Militär-Wochenblatt* 122, no. 4, July 27, 1937, pp. 210–214. For the Carlist role in the Spanish civil war, the "Fourth Carlist War," along with a great deal of information on the Requeté, see Martin Blinkhorn, *Carlism and Crisis in Spain, 1931–1939* (Cambridge: Cambridge University Press, 1975), especially pp. 251–261.

54. For Brunete, see Thomas, *Spanish Civil War,* pp. 710–717; Jackson, *Spanish Republic,* pp. 394–396, and *Spanish Civil War,* pp. 129–131; Xylander, *Vom spanischen*

· ·

Krieg, pt. 33, "Die erste Schlacht bei Brunete," *Militär-Wochenblatt* 122, no. 7, August 13, 1937, pp. 391–395; and pt. 34, "Die zweite Schlacht bei Brunete," *Militär-Wochenblatt* 122, no. 9, August 27, 1937, pp. 529–532.

55. Candil, "Soviet Armor in Spain," p. 37.

56. Ibid.

57. Howard, *Mackenzie-Papineau Battalion,* pp. 144–145.

58. Ibid., p. 145.

59. Ibid., p. 146.

60. Quoted in an article by General H. J. Reilly that appeared in *Illustration* (Paris), January 28, 1939. A translation entitled "The Queen of Battle Versus the Tanks" is on file at the MHI. The citation is from the translation, pp. 3–4.

61. Ibid., p. 5.

62. Ibid., p. 6.

63. V. Gusew, "Antitank Defense," *Krasnaya Zvesda,* Moscow, May 21, 1938. The Translation Section of the Army War College translated it into English, and it is on file at the MHI. Citation from the English translation, pp. 4–5.

64. Ibid., p. 5.

65. For Teruel, see Thomas, *Spanish Civil War,* pp. 788–794; Jackson, *Spanish Civil War,* pp. 133–138; Xylander, *Vom spanischen Krieg,* pt. 41, "Der rote Angriff gegen Teruel," *Militär-Wochenblatt* 122, no. 29, January 14, 1938, pp. 1825–1829; pt. 42, "Der Verlust Teruels," *Militär-Wochenblatt* 122, no. 32, February 4, 1938, pp. 2029–2032; pt. 43, "Eroberung der Sierra Palomera," *Militär-Wochenblatt* 122, no. 36, March 4, 1938, pp. 2301–2305; and pt. 45, "Die Wiedereroberung von Teruel," *Militär-Wochenblatt* 122, no. 40, April 1, 1938, pp. 2572–2573.

66. Quoted in Thomas, *Spanish Civil War,* p. 791.

67. For Franco's great breakthrough in Aragon, see Jackson, *Spanish Republic,* pp. 398–400; Jackson, *Spanish Civil War,* pp. 138–143; Thomas, *Spanish Civil War,* pp. 797–803; Xylander, *Vom spanischen Krieg,* pt. 46, "Der Durchbruch südlich des Ebro," *Militär-Wochenblatt* 122, no. 40, April 1, 1938, pp. 2574–2576; pt. 47, "Eindruck der Erfolge der Nationalen," pt. 48, "Neuer Angriff südlich des Ebro," and part 49, "Der Angriff nördlich des Ebro," *Militär-Wochenblatt* 122, no. 42, April 15, 1938, pp. 2695–2701; pt. 50, "Kampf um der Segre-Noguera Abschnitt," and pt. 51, "Schlacht von Tortosa," *Militär-Wochenblatt* 122, no. 43, April 22, 1938, pp. 2768–2771; pt. 52, "Durchbruch zum Meere," and pt. 53, "Rückwirkungen des nationalen Erfolges," *Militär-Wochenblatt* 122, no. 45, May 6, 1938, pp. 2894–2899.

68. For the Republic's Ebro offensive, see Xylander, *Vom spanischen Krieg,* pt. 64, "Die Roten gehen über den unteren Ebro," *Militär-Wochenblatt* 123, no. 10, September 2, 1938, pp. 620–624; pt. 65, "Ebro-Kämpfe und Entlastungsangriffe," *Militär-Wochenblatt* 123, no. 12, September 16, 1938, pp. 756–758; pt. 67, "Kämpfe in der ersten Septemberhälfte," *Militär-Wochenblatt* 123, no. 14, September 30, 1938, pp. 876–879; pt. 68, "Kämpfe von Mitte September bis zum ersten November-Drittel," *Militär-Wochenblatt* 123, no. 22, November 26, 1938, pp. 1430–1434; and pt. 69, "Das Ende der Ebroschlacht," *Militär-Wochenblatt* 123, no. 24, December 9, 1938, pp. 1575–1577.

69. B. H. Liddell Hart, *The German Generals Talk* (New York: Quill, 1979), pp. 92–93. See also Michael Alpert, "The Clash of Spanish Armies," *War in History* 6, no. 3, 1999, pp. 338–341. There were voices in Germany arguing against viewing Spain as a proving ground for tank doctrine. See, for example, Major Sieberg, "Beantwort der Krieg in Spanien die Frange, ob der moderne Panzerkampfwagen oder das moderne Abwehrgeschütz überlegen ist?" *Militär-Wochenblatt* 122, no. 33, February 11, 1938, pp. 2092–2097: "It would be a disastrous error to use events in Spain to draw conclusions that the massed use of tanks or the use of panzer divisions in a future war would have no hope of success. Massed tank attacks have not taken place, because neither side has the necessary numbers" (p. 2097).

70. Miksche, *Attack,* p. 171.

71. Thomas, *Spanish Civil War,* pp. 468.

72. Jackson, *Spanish Civil War,* p. 138.

73. See Daley, "Theory and Practice of Armored Warfare in Spain," p. 43.

74. Wanty, "A Year of War in Spain," pp. 22–23.

75. Daley, "Theory and Practice of Armored Warfare in Spain," pp. 41–42.

76. B. H. Liddell Hart, *The British Way in Warfare* (London: Faber and Faber, 1932).

77. For a German analysis of the "heavy tank" concept, see Helmut Burckhardt, "Grosstanks oder Massenangriff mit unzureichend gepanzerten Tanks?" *Militär-Wochenblatt* 122, no. 3, July 16, 1937, pp. 143–144. He argued that the notion of an "antitank-proof heavy tank" *(pak-sichere Grosstank)* was a myth, because technology guarantees that it would not be "antitank-proof" for long.

78. For the Carden-Lloyd and Morris-Martel, see Robert M. Citino, *Armored Forces: History and Sourcebook* (Westport, Conn.: Greenwood Press, 1994), pp. 45, 48, and the biographical profile of tank designer Giffard le Quesne Martel, p. 256.

79. On the limits of armor, see, for example, the article by Rittmeister Gerhard, "Oberstleutnant Perré, Hauptmann Liddell Hart—und wir," *Militär-Wochenblatt* 120, no. 3, July 18, 1935, pp. 105–106.

80. General Ludwig von Eimannsberger, "Panzertaktik," pt. 2, *Militär-Wochenblatt* 120, no. 24, December 25, 1935, p. 1028.

81. Quoted in Thomas, *Spanish Civil War,* p. 603.

82. Matthews, *Two Wars and More to Come,* p. 254.

83. Wanty, "A Year of War in Spain," pp. 23–25, 32–33.

84. A. Shebanow, "Infantry in Offensive Combat: Experience of the Spanish Civil War," *Krasnaya Zvesda,* Moscow, May 27, 1938, p. 4. An English translation, prepared by the Translation Section of the U.S. Army War College, is on file at the MHI.

85. Arthur Ehrhardt, "Airplane Versus Ground Motor: Lessons Gained from the Battle of Guadalajara," p. 6, originally published in *Wissen und Wehr,* Berlin, July 1938. An English translation, prepared by the Translation Section of the U.S. Army War College, is on file at the MHI. All citations are from the English translation.

86. Ibid., pp. 9–10. Ehrhardt quotes extensively from a report by Captain Didier Poulain, "Aircraft and Mechanized Land Warfare: The Battle of Guadalajara, 1937,"

Journal of the Royal United Service Institution 83, no. 530, May 1938, pp. 363–367. See also Poulain, "The Role of Aircraft in the Spanish Civil War," *Journal of the Royal United Service Institution* 83, no. 531, August 1938, pp. 581–586.

87. Liddell Hart, *Europe in Arms,* pp. 323–324, 331.

88. One contemporary officer accused Liddell Hart of preaching a "cult of the defensive," and it is a fair criticism. See Colonel R. H. Beadon, "Defence and Defeat," *Journal of the Royal United Service Institution* 83, no. 529, February 1938, pp. 59–61. It brought forth a spirited but not altogether convincing defense of Liddell Hart: Major E. W. Sheppard, "Does Defence Mean Defeat?" *Journal of the Royal United Service Institution* 83, no. 530, May 1938, pp. 291–298; a retort from Beadon in the correspondence section, *Journal of the Royal United Service Institution* 83, no. 531, August 1938, pp. 629–630; and another article attacking Liddell Hart: Captain H. M. Curteis, "The Doctrine of Limited Liability," *Journal of the Royal United Service Institution* 83, no. 532, November 1938, pp. 695–701. More recently, Antulio J. Echevarria II, *After Clausewitz: German Military Thinkers Before the Great War* (Lawrence: University Press of Kansas, 2000), pp. 4–5, has applied the same term, "cult of the defensive," to the writings of many modern historians of 1914.

89. For a contemporary German view of the difficulty in comparing different wars and eras, and the special danger in using the *Stellungskrieg* of World War I as a test of generalship, see General Georg Wetzell, "Kriegsgeschichtliche Vergleiche: Der Vernichtungsgedanke," *Militär-Wochenblatt* 124, no. 20, November 10, 1939, pp. 1051–1053.

90. See the considerable body of work by James S. Corum on this topic, especially *Luftwaffe*, pp. 219–223; "Spanish Civil War"; "The Luftwaffe's Army Support Doctrine, 1918–1941," *Journal of Military History* 59, no. 1, January 1995, pp. 53–76; and "From Biplanes to Blitzkrieg: The Development of German Air Doctrine Between the Wars," *War in History* 3, no. 1, 1996, pp. 85–101. Corum effectively refutes what had long been the scholarly consensus: that Spain retarded Germany's strategic bombing effort and recast the Luftwaffe in a narrow "tactical" role. See Proctor, *Hitler's Luftwaffe in the Spanish Civil War.*

Chapter 8. Operational Art Reborn

1. See, for example, Philip S. Meilinger, "Trenchard and 'Morale Bombing': The Evolution of Royal Air Force Doctrine Before World War II," *Journal of Military History* 60, no. 2, April 1996, pp. 243–270.

2. See James S. Corum, *The Luftwaffe: Creating the Operational Air War, 1918–1940* (Lawrence: University Press of Kansas, 1997), which stresses the operational significance of the 1935 Luftwaffe regulations, *The Conduct of the Air War.*

3. Review of Air Commodore L. E. O. Charlton, *War over England* (London: Longmans, Green, 1936), in *Journal of the Royal United Service Institution* 81, no. 524, November 1936, p. 922. The reviewer mocks the author's ideal world as "incidentally, a world in which all sensational journalism would be rigorously repressed as tending to upset the complete equality of life." For an overview of lit-

erature by Charlton and other "prophets of doom," see Philip S. Meilinger, "The Historiography of Airpower: Theory and Doctrine," *Journal of Military History* 64, no. 2, April 2000, pp. 467–501.

4. "Army Notes: France," *Journal of the Royal United Service Institution* 81, no. 521, February 1936, pp. 209–212.

5. For Italian doctrine in the interwar period, see John J. T. Sweet, *Iron Arm: The Mechanization of Mussolini's Army, 1920–1940* (Westport, Conn.: Greenwood Press, 1980). On Maltese, see pp. 56–58; for Zoppi, pp. 80–82; and for Bitossi, pp. 82–84. See also Enzio Rivus, "Die Tankwaffe Italiens," *Militär-Wochenblatt* 121, no. 4, July 25, 1936, pp. 179–182, for descriptions, photographs, and line drawings of Italian tanks.

6. Lieutenant Colonel M. Braun, "Motorisierte Gedankensplitter aus aller Welt," pt. 6, "Die neue italienische Inf.-Versuchsdivision 'Binaria,'" *Militär-Wochenblatt* 123, no. 21, November 18, 1938, pp. 1345–1347. For a modern verdict, see Brian R. Sullivan, "Fascist Italy's Military Involvement in the Spanish Civil War," *Journal of Military History* 59, no. 4, October 1995, p. 709: the divisions were "too weak against opponents better armed than the Ethiopians and—lacking a third infantry regiment—too inflexible in maneuver."

7. Lieutenant Colonel Himpe, "Die italienischen Manöver in den Abruzzen," *Militär-Wochenblatt* 123, no. 11, September 9, 1938, pp. 679–684. The cover of this issue sports a very interesting photograph of Bersaglieri advancing up a mountain road by bicycle column. Sweet, *Iron Arm,* pp. 146–147, downplays the maneuvers and does not discuss the binary division at all. For the fall 1939 Italian maneuvers of the "Po Army," see Lieutenant Colonel Himpe, "Die grossen Manöver der Po-Armee," pt. 1, *Militär-Wochenblatt* 124, no. 10, September 1, 1939, pp. 605–609; and pt. 2, *Militär-Wochenblatt* 124, no. 11, September 8, 1939, pp. 671–674.

8. During the interwar era, German military authors habitually labeled diagrams with the admonition "Nicht ein Schema!" ("Not a formula!"). See John A. English and Bruce I. Gudmundsson, *On Infantry* (Westport, Conn.: Praeger, 1994), p. 51.

9. Major J. K. Edwards, "The Functions of Tanks," *Journal of the Royal United Service Institution* 80, no. 517, February 1935, p. 104.

10. For the German conquest of Poland, see the recent article by David T. Zabecki, "Invasion of Poland: Campaign That Launched a War," *World War II* 14, no. 3, September 1999, pp. 26ff. Robert M. Kennedy, *The German Campaign in Poland, 1939,* Department of the Army Pamphlet no. 20-255 (Washington, D.C.: Department of the Army, 1956), continues to be useful, as does Matthew Cooper, *The German Army, 1933–1945* (Chelsea, Mich.: Scarborough House, 1978), pp. 169–176. See also the pertinent sections in the memoir literature: Heinz Guderian, *Panzer Leader* (New York: Ballantine, 1957), pp. 46–63; Erich von Manstein, *Lost Victories* (Novato, Calif.: Presidio, 1982), pp. 22–63; and F. W. von Mellenthin, *Panzer Battles: A Study of the Employment of Armor in the Second World War* (New York: Ballantine, 1956), pp. 3–9. A recent work, drawn from Polish sources, is Steven J. Zaloga and Victory Madej, *The Polish Campaign* (New York: Hippocrene, 1991). For a blow-by-blow account while it was happening, see *Deutschlands Abwehrkrieg*

von 1939, pt. 1, "Die Ereignisse im Osten vom 1. bis 9. September," *Militär-Wochenblatt* 124, no. 12, September 15, 1939, pp. 729–733; pt. 2, "Die Ereignisse im Osten vom 9. September bis 16. September," *Militär-Wochenblatt* 124, no. 13, September 22, 1939, pp. 769–774; and pt. 3, "Die Ereignisse in Polen vom 17. bis 24. September," *Militär-Wochenblatt* 124, no. 14, October 1, 1939, pp. 809–813.

11. Dennis Showalter, "Blitzkrieg," in *Reader's Companion to Military History,* ed. Robert Cowley and Geoffrey Parker (Boston: Houghton Mifflin, 1996), p. 57, gives the September 1939 date, which has been generally accepted. But see, for example, Major E. W. Sheppard, "How Wars End," *Journal of the Royal United Service Institution* 84, no. 535, August 1939, p. 533: "Incidentally, history lends little support to the theory of the *Blitzkrieg,* that a sudden overwhelming blow at the very outset of a war can paralyze all hostile means of resistance and ensure a lightning victory," a passage written before the start of the war. See also the review of Fritz Sternberg, *Germany and a Lightning War* (London: Faber and Faber, 1939), in *Journal of the Royal United Service Institution* 84, no. 534, May 1939, p. 449, which specifies its being "translated by Edward Fitzgerald" (presumably from the German?). For the most recent analyses, see George Raudzens, "Blitzkrieg Ambiguities: Doubtful Usage of a Famous Word," *War and Society* 7, September 1989, pp. 77–94; and William A. Fanning Jr., "The Origins of the Term 'Blitzkrieg': Another View," *Journal of Military History* 61, no. 61 (April 1997): 283–302. No doubt there is more to be said on this topic.

12. Rolf Bathe, *Der Feldzug der 18 Tage: Die Chronik des polnischen Dramas* (Oldenburg: Gerhard Stalling, 1939). Zaloga and Madej address the "myth of the 'eighteen-day war'" in *Polish Campaign,* p. 158, pointing out that Army Group South "lost more men killed in the final half of the war than in the first two weeks."

13. Nis Petersen, "Polens Vernichtung als Vorschule für den genialen Durchbruch der deutschen Panzerwaffe im Westen," *Militär-Wochenblatt* 125, no. 10, September 6, 1940, p. 377.

14. For a detailed operational account of the fighting around Modlin, see Major Wim Brandt, "Bilder aus der Belagerung von Modlin," *Militär-Wochenblatt* 124, no. 30, January 19, 1940, pp. 1451–1454.

15. Corum, *Luftwaffe,* pp. 272–275.

16. For the battle of the Bzura, see Zaloga and Madej, *Polish Campaign,* pp. 131–138.

17. Ibid., pp. 138–141.

18. The original Halder plan is discussed and diagrammed in Cooper, *German Army,* pp. 196–197.

19. General Walter Warlimont of the Armed Forces High Command (OKW) described the revised plan as resulting from "considerable further discussion between Hitler and the senior officers of the OKW on the one side and the Army Commander-in-Chief [Brauchitsch] and Chief of Staff [Halder] on the other." See Warlimont, *Inside Hitler's Headquarters* (Novato, Calif.: Presidio, 1991), p. 51.

20. A number of published works chronicle the controversy over the German operational plan in 1940; none do so more passionately than Erich von Manstein,

Lost Victories, pp. 94–126; the quotation is taken from p. 98. See also J. F. C. Fuller, *A Military History of the Western World,* vol. 3, *From the American Civil War to the End of World War II* (New York: Da Capo, 1956), pp. 386–389; John Williams, *The Ides of May: The Defeat of France, May–June 1940* (New York: Knopf, 1968), pp. 63–72; Alistair Horne, *To Lose a Battle: France 1940* (Boston: Little, Brown, 1969), pp. 138–168; Cooper, *German Army,* pp. 198–216; Jeffrey A. Gunsburg, *Divided and Conquered: The French High Command and the Defeat in the West, 1940* (Westport, Conn.: Greenwood Press, 1979), pp. 148–150; B. H. Liddell Hart, *The German Generals Talk* (New York: Quill, 1979), pp. 105–117; Robert A. Doughty, *The Breaking Point: Sedan and the Fall of France, 1940* (Hamden, Conn.: Archon, 1990), pp. 19–26; Florian K. Rothbrust, *Guderian's XIXth Panzer Corps and the Battle of France: Breakthrough in the Ardennes, May 1940* (Westport, Conn.: Praeger, 1990), pp. 1–15; and Robert M. Citino, *Armored Forces: History and Sourcebook* (Westport, Conn.: Greenwood Press, 1994), pp. 69–75.

21. Manstein, *Lost Victories,* p. 99.

22. Rothbrust, *Guderians' XIXth Panzer Corps,* pp. 114–118, contains diagrams of all the various permutations of the Halder plan, as well as the Manstein proposal.

23. Guderian, *Panzer Leader,* pp. 67–68.

24. For the Mechelen incident, see Gunsburg, *Divided and Conquered,* pp. 136–148 and Doughty, *Breaking Point,* pp. 23–24.

25. Liddell Hart, *German Generals Talk,* p. 117.

26. The Churchillian term has entered the military history of the campaign. See Rothbrust, *Guderians' XIXth Panzer Corps,* p. 15. It even appears as the German term *Sichelschnitt,* although the Germans do not appear to have used it. See Horne, *To Lose a Battle,* p. 167.

27. Quoted in Horne, *To Lose a Battle,* p. 164.

28. For a German view of the "Saar offensive," see *Deutschlands Abwehrkrieg von 1939,* pt. 5, "Der Kampf gegen Frankreich vom 3. bis 30. September," *Militär-Wochenblatt* 124, no. 16, October 13, 1939, p. 890.

29. For "Plan D," see Doughty, *Breaking Point,* pp. 8–18; as well as Gunsburg, *Divided and Conquered,* pp. 119–146, 270–274, who argues that the move into Belgium was necessary "in order to solder the Dutch, Belgian, and British forces together with the French into a coherent front in an advantageous position" and "to build an Allied front in northeastern Belgium and the southeastern Netherlands—near the Ruhr—in which all the Allies shared a vital interest" (p. 270).

30. The extremely short duration of the 1940 campaign in the west ("the Flanders campaign," the Germans called it) has lent itself to detailed historical treatment. For day-to-day accounts, see Rothbrust, *Guderians' XIXth Panzer Corps,* pp. 45–88; Gunsburg, *Divided and Conquered,* pp. 168–228. Doughty, *Breaking Point,* is the most meticulous and detailed, subjecting the battle of Sedan to careful scrutiny and examining the operations and tactics of both sides. See also the general accounts (Horne, *To Lose a Battle;* Williams, *Ides of May*), as well as the memoirs of Guderian, *Panzer Leader,* pp. 67–98, and Mellenthin, *Panzer Battles,* pp. 10–30. For the German view of the campaign as it was unfolding, see the series of articles entitled

Grossdeutschlands Freiheitskrieg 1940, pt. 41, "Die deutsche Maioffensive and der Westfront in den Tagen vom 10. bis 17. Mai 1940," *Militär-Wochenblatt* 124, no. 47, May 24, 1940, pp. 2121–2127; pt. 42, "Die deutsche Maioffensive and der Westfront in den Tagen vom 17. bis 23. Mai 1940," *Militär-Wochenblatt* 124, no. 48, May 31, 1940, pp. 2161–2170; and especially pt. 43, "Die Kapitulation der belgischen Armee und die Vernichtung der englischen und französischen Armeen in Flandern und im Artois in den Tagen von 24. Mai bis 1. Juni 1940," *Militär-Wochenblatt* 124, no. 49, June 7, 1940, pp. 2201–2207.

31. For the campaign in the Netherlands, see two articles by David Meyler in *Command* 42, March 1997: "Missed Opportunities: the Ground War in Holland," pp. 58–69, and "To Sow the Wind: The Luftwaffe's Campaign in the Netherlands, 10–14 May 1940," pp. 70–76. For the consequences of the Dutch surrender, see *Grossdeutschlands Freiheitskrieg, 1940*, pt. 41, "Die deutsche Maioffensive an der Westfront in den Tagen von 10. bis 17 Mai, 1940," *Militär-Wochenblatt* 124, no. 47, May 24, 1940, pp. 2125–2126.

32. For the glider assault on Eben Emael, see James E. Mrazek, *The Fall of Eben Emael* (Novato, Calif.: Presidio, 1991). For the armored battle near Gembloux, see Jeffrey A. Gunsburg, "The Battle of the Belgian Plain, 12–14 May 1940: The First Great Tank Battle," *Journal of Military History* 56, no. 2, April 1992, pp. 207–244.

33. For the crossing of the 7th Panzer Division, see Williams, *Ides of May*, pp. 125–126; and Russel H. S. Stolfi, *A Bias for Action: The German 7th Panzer Division in France and Russia, 1940–1941*, Marine Corps University Series Perspectives on Warfighting 1 (Quantico, Va.: Marine Corps Association, 1991), pp. 1–17.

34. For French defenses along the Meuse, see Williams, *Ides of May*, pp. 108–122; Gunsburg, *Divided and Conquered*, pp. 185–186, 189–192; and Doughty, *Breaking Point*, pp. 101–130.

35. Quoted in Williams, *Ides of May*, p. 130.

36. Guderian, *Panzer Leader*, p. 79; Doughty, *Breaking Point*, p. 133; Rothbrust, *Guderian's XIXth Panzer Corps*, p. 69.

37. Quoted in Fuller, *Military History of the Western World*, 3:393 n. 2.

38. One British officer characterized the air attacks as "caution, safety first, and too late, the usual sequence. . . . All the dash and drive is left to the Germans." Quoted in Williams, *Ides of May*, p. 155.

39. For the destruction of the 1st DCR, see Kenneth Macksey, *Tank Versus Tank: The Illustrated Story of Armored Battlefield Conflict in the Twentieth Century* (New York: Barnes and Noble, 1999), pp. 68–74.

40. *Grossdeutschlands Freiheitskrieg 1940*, pt. 42, "Die deutsche Maioffensive in den Tagen von 17. bis 23. Mai 1940," *Militär-Wochenblatt* 124, no. 48, May 31, 1940, pp. 2162–2163.

41. Stolfi, *Bias for Action*, pp. 13, 32, 100–119. For the *eingeschlossen-eingetroffen* mix-up, see p. 10. For the importance of radio in the campaign, see also Heinz Guderian's little-known article, "Armored Warfare: Consideration of the Past and Future," *Armored Cavalry Journal* 58, no. 1, January–February, 1949, p. 3.

42. Quoted in Liddell Hart, *German Generals Talk,* p. 128.

43. Quoted in Cooper, *German Army,* p. 224.

44. For the "reconnaissance in force," see Guderian, *Panzer Leader,* p. 88.

45. For the Allied attacks at Montcornet, Crécy, and Arras, see Horne, *To Lose a Battle,* pp. 425–430, 498–509; Gunsburg, *Divided and Conquered,* pp. 231–234, 245–246, 249–250. Macksey, *Tank Versus Tank,* pp. 74–80, is especially good on Arras.

46. See Corum, *Luftwaffe,* pp. 275–280.

47. See, for example, the speech by President Roosevelt to a joint session of the Senate and House of Representatives on May 16, 1940, in which he warned that "motorized armies can now sweep through enemy territories at the rate of two hundred miles per day." Quoted in Doughty, *Breaking Point,* p. 2.

48. For the most detailed examination of the campaign in Norway, as well as the fighting there throughout the whole war, see Adam Claasen, *Hitler's Northern War: The Luftwaffe's Ill-Fated Campaign, 1940–1945* (Lawrence: University Press of Kansas, 2001).

49. A point emphasized by Larry H. Addington, *The Blitzkrieg Era and the German General Staff, 1865–1941* (New Brunswick, N.J.: Rutgers University Press, 1971).

50. See Lieutenant Colonel Gaul, "Der Blitzkrieg in Frankreich," *Militär-Wochenblatt* 125, no. 35, February 28, 1941, pp. 1513–1517, a discussion of the French General Staff's report on the 1940 campaign.

51. See Russel H. S. Stolfi, "Equipment for Victory in France in 1940," *History* 52, February 1970, pp. 1–20, which exploded the myth of the technical superiority of German tanks in the French campaign. For a more recent analysis, see K. H. Frieser, *Blitzkrieg Legende: Der Westfeldzug 1940* (Munich: R. Oldenburg, 1995).

52. Marc Bloch, *Strange Defeat: A Statement of Evidence Written in 1940* (New York: Norton, 1968), pp. 47–48.

53. *Grossdeutschlands Freiheitskrieg 1940,* pt. 44, "Der Abschluss der Vernichtungschlacht in Flandern und im Artois sowie der Beginn der neuen deutschen Offensive über die Somme und den Oise–Aisne-Kanal in der Woche vom 2. bis 8.6.1940," *Militär-Wochenblatt* 124, no. 50, June 14, 1940, p. 2245.

54. Lieutenant Colonel Guse, "Ein modernes Austerlitz," *Militär-Wochenblatt* 125, no. 20, November 15, 1940, pp. 947–949.

55. Lieutenant Colonel Köhn, "Die Infanterie im 'Blitzkrieg,'" *Militär-Wochenblatt* 125, no. 5, August 2, 1940, p. 165.

56. Ibid., p. 166.

57. Rittmeister F. Kronberger, "'Es gibt Fälle, wo das höchste Wagen die höchste Weisheit ist,'" *Militär-Wochenblatt* 125, no. 7, August 16, 1940, p. 249.

58. Ibid., p. 250.

59. Colonel Rudolf Theiss, "Der Panzer in der Weltgeschichte," *Militär-Wochenblatt* 125, no. 15, October 11, 1940, pp. 705–708.

60. Ibid., p. 706.

61. Ibid., p. 708.

62. Ibid., p. 706.

63. Ibid., p. 708.

64. Lieutenant Colonel Völkel, "Tchingis-Chan als Vorbild und Lehrmeister des modernen Pz.-Kavalleristen," *Militär-Wochenblatt* 126, no. 12, September 19, 1941, p. 322.

65. General Fritz Willich, "Clausewitz und der jetzige Krieg," *Militär-Wochenblatt* 125, no. 1, July 5, 1940, p. 9.

66. General of Artillery Ludwig, "Die Operation auf der inneren und der äußeren Linie im Lichte unserer Zeit," *Militär-Wochenblatt* 126, no. 1, July 4, 1941, pp. 7–10.

67. Colonel Achsenbrandt, "Die Bedeutung des Anfangserfolges im Kriege," *Militär-Wochenblatt* 125, no. 51, June 20, 1941, pp. 1965–1968.

68. The article is by a Hungarian general, Otto Tövisházy-Ferjentsik, "Adolf Hitler als Feldherr: Der Meister des Überraschungskrieges," *Militär-Wochenblatt* 125, no. 48, May 30, 1941, pp. 1875–1877.

69. Hans Wolf Rode, "Das Kriegserlebnis von 1939 und 1914," *Militär-Wochenblatt* 125, no. 46, May 16, 1941, p. 1826.

70. Lieutenant Colonel Oheimb, "Motor und Kriegführung," *Militär-Wochenblatt* 125, no. 36, March 7, 1941, pp. 1547–1549; and General Liebmann, "Der Anteil des Motors am deutschen Siege," *Militär-Wochenblatt* 126, no. 1, July 4, 1941, pp. 10–12.

71. General of Artillery Ludwig, "Die Einkesselung," *Militär-Wochenblatt* 126, no. 11, September 12, 1941, p. 286.

72. General Ernst Kabisch, "Systemlose Strategie," *Militär-Wochenblatt* 125, no. 26, December 27, 1940, pp. 1234–1237.

73. Nis Petersen, "Die deutsche Land- und Luftkriegführung im ersten Kriegsjahre," *Militär-Wochenblatt* 125, no. 24, December 13, 1940, p. 1147.

74. Showalter, "Blitzkrieg," p. 58.

75. Colonel Rudolf Theiss, "Vom Tank zur Panzerwaffe," *Militär-Wochenblatt* 126, no. 7, August 15, 1941, pp. 176–180.

76. This is the response of many who resist the notion that the U.S. Army might profit from a study of German doctrinal transformation in the 1930s. See Bruce I. Gudmundsson, "Maneuver Warfare: The German Tradition," in *Maneuver Warfare: An Anthology*, ed. Richard D. Hooker (Novato, Calif.: Presidio, 1993), p. 287. For a strongly worded essay on the way in which German terms and concepts can be misused within the contemporary U.S. Army, see Daniel J. Hughes, "Abuses of German Military History," *Military Review* 65, no. 12, December 1986, pp. 66–76. See also the two-round debate between John Sloan Brown and Colonel Trevor N. Dupuy in the pages of *Military Affairs*, in which Brown took issue with Dupuy's mathematical model for assessing combat effectiveness: Brown, "Colonel Trevor N. Dupuy and the Mythos of Wehrmacht Superiority: A Reconsideration," *Military Affairs* 50, no. 1, January 1986, pp. 16–20; Dupuy, "The Quantified Judgment Model and German Combat Effectiveness," *Military Affairs* 50, no. 4, October 1986, pp. 204–210; Brown, "The Wehrmacht Mythos Revisited: A Challenge for Colonel Trevor N. Dupuy," *Military Affairs* 51, no. 3, July 1987, pp. 146–147; and Dupuy, "A Response to 'The Wehrmacht Mythos Revisited,'" *Military Affairs* 51, no. 4, October 1987, pp. 196–197.

WORKS CITED

Achsenbrandt, Colonel. "Die Bedeutung des Anfangserfolges im Kriege." *Militär-Wochenblatt* 125, no. 51, June 20, 1941.

Addington, Larry H. *The Blitzkrieg Era and the German General Staff, 1865–1941.* New Brunswick, N.J.: Rutgers University Press, 1971.

———. *The Patterns of War Since the Eighteenth Century.* Bloomington: Indiana University Press, 1994.

Allison, Brigadier General James N. "Notes on the War in the Balkans." *Journal of the Military Service Institution* 3, no. 182, March–April 1913.

Alpert, Michael. "The Clash of Spanish Armies." *War in History* 6, no. 3, 1999.

———. *A New International History of the Spanish Civil War.* New York: St. Martin's Press, 1994.

"Army Notes: France." *Journal of the Royal United Service Institution* 81, no. 521, February 1936.

Arnold, Lieutenant Colonel A. C. "The Italo-Abyssinian Campaign, 1935–36." *Journal of the Royal United Service Institution* 82, no. 525, February 1937.

Arnold, Joseph C. "French Tactical Doctrine, 1870–1914." *Military Affairs* 42, no. 2, April 1978.

Ashmead-Bartlett, Ellis. *With the Turks in Thrace.* New York: George H. Doran, 1913.

Asprey, Robert B. *The First Battle of the Marne.* Philadelphia: Lippincott, 1962.

Badoglio, Marshal Pietro. *The War in Abyssinia.* London: Methuen, 1937.

Badsey, Stephen. "Cavalry and the Development of Breakthrough Doctrine." In *British Fighting Methods in the Great War,* edited by Paddy Griffith. London: Frank Cass, 1996.

Baentsch, Lieutenant Colonel Alfred. "Der Motor in der Durchbruchsschlacht." *Militärwissenschaftliche Rundschau* 3, no. 1, 1938.

Baldwin, Hanson. *World War I: An Outline History.* New York: Harper and Row, 1962.

Barbary, James. *The Crimean War.* New York: Hawthorn, 1970.

Barbusse, Henri. *Le Feu: Journal d'une Escouade.* Paris: E. Flammarion, 1916.

Barker, A. J. *The Rape of Ethiopia, 1936.* New York: Ballantine, 1971.

Barnett, Correlli. *The Swordbearers: Supreme Command in the First World War.* Bloomington: Indiana University Press, 1963.

Barthorp, Michael. *The Anglo-Boer Wars: The British and the Afrikaners, 1815–1902.* New York: Blandford Press, 1987.

Bateman, Robert L., III. "Avoiding Information Overload." *Military Review* 78, no. 4, July 1998.

Bathe, Rolf. *Der Feldzug der 18 Tage: Die Chronik des polnischen Dramas.* Oldenburg: Gerhard Stalling, 1939.

Bauer, Colonel Max. *Der grosse Krieg in Feld und Heimat.* Tübingen: Osiander'sche Buchhandlung, 1921.

Beadon, Colonel R. H. "Defence and Defeat." *Journal of the Royal United Service Institution* 83, no. 529, February 1938.

———. "Some Strategical Theories of Captain Liddell Hart." *Journal of the Royal United Service Institution* 81, no. 524, November 1936.

Beevor, Antony. *The Spanish Civil War.* London: Orbis, 1982.

Bell, P. M. H. *The Origins of the Second World War in Europe.* London: Longman, 1986.

Bell, Ron. "The Russo-Japanese War, 1904–1905: The Land Campaigns." *Command* 19, November–December 1992.

Bertkau, Major Friedrich. "Die nachrichtentechnische Führung mechanisierter Verbände." *Militär-Wochenblatt* 120, no. 15, October 18, 1935.

Bidwell, Shelford, and Dominick Graham. *Fire-Power: British Army Weapons and Theories of War, 1904–1945.* London: Allen and Unwin, 1982.

Bird, Major-General W. D. *An Account of the Battle of Liao-yang.* Aldershot: Gale and Polden, n.d.

———. *Lectures on the Strategy of the Russo-Japanese War.* London: Hugh Rees, 1911.

Birkbeck, Colonel W. H. "The Battle of Mukden: Action of the Cavalry of the Third Army." In *The Russo-Japanese War: Reports from British Officers Attached to the Japanese Forces in the Field.* London: General Staff, 1907.

———. "The Battle of Mukden: Operations of the Third Japanese Army." In *The Russo-Japanese War: Reports from British Officers Attached to the Japanese Forces in the Field.* London: General Staff, 1907.

Blinkhorn, Martin. *Carlism and Crisis in Spain, 1931–1939.* Cambridge: Cambridge University Press, 1975.

Bloch, Marc. *Strange Defeat: A Statement of Evidence Written in 1940.* New York: Norton, 1968.

Blond, Georges. *The Marne.* London: Macdonald, 1965.

Bolloten, Burnett. *The Spanish Civil War: Revolution and Counterrevolution.* Chapel Hill: University of North Carolina Press, 1991.

Bond, Brian. *British Military Policy Between the Two World Wars.* Oxford: Clarendon Press, 1980.

———. *Liddell Hart: A Study of His Military Thought.* New Brunswick, N.J.: Rutgers University Press, 1977.

———. *The Pursuit of Victory: From Napoleon to Saddam Hussein.* Oxford: Oxford University Press, 1996.

Bond, Brian, and Nigel Cave, eds. *Haig: A Reappraisal 70 Years On.* London: Leo Cooper, 1999.

Borgert, Heinz-Ludger. "Grundzüge der Landkriegführung von Schlieffen bis Guderian." *Handbuch zur deutschen Militärgeschichte 1648–1939,* Vol. 9, *Grundzüge der militärischen Kriegführung.* Munich: Bernard & Graefe, 1979.

Boucabeille, Lieutenant-Colonel. *La Guerre Turco-Balkanique 1912–1913: Thrace—Macédoine—Albanie—Epire.* Paris: Librairie Chapelot, 1914.

Brandt, Major Wim. "Bilder aus der Belagerung von Modlin." *Militär-Wochenblatt* 124, no. 30, January 19, 1940.

———. "Die Tankerfahrungen des Chacokrieges." *Militär-Wochenblatt* 120, no. 35, March 18, 1936.

Braun, Major M. "Gedanken über Kampfwagen- und Fliegerverwendung bei den russischen Herbstmanövern 1936." *Militär-Wochenblatt* 121, no. 28, January 22, 1937.

———. "Kriegseindrücke von der Somalifront." *Militär-Wochenblatt* 121, no. 5, August 4, 1936.

———. "Motorisierte Gedankensplitter aus aller Welt," pt. 6, "Die neue italienische Inf.-Versuchsdivision 'Binaria.'" *Militär-Wochenblatt* 123, no. 21, November 18, 1938.

British Army. *The Russo-Japanese War: Reports from British Officers Attached to the Japanese Forces in the Field,* 3 vols. London: General Staff, 1907.

Brooks, Richard. "The Italian Campaign of 1859." *Military History* 16, no. 2, June 1999.

Brown, John Sloan. "Colonel Trevor N. Dupuy and the Mythos of Wehrmacht Superiority: A Reconsideration." *Military Affairs* 50, January 1986.

———. "The Wehrmacht Mythos Revisited: A Challenge for Colonel Trevor N. Dupuy." *Military Affairs* 51, July 1987.

Brown, Major R. A. "Why the Bulgarians Did Not Enter Constantinople: Bulgarian Operations Ending with the Battle of Tchataldja, November 17 and 18, 1912." *Journal of the Military Service Institution* 53, no. 185, September–October 1913.

Browne, Harry. *Spain's Civil War.* London: Longman, 1996.

Brückner, Lieutenant Colonel. "Der Durchbruchsangriff vor dem Weltkriege in Anwendung und Theorie." *Militärwissenschaftliche Rundschau* III, 6, 1938.

Bucholz, Arden. *Moltke, Schlieffen, and Prussian War Planning.* Providence, R.I.: Berg, 1991.

Büdingen, Lieutenant Colonel. "Flak gegen Tanks im Weltkriege." *Militär-Wochenblatt* 125, no. 11, September 13, 1941.

Burckhardt, Helmut. "Grosstanks oder Massenangriff mit unzureichend gepanzerten Tanks?" *Militär-Wochenblatt* 122, no. 3, July 16, 1937.

Candil, Colonel Antonio J. "Soviet Armor in Spain: Aid Mission to the Republicans Tested Doctrine and Equipment." *Armor* 108, no. 2, March–April 1999.

Carr, Raymond. *The Republic and the Civil War in Spain.* New York: St. Martin's Press, 1971.

———. *The Spanish Tragedy: The Civil War in Perspective.* London: Weidenfeld and Nicolson, 1977.

Carroll, Peter N. *The Odyssey of the Abraham Lincoln Brigade: Americans in the Spanish Civil War.* Stanford, Calif.: Stanford University Press, 1994.

Carver, Field Marshal Lord Michael. *The Apostles of Mobility.* London: Weidenfeld and Nicolson, 1979.

Chandler, David G. "Cambrai: The British Onslaught." In *Tanks and Weapons of World War I*, edited by Bernard Fitzsimons. London: Phoebus, 1973.

———. *The Campaigns of Napoleon.* New York: Macmillan, 1966.

Charlton, L. E. O. *War over England.* London: Longmans, Green, 1936.

Cherry, R. G. "Synopsis of the Battle of the Sha-Ho, October 1904." *Journal of the Royal Artillery* 40, no. 9, December 1913.

Childers, Erskine. *In the Ranks of the C.I.V.* London: Smith, Elder, 1901.

Childs, David J. *A Peripheral Weapon: The Production and Employment of British Tanks in the First World War.* Westport, Conn.: Greenwood Press, 1999.

Churchill, Winston. *The Boer War.* New York: Dorset Press, 1991.

———. *The Unknown War: The Eastern Front.* New York: Scribner's, 1932.

Citino, Robert M. *Armored Forces: History and Sourcebook.* Westport, Conn.: Greenwood Press, 1994.

———. *The Evolution of Blitzkrieg Tactics: Germany Defends Itself Against Poland, 1918–1933.* Westport, Conn.: Greenwood Press, 1987.

———. *The Path to Blitzkrieg: Doctrine and Training in the German Army, 1920–1939.* Boulder, Colo.: Lynne Rienner, 1998.

———. "The Weimar Roots of German Military Planning." In *Military Planning and the Origins of the Second World War in Europe*, edited by B. J. C. McKercher and Roch Legault. Westport, Conn.: Praeger, 2001.

Claasen, Adam. *Hitler's Northern War: The Luftwaffe's Ill-Fated Campaign, 1940–1945.* Lawrence: University Press of Kansas, 2001.

Clark, Alan. *Suicide of the Empires: The Battles on the Eastern Front, 1914–18.* New York: American Heritage Press, 1971.

Clausewitz, Carl von. *On War.* Translated and edited by Michael Howard and Peter Paret. Princeton, N.J.: Princeton University Press, 1984.

Coffey, Thomas M. *Lion by the Tail: The Story of the Italian-Ethiopian War.* London: Hamish Hamilton, 1974.

Colodny, Robert Garland. *The Struggle for Madrid: The Central Epic of the Spanish Conflict, 1936–37.* New York: Paine-Whitman, 1958.

Connaughton, R. M. *The War of the Rising Sun and Tumbling Bear: A Military History of the Russo-Japanese War.* London: Routledge, 1988.

"Controversy Between Generals Fitcheff and Dimitrieff on the Conduct of Affairs in the Bulgarian Army During the Recent Balkan Wars." *Journal of the Military Service Institution* 55, no. 191, September–October 1914.

Cooper, Bryan. *The Battle of Cambrai.* New York: Stein and Day, 1968.

Cooper, Matthew. *The German Army, 1933–1945.* Chelsea, Mich.: Scarborough House, 1978.

Corum, James S. "From Biplanes to Blitzkrieg: The Development of German Air Doctrine Between the Wars." *War in History* 3, no. 1, 1996.

———. *The Luftwaffe: Creating the Operational Air War, 1918–1940.* Lawrence: University Press of Kansas, 1997.

———. "The Luftwaffe's Army Support Doctrine, 1918–1941." *Journal of Military History* 59, no. 1, January 1995.

———. *The Roots of Blitzkrieg: Hans von Seeckt and German Military Reform.* Lawrence: University Press of Kansas, 1992.

———. "The Spanish Civil War: Lessons Learned and Not Learned by the Great Powers." *Journal of Military History* 62, no. 2, April 1998.

Cowley, Robert, and Geoffrey Parker, eds. *Reader's Companion to Military History.* Boston: Houghton Mifflin, 1996.

Cox, Gary P. "Of Aphorisms, Lessons, and Paradigms: Comparing the British and German Official Histories of the Russo-Japanese War." *Journal of Military History* 56, no. 3, July 1992.

Craig, Gordon A. *The Battle of Königgrätz.* Philadelphia: Lippincott, 1964.

———. *The Politics of the Prussian Army, 1640–1945.* Oxford: Oxford University Press, 1955.

Crawford, Major C. M. "Diary of the Officers Attached to the Third Japanese Army from 29th July 1904 to the Fall of the Fortress." In *Reports from British Officers Attached to the Japanese Forces in the Field.* London: General Staff, 1907.

Creveld, Martin van. *Command in War.* Cambridge, Mass.: Harvard University Press, 1985.

———. *Supplying War: Logistics from Wallenstein to Patton.* Cambridge: Cambridge University Press, 1977.

———. *Technology and War: From 2000 B.C. to the Present.* New York: Free Press, 1991.

Crow, Duncan, ed. *AFVs of World War One.* Vol. 1. Windsor, Ontario: Profile Publications, 1970.

Crum, F. M. *With the Mounted Rifles in South Africa.* Cambridge: Macmillan, 1903.

Crutwell, C. R. M. F. *A History of the Great War, 1914–1918.* Chicago: Academy Chicago, 1991.

Curteis, Captain H. M. "The Doctrine of Limited Liability." *Journal of the Royal United Service Institution* 83, no. 532, November 1938.

Dahms, Hellmuth. *Der spanische Bürgerkrieg 1936–1939.* Tübingen: R. Wunderlich, 1962.

Daley, John L. S. "An Experiment Reconsidered: The Theory and Practice of Armored Warfare in Spain: October 1936–February 1937." *Armor* 108, no. 2, March–April 1999.

———. "Soviet and German Advisors Put Doctrine to the Test: Tanks in the Siege of Madrid." *Armor* 108, no. 3, May 1999.

Danchev, Alex. "Liddell Hart and the Indirect Approach." *Journal of Military History* 63, no. 2, April 1999.

Dangel, Paul. "Blood and Iron." *Command* 21, March–April 1993.

Dastrup, Boyd L. *The Field Artillery: History and Sourcebook.* Westport, Conn.: Greenwood Press, 1994.

David, Daniel. *The 1914 Campaign.* New York: Wieser and Wieser, 1987.

Davies, Norman. *White Eagle—Red Star.* London: Macdonald, 1972.

Davis, Richard Harding. *With Both Armies in South Africa.* New York: Scribner's, 1900.

De Wet, Christiaan. *Three Years' War.* New York: Scribner's, 1903.

del Boca, Angelo. *The Ethiopian War, 1935–1941.* Chicago: University of Chicago Press, 1965.

———. *I gas di Mussolini: Il Fascismo e la Guerra d'Etiopia.* Rome: Editori Riuniti, 1996.

"Die spanische Legionen." *Militär-Wochenblatt* 121, no. 46, May 28, 1937.

DiNardo, R. L. "French Military Planning, 1871–1914." *Strategy and Tactics* 118, March–April 1988.

———. *Germany's Panzer Arm.* Westport, Conn.: Greenwood Press, 1997.

———. *Mechanized Juggernaut or Military Anachronism? Horses and the German Army of World War II.* Westport, Conn.: Greenwood Press, 1991.

"Divisionsführung und Befehlstechnik." *Militär-Wochenblatt* 126, no. 44, May 18, 1932.

Djordjevic, Dimitrije. "*Vojvoda* Radomir Putnik." In *War and Society in East Central Europe.* Vol. 25, *East Central European War Leaders: Civilian and Military,* edited by Béla K. Király and Albert A. Nofi. Boulder, Colo.: Social Science Monographs, 1988.

Dodge, Theodore Ayrault. *The Campaign of Chancellorsville.* New York: Da Capo, 1999.

Doughty, Robert A. *The Breaking Point: Sedan and the Fall of France, 1940.* Hamden, Conn.: Archon, 1990.

Duffield, Michael. "Ethiopia: The Unconquered Lion of Africa." *Command* 4, May–June 1990.

Dupuy, Trevor N. "The Quantified Judgment Model and German Combat Effectiveness." *Military Affairs* 50, October 1986.

———. "A Response to 'The Wehrmacht Mythos Revisited.'" *Military Affairs* 51, October 1987.

Durfee, Major L. L. "Mobilization and Concentration of the Bulgarian Army in 1912." Carlisle, Pa.: U.S. Army Military History Institute, 1914–15.

Earle, Edward Mead, ed. *Makers of Modern Strategy: Military Thought from Machiavelli to Hitler.* New York: Atheneum, 1966.

Eby, Cecil D. *Between the Bullet and the Lie: American Volunteers in the Spanish Civil War.* New York: Holt, Rinehart and Winston, 1969.

———. *The Siege of the Alcazar.* New York: Random House, 1965.

Echevarria, Antulio J., II. *After Clausewitz: German Military Thinkers Before the Great War.* Lawrence: University Press of Kansas, 2000.

Edwards, Major J. K. "The Functions of Tanks." *Journal of the Royal United Service Institution* 80, no. 517, February 1935.

Ehrhardt, Arthur. "Airplane Versus Ground Motor: Lessons Gained from the Battle of Guadalajara." *Wissen und Wehr,* Berlin, July 1938 (translated). Carlisle, Pa.: U.S. Army Military History Institute, 1938.

Eimannsberger, General Ludwig von. *Der Kampfwagenkrieg.* 2d ed. Munich: J. F. Lehmann, 1938.

———. "Panzertaktik," pt. 1, *Militär-Wochenblatt* 120, no. 23, December 18, 1935, and pt. 2, *Militär-Wochenblatt* 120, no. 24, December 25, 1935.

Ellis, Chris, and Peter Chamberlain. "Medium Tanks Marks A to D." In *AFVs of World War One,* vol 1, edited by Duncan Crow. Windsor: Profile Publications, 1970.

English, John A., and Bruce I. Gudmundsson. *On Infantry.* Westport, Conn.: Praeger, 1994.

Epitome of the Russo-Japanese War (U.S. Army). Washington, D.C.: Government Printing Office, 1907.

Epstein, Robert M. *Napoleon's Last Victory and the Emergence of Modern War.* Lawrence: University Press of Kansas, 1994.

———. "Patterns of Change and Continuity in Nineteenth-Century Warfare." *Journal of Military History* 56, no. 3, July 1992.

"Erfahrungen Badoglios mit den einzelnen Waffengattungen." *Militär-Wochenblatt* 121, no. 19, November 18, 1936.

Esenwein, George, and Adrian Schubert. *Spain at War: The Spanish Civil War in Context, 1931–1939.* London: Longman, 1995.

Falls, Cyril. *The Art of War: From the Age of Napoleon to the Present Day.* New York: Oxford University Press, 1961.

———. *The Great War.* New York: Capricorn, 1959.

Fanning, William A., Jr. "The Origins of the Term 'Blitzkrieg': Another View." *Journal of Military History* 61, no. 61, April 1997.

Farcau, Bruce W. *The Chaco War: Bolivia and Paraguay, 1932–1935.* Westport, Conn.: Praeger, 1996.

Farnsworth, Lieutenant E. E. "The War in the Chaco." *Infantry Journal* 42, no. 3, May–June 1935.

Farwell, Byron. *The Great Anglo-Boer War.* New York: Norton, 1976.

Ferreira, O. J. O., ed. *Memoirs of General Ben Bouwer.* Pretoria: Human Sciences Research Council, 1980.

Fitzsimons, Bernard, ed. *Tanks and Weapons of World War I.* London: Phoebus, 1973.

Fleck, General D. E. "Die Leere des Schlachtfelds." *Militär-Wochenblatt* 116, no. 25, January 4, 1932.

Fletcher, D. J. "The Origins of Armour." In *Armoured Warfare,* edited by J. P. Harris and F. H. Toase. London: B. T. Batsford, 1990.

Fraser, Ronald. *Blood of Spain: An Oral History of the Spanish Civil War.* New York: Pantheon, 1979.

Freytag–Loringhoven, Hugo von. *The Power of Personality in War.* Roots of Strategy 3. Harrisburg, Pa.: Stackpole Books, 1991.

Frieser, K. H. *Blitzkrieg Legende: Der Westfeldzug 1940.* Munich: R. Oldenburg, 1995.

Fugate, Bryan. "On Inventing History." *Air University Review* 26, no. 6, September–October 1985.

———. *Operation Barbarossa.* Novato, Calif.: Presidio, 1984.

Fuller, J. F. C. *The Conduct of War, 1789–1961.* New York: Da Capo, 1992.

———. *The First of the League Wars: Its Lessons and Omens.* London: Eyre and Spottiswoode, 1936.

———. *Grant and Lee: A Study in Personality and Generalship.* Bloomington: Indiana University Press, 1957.

———. "The Italo-Ethiopian War: Military Analysis by an Eyewitness Observer." *Army Ordnance* 16, no. 96, May–June 1936.

———. *The Last of the Gentlemen's Wars.* London: Faber and Faber, 1937.

———. *Memoirs of an Unconventional Soldier.* London: Ivor Nicholson and Watson, 1936.

———. *A Military History of the Western World.* Vol. 3, *From the American Civil War to the End of World War II.* New York: Da Capo, 1956.

———. *The Reformation of War.* London: Hutchinson, 1923.

———. *Tanks in the Great War, 1914–1918.* New York: Dutton, 1920.

Fuppe, Colonel. "Neuzeitliches Nachrichtenverbindungswesen als Führungsmittel im Kriege." *Militärwissenschaftliche Rundschau* 3, no. 6, 1938.

Fussell, Paul. *The Great War and Modern Memory.* Oxford: Oxford University Press, 1975.

Gardner, Nikolas. "Command and Control in the 'Great Retreat' of 1914: The Disintegration of the British Cavalry Division." *Journal of Military History* 63, no. 1, January 1999.

Garratt, Geoffrey T. *Mussolini's Roman Empire.* New York: Bobbs-Merrill, 1938.

Gat, Azar. *Fascist and Liberal Visions of War: Fuller, Liddell Hart, Douhet, and Other Modernists.* Oxford: Oxford University Press, 1998.

Gaul, Lieutenant Colonel. "Der Blitzkrieg in Frankreich." *Militär-Wochenblatt* 125, no. 35, February 28, 1941.

Gaulle, Charles de. *The Army of the Future.* London: Hutchinson, 1940.

Geiser, Carl. *Prisoners of the Good Fight: The Spanish Civil War, 1936–1939.* Westport, Conn.: L. Hill, 1986.

"Generalfeldmarschall Graf von Schlieffen über den großen Feldherrn der preußisch-deutschen Armee." *Militär-Wochenblatt* 125, no. 17, October 25, 1940.

Gerassi, John. *The Premature Antifascists: North American Volunteers in the Spanish Civil War, 1936–39, an Oral History.* New York: Praeger, 1986.

Gerhard, Rittmeister. "Oberstleutnant Perré, Hauptmann Liddell Hart—und wir." *Militär-Wochenblatt* 120, no. 3, July 18, 1935.

Gibbs, Jack. *The Spanish Civil War.* London: E. Benn, 1973.

Gibbs, Peter. *The Battle of the Alma.* Philadelphia: Lippincott, 1963.

Gibbs, Philip, and Bernard Grant. *The Balkan War: Adventures of War with Cross and Crescent.* Boston: Small, Maynard, and Company, 1913.

Gilmore, Russell. "'The New Courage': Rifles and Soldier Individualism, 1876–1918." *Military Affairs* 40, no. 3, October 1976.

Glantz, David M. "Observing the Soviets: U.S. Army Attachés in Eastern Europe During the 1930s." *Journal of Military History* 55, no. 2, April 1991.

Graves, Robert. *Good-Bye to All That: An Autobiography.* London: J. Cape, 1929.

Griffith, Paddy. *Battle Tactics of the Western Front: The British Army's Art of Attack, 1916–1918.* New Haven, Conn.: Yale University Press, 1994.

———. *Forward into Battle: Fighting Tactics from Waterloo to the Near Future.* Novato, Calif.: Presidio, 1990.

———, ed., *British Fighting Methods in the Great War.* London: Frank Cass, 1996.

Groener, Wilhelm. *Der Feldherr wider Willen: Operative Studien über den Weltkrieg.* Berlin: E. S. Mittler and Son, 1927.

Guderian, Heinz. *Achtung—Panzer! The Development of Armored Forces, Their Tactics, and Operational Potential.* London: Arms and Armor, 1992.

———. "Armored Warfare: Consideration of the Past and Future." *Armored Cavalry Journal* 58, no. 1, January–February 1949.

———. "Kraftfahrtruppen." *Militärwissenschaftliche Rundschau* 1, no. 1, 1936.

———. *Panzer Leader.* New York: Ballantine, 1957.

———. "Die Panzertruppen und ihr Zusammenwirken mit den anderen Waffen." *Militärwissenschaftliche Rundschau* 1, no. 5, 1936.

Gudmundsson, Bruce I. "Maneuver Warfare: The German Tradition." In *Maneuver Warfare: An Anthology,* edited by Richard D. Hooker. Novato, Calif.: Presidio, 1993.

———. *Stormtroop Tactics: Innovation in the German Army, 1914–1918.* Westport, Conn.: Praeger, 1989.

Gunsburg, Jeffrey A. "The Battle of the Belgian Plain, 12–14 May 1940: The First Great Tank Battle." *Journal of Military History* 56, no. 2, April 1992.

———. *Divided and Conquered: The French High Command and the Defeat in the West, 1940.* Westport, Conn.: Greenwood Press, 1979.

Guse, Lieutenant Colonel. "Ein modernes Austerlitz." *Militär-Wochenblatt* 125, no. 20, November 15, 1940.

Gusew, V. "Antitank Defense." *Krasnaya Zvesda,* Moscow, May 21, 1938 (translated). Carlisle, Pa.: U.S. Army Military History Institute, 1938.

Habeck, Mary Ruth. "Imagining War: The Development of Armored Doctrine in Germany and the Soviet Union, 1919–1939." Ph.D. diss., Yale University, 1996.

Haldane, Lieutenant-Colonel A.L. "The Battle of Mudken: Operations of the Second Japanese Army." In *The Russo-Japanese War: Reports from British Officers Attached to the Japanese Forces in the Field.* London: General Staff, 1907.

———. "Second Japanese Army—Operations from 20th October 1904 to 29th January 1905, Including General Mishchenko's Raid and the Battle of Hei-kou-tai." In *The Russo-Japanese War: Reports from British Officers Attached to the Japanese Forces in the Field.* London: General Staff, 1907.

Hamilton, Sir Ian. *A Staff Officer's Scrap-Book.* London: Edward Arnold, 1912.

Hamilton, Ralph G. A. *The War Diary of the Master of Belhaven (Ralph Hamilton), 1914–1918.* Barnsley: Wharncliffe, 1990.

Hamley, Edward. *The War in the Crimea.* London: Seeley, 1910.

Hargreaves, Reginald. *Red Sun Rising: The Siege of Port Arthur.* Philadelphia: Lippincott, 1962.

Harris, J. P. "British Armour 1918–1940: Doctrine and Development." In *Armoured Warfare,* edited by J. P. Harris and F. H. Toase. London: B. T. Batsford, 1990.

———. *Men, Ideas, and Tanks: British Military Thought and Armoured Forces, 1903–1939.* Manchester: Manchester University Press, 1995.

Harris, J. P., and F. H. Toase, eds. *Armoured Warfare.* London: B. T. Batsford, 1990.

Harrison, Richard W. *The Russian Way of War: Operational Art, 1904–1940.* Lawrence: University Press of Kansas, 2001.

Heinemann, W. "The Development of German Armoured Forces, 1918–1940." In *Armoured Warfare,* edited by J. P. Harris and F. H. Toase. London: B. T. Batsford, 1990.

Herwig, Holger. *The First World War: Germany and Austria-Hungary, 1914–1918.* London: Arnold, 1997.

———. *Hammer or Anvil: Modern Germany, 1648–Present.* Lexington, Mass.: Heath, 1994.

———. "Stategic Uncertainties of a Nation-State: Prussia-Germany, 1871–1918." In *The Making of Strategy: Rulers, States, and War,* edited by Williamson Murray, MacGregor Knox, and Alvin Berstein. Cambridge: Cambridge University Press, 1994.

Himpe, Lieutenant Colonel. "Die grossen Manöver der Po-Armee," pt. 1, *Militär-Wochenblatt* 124, no. 10, September 1, 1939, and pt. 2, *Militär-Wochenblatt* 124, no. 11, September 8, 1939.

———. "Die italienischen Manöver in den Abruzzen." *Militär-Wochenblatt* 123, no. 11, September 9, 1938.

Hindenburg, Field Marshal Paul von. *Out of My Life.* 2 vols. New York: Harper and Brothers, 1921.

Holt, Edgar. *The Boer War.* London: Putnam, 1958.

Holtman, Robert. *The Napoleonic Revolution.* New York: Lippincott, 1967.

Home, Major J. M. "General Report on the Russo-Japanese War up to the 15th August 1904." In *The Russo-Japanese War: Reports from British Officers Attached to the Japanese Forces in the Field.* London: General Staff, 1907.

———. "Historical Narrative from the Outbreak of the War to the 15th August 1904." In *Reports from British Officers Attached to the Japanese Forces in the Field.* London: General Staff, 1907.

Hooker, Richard D., ed. *Maneuver Warfare: An Anthology.* Novato, Calif.: Presidio, 1993.

Horne, Alistair. *The Price of Glory: Verdun 1916.* New York: Penguin, 1964.

———. *To Lose a Battle: France 1940.* Boston: Little, Brown, 1969.

Howard, Michael. *The Franco-Prussian War.* New York: Macmillan, 1962.

———. "Jomini and the Classical Tradition in Military Thought." In *The Theory and Practice of War,* edited by Michael Howard. Bloomington: Indiana University Press, 1965.

———. "Men Against Fire: The Doctrine of the Offensive in 1914." In *Makers of Modern Strategy from Machiavelli to the Nuclear Age,* edited by Peter Paret. Princeton, N.J.: Princeton University Press, 1986.

———. "World War One: The Crisis in European History, the Role of the Military Historian." *Journal of Military History* 57, no. 1, October 1993.

———, ed. *The Theory and Practice of War.* Bloomington: Indiana University Press, 1965.

Howard, Victor, with Mac Reynolds. *The Mackenzie-Papineau Battalion: The Canadian Contingent in the Spanish Civil War.* Ottawa: Carleton University Press, 1986.

Howland, Frederick Hoppin. *The Chase of De Wet.* Providence, R.I.: Preston and Rounds, 1901.

Howson, Gerald. *Aircraft in the Spanish Civil War.* Washington, D.C.: Smithsonian Institution Press, 1990.

———. *Arms for Spain: The Untold Story of the Spanish Civil War.* New York: St. Martin's Press, 1999.

Hudson, Roger, ed. *William Russell: Special Correspondent of* The Times. London: Folio Society, 1995.

Hughes, Daniel J. "Abuses of German Military History." *Military Review* 65, no. 12, December 1986.

———. "Schlichting, Schlieffen, and the Prussian Theory of War in 1914." *Journal of Military History* 59, no. 2, April 1995.

———, ed. *Moltke on the Art of War: Selected Writings.* Novato, Calif.: Presidio, 1993.

Ironside, Sir Edmund. *Tannenberg: The First Thirty Days in East Prussia.* Edinburgh: William Blackwood, 1933.

Jackson, Gabriel. *A Concise History of the Spanish Civil War.* New York: John Day, 1974.

———. *The Spanish Republic and the Civil War.* Princeton, N.J.: Princeton University Press, 1965.

James, David H. *The Siege of Port Arthur.* London: T. Fisher Unwin, 1905.

Jarymowycz, Roman Johann. "Jedi Knights in the Kremlin: The Soviet Military in the 1930s and the Genesis of Deep Battle." In *Military Planning and the Origins of the Second World War in Europe,* edited by B. J. C. McKercher and Roch Legault. Westport, Conn.: Praeger, 2001.

Jelavich, Barbara. *History of the Balkans.* 2 vols. Cambridge: Cambridge University Press, 1983.

————. *St. Petersburg and Moscow: Tsarist and Soviet Foreign Policy, 1814–1974.* Bloomington: Indiana University Press, 1974.

Jellinek, Frank. *The Civil War in Spain.* New York: H. Fertig, 1969.

Johnson, David E. *Fast Tanks and Heavy Bombers: Innovation in the U.S. Army, 1917–1945.* Ithaca, N.Y.: Cornell University Press, 1998.

Johnson, Hubert C. *Breakthrough: Tactics, Technology, and the Search for Victory on the Western Front in World War I.* Novato, Calif.: Presidio, 1994.

Johnston, Douglas V., II, and Rolfe Hillman Jr. *Soissons 1918.* College Station: Texas A&M University Press, 1999.

Jomini, Baron Antoine Henri de. *The Art of War.* 1862. Reprint, Westport, Conn.: Greenwood Press, 1971.

Kabisch, General Ernst. "Systemlose Strategie." *Militär-Wochenblatt* 125, no. 26, December 27, 1940.

Keegan, John. *The First World War.* London: Hutchinson, 1998.

Kellie, Major G. B. J. "The Support of Infantry Tanks in the Attack." *Journal of the Royal United Service Institution* 83, no. 531, August 1938.

Kennedy, Robert M. *The German Campaign in Poland, 1939.* Department of the Army Pamphlet no. 20-255. Washington, D.C.: Department of the Army, 1956.

Kiesling, Eugenia C. *Arming Against Hitler: France and the Limits of Military Planning.* Lawrence: University Press of Kansas, 1996.

Kinglake, Alexander William. *The Invasion of the Crimea: Its Origin, and an Account of Its Progress Down to the Death of Lord Raglan.* 6 vols. New York: Harper, 1863–88.

Kipp, Jacob W. "Barbarossa, Soviet Covering Forces and the Initial Period of War: Military History and AirLand Battle." *Journal of Soviet Military Studies* 1, no. 2, June 1988.

Köhn, Lieutenant Colonel. "Die Infanterie im 'Blitzkrieg.'" *Militär-Wochenblatt* 125, no. 5, August 2, 1940.

Kronberger, Rittmeister F. "'Es gibt Fälle, wo das höchste Wagen die höchste Weisheit ist.'" *Militär-Wochenblatt* 125, no. 7, August 16, 1940.

Kühn, Dr. Arthur. "Raum und Gelände in den deutschen und gegnerischen Operationsplänen Frühjahr 1918." *Militär-Wochenblatt* 123, no. 4, July 22, 1938.

Kuhn, Major Joseph E. "Report on Engineering Aspects of the Port Arthur Operation." In *Reports of Military Observers Attached to the Armies in Manchuria During the Russo-Japanese War* (U.S. Army). Washington, D.C.: Government Printing Office, 1906.

Kuropatkin, Marshal Alexei N. *The Russian Army and the Japanese War.* 2 vols. Westport, Conn.: Hyperion, 1977.

Kurzman, Dan. *Miracle of November: Madrid's Epic Stand, 1936.* New York: Putnam, 1980.

Kutschbach, A. *Die Serben im Balkankrieg 1912–1913 und im Kriege gegen die Bulgaren.* Stuttgart: Frank'sche Verlagshandlung, 1913.

Lackey, Scott W. *The Rebirth of the Habsburg Army: Friedrich Beck and the Rise of the General Staff.* Westport, Conn.: Greenwood Press, 1995.

Laderchi, Colonel Count Ruggeri. "Tactical and Administrative Lessons of the War in Abyssinia." *Journal of the Royal United Service Institution* 83, no. 530, May 1938.

Laffin, John. *High Command.* New York: Barnes and Noble, 1995.

Larrazabal, Jesus Salas. *Air War over Spain.* London: Ian Allen, 1969.

Larson, Robert H. *The British Army and the Theory of Armored Warfare.* Newark: University of Delaware Press, 1984.

Lechowich, Captain Richard. "Balkan Wars: Prelude to Disaster, 1912–1913." *Strategy and Tactics* 164, November 1993.

Lewis, S. J. *Forgotten Legions: German Infantry Policy, 1918–1941.* Westport, Conn.: Praeger, 1985.

Liddell Hart, B. H. *The British Way in Warfare.* London: Faber and Faber, 1932.

———. *The Decisive Wars of History.* London: G. Bell, 1929.

———. *Europe in Arms.* London: Faber and Faber, 1937.

———. *The German Generals Talk.* New York: Quill, 1979.

———. *A Greater Than Napoleon: Scipio Africanus.* London: Blackwood, 1926.

———. *Memoirs.* London: Cassell, 1965.

———. *Paris, or the Future of War.* London: Kegan Paul, 1925.

———. *The Real War, 1914–1918.* Boston: Little, Brown, 1930.

———. *The Remaking of Modern Armies.* Boston: Little, Brown, 1927.

———. *Sherman: Soldier, Realist, American.* London: Eyre and Spottiswoode, 1930.

———. *Strategy.* New York: Penguin, 1967.

———. *The Tanks.* Vol. 1. London: Cassell, 1959.

Liddle, Peter H., ed. *Passchendaele in Perspective: The Third Battle of Ypres.* London: Leo Cooper, 1997.

Liebmann, General. "Der Anteil des Motors am deutschen Siege." *Militär-Wochenblatt* 126, no. 1, July 4, 1941.

Lincoln, W. Bruce. *Passage Through Armageddon: The Russians in War and Revolution, 1914–1918.* New York: Simon and Schuster, 1986.

[Linesman]. *Words by an Eyewitness: The Struggle in Natal.* London: William Blackwood, 1901.

Ludwig, General of Artillery. "Die Einkesselung." *Militär-Wochenblatt* 126, no. 11, September 12, 1941.

———. "Gedanken über den Angriff im Bewegungskriege." *Militärwissenschaftliche Rundschau* 1, no. 2, 1936.

———. "Moltke als Erzieher." *Militär-Wochenblatt* 125, no. 17, October 25, 1940.

———. "Die Operation auf der inneren und der äußeren Linie im Lichte unserer Zeit." *Militär-Wochenblatt* 126, no. 1, July 4, 1941.

Lupfer, Timothy S. *The Dynamics of Doctrine: The Changes in German Tactical Doctrine During the First World War.* Ft. Leavenworth, Kans.: U.S. Army Command and General Staff College, 1981.

Luvaas, Jay. *The Education of an Army: British Military Thought, 1815–1940.* London: Cassell, 1965.

Luvaas, Jay, and Harold W. Nelson, eds. *The U.S. Army War College Guide to the Battles of Chancellorsville and Fredericksburg.* Lawrence: University Press of Kansas, 1994.

Lynn, John. *The Bayonets of the Republic: Motivation and Tactics in the Army of Revolutionary France, 1791–94.* Chicago: University of Illinois Press, 1984.

———. "The History of Logistics and *Supplying War.*" In *Feeding Mars: Logistics in Western Warfare from the Middle Ages to the Present,* edited by John Lynn. Boulder, Colo.: Westview Press, 1993.

Lyon, James B. "'A Peasant Mob': The Serbian Army on the Eve of the Great War." *Journal of Military History* 61, no. 3, July 1997.

———. "Serbia and the Balkan Front, 1914." Ph.D. diss., University of California, Los Angeles, 1995.

Mack Smith, Denis. *Mussolini.* New York: Knopf, 1982.

———. *Mussolini's Roman Empire.* New York: Viking, 1976.

Macksey, Kenneth. *Armoured Crusader.* London: Hutchinson, 1967.

———. "Tank Development." In *Tanks and Weapons of World War I,* edited by Bernard Fitzsimons. London: Phoebus, 1973.

———. *Tank Versus Tank: The Illustrated Story of Armored Battlefield Conflict in the Twentieth Century.* New York: Barnes and Noble, 1999.

———. *Tank Warfare: A History of Tanks in Battle.* New York: Stein and Day, 1972.

Mahan, Admiral Alfred T. *The Story of the War in South Africa, 1899–1900.* London: Samson Low, Marston, and Company, 1901.

Mahmud Mukhtar, Pasha. *Meine Führung im Balkankriege 1912.* Berlin: E. S. Mittler and Son, 1913.

Manstein, Erich von. *Lost Victories.* Novato, Calif.: Presidio, 1982.

Mantey, Colonel von. "Nachschub und Operationsplan," pt. 1, *Militär-Wochenblatt* 124, no. 1, July 1, 1939, and pt. 2, *Militär-Wochenblatt* 124, no. 2, July 7, 1939.

March, Captain Peyton C. "Reports of Captain Peyton C. March, General Staff, Observer with the Japanese Army." In *Reports of Military Observers Attached to the Armies in Manchuria During the Russo-Japanese War* (U.S. Army). Washington, D.C.: Government Printing Office, 1906.

Martelli, George. *Italy Against the World.* New York: Harcourt, Brace, 1938.

Matthews, Herbert. *Two Wars and More to Come.* New York: Carrick and Evans, 1938.

Maurice, Frederick. *History of the War in South Africa, 1899–1902.* Vol. 1. London: Hurst and Blackett, 1906.

Mayne, Colonel C. B. "The Balkan War and Some of Its Lessons." *Journal of the Royal United Service Institution* 57, no. 423, May 1913.

McElwee, William. *The Art of War: Waterloo to Mons.* Bloomington: Indiana University Press, 1974.

McKercher, B. J. C., and Roch Legault, eds. *Military Planning and the Origins of the Second World War in Europe.* Westport, Conn.: Praeger, 2001.

Mearsheimer, John J. *Liddell Hart and the Weight of History.* Ithaca, N.Y.: Cornell University Press, 1988.

Meilinger, Philip S. "The Historiography of Airpower: Theory and Doctrine." *Journal of Military History* 64, no. 2, April 2000.

———. "Trenchard and 'Morale Bombing': The Evolution of Royal Air Force Doctrine Before World War II." *Journal of Military History* 60, no. 2, April 1996.

Mellenthin, F. W. von. *Panzer Battles: A Study of the Employment of Armor in the Second World War.* New York: Ballantine, 1956.

Menning, Bruce. *Bayonets Before Bullets: The Imperial Russian Army, 1861–1914.* Bloomington: Indiana University Press, 1992.

———. "The Deep Strike in Russian and Soviet Military History." *Journal of Soviet Military Studies* 1, no. 1, April 1988.

Meyler, David. "Missed Opportunities: The Ground War in Holland." *Command* 42, March 1997.

———. "To Sow the Wind: The Luftwaffe's Campaign in the Netherlands, 10–14 May 1940." *Command* 42, March 1997.

Middlebrook, Martin. *The First Day on the Somme: 1 July 1916.* New York: Norton, 1971.

Miksche, Ferdinand O. *Attack: A Study of Blitzkrieg Tactics.* New York: Random House, 1942.

Miller, David. *Illustrated Directory of Tanks of the World: From World War I to the Present Day.* London: Salamander Books, 2000.

Miller, Stephen M. *Lord Methuen and the British Army.* London: Frank Cass, 1999.

Mockler, Anthony. *Haile Selassie's War: The Italian-Ethiopian Campaign, 1935–1941.* New York: Random House, 1984.

Moltke, Helmuth von. *Militärische Werke.* 14 vols. Berlin: E. S. Mittler and Son, 1892–1912.

Morris, Eric. *Tanks.* London: Octopus Books, 1975.

Morrison, Captain John F. "Report of Captain John F. Morrison, Twentieth Infantry (Now Major Thirteenth Infantry), Observer with the Japanese Army." In *Reports of Military Observers Attached to the Armies in Manchuria During the Russo-Japanese War* (U.S. Army). Washington, D.C.: Government Printing Office, 1906.

Mrazek, James E. *The Fall of Eben Emael.* Novato, Calif.: Presidio, 1991.

Muir, Rory. *Tactics and the Experience of Battle in the Age of Napoleon.* New Haven, Conn.: Yale University Press, 1998.

Murray, Williamson, MacGregor Knox, and Alvin Bernstein. *The Making of Strategy: Rulers, States, and War.* Cambridge: Cambridge University Press, 1994.

Murray, Williamson, and Allan R. Millett, eds. *Military Innovation in the Interwar Period.* Cambridge: Cambridge University Press, 1996.

"Die Nachschubfrage im Abessinischen Feldzug." *Militär-Wochenblatt* 121, no. 39, April 9, 1937.

Nasson, Bill. *The South African War, 1899–1902.* Oxford: Oxford University Press, 2000.

Naudeau, Ludovic. "Battles of Which One Never Heard." *Le Journal,* Paris, December 25, 1912 (translated). Carlisle, Pa.: U.S. Army Military History Institute, 1913.

Naveh, Shimon. *In Pursuit of Excellence: The Evolution of Operational Theory.* London: Frank Cass, 1997.

Noel-Buxton, N. E. *With the Bulgarian Staff.* New York: Macmillan, 1913.

Nofi, Albert A., ed. *Napoleon at War: Selected Writings of F. Loraine Petre.* New York: Hippocrene, 1984.

Nojine [Nozhin], E. K. *The Truth About Port Arthur.* London: John Murray, 1908.

Nosworthy, Brent. *The Anatomy of Victory: Battle Tactics, 1689–1763.* New York: Hippocrene, 1990.

Obkircher, Lieutenant Colonel. "Moltke, der 'unbekannte' General von Königgrätz: Zur Errinerung an den 75. Gedenktag der Schlacht bei Königgrätz am 3. Juli 1866." *Militär-Wochenblatt* 125, no. 52, June 27, 1941.

Odom, William O. *After the Trenches: The Transformation of U.S. Army Doctrine, 1918–1939.* College Station: Texas A&M University Press, 1999.

Ogorkiewicz, Richard M. *Armoured Forces: A History of Armoured Forces and Their Vehicles.* New York: Arco, 1970.

Oheimb, Lieutenant Colonel. "Motor und Kriegführung." *Militär-Wochenblatt* 125, no. 36, March 7, 1941.

Orgill, Douglas. *The Tank: Studies in the Development and Use of a Weapon.* London: Heinemann, 1970.

Orwell, George. *Homage to Catalonia.* New York: Harcourt, Brace, 1952.

Oven, Wilfred von. *Hitler und der spanische Bürgerkrieg: Mission und Schicksal der Legion Condor.* Tübingen: Grabert, 1978.

Pakenham, Thomas. *The Boer War.* New York: Random House, 1979.

Palmer, Alan. *The Crimean War.* New York: Dorset Press, 1987.

Paret, Peter. "Clausewitz." In *Makers of Modern Strategy from Machiavelli to the Nuclear Age,* edited by Peter Paret. Princeton, N.J.: Princeton University Press, 1986.

———. "Clausewitz and the Nineteenth Century." In *The Theory and Practice of War,* edited by Michael Howard. Bloomington: Indiana University Press, 1965.

———. ed. *Makers of Modern Strategy from Machiavelli to the Nuclear Age.* Princeton, N.J.: Princeton University Press, 1986.

Parrish, Michael. "Formation and Leadership of the Soviet Mechanized Corps in 1941." *Military Affairs,* 47, no. 2, April 1983.

Paschall, Rod. *The Defeat of Imperial Germany, 1917–1918.* Chapel Hill, N.C.: Algonquin, 1989.

Passingham, Ian. *Pillars of Fire: The Battle of Messines Ridge, June 1917.* Stroud: Sutton Publishing, 1999.

Pélissier, Jean. *Dix mois de guerre dans les Balkans, Octobre 1912–Aout 1913.* Paris: Perrin, 1914.

Pemberton, W. Baring. *Battles of the Boer War.* London: Batsford, 1964.

Petersen, Nis. "Die deutsche Land- und Luftkriegführung im ersten Kriegsjahre." *Militär-Wochenblatt* 125, no. 24, December 13, 1940.

———. "Polens Vernichtung als Vorschule für den genialen Durchbruch der deutschen Panzerwaffe im Westen." *Militär-Wochenblatt* 125, no. 10, September 6, 1940.

Petrov, Ljudmil. "The Training of Bulgarian Officers, 1878–1918." In *War and Society in East Central Europe.* Vol. 24, *The East Central European Officer Corps 1740–*

1920s: Social Origins, Selection, Education, and Training, edited by Béla K. Király and Walter Scott Dillard. Boulder, Colo.: Social Science Monographs, 1988.

Picq, Charles-Ardant du. *Battle Studies: Ancient and Modern Battle.* New York: Macmillan, 1921.

Pilsudksi, Jozef. *Year 1920.* London: Pilsudski Institute of London, 1972.

Pitreich, Max Freiherr von. "Osterreich-Ungarns Kriegsbeginn gegen Russland und das Siedlecproblem." *Militär-Wochenblatt* 122, no. 8, August 20, 1937.

Polson Newman, Major E. W. *Italy's Conquest of Ethiopia.* London: Thornton Butterworth, 1937.

Ponath, Lieutenant Colonel. "Die Schlacht bei Tannenberg 1914 in kriegsgeschicht-licher, taktischer, und erzieherischer Auswertung." *Militär-Wochenblatt* 124, no. 8, August 18, 1939.

Porch, Douglas. *The March to the Marne: The French Army, 1871–1914.* Cambridge: Cambridge University Press, 1981.

Possony, Stefan T., and Etienne Mantoux. "Du Picq and Foch: The French School." In *Makers of Modern Strategy: Military Thought from Machiavelli to Hitler,* edited by Edward Mead Earle. New York: Atheneum, 1966.

Poulain, Captain Didier. "Aircraft and Mechanized Land Warfare: The Battle of Guadalajara, 1937." *Journal of the Royal United Service Institution* 83, no. 530, May 1938.

———. "The Role of Aircraft in the Spanish Civil War." *Journal of the Royal United Service Institution* 83, no. 531, August 1938.

Preston, Paul. *Franco: A Biography.* New York: Basic Books, 1994.

Preston, Paul, and Ann L. Mackenzie, eds. *The Republic Besieged: Civil War in Spain 1936–1939.* Edinburgh: Edinburgh University Press, 1996.

Prior, Robin, and Trevor Wilson. *Passchendaele: The Untold Story.* New Haven, Conn.: Yale University Press, 1996.

Proctor, Raymond L. *Hitler's Luftwaffe in the Spanish Civil War.* Westport, Conn.: Greenwood Press, 1983.

Raicer, Ted S. "When Eagles Fight: The Eastern Front in World War I." *Command* 25, November–December 1993.

Raudzens, George. "Blitzkrieg Ambiguities: Doubtful Usage of a Famous Word." *War and Society* 7, September 1989.

Ravenhill, Lieutenant C. "Tactics Employed by the Japanese Army in the War of 1904–5." *Journal of the Royal United Service Institution* 82, no. 527, August 1937.

Reichmann, Captain Carl. "Report of Captain Carl Reichmann, Seventeenth Infantry, Observer with the Russian Forces." In *Reports of Military Observers Attached to the Armies in Manchuria During the Russo-Japanese War* (U.S. Army). Washington, D.C.: Government Printing Office, 1906.

Reid, Brian Holden. "Colonel J. F. C. Fuller and the Revival of Classical Military Thinking in Britain, 1918–1926." *Military Affairs* 49, no. 4, October 1985.

———. *J. F. C. Fuller: Military Thinker.* New York: St. Martin's Press, 1987.

———. *Studies in British Military Thought: Debates with Fuller and Liddell Hart.* Lincoln: University of Nebraska Press, 1998.

Reilly, General H. J. "The Queen of Battle Versus the Tanks." *Illustration,* Paris, January 28, 1939 (translated). Carlisle, Pa.: U.S. Army Military History Institute, 1939.

Reinicke, Adolf. *Das Reichsheer 1921–1934: Ziele, Methoden der Ausbildung und Erziehung sowie der Dienstgestaltung.* Osnabrück: Biblio Verlag, 1986.

Reitz, Deneys. *Boer Commando: An Afrikaner Journal of the Boer War.* New York: Sarpedon, 1993.

———. *Trekking On.* Prescott, Ariz.: Wolfe, 1994.

Remarque, Erich Maria. *All Quiet on the Western Front.* New York: Grosset and Dunlap, 1929.

Rich, Norman. *Why the Crimean War? A Cautionary Tale.* Hanover, N.H.: University Press of New England, 1985.

Richardson, R. Dan. "The Defense of Madrid: Mysterious Generals, Red Front Fighters, and the International Brigades." *Military Affairs* 43, no. 4, December 1979.

Richey, Stephen W. "Auftragstaktik, Schwerpunkt, Aufrollen: The Philosophical Basis of the AirLand Battle." *Military Review* 64, no. 5, May 1984.

Ries, Karl, and Hans Ring. *The Legion Condor: A History of the Luftwaffe in the Spanish Civil War, 1939–1939.* West Chester, Pa.: Schiffer Military History, 1992.

Ripperger, Robert M. "The Development of the French Artillery for the Offensive, 1890–1914." *Journal of Military History* 59, no. 4, October 1995.

Ritter, Gerhard. *Der Schlieffenplan: Kritik eines Mythos.* Munich: R. Oldenbourg, 1956.

Rivus, Enzio. "Die Tankwaffe Italiens." *Militär-Wochenblatt* 121, no. 4, July 25, 1936.

Robinson, Major-General H. Rowan. *The Infantry Experiment.* London: William Clowes and Sons, 1935.

Rochat, Giorgio. "Badoglio e le Operazioni contro L'Etiopia, 1935–1936." In *Guerre Italiane in Libia e in Etiopia: Studi Militari, 1921–1939.* Paese: Pagus Edizioni, 1991.

Rode, Hans Wolf. "Das Kriegserlebnis von 1939 und 1914." *Militär-Wochenblatt* 125, no. 46, May 16, 1941.

Rogers, H. C. B. *Tanks in Battle.* London: Seeley Service, 1965.

Romilly, Esmond. *Boadilla.* London: Macdonald, 1971.

Rosenstone, Robert A. *Crusade of the Left: The Lincoln Battalion in the Spanish Civil War.* New York: Pegasus, 1969.

Ross, Steven S. *From Flintlock to Rifle: Infantry Tactics, 1740–1866.* London: Frank Cass, 1996.

Rothbrust, Florian K. *Guderian's XIXth Panzer Corps and the Battle of France: Breakthrough in the Ardennes, May 1940.* Westport, Conn.: Praeger, 1990.

Rothenberg, Gunther E. *The Army of Francis Joseph.* West Lafayette, Ind.: Purdue University Press, 1976.

———. *The Art of Warfare in the Age of Napoleon.* Bloomington: Indiana University Press, 1978.

———. "The Austro-Hungarian Campaign Against Serbia in 1914." *Journal of Military History* 53, no. 2, April 1989.

———. *Napoleon's Great Adversaries: The Archduke Charles and the Austrian Army, 1792–1814.* Bloomington: Indiana University Press, 1982.

Royle, Trevor. *Crimea: The Great Crimean War, 1854–1856.* New York: St. Martin's Press, 2000.

Saab, Ann Pottinger. *The Origins of the Crimean Alliance.* Charlottesville: University Press of Virginia, 1977.

Sadkovich, James J. "The Development of the Italian Air Force Prior to World War II." *Military Affairs* 51, no. 3, July 1987.

Sakurai, Tadayoshi. *Human Bullets: A Soldier's Story of the Russo-Japanese War.* Lincoln: University of Nebraska Press, 1999.

Schulz, General Otto. "Die italienische Denkschrift über die Verwendung der grossen Einheiten in Abessinien." *Militär-Wochenblatt* 122, no. 10, September 3, 1937.

———. "Die serbische Armee in der Schlacht bei Kumanovo am 10. und 11. Oktober 1912." *Militär-Wochenblatt* 123, no. 15, October 7, 1938.

Schüttel, Major. "Die Mitwirkung der italienischen Luftwaffe am Niederbruch Abessiniens." *Militärwissenschaftliche Rundschau* 1, no. 4, 1936.

Schuyler, Lieutenant Colonel Walter S. "Report of Lieutenant Colonel Walter S. Schuyler, General Staff, Observer with the Russian Army." *Reports of Military Observers Attached to the Armies in Manchuria During the Russo-Japanese War* (U.S. Army). Washington, D.C.: Government Printing Office, 1906.

Sears, Stephen W. *Chancellorsville.* Boston: Houghton Mifflin, 1996.

———. "Modernes Heer." In *Gedanken eines Soldaten.* Leipzig: K. F. Koehler, 1935.

Seeckt, General Hans von. *Gedanken eines Soldaten.* Leipzig: K. F. Koehler, 1929.

———. "Grundsätze moderner Landesverteidigung." In *Gedanken eines Soldaten.* Leipzig: K. F. Koehler, 1935.

Shebanow, A. "Infantry in Offensive Combat: Experience of the Spanish Civil War." *Krasnaya Zvesda,* Moscow, May 27, 1938 (translated). Carlisle: Pa.: U.S. Army Military History Institute, 1938.

Sheppard, Major E. W. "Does Defence Mean Defeat?" *Journal of the Royal United Service Institution* 83, no. 530, May 1938.

———. "How Wars End." *Journal of the Royal United Service Institution* 84, no. 535, August 1939.

Showalter, Dennis E. "Even Generals Wet Their Pants: The First Three Weeks in East Prussia, August 1914." *War and Society* 2, no. 2, 1984.

———. "For Deterrence to Doomsday Machine: The German Way of War, 1890–1914." *Journal of Military History* 64, no. 3, July 2000.

———. "Manifestation of Reform: The Rearmament of the Prussian Infantry, 1806–1813." *Journal of Modern History* 44, no. 3, September 1972.

———. "Mass Multiplied by Impulsion: The Influence of Railroads on Prussian Planning for the Seven Weeks' War." *Military Affairs* 38, no. 2, April 1974.

———. *Railroads and Rifles: Soldiers, Technology, and the Unification of Germany.* Hamden, Conn.: Archon, 1975.

———. "The Retaming of Bellona: Prussia and the Institutionalization of the Napoleonic Legacy, 1815–1876." *Military Affairs* 44, no. 2, April 1980.

————. *Tannenberg: Clash of Empires.* Hamden, Conn.: Archon, 1991.

Shy, John. "Jomini." In *Makers of Modern Strategy from Machiavelli to the Nuclear Age,* edited by Peter Paret. Princeton, N.J.: Princeton University Press, 1986.

Sieberg, Major. "Beantwort der Krieg in Spanien die Frange, ob der moderne Panzerkampfwagen oder das moderne Abwehrgeschütz überlegen ist?" *Militär-Wochenblatt* 122, no. 33, February 11, 1938.

Sigerfoos, Major Edward. "The Campaign of Kirk Kilissé." Carlisle, Pa.: U.S. Army Military History Institute, 1913.

Simpkin, Richard E. *Deep Battle: The Brainchild of Marshal Tukhachevskii.* New York: Pergamon, 1987.

Sinnema, Robert J. "General Mangin and the Tenth Army, 1918." Master's thesis, University of Calgary, 1996.

Skoko, Savo. "An Analysis of the Strategy of *Vojvoda* Putnik During the Balkan Wars." In *War and Society in East Central Europe.* Vol. 18, *East Central European Society and the Balkan Wars,* edited by Béla K. Király and Dimitrije Djordjevic. Boulder, Colo.: Social Science Monographs, 1987.

Snellgrove, Laurence Ernest. *Franco and the Spanish Civil War.* New York: McGraw-Hill, 1968.

[Solaire]. "The Hare, the Tortoise, and the Eagle." *Journal of the Royal United Service Institution* 81, no. 521, February 1936.

Southworth, Herbert. *Guernica, Guernica: A Study of Journalism, Diplomacy, Propaganda, and History.* Berkeley: University of California Press, 1977.

Spannenkrebs, Colonel Walter. *Angriff mit Kampfwagen.* Oldenburg: Gerhard Stalling, 1939.

————. "Infanterie und Panzer." *Militär-Wochenblatt* 123, no. 7, August 12, 1938.

[A Special Correspondent]. *The Balkan War Drama.* London: Andrew Melrose, 1913.

Steevens, G. W. *From Cape Town to Ladysmith.* New York: Dodd, Mead, 1900.

Stentzler, Captain. "Gedanken über die Tätigkeit der Fliegertruppe bei der Verfolgung einer im Rückzug befindlichen Erdtruppe." *Militär-Wochenblatt* 122, no. 47, May 20, 1938.

Sternberg, Fritz. *Germany and a Lightning War.* London: Faber and Faber, 1939.

Stoecker, Sally Webb. *Forging Stalin's Army: Marshal Tukhachevsky and the Politics of Military Innovation.* Boulder, Colo.: Westview Press, 1998.

Stoilov, Petar. "General of Infantry Nikola Ivanov." In *War and Society in East Central Europe.* Vol. 25, *East Central European War Leaders: Civilian and Military,* edited by Béla K. Király and Albert A. Nofi. Boulder, Colo.: Social Science Monographs, 1988.

Stokesbury, James L. *A Short History of World War I.* New York: William Morrow, 1981.

Stolfi, Russel H. S. *A Bias for Action: The German 7th Panzer Division in France and Russia, 1940–1941.* Marine Corps University Series Perspectives on Warfighting 1. Quantico, Va.: Marine Corps Association, 1991.

————. "Equipment for Victory in France in 1940." *History* 52, February 1970.

Stone, Norman. *The Eastern Front, 1914–1917.* London: Hodder and Stoughton, 1975.

Sullivan, Brian R. "Fascist Italy's Military Involvement in the Spanish Civil War." *Journal of Military History* 59, no. 4, October 1995.

———. "The Italian-Ethiopian War, October 1935–November 1941: Causes, Conduct, and Consequences." In *Great Powers and Little Wars: The Limits of Power,* edited by A. Hamish Ion and E. J. Errington. Westport, Conn.: Praeger, 1993.

———. "A Thirst for Glory: Mussolini, the Italian Military and the Fascist Regime, 1922–1936." Ph.D. diss., Columbia University, 1984.

Sutherland, Daniel E. *Fredericksbsurg and Chancellorsville: The Dare Mark Campaign.* Lincoln: University of Nebraska Press, 1998.

Sweet, John J. T. *Iron Arm: The Mechanization of Mussolini's Army, 1920–1940.* Westport, Conn.: Greenwood Press, 1980.

Sweetman, John. "'Ad Hoc' Support Services During the Crimean War, 1854–6: Temporary, Ill-Planned, and Largely Unsuccessful." *Military Affairs* 52, no. 3, July 1988.

Swinton, Ernest. "The Defence of Duffer's Drift." Ft. Leavenworth, Kans.: U.S. Army Command and General Staff College, 1905.

Talbot, Randy R. "General Hermann von François and Corps-Level Operations During the Tannenberg Campaign, August 1914." Master's thesis, Eastern Michigan University, 1999.

Taylor, William L. "The Debate over Changing Cavalry Tactics and Weapons, 1900–1914." *Military Affairs* 28, no. 4, winter 1964–1965.

Terraine, John. *The Road to Passchendaele: The Flanders Offensive of 1917: A Study in Inevitability.* London: Leo Cooper, 1977.

Theiss, Colonel Rudolf, "Der 'Augenzeuge.'" *Militär-Wochenblatt* 125, no. 11, September 13, 1940.

———. "Der Panzer in der Weltgeschichte." *Militär-Wochenblatt* 125, no. 15, October 11, 1940.

———. "Vom Tank zur Panzerwaffe." *Militär-Wochenblatt* 126, no. 7, August 15, 1941.

Thomas, Gordon, and Max Morgan Witts. *Guernica: The Crucible of World War II.* New York: Stein and Day, 1975.

Thomas, Hugh. *The Spanish Civil War.* New York: Touchstone, 1986.

Touzin, Pierre, and Christian Gurtner. "Renault F.T." In *AFVs of World War One,* edited by Duncan Crow. Vol. 1. Windsor: Profile Publications, 1970.

Tövisházy-Ferjentsik, Otto. "Adolf Hitler als Feldherr: Der Meister des Überraschungskrieges." *Militär-Wochenblatt* 125, no. 48, May 30, 1941.

Travers, Tim. "Could the Tanks of 1918 Have Been War-Winners for the British Expeditionary Force?" *Journal of Contemporary History* 27, no. 3, July 1992.

———. "The Evolution of British Strategy and Tactics on the Western Front in 1918: GHQ, Manpower, and Technology." *Journal of Military History* 54, no. 2, April 1990.

————. *How the War Was Won: Command and Technology in the British Army on the Western Front, 1917–1918.* New York: Routledge, 1992.

————. *The Killing Ground: The British Army, the Western Front, and the Emergence of Modern Warfare, 1900–1918.* London: Allen and Unwin, 1987.

————. "Technology, Tactics, and Morale: Jean de Bloch, the Boer War, and British Military Theory." *Journal of Modern History* 51, no. 2, June 1979.

Turner, Frederick Carleton. "The Genesis of the Soviet 'Deep Operation': The Stalin-Era Doctrine for Large-Scale Offensive Maneuver Warfare." Ph.D. diss., Duke University, 1988.

[Ubique]. "The Offensive Spirit in War." *United Service Magazine* 47, no. 1018, September 1913.

Uffindell, Andrew. "Soldiers' Victory at Magenta." *Military History* 16, no. 2, June 1999.

United States Military Intelligence Reports: Germany, 1919–1941. Frederick, Md.: University Publications of America, 1983.

U.S. Army. *Reports of Military Observers Attached to the Armies in Manchuria During the Russo-Japanese War.* Washington, D.C.: Government Printing Office, 1906.

U.S. Army. Military Intelligence Division, War Department. "Subject: Certain Studies on and Deductions from Operations of Italian Army in East Africa, October 1935–May 1936." Carlisle, Pa.: U.S. Army Military History Institute, 1937.

Usborne, Vice-Admiral C. V. "The Influence of Sea Power on the Fighting in Spain." *Journal of the Royal United Service Institution* 83, no. 529, February 1938.

van Hartesveldt, Fred R. *The Boer War: Historiography and Annotated Bibliography.* Westport, Conn.: Greenwood Press, 2000.

Viljoen, Ben. *My Reminiscences of the Anglo-Boer War.* Cape Town: C. Struik, 1972.

Völkel, Lieutenant Colonel. "Tchingis-Chan als Vorbild und Lehrmeister des modernen Pz.-Kavalleristen." *Militär-Wochenblatt* 126, no. 12, September 19, 1941.

Wagner, Lieutenant Hermenegild. *With the Victorious Bulgarians.* Boston: Houghton Mifflin, 1913.

Wallach, Jehuda L. *The Dogma of the Battle of Annihilation: The Theories of Clausewitz and Schlieffen and Their Impact on the German Conduct of Two World Wars.* Westport, Conn.: Greenwood Press, 1986.

Wanty, Major. "A Year of War in Spain: Facts and Lessons." *La Revue d'Infanterie*, Paris, April 1938 (translated). Carlisle, Pa.: U.S. Army Military History Institute, 1938.

The War in the Far East by the Military Correspondent of The Times. New York: Dutton, 1905.

Warlimont, General Walter. *Inside Hitler's Headquarters.* Novato, Calif.: Presidio, 1991.

Waters, Colonel H.-H. "The Battle of Liao-Yang, the 30th August to the 5th September 1904." In *Reports from British Officers Attached to the Japanese Forces in the Field.* London: General Staff, 1907.

———. "The Battle of Tel-li-ssu (Wa-fang-kou), the 14th and 15th June 1904." In *Reports from British Officers Attached to the Japanese Forces in the Field.* London: General Staff, 1907.

Watteville, Lieutenant-Colonel H. de. "The German Army Maneuvers, 1936." *Journal of the Royal United Service Institution* 81, no. 524, November 1936.

Watts, Barry D., and Williamson Murray. "Inventing History: Soviet Military Genius Revealed." *Air University Review* 26, no. 3, March–April 1985.

Wawro, Geoffrey. "'An Army of Pigs': The Technical, Social, and Political Bases of Austrian Shock Tactics, 1859–1866." *Journal of Military History* 59, no. 3, July 1995.

———. *The Austro-Prussian War: Austria's War with Prussia and Italy in 1866.* Cambridge: Cambridge University Press, 1996.

———. *Warfare and Society in Europe, 1792–1914.* London: Routledge, 2000.

Weeks, John. *Men Against Tanks: A History of Antitank Warfare.* New York: Mason/Charter, 1975.

Werbaneth, James P. "Fletching the Arrows: The Luftwaffe in Spain." *Command* 1, November–December 1989.

Wetzell, General Georg. "Britische Strategie." *Militär-Wochenblatt* 121, no. 48, June 11, 1937.

———. "Gedanken zum X. Band des Weltkriegswerkes über das Kriegsjahr 1916." *Militär-Wochenblatt* 121, no. 8, August 25, 1936.

———. "Kriegsgeschichtliche Vergleiche: Der Vernichtungsgedanke." *Militär-Wochenblatt* 124, no. 20, November 10, 1939.

———. "Verdun in der kriegswissenschaftlichen Kritik." *Militär-Wochenblatt* 121, no. 9, September 4, 1936.

Whealey, Robert H. *Hitler and Spain: The Nazi Role in the Spanish Civil War, 1936–1939.* Lexington: University Press of Kentucky, 1989.

Wheeler-Bennett, J. W. *Brest-Litovsk: The Forgotten Peace: March 1918.* New York: Norton, 1971.

Williams, John. *The Ides of May: The Defeat of France, May–June 1940.* New York: Knopf, 1968.

Williams-Ellis, Clough, and A. Williams-Ellis. *The Tank Corps.* New York: George H. Doran, 1919.

Willich, General Fritz. "Clausewitz und der jetzige Krieg." *Militär-Wochenblatt* 125, no. 1, July 5, 1940.

Winter, Denis. *Death's Men: Soldiers of the Great War.* New York: Penguin, 1978.

Winton, Harold R. *To Change an Army: General Sir John Burnett-Stuart and British Armored Doctrine, 1927–1938.* Lawrence: University Press of Kansas, 1988.

Winton, Harold R., and David R. Mets, eds. *The Challenge of Change: Military Institutions and New Realities, 1918–1941.* Lincoln: University of Nebraska Press, 2000.

Xylander, Colonel Rudolf von. "Military Problems in Ethiopia" (translated). Carlisle, Pa.: U.S. Army War Military History Institute, 1938.

———. *Vom spanischen Krieg. Militär-Wochenblatt* 121–123.

Yonov, Momchil. "Bulgarian Military Operations in the Balkan Wars." In *War and Society in East Central Europe*. Vol. 18, *East Central European Society and the Balkan Wars*, edited by Béla K. Király and Dimitrije Djordjevic. Boulder, Colo.: Social Science Monographs, 1987.

Zabecki, David T. "The Dress Rehearsal: Lost Artillery Lessons of the 1912–1913 Balkan Wars." *Field Artillery*, August 1988.

———. "The Guns of Manchuria." *Field Artillery*, April 1988.

———. "Invasion of Poland: Campaign That Launched a War." *World War II* 14, no. 3, September 1999.

———. *Steel Wind: Colonel Georg Bruchmüller and the Birth of Modern Artillery*. Westport, Conn.: Praeger, 1994.

Zaloga, Steven J. "Soviet Tank Operations in the Spanish Civil War." *Journal of Slavic Military Studies* 12, no. 3, September 1999.

Zaloga, Steven J., and Victory Madej. *The Polish Campaign*. New York: Hippocrene, 1991.

Zamoyski, Adam. *The Battle for the Marchlands*. Boulder, Colo.: East European Monographs, 1981.

Zentner, Joe. "The Destruction of a Basque Town Served as a Model for Terror Bombing and Inspired an Anti-war Masterpiece." *Military History* 14, no. 2, June 1997.

Zola, Emile. *The Debacle*. New York: Penguin, 1972.

Zook, David. *The Conduct of the Chaco War*. New York: Bookman Associates, 1961.

Zuber, Terence. "The Schlieffen Plan Reconsidered." *War in History* 6, no. 3, 1999.

INDEX